PETERSON'S®

ACT® PREP GUIDE ASAP:
THE ULTIMATE
QUICK-STUDY GUIDE

PETERSON'S®

About Peterson's®

Peterson's is everywhere that education happens. For over five decades, Peterson's has provided products and services that keep students and their families engaged throughout the pre-college, college, and post-college experience. From the first day of kindergarten through high school graduation and beyond, Peterson's is a single source of educational content to help families maximize their student's learning and opportunities for success. Whether a fifth-grader needs help with geometry or a high school junior could benefit from essay-writing tips, Peterson's is the ultimate source for the highest quality educational resources.

Since 2005, Peterson's has been the leading publisher of prep guides for the ACT. Over the past ten years, more than one million students across 60 countries have prepared for the ACT with Peterson's titles.

For additional information about Peterson's range of educational products, please visit http://www.petersons.com.

ACT® is a registered trademark of ACT, Inc., which did not collaborate in the development of, and does not endorse, this product.

ACT® is a registered trademark of ACT, Inc., in the U.S.A. and other countries.

For more information, contact Peterson's, 3 Columbia Circle, Suite 205, Albany, NY 12203, 800-338-3282 Ext. 54229; or find us online at www.petersons.com.

Peterson's ACT® Prep Guide ASAP
ISBN 978-0-7689-4121-0

Printed in the United States of America

10 9 8 7 6 5 4 3 2   18 17 16

First Edition

TABLE OF CONTENTS

5

THE ACT® READING TEST

6

THE ACT® SCIENCE TEST

7

THE ACT® WRITING TEST

CHAPTER 1
ALL ABOUT THE ACT® AND HOW TO USE THIS BOOK

OVERVIEW

- How to Use This Book—*FAST*
- Test Overview
- Registering for the ACT®
- Scoring
- Getting Ready for Test Day
- Summing It Up

We know that you're gearing up to prepare for the ACT and you don't have much time—there's likely 30 or fewer days between now and test day, and you're eager to get started with quick, effective, and no-nonsense strategies and review to help you conquer the exam.

We completely get it—and we're here to help!

Consider *Peterson's ACT® Prep Guide ASAP* your quick, last-minute ACT study buddy, the test coach that's going to help you make the most of your time, even if it's just a few days or weeks, to get ready for this super-important exam and, most important, **make up for lost time!**

That's right—if you're nervous, anxious, or stressing out because you think you've waited too long to study or you feel the pressure of the ticking clock and are worried that you don't have enough time to prepare effectively—think again. No matter how much time you have left, if you use it wisely you can achieve your goals for the ACT.

Here's the message at the heart of *Peterson's ACT® Prep Guide ASAP*: it's *never* too late to build your skills and get ready for the ACT, and this book *will* help you make the most of the time you have left. We'll keep things moving forward at a brisk pace, focusing on just what you need to reach your target score on the ACT. You'll get:

- **Quick and complete coverage** of the structure and format of the ACT. No time wasting here, just exactly what you need to know about the ACT to get ready for test day and be ahead of the competition.

- **Straightforward and efficient review** of each section of the test. Each chapter cuts straight to the core with the most essential topics and concepts that you'll need to know for test day.
- **Effective tips that *really* work** on the exam. You'll show up on test day confident and ready with proven and time-saving strategies and advice for every section of the exam to get your absolute best scores possible in a short amount of time.
- **No-nonsense practice** for all types of questions that you may encounter on test day, to get in good test-taking shape—fast!

Bottom line: We're with you on this ACT journey, no matter how long you have to get ready. Feel better? Great! Let's not waste any time getting started!

HOW TO USE THIS BOOK—*FAST*

You know better than anyone exactly how much time you have between now and test day. It's our job to help you make the most of that time.

Is it a few weeks or just a few days? We suggest two possible approaches for using this book and making the most of the time you have.

THE FULL REVIEW STRATEGY

This approach gives you an *equal* amount of time for each ACT test section, for a comprehensive review of the entire exam. You'll also dedicate a chunk of time to taking a test-like diagnostic exam that will let you assess your strengths and weaknesses going in to your study period.

- **Step 1:** List the number of days you have until test day: _____ days

- **Step 2:** Take a few hours off the top—*no more than a day*—reading this chapter to learn just what you need to know about the ACT, including registration, scoring, and getting comfortable with the general format of each test section.

- **Step 3:** Take 1 day to find a quiet space and attack the Diagnostic Test in Chapter 2. The test itself (including a short break) will take you approximately 3 hours and 30 minutes. When you're done, allot the rest of the day's study time to review all answer explanations and assess where you need to focus your study.

- **Step 4:** Build your study plan. Divide the remaining number of days you have to prepare equally for each test section, splitting that time (days or hours) between *topic review* and *question practice*.

English Test Section

Topic review: _____

Question practice: _____

Mathematics Test Section

    Topic review: _____

    Question practice: _____

Reading Test Section

    Topic review: _____

    Question practice: _____

Science Test Section

    Topic review: _____

    Question practice: _____

Writing Test Section (*Optional*)

    Topic review: _____

    Question practice: _____

- **Step 5:** Structure your study calendar. Now that you know the number of days you have to devote to topic review and question practice for each test section of the ACT, take some time to fill in a study calendar so you'll know exactly what preparation you'll be tackling each day between now and test day. Structure your calendar to suit your study style—devote each day to a single test section or divide your days so you can work on a section for a set number of hours and switch things up—whatever keeps you interested, focused, and on track!

THE WEAKNESS TARGETING STRATEGY

This approach lets you allocate the time you have between now and test day to target your weak areas and build your skills where you need to most.

- **Step 1:** List the number of days you have until test day: _____ days

- **Step 2:** Take a few hours off the top—*no more than a day*—reading this chapter to learn just what you need to know about the ACT, including registration, scoring, and getting comfortable with the general format of each test section.

- **Step 3:** Take 1 day to find a quiet space and attack the Diagnostic Test in Chapter 2. The exam itself (including a short break) will take you approximately 3 hours and 30 minutes. When you're done, allot the rest of the day's study time to review the detailed explanations of the questions you answered incorrectly and the questions that gave you the most trouble.

- **Step 4:** Assess your strengths and weaknesses. Use your diagnostic test results to rank each test section based on your strengths and weaknesses in each test subject. We recommend you use your class grades as a guide. Are you a science whiz? Have you always gotten great grades in English classes but struggled in math?

Using your academic history as a guide, rank each test section from 1 (weakest subject) to 5 (best subject).

English Test Section: _____

Mathematics Test Section: _____

Reading Test Section: _____

Science Test Section: _____

Writing Test Section (*Optional*): _____

Keep in mind that you will need to adjust your rankings as you move through your study schedule and calendar. Your skill levels may shift, and your study plan should follow suit so that you're always spending your time working on your weakest areas.

- **Step 5:** Build your study plan: Divide the number of days/hours you have to prepare among the test sections, splitting your time (days or hours) based on your rankings. You can divide your time however you see fit, as long as you're dedicating the majority of your time to improving your weak spots. One example for allocating your time is as follows:

  ○ 30% of your time for the section you ranked 1

  ○ 25% of your time for the section you ranked 2

  ○ 20% of your time for the section you ranked 3

  ○ 15% of your time for the section you ranked 4

  ○ 10% of your time for the section you ranked 5

Once you're comfortable with your initial study plan, fill in your initial study time for each section.

English Test Section: _____

Mathematics Test Section: _____

Reading Test Section: _____

Science Test Section: _____

Writing Test Section (*Optional*): _____

Now, decide how you want to divide your time for each section between *topic review* and *question practice*. Is your math knowledge strong but you aren't a great test-taker and need more question practice? Is the reverse true? For each test section, decide how you want to break up the time you allotted between topic review and question practice.

English Test Section

Topic review: _____

Question practice: _____

Mathematics Test Section

Topic review: _____

Question practice: _____

Reading Test Section

Topic review: _____

Question practice: _____

Science Test Section

Topic review: _____

Question practice: _____

Writing Test Section (*Optional*)

Topic review: _____

Question practice: _____

- **Step 6:** Structure your study calendar. Now that you know the amount of time you have to devote to topic review and question practice for each section of the ACT, take some time to fill in a study calendar so you'll know exactly what you'll be tackling each day between now and test day. Feel free to structure your calendar to suit your study style—devote each day to a single test section or divide your days so you can work on a section for a set number of hours and switch—whatever will keep you interested, focused, and on track!

Remember, as your skill levels shift, you should reweigh and re-rank each test section so that you're always giving sufficient focus to your weakest subject areas.

TEST OVERVIEW

We know you're feeling under pressure and are eager to quickly dive into the practice and review that'll get you ready for the ACT—but a quick overview of exam basics will help you be better prepared for test day.

NOTE: Make sure you're *fully* aware of the admissions requirements of each college or university that you're applying to, including which schools accept or require ACT scores!

The ACT is designed to test your abilities in the following core subjects: **English, Mathematics, Reading, Science,** and **Writing.** Most of the questions on the exam are multiple choice, the kind that require you to select the best option among several possible answer choices. There's also a written essay on the optional Writing section if you choose to take this test.

ACT® Timing

The ACT is a **2-hour-and-55-minute test** consisting of **215 multiple-choice questions.** There's a short break between the Mathematics and Reading tests, and a short break before the 40-minute optional Writing test. If you are taking the ACT without the Writing test, expect to be dismissed by 12:15 p.m.; if you are taking the ACT with Writing, expect to wrap things up by 1:15 p.m.

Make sure you're comfortable with the format and timing of the exam and each test section before test day, and if your schedule allows, practice working in simulated timed conditions so you can develop an effective test-taking pace.

Each chapter in *Peterson's ACT® Prep Guide ASAP* focuses on a specific test section, with a review of essential topics that are often tested on the exam and practice with questions similar to those you'll encounter on test day.

For now, let's take a quick look at what you'll encounter in each test section.

THE ENGLISH TEST

The ACT English test is 45 minutes long and consists of 75 questions. It's designed to test your skills in the core elements of effective writing, including **usage and mechanics** and **rhetorical skills:**

- **Usage and mechanics** questions test your knowledge and understanding of punctuation, grammar, and sentence structure.
- **Rhetorical skills** questions test your knowledge and understanding of writing strategy, organization, and style.

On the exam, you'll encounter five reading passages, each of which will contain various underlined portions that may include errors that you must address and fix.

- **If there is an error or multiple errors**, you will select the best correction offered from among the available answer choices that accompany a given passage.
- **If there aren't any errors**, you'll select the choice that reads NO CHANGE. The majority of usage and mechanics questions on the exam will adhere to this format.

The rhetorical skills questions will typically ask you a question about the *best* way to **rethink, reorganize,** or **restyle** a specific portion of each passage or perhaps an entire passage itself. The relevant portion in each passage will be numbered, and those numbers will refer to the numbers of the particular questions that relate to those portions.

THE MATHEMATICS TEST

The ACT Mathematics test is 60 minutes long and consists of 60 questions. It's designed to test your ability in the following core subject areas:

- Pre-algebra/elementary algebra
- Intermediate algebra/coordinate geometry
- Plane geometry/trigonometry

Each question is multiple-choice; however, unlike the other ACT test sections, there are *five* possible answer choices for each question.

While you'll have to know basic formulas and computations for the math test, you will *not* be expected to remember more complex ones—they'll be provided for you along with the questions.

You'll also be permitted to use certain calculators on the math test, though a calculator is *not* required. You'll learn which kinds of calculators are permitted on the ACT later on in this chapter.

THE READING TEST

The ACT Reading test is 35 minutes long and consists of 40 questions. You'll encounter four different kinds of passages on this test:

1. **Literary narrative** passages include portions of text from short stories, novels, memoirs, or personal essays.

2. **Social studies** passages discuss anthropology, archaeology, biography, business, economics, education, geography, history, political science, psychology, and sociology.

3. **Natural science** passages discuss anatomy, astronomy, biology, botany, chemistry, ecology, geology, medicine, meteorology, microbiology, natural history, physiology, physics, technology, and zoology.

4. **Humanities** passages discuss architecture, art, dance, ethics, film, language, literary criticism, music, philosophy, radio, television, and theater.

The questions on this section of the exam are multiple choice, each with four possible answer choices.

Reading test questions require you to determine meanings that are both explicit and implicit, recognize main ideas, and identify the meanings of words as they are used in context. You'll also have to locate and interpret significant details, understand the correct sequence of events, comprehend cause-and-effect relationships, analyze tone and mood, and draw generalizations.

Some passages will consist of a pair of shorter passages, and some of the accompanying questions will test your ability to analyze how those two passages relate to each other—including differences and similarities.

THE SCIENCE TEST

The ACT Science test lasts 35 minutes and consists of 40 questions. The test includes various passages with key scientific information, each followed by multiple-choice questions with four possible answer choices.

The science skills tested cover the following core topic areas: biology, chemistry, physics, Earth science, and astronomy.

You'll encounter the following distinct question types:

- **Data representation** questions require you to read and interpret information on graphs, scatterplots, and tables.

- **Research summary** questions require you to read about experiments and draw conclusions about their designs and results.

- **Conflicting viewpoints** questions feature pairs of contrasting hypotheses about data or premises and require you to understand, analyze, compare, and contrast those viewpoints.

 ALERT: Calculators are *not* allowed on the Science section of the exam because you will not be required to make any calculations.

THE OPTIONAL WRITING TEST

The optional ACT Writing test is 40 minutes long and consists of a single essay writing task. You'll receive an essay prompt alongside three different perspectives on a particular issue. After reading the prompt and each perspective carefully, you'll compose an essay that evaluates the issue in the prompt and supports your distinct perspective on the issue while also taking into account the other perspectives.

Again, this is an optional section and not every college requires that you take it. You can find the Writing section requirements for your target colleges on the official ACT website: ***www.actstudent.org/writing/.***

NOTE: Your opinions will *not* affect your score, but the quality of your ideas and writing will. There are no multiple-choice questions on the Writing test.

REGISTERING FOR THE ACT®

Registering online for the ACT is the quickest method. Go to **www.actstudent.org /regist/**, follow the instructions, and create an online account to get started and register.

You can use the official ACT website to request extended time to take the test if you have a disability, and you can request a standby online test if you missed the late registration deadline. You may also request an online test if you are homebound or confined or are not within 75 miles of a testing center.

If you are under 13 years old or cannot pay with a credit card, don't worry! You can request a Register-By-Mail packet by filling out a form online at **www.actstudent.org /forms/stud_req/**.

REGISTRATION FEES*

The fee for taking the ACT without the optional Writing test is $42.50, which includes having your score report sent to you, your high school, and as many as four colleges of your choice. If you're taking the optional Writing test, the total fee is $58.50 (the extra $16 fee is refundable in the event you either cannot make it to test day or you decide to take the ACT without the Writing test before the test begins).

If you decide to have your score report sent to a fifth and sixth college, there is a $12 fee for each additional school.

Other options and fees include:

- Standby testing: $51
- Late registration (available only in the U.S. and Canada): $27
- International testing (outside the U.S. and Canada): $41
- Changing the date of your test: $24
- Changing the location of your test: $25
- Requesting a copy of your test and answers (Test Information Release, or TIR): $20 (where available)

You may be eligible for a fee waiver to help cover the cost of the exam. To find out if you're eligible, and for additional fee information, check out the official ACT website: **www.act.org/content/act/en/products-and-services/the-act/taking-the-test.html**.

---

* Registration fees at the time of publication. Go to **www.petersons.com/act** for up-to-date information.

Photo ID

For security purposes, you must provide a photo ID to register for the ACT. Your photo ID must be current, valid, and legal. Your ID must be hard plastic, such as a student ID or driver's license. If you do not have an acceptable photo ID, you must obtain an ACT Student Identification Letter with Photo from the ACT website here: ***http://www.act .org/content/dam/act/unsecured/documents/Identification-Letter-Form.pdf.***

You can learn how to upload a photo of yourself using your computer or mobile device on the official ACT website (***www.actstudent.org/regist/add-photo.html***). You can also learn how to submit a paper photo by visiting ***www.actstudent.org/regist/add-photo .html#paper***.

After you register for the ACT, you'll receive a registration ticket with your photo. You *MUST* bring this ticket and your photo ID with you on test day!

Students taking the test on standby—those who missed the late registration date or requested a test date or test center change—must also bring a standby ticket with a photo of themselves on test day. (Find out more about obtaining this ticket on the ACT site: ***www.actstudent.org/regist/standbytest.html***).

WHEN AND HOW OFTEN TO TAKE THE ACT®

In the Unites States, the ACT is given six times a year—in September, October, December, February, April, and June. Select the test date that works best for you and your specific goals, and be sure to check out the registration deadlines on the official ACT website. In addition, if you require information for testing outside of the United States, visit the official ACT website.

You can take the test more than once (actually, you can take the exam up to twelve times), if you feel the need to. A separate record will be kept for each test date on which you've taken the exam. When you request that ACT send a score report to a college, ACT will release *only* the score record from the test date you request. This means that you're in control of which scores colleges see.

You can also ask ACT to send more than one score report from more than one test date to a college. However, ACT will *not* create a new record for you by selecting and combining scores from different test dates—you can only send entire test date records as they stand. There is a process known as **superscoring,** which you can use to your advantage if you're applying to colleges that utilize the Common Application form (read the Scoring section for more info).

SCORING

Let's quickly explore how the exam is scored. The ACT is a multiple-choice test (the optional Writing test is an essay writing task), which does *not* penalize you for selecting a wrong answer. However, a blank answer *will* be marked as incorrect. Therefore, it is important to answer *every* question on the test, even if you only guess. ***Never* leave an answer blank!**

Each of the four multiple-choice tests—English, Mathematics, Reading, and Science—is worth 36 points. Your total score, also known as your **composite score,** is the average score of these tests, and the best possible score on the ACT is a composite score of 36.

The optional Writing test is scored a bit differently. Two official essay readers will score your essay independently on a scale from 1–6 for each of the four domains. Each domain will be given a score ranging from 2–12 based on the combined readers' scores. Your final score will be the average of the four domain scores. The highest possible score you can earn for the Writing test is 12.

Superscoring

Did you know that certain colleges (more than 500 as of this writing) allow you to take the ACT multiple times and average together your best scores on each of the multiple-choice tests? This is known as superscoring.

These colleges use the Common Application form, which gives you the option of entering your highest scores for the ACT English, Mathematics, Reading, and Science tests. It does not matter if you earned each of these scores on different dates. The application averages these high scores, giving you your best possible score. Superscoring is a compelling reason to consider taking the ACT more than once, especially if you did great on a few of the test sections but fell short of your perfect score goal.

VIEWING YOUR SCORES

You'll be able to view your scores online by logging into your account on the official ACT website. Scores are generally available for online viewing approximately 2 weeks after your test date, and score reports are typically released within three to eight weeks of your test date. If you've decided to take the optional Writing test, your score report (with writing score) will be released within five to eight weeks of your test date.

REPORTING YOUR SCORES

Once your score report is available, ACT will automatically send it to you and the schools you've requested while registering (up to four free). If there are additional institutions that you'd like to have your scores sent to, you can request additional reports.

You can request an additional regular report, which is processed within one week from receipt of request, for $12 per report (per test date), or a priority report (available only in the U.S.), which is processed within two working days from receipt of request, for $16.50 per report (per test date).

Requesting a report can be done from the official ACT website by logging into your ACT account and completing a PDF request form (payment must be made by credit card), by phone (319-337-1270), or by sending a letter of request (must include your full name; current mailing address and address used during registration, if different; ACT ID; date of birth; phone number; test date; names and codes of additional institutions you'd like your score report sent to, including city and state; and your signature) and a check or money order payable to ACT to the following:

> ACT Student Services—Score Reports
> PO Box 451
> Iowa City, IA 52243-0451

For complete information regarding ACT scoring policies and procedures, visit the official ACT website.

GETTING READY FOR TEST DAY

We know that you don't have much time to study and prepare for the ACT, so we'll get you moving in the right direction with a quick review of what you need to know to be ready for test day—including selecting a test day and location, what to expect when you arrive at your test center, what to bring, and what to leave home—so you can avoid surprises, reduce anxiety, and be ready to attack every exam section and question!

CHOOSING YOUR TEST DAY AND LOCATION

Be sure to choose a test day strategically—choose a day that is convenient for you and will not conflict with other activities on your schedule. The last thing you want on the day of this important exam is to be overbooked or racing around to the point of exhaustion. There are a limited number of test administrations each year, and you know just how important this test is, so choose wisely!

Also be sure that the location you choose to take the exam is convenient for you, and—this is important—make sure you know *precisely* how long it will take you to get to the testing center. Make a few practice runs, have a route as well as an alternate route to the test location just in case, and don't leave anything to chance. Be sure to take all possible factors into account to ensure you don't arrive late to the test center: traffic, adverse weather conditions, a detour to the gas station, etc.

Visit the official ACT website to find the best test location for you—and register as early as possible to avoid having your preferred test location fill up before you sign up: ***http://www .act.org/content/act/en/products-and-services/the-act/taking-the-test/test-center -locator.html***.

WHAT TO EXPECT, WHAT TO BRING, AND WHAT TO LEAVE HOME

Test time *always* begins at 8:00 a.m., and by this time you should be present and in your seat. Plan to arrive early, giving you time to relax, get comfortable, and get settled into test-taking mode; you *definitely* don't want to have to deal with the stress of racing the clock to avoid missing the start of the test, and you will *not* be admitted to take the test if you arrive late.

When you arrive at your test center, the staff will check your photo ID and ticket, admit you into the room, bring you to your seat, and provide you with the required test materials.

The sections on the ACT are administered in the following order: English, Mathematics, Reading, Science, and, finally, Writing. Your 30-minute break occurs after the Mathematics test. There is also an extra 10-minute break before the Writing test if you're taking it.

NOTE: Individuals taking the ACT without the Writing test are generally dismissed at 12:15 p.m. Those taking the optional Writing test are generally dismissed at 1:15 p.m.

Your Test Day Checklist

Make absolutely certain that you bring the following items with you on test day:

- Your test ticket
- Acceptable photo ID (visit the official ACT website for what constitutes acceptable ID)
- Sharpened No. 2 pencils with erasers

Consider bringing the following optional items to help maximize your test-taking experience:

- Permissible calculator for the Mathematics test (see the guidelines that follow)
- A watch (without an alarm) to help pace yourself through each test section
- A sweater to help you adapt to the test center temperature

Do not bring the following items with you to the test room—you absolutely will not be able to use them:

- Electronic devices: smartphone, cell phone, iPad or tablet, camera, and headphones
- Reading material, textbooks, reference materials (including dictionaries and other study aids), and outside notes
- Extra scratch paper
- Highlighters, colored pens and pencils, or correction tape/fluid
- Food or beverages
- Tobacco

CALCULATORS AND THE ACT®

Here's everything you need to know about using a calculator on test day:

- You may bring any 4-function, scientific, or graphing calculator for use on test day, as long as it does not violate any of the rules listed here.

- You'll be allowed to use a calculator only on the Mathematics test.

- If you bring or attempt to use a prohibited device on test day, you'll be dismissed from the exam and will not receive a test score.

- Sharing calculators during the ACT is prohibited.

- You will not be able to obtain a calculator from the test proctor—it is your responsibility to know which calculators are permitted and to bring an acceptable device.

- You are responsible for the proper functioning of your calculator, and you are allowed to bring a spare calculator and batteries.

- An on-screen calculator may be provided in a computer-based testing environment.

- Accessible calculators, including audio/"talking" or Braille calculators, may be allowed under the accessibility policies for the ACT (visit the official website for details).

The following calculators are *not* permitted for use on the ACT®:

- Any calculator with built-in or downloaded computer algebra system functionality
- Handheld, tablet, or laptop computers, including PDAs
- Calculators built into cell phones or any other electronic communication devices
- Calculators with a typewriter keypad (letter keys in QWERTY format; letter keys not in QWERTY format are permitted)
- Electronic writing pads or pen-input devices
    - **Note:** The Sharp EL 9600 is permitted
- Any of the following brands:
    - **Texas Instruments**

        ◊ All model numbers that begin with TI-89 or TI-92

        ◊ TI-Nspire CAS (*Note:* The TI-Nspire (non-CAS) is permitted)

    - **Hewlett-Packard**

        ◊ HP Prime

        ◊ HP 48GII

        ◊ All model numbers that begin with HP40G, HP49G, or HP50G

    - **Casio**

        ◊ fx-CP400 (ClassPad 400)

        ◊ ClassPad 300

        ◊ ClassPad 330

        ◊ Algebra fx 2.0

        ◊ All model numbers that begin with CFX-9970G

The following types of calculators are permitted—but only after they are modified as indicated:

- Calculators that can hold programs or documents—remove all documents and remove all programs that have computer algebra system functionality
- Calculators with paper tape—remove the tape
- Calculators that make noise—turn off the sound
- Calculators with an infrared data port—completely cover the infrared data port with heavy opaque material such as duct tape or electrician's tape (includes Hewlett-Packard HP38G series, HP39G series, and HP48G)
- Calculators that have power cords—remove all power/electrical cords

Bottom line: Yes, you're short on time to prepare for the ACT, but it's *never* too late to build your skills and get ready for test success—and this book *will* help you make the most of the time you have left—so keep reading!

SUMMING IT UP

- The ACT consists of four multiple-choice tests in **English**, **Mathematics**, **Reading**, and **Science**, with a total of 215 questions.
  - ○ There is also an optional Writing test, which takes an additional 40 minutes to complete. Some colleges do not require the Writing test—make sure you know the requirements of the schools you're applying to.

- Your score on the ACT will be among the most important factors that college admissions panels will use to make admissions decisions. It also gives colleges a good idea of your skills in each tested area and will help guide decisions regarding class level placement.

- **The English test** lasts 45 minutes and consists of 75 questions that test your grammar and usage and rhetorical skills.

- **The Mathematics test** lasts 60 minutes and consists of 60 questions that test your knowledge of pre-algebra, elementary algebra, intermediate algebra, coordinate geometry, plane geometry, and trigonometry.

- **The Reading test** lasts for 35 minutes and consists of 40 questions that test your ability to analyze and comprehend four distinct passages.

- **The Science test** lasts for 35 minutes and consists of 40 questions that test your knowledge of biology, chemistry, physics, Earth science, and astronomy.

- **The optional Writing test** lasts for 40 minutes and consists of an essay task, which requires you to evaluate a prompt and three perspectives on an issue, create your own perspective on that issue, and explain how your perspective relates to the ones provided.

- **Registering online for the ACT is the quickest method**—go to *www.actstudent .org/regist/*, follow the instructions, and create an online account to get started and register.

- **Verify the cost of the test.** Make sure you're fully aware of all applicable test fees, based on your specific testing and reporting needs.

- **Choose the test date and location that works best for you,** and make sure you register before the deadline.

- **Plan your travel route.** Make sure you have at least one, and preferably an alternate, route to your test location that will get you there with plenty of time to spare.

- **The test begins at 8:00 a.m.** Arrive at the test center well before test time.
  - ○ Individuals taking the ACT without Writing are generally dismissed at 12:15 p.m. Those taking the Writing test are generally dismissed at 1:15 p.m.

- **Don't bring unnecessary items.** Make sure you're fully aware of what you *must bring*, *can bring*, and *cannot bring* with you on test day, including calculator guidelines.

- **The maximum score you can get on the ACT is a composite score of 36**, and that score is determined by averaging your score on each of the four multiple-choice tests.

- **The Writing test essay is scored on a scale from 1 to 6 in each of four writing domains.** The maximum score you can get is 12, which is the average of the four domain scores your essay receives from two essay readers

- **There is no penalty for choosing an incorrect answer on the ACT**, so you should answer every question. Unanswered questions are considered to be wrong answers.

- **ACT scores are generally available for online viewing approximately two weeks after your test date**, and score reports are typically released within three to eight weeks of your test date. If you're taking the optional Writing test, your score report (with writing score) will be released within five to eight weeks of your test date.

- **Be sure to request that ACT send your score report to each college that you're interested in applying to**; this includes the colleges you indicate while registering for the test (up to four), as well as any additional schools later on.

- **The path to a perfect score on the ACT is *not* an easy one.** Your skills on each section of the exam have to be razor sharp if you're going to achieve your goal. Your best approach is to get plenty of practice and review between now and test day and to target your weakest areas for improvement.

- **Commit** to a prep strategy and structured study calendar to make the most of your time between now and test day. Consider these options:
    - **The Full Review Strategy:** This approach gives you an *equal* amount of time for each section of the exam, for a comprehensive review of the entire test.

    - **The Weakness Targeting Strategy:** This approach lets you allocate the time you have between now and test day to target your weak areas and build your skills where you need to most.

DIAGNOSTIC TEST INTRODUCTION

Now that you know what to expect on the ACT, it's time for you to assess your strengths and weaknesses before you dive into your study plan. The following diagnostic test mirrors the structure of the ACT you will see on test day. It can be tempting to rush through this practice test and answer questions here and there (you *are* in a hurry, after all), but trust us—you'll really want to treat this seriously and approach this diagnostic like you would the actual test. It's the only opportunity you'll have to get a sense of how your knowledge translates to taking the ACT and how you handle sitting and answering questions for 3 or more hours straight!

So if you have the time and opportunity, we hope you will take this exam under "test-like" conditions. That means you should ideally find a super-quiet spot with limited interruptions. Silence your phone, turn off the television, and don't listen to any music—do your best to create the conditions you will have on the actual test day.

Each subject test will have a time limit listed at its start. Set a timer and try to answer all of the test questions in the allotted time. If you find you can't, take note—timing is an issue you will have to practice before test day. Also note throughout the exam which sections give you the most trouble and what types of questions *within* each section take you the most time to answer. With your test date approaching soon, you'll really want to use this diagnostic test as a tool to help you focus your study so you don't waste any time.

After completing this diagnostic test, be sure to review the test section answer keys, detailed explanations for each question, and sample essays at different levels. Even in your haste to begin studying, don't skip over these detailed explanations—they're study tools themselves and really get into why every answer choice is right or wrong. Learning from your mistakes is key to advancing your study and increasing your score.

CHAPTER 2:
THE DIAGNOSTIC TEST

OVERVIEW

- Answer Sheets
- English Test
- Mathematics Test
- Reading Test
- Science Test
- Writing Test
- Answer Keys and Explanations
- Diagnostic Test Assesment Grid
- Diagnostic Test Conclusion

English Test

1. Ⓐ Ⓑ Ⓒ Ⓓ   16. Ⓕ Ⓖ Ⓗ Ⓙ   31. Ⓐ Ⓑ Ⓒ Ⓓ   46. Ⓕ Ⓖ Ⓗ Ⓙ   61. Ⓐ Ⓑ Ⓒ Ⓓ

2. Ⓕ Ⓖ Ⓗ Ⓙ   17. Ⓐ Ⓑ Ⓒ Ⓓ   32. Ⓕ Ⓖ Ⓗ Ⓙ   47. Ⓐ Ⓑ Ⓒ Ⓓ   62. Ⓕ Ⓖ Ⓗ Ⓙ

3. Ⓐ Ⓑ Ⓒ Ⓓ   18. Ⓕ Ⓖ Ⓗ Ⓙ   33. Ⓐ Ⓑ Ⓒ Ⓓ   48. Ⓕ Ⓖ Ⓗ Ⓙ   63. Ⓐ Ⓑ Ⓒ Ⓓ

4. Ⓕ Ⓖ Ⓗ Ⓙ   19. Ⓐ Ⓑ Ⓒ Ⓓ   34. Ⓕ Ⓖ Ⓗ Ⓙ   49. Ⓐ Ⓑ Ⓒ Ⓓ   64. Ⓕ Ⓖ Ⓗ Ⓙ

5. Ⓐ Ⓑ Ⓒ Ⓓ   20. Ⓕ Ⓖ Ⓗ Ⓙ   35. Ⓐ Ⓑ Ⓒ Ⓓ   50. Ⓕ Ⓖ Ⓗ Ⓙ   65. Ⓐ Ⓑ Ⓒ Ⓓ

6. Ⓕ Ⓖ Ⓗ Ⓙ   21. Ⓐ Ⓑ Ⓒ Ⓓ   36. Ⓕ Ⓖ Ⓗ Ⓙ   51. Ⓐ Ⓑ Ⓒ Ⓓ   66. Ⓕ Ⓖ Ⓗ Ⓙ

7. Ⓐ Ⓑ Ⓒ Ⓓ   22. Ⓕ Ⓖ Ⓗ Ⓙ   37. Ⓐ Ⓑ Ⓒ Ⓓ   52. Ⓕ Ⓖ Ⓗ Ⓙ   67. Ⓐ Ⓑ Ⓒ Ⓓ

8. Ⓕ Ⓖ Ⓗ Ⓙ   23. Ⓐ Ⓑ Ⓒ Ⓓ   38. Ⓕ Ⓖ Ⓗ Ⓙ   53. Ⓐ Ⓑ Ⓒ Ⓓ   68. Ⓕ Ⓖ Ⓗ Ⓙ

9. Ⓐ Ⓑ Ⓒ Ⓓ   24. Ⓕ Ⓖ Ⓗ Ⓙ   39. Ⓐ Ⓑ Ⓒ Ⓓ   54. Ⓕ Ⓖ Ⓗ Ⓙ   69. Ⓐ Ⓑ Ⓒ Ⓓ

10. Ⓕ Ⓖ Ⓗ Ⓙ   25. Ⓐ Ⓑ Ⓒ Ⓓ   40. Ⓕ Ⓖ Ⓗ Ⓙ   55. Ⓐ Ⓑ Ⓒ Ⓓ   70. Ⓕ Ⓖ Ⓗ Ⓙ

11. Ⓐ Ⓑ Ⓒ Ⓓ   26. Ⓕ Ⓖ Ⓗ Ⓙ   41. Ⓐ Ⓑ Ⓒ Ⓓ   56. Ⓕ Ⓖ Ⓗ Ⓙ   71. Ⓐ Ⓑ Ⓒ Ⓓ

12. Ⓕ Ⓖ Ⓗ Ⓙ   27. Ⓐ Ⓑ Ⓒ Ⓓ   42. Ⓕ Ⓖ Ⓗ Ⓙ   57. Ⓐ Ⓑ Ⓒ Ⓓ   72. Ⓕ Ⓖ Ⓗ Ⓙ

13. Ⓐ Ⓑ Ⓒ Ⓓ   28. Ⓕ Ⓖ Ⓗ Ⓙ   43. Ⓐ Ⓑ Ⓒ Ⓓ   58. Ⓕ Ⓖ Ⓗ Ⓙ   73. Ⓐ Ⓑ Ⓒ Ⓓ

14. Ⓕ Ⓖ Ⓗ Ⓙ   29. Ⓐ Ⓑ Ⓒ Ⓓ   44. Ⓕ Ⓖ Ⓗ Ⓙ   59. Ⓐ Ⓑ Ⓒ Ⓓ   74. Ⓕ Ⓖ Ⓗ Ⓙ

15. Ⓐ Ⓑ Ⓒ Ⓓ   30. Ⓕ Ⓖ Ⓗ Ⓙ   45. Ⓐ Ⓑ Ⓒ Ⓓ   60. Ⓕ Ⓖ Ⓗ Ⓙ   75. Ⓐ Ⓑ Ⓒ Ⓓ

Math Test

1. Ⓐ Ⓑ Ⓒ Ⓓ Ⓔ   16. Ⓕ Ⓖ Ⓗ Ⓙ Ⓚ   31. Ⓐ Ⓑ Ⓒ Ⓓ Ⓔ   46. Ⓕ Ⓖ Ⓗ Ⓙ Ⓚ
2. Ⓕ Ⓖ Ⓗ Ⓙ Ⓚ   17. Ⓐ Ⓑ Ⓒ Ⓓ Ⓔ   32. Ⓕ Ⓖ Ⓗ Ⓙ Ⓚ   47. Ⓐ Ⓑ Ⓒ Ⓓ Ⓔ
3. Ⓐ Ⓑ Ⓒ Ⓓ Ⓔ   18. Ⓕ Ⓖ Ⓗ Ⓙ Ⓚ   33. Ⓐ Ⓑ Ⓒ Ⓓ Ⓔ   48. Ⓕ Ⓖ Ⓗ Ⓙ Ⓚ
4. Ⓕ Ⓖ Ⓗ Ⓙ Ⓚ   19. Ⓐ Ⓑ Ⓒ Ⓓ Ⓔ   34. Ⓕ Ⓖ Ⓗ Ⓙ Ⓚ   49. Ⓐ Ⓑ Ⓒ Ⓓ Ⓔ
5. Ⓐ Ⓑ Ⓒ Ⓓ Ⓔ   20. Ⓕ Ⓖ Ⓗ Ⓙ Ⓚ   35. Ⓐ Ⓑ Ⓒ Ⓓ Ⓔ   50. Ⓕ Ⓖ Ⓗ Ⓙ Ⓚ
6. Ⓕ Ⓖ Ⓗ Ⓙ Ⓚ   21. Ⓐ Ⓑ Ⓒ Ⓓ Ⓔ   36. Ⓕ Ⓖ Ⓗ Ⓙ Ⓚ   51. Ⓐ Ⓑ Ⓒ Ⓓ Ⓔ
7. Ⓐ Ⓑ Ⓒ Ⓓ Ⓔ   22. Ⓕ Ⓖ Ⓗ Ⓙ Ⓚ   37. Ⓐ Ⓑ Ⓒ Ⓓ Ⓔ   52. Ⓕ Ⓖ Ⓗ Ⓙ Ⓚ
8. Ⓕ Ⓖ Ⓗ Ⓙ Ⓚ   23. Ⓐ Ⓑ Ⓒ Ⓓ Ⓔ   38. Ⓕ Ⓖ Ⓗ Ⓙ Ⓚ   53. Ⓐ Ⓑ Ⓒ Ⓓ Ⓔ
9. Ⓐ Ⓑ Ⓒ Ⓓ Ⓔ   24. Ⓕ Ⓖ Ⓗ Ⓙ Ⓚ   39. Ⓐ Ⓑ Ⓒ Ⓓ Ⓔ   54. Ⓕ Ⓖ Ⓗ Ⓙ Ⓚ
10. Ⓕ Ⓖ Ⓗ Ⓙ Ⓚ   25. Ⓐ Ⓑ Ⓒ Ⓓ Ⓔ   40. Ⓕ Ⓖ Ⓗ Ⓙ Ⓚ   55. Ⓐ Ⓑ Ⓒ Ⓓ Ⓔ
11. Ⓐ Ⓑ Ⓒ Ⓓ Ⓔ   26. Ⓕ Ⓖ Ⓗ Ⓙ Ⓚ   41. Ⓐ Ⓑ Ⓒ Ⓓ Ⓔ   56. Ⓕ Ⓖ Ⓗ Ⓙ Ⓚ
12. Ⓕ Ⓖ Ⓗ Ⓙ Ⓚ   27. Ⓐ Ⓑ Ⓒ Ⓓ Ⓔ   42. Ⓕ Ⓖ Ⓗ Ⓙ Ⓚ   57. Ⓐ Ⓑ Ⓒ Ⓓ Ⓔ
13. Ⓐ Ⓑ Ⓒ Ⓓ Ⓔ   28. Ⓕ Ⓖ Ⓗ Ⓙ Ⓚ   43. Ⓐ Ⓑ Ⓒ Ⓓ Ⓔ   58. Ⓕ Ⓖ Ⓗ Ⓙ Ⓚ
14. Ⓕ Ⓖ Ⓗ Ⓙ Ⓚ   29. Ⓐ Ⓑ Ⓒ Ⓓ Ⓔ   44. Ⓕ Ⓖ Ⓗ Ⓙ Ⓚ   59. Ⓐ Ⓑ Ⓒ Ⓓ Ⓔ
15. Ⓐ Ⓑ Ⓒ Ⓓ Ⓔ   30. Ⓕ Ⓖ Ⓗ Ⓙ Ⓚ   45. Ⓐ Ⓑ Ⓒ Ⓓ Ⓔ   60. Ⓕ Ⓖ Ⓗ Ⓙ Ⓚ

Reading Test

1. Ⓐ Ⓑ Ⓒ Ⓓ   11. Ⓐ Ⓑ Ⓒ Ⓓ   21. Ⓐ Ⓑ Ⓒ Ⓓ   31. Ⓐ Ⓑ Ⓒ Ⓓ
2. Ⓕ Ⓖ Ⓗ Ⓙ   12. Ⓕ Ⓖ Ⓗ Ⓙ   22. Ⓕ Ⓖ Ⓗ Ⓙ   32. Ⓕ Ⓖ Ⓗ Ⓙ
3. Ⓐ Ⓑ Ⓒ Ⓓ   13. Ⓐ Ⓑ Ⓒ Ⓓ   23. Ⓐ Ⓑ Ⓒ Ⓓ   33. Ⓐ Ⓑ Ⓒ Ⓓ
4. Ⓕ Ⓖ Ⓗ Ⓙ   14. Ⓕ Ⓖ Ⓗ Ⓙ   24. Ⓕ Ⓖ Ⓗ Ⓙ   34. Ⓕ Ⓖ Ⓗ Ⓙ
5. Ⓐ Ⓑ Ⓒ Ⓓ   15. Ⓐ Ⓑ Ⓒ Ⓓ   25. Ⓐ Ⓑ Ⓒ Ⓓ   35. Ⓐ Ⓑ Ⓒ Ⓓ
6. Ⓕ Ⓖ Ⓗ Ⓙ   16. Ⓕ Ⓖ Ⓗ Ⓙ   26. Ⓕ Ⓖ Ⓗ Ⓙ   36. Ⓕ Ⓖ Ⓗ Ⓙ
7. Ⓐ Ⓑ Ⓒ Ⓓ   17. Ⓐ Ⓑ Ⓒ Ⓓ   27. Ⓐ Ⓑ Ⓒ Ⓓ   37. Ⓐ Ⓑ Ⓒ Ⓓ
8. Ⓕ Ⓖ Ⓗ Ⓙ   18. Ⓕ Ⓖ Ⓗ Ⓙ   28. Ⓕ Ⓖ Ⓗ Ⓙ   38. Ⓕ Ⓖ Ⓗ Ⓙ
9. Ⓐ Ⓑ Ⓒ Ⓓ   19. Ⓐ Ⓑ Ⓒ Ⓓ   29. Ⓐ Ⓑ Ⓒ Ⓓ   39. Ⓐ Ⓑ Ⓒ Ⓓ
10. Ⓕ Ⓖ Ⓗ Ⓙ   20. Ⓕ Ⓖ Ⓗ Ⓙ   30. Ⓕ Ⓖ Ⓗ Ⓙ   40. Ⓕ Ⓖ Ⓗ Ⓙ

Science Test

1. Ⓐ Ⓑ Ⓒ Ⓓ   11. Ⓐ Ⓑ Ⓒ Ⓓ   21. Ⓐ Ⓑ Ⓒ Ⓓ   31. Ⓐ Ⓑ Ⓒ Ⓓ

2. Ⓕ Ⓖ Ⓗ Ⓙ   12. Ⓕ Ⓖ Ⓗ Ⓙ   22. Ⓕ Ⓖ Ⓗ Ⓙ   32. Ⓕ Ⓖ Ⓗ Ⓙ

3. Ⓐ Ⓑ Ⓒ Ⓓ   13. Ⓐ Ⓑ Ⓒ Ⓓ   23. Ⓐ Ⓑ Ⓒ Ⓓ   33. Ⓐ Ⓑ Ⓒ Ⓓ

4. Ⓕ Ⓖ Ⓗ Ⓙ   14. Ⓕ Ⓖ Ⓗ Ⓙ   24. Ⓕ Ⓖ Ⓗ Ⓙ   34. Ⓕ Ⓖ Ⓗ Ⓙ

5. Ⓐ Ⓑ Ⓒ Ⓓ   15. Ⓐ Ⓑ Ⓒ Ⓓ   25. Ⓐ Ⓑ Ⓒ Ⓓ   35. Ⓐ Ⓑ Ⓒ Ⓓ

6. Ⓕ Ⓖ Ⓗ Ⓙ   16. Ⓕ Ⓖ Ⓗ Ⓙ   26. Ⓕ Ⓖ Ⓗ Ⓙ   36. Ⓕ Ⓖ Ⓗ Ⓙ

7. Ⓐ Ⓑ Ⓒ Ⓓ   17. Ⓐ Ⓑ Ⓒ Ⓓ   27. Ⓐ Ⓑ Ⓒ Ⓓ   37. Ⓐ Ⓑ Ⓒ Ⓓ

8. Ⓕ Ⓖ Ⓗ Ⓙ   18. Ⓕ Ⓖ Ⓗ Ⓙ   28. Ⓕ Ⓖ Ⓗ Ⓙ   38. Ⓕ Ⓖ Ⓗ Ⓙ

9. Ⓐ Ⓑ Ⓒ Ⓓ   19. Ⓐ Ⓑ Ⓒ Ⓓ   29. Ⓐ Ⓑ Ⓒ Ⓓ   39. Ⓐ Ⓑ Ⓒ Ⓓ

10. Ⓕ Ⓖ Ⓗ Ⓙ   20. Ⓕ Ⓖ Ⓗ Ⓙ   30. Ⓕ Ⓖ Ⓗ Ⓙ   40. Ⓕ Ⓖ Ⓗ Ⓙ

WRITING TEST

PLAN YOUR ESSAY

_____

_____

_____

_____

_____

_____

_____

_____

_____

_____

_____

_____

_____

_____

_____

_____

_____

_____

_____

_____

_____

_____

_____

_____

_____

_____

_____

_____

WRITE YOUR ESSAY

_____

_____

_____

_____

_____

_____

_____

_____

_____

_____

_____

_____

_____

_____

_____

_____

_____

_____

_____

_____

_____

_____

_____

_____

_____

_____

_____

_____

_____

_____

ENGLISH TEST

45 MINUTES—75 QUESTIONS

> **DIRECTIONS:** In this section, you will see passages with words and phrases that are underlined and numbered. Below each passage you will find questions corresponding to each number that provides alternatives to the underlined part. In most of the items, you are to choose the best alternative. If no change is needed, choose NO CHANGE.
>
> In other items, there will be either a question about an underlined portion of the passage or a question about a section of the passage or about the passage as a whole. This question type will correspond to a number or numbers in a box.
>
> For each question, choose the best alternative or answer and fill in the corresponding circle on the answer sheet.

PASSAGE I

The Right Fit

[1]

If you're in the market for a fitness tracker, you are shopping for a fitness tracker.
‾‾‾
                   1
Wearable technology is all the rage these days, giving us statistics and milestones we can use with downloadable apps to improve our daily habits. Our exercise gets better
‾‾‾‾‾‾‾‾‾‾‾‾‾‾‾‾‾‾‾‾‾‾‾
                                              2
with data, or our eating. There are many tracker options available for every kind of fitness
‾‾‾‾‾‾‾‾‾‾‾‾‾‾‾‾‾‾‾
        2
buff. 3

[2]

The MyFit bracelet is frequent considered the gold standard of trackers. It is covered
                       ‾‾‾‾‾‾‾‾‾   ‾‾‾‾‾‾‾‾‾
                             4   5
in durable silicone rubber, it is completely waterproof. You can even wear it in the
‾‾‾   ‾‾‾‾‾
                              5   6
following situations, the pool, the shower, or the rain. The latest version of the MyFit sinks
‾‾   ‾‾‾‾‾
                              6   7
seamlessly with your smartphone or tablet, so you can track your exercise and calories burned no matter where you go. If the MyFit has a drawback, it is that it's only available
‾‾‾‾‾‾‾‾‾
                                                                      8
in a limited range of colors. Also the price.
                      ‾‾‾‾‾‾‾‾‾‾‾‾‾‾‾‾‾‾‾
                               9

CONTINUE

[3]

Unlike the MyFit, the Fitness Buddy <u>needs plugged</u> into your computer or smart-
10
phone's earphone jack to sync its data. This is what makes it less user-friendly <u>on the</u>
11
<u>go?</u> The Fitness Buddy looks and feels similar to the MyFit (and is even lighter) and comes
11
in sixteen different colors. However, it's not as watertight, <u>or don't take it in the water.</u>
12
Field tests have shown that when the Fitness Buddy is submerged in water for more

than a few seconds, it stops working.

[4]

If a bracelet tracker isn't for you, consider the <u>newer</u> entry into the tracker market:
13
the VivaLife pendant. This isn't your momma's necklace! The small, lightweight pendant

is connected to a lanyard that fits around your neck. Ideally, you forget <u>its</u> there while
14
it records data like your heart rate, the number of steps you've taken today, and the

calories you've burned. Like the MyFit, it syncs wirelessly with an app on your smartphone.

Like the Fitness Buddy, it is available in a number of colors—with the added bonus of

different silicone "skins" you can purchase to make it blend in with your clothes. 15

1. **A.** NO CHANGE
    B. If you're in the market for a fitness tracker, your options have never been better.
    C. You are already shopping for a fitness tracker.
    D. Shopping for a fitness tracker has never been more challenging.

2. **F.** NO CHANGE
    G. That data can help us make better choices about exercise and eating.
    H. The data, it helps us eat and exercise better.
    J. The data is better exercise and eating.

3. Which of the following sentences could be added to Paragraph 1?

    A. A gym membership also encourages more exercise.
    B. Fitness trackers can often be used underwater, but this is not always the case.
    C. I never used a fitness tracker before last year.
    D. Trackers can tell you how many calories you've burned and how intense your exercise was.

4. **F.** NO CHANGE
   G. hardly
   H. frequently
   J. frequenting

5. **A.** NO CHANGE
   B. Although it is covered in durable silicone rubber, it is completely waterproof.
   C. It is covered in durable silicone rubber, so it is completely waterproof.
   D. It is covered in durable silicone rubber, why it is waterproof.

6. **F.** NO CHANGE
   G. the pool, the shower, or the rain.
   H. the following situations like the pool, the shower, or the rain.
   J. the following situations: the pool. The shower. Or the rain.

7. **A.** NO CHANGE
   B. streams
   C. syncs
   D. sings

8. **F.** NO CHANGE
   G. they are that
   H. it were that
   J. it will be that

9. **A.** NO CHANGE
   B. Also, the price is among the highest in the market.
   C. Also the price is not so bad.
   D. The price is also a drawback.

10. **F.** NO CHANGE
    G. needs should plugged
    H. needs to be plugged
    J. to be plugged

11. **A.** NO CHANGE
    B. on the go;
    C. on the go,
    D. on the go.

12. **F.** NO CHANGE
    G. for
    H. so
    J. nor

13. **A.** NO CHANGE
    B. newest
    C. new
    D. news

14. **F.** NO CHANGE
    G. its'
    H. it were
    J. it's

15. Which of the following would be an appropriate closing sentence for Paragraph 4?

    A. Another fitness tracker available today is the TrackStar.
    B. In some ways, the VivaLife is the best of both worlds.
    C. The MyFit is not available for sale in stores, only online.
    D. The VivaLife app is available to download for $1.99.

CONTINUE

The Critic

[1]

Well, readers, this year's Student Playwright Festival has come and gone. <u>And me,</u>
<u>16</u>
your faithful theater critic for the *Garfield High Gazette*, <u>has</u> attended every single one
<u>17</u>
of this year's plays. The theater scene here at the school is strong, but I have to say that

this year's productions were somewhat of a mixed bag.

[2]

Every year around this time, the festival gives our resident writers and actors a

chance to shine by <u>writing their own shows, producing, and stage their own shows.</u>
<u>18</u>
<u>Sponsorship</u> by Ms. Campbell and Mr. Rodriguez as faculty advisors this year, the festival
<u>19</u>
<u>has been actually</u> a Garfield tradition since 1987.
<u>20</u>

[3]

[21] The good ones I liked were the following. Marguerite Jackson's play *The Armchair*

Quarterback was a searing look at the dangers of becoming addicted to fantasy football.

Her lead actor, Colin Bronson, showed great vulnerability and sensitivity in his role

(a welcome change from his <u>last year</u> lackluster performance as Edward Cullen in the
<u>22</u>
Garfield Drama <u>Clubs'</u> adaptation of *Twilight!: The Musical*).
<u>23</u>

[4]

Honorable mention goes to Joey Mirabelli's one-act, one-man show *Deep Space*.

<u>In which,</u> the playwright <u>starred also</u> as an astronaut who lost contact with his ship. Sure,
<u>24</u>   <u>25</u>
the plot was similar to <u>*Gravity*</u>, but his performance was so good that I forgot that after
<u>26</u>
a while. <u>Watch out for competition, *Gravity* stars Sandra Bullock and George Clooney!</u>
<u>27</u>

[5]

Now for the bad: Andrea Medeiros's play *The Hunger Games!: The Musical* was rather

disappointing. If you'll recall, Andrea was the driving force behind *Twilight!: The Musical*;

also recall that yours truly walked out before the end of that <u>show, Sorry</u> Andrea, some
28

books are better left un-adapted.

[6]

Other plays at this year's festival included *Stranded*, *Life in the Dollhouse*, *The Bell Mason Jar*, and *My Inner Monologues During Algebra II.* 29

Overall, readers, this year's festival was a success. 30

16. **F.** NO CHANGE
    G. And you
    H. And I
    J. And myself

17. **A.** NO CHANGE
    B. have
    C. will have
    D. has been

18. **F.** NO CHANGE
    G. writing, producing, and staging.
    H. write, produce, and stage their own shows.
    J. writing, producing, and staging their own shows.

19. **A.** NO CHANGE
    B. Sponsoring
    C. Sponsors
    D. Sponsored

20. **F.** NO CHANGE
    G. has actually been
    H. actually been
    J. actually has been

21. Which of the following would be a more effective opening sentence for Paragraph 3?
    A. First, let's talk about the plays I enjoyed.
    B. Not all of the plays were terrible.
    C. year's festival was held in Brownwell Auditorium.
    D. Student playwright Marguerite Jackson is my friend.

22. The best placement for the underlined portion would be:
    F. where it is now.
    G. after *lackluster*.
    H. before *his*.
    J. after *performance*.

23. **A.** NO CHANGE
    B. Clubs's
    C. Club's
    D. Clubs

24. **F.** NO CHANGE
    G. In that,
    H. In what,
    J. In it,

CONTINUE

25. **A.** NO CHANGE
    B. also starred
    C. starred as well
    D. too starred

26. What context detail could the writer add to the underlined text?
    F. A long, detailed explanation of *Gravity's* plot
    G. A list of other space-themed movies
    H. That *Gravity* was a movie released in 2014
    J. His personal thoughts on *Gravity*

27. **A.** NO CHANGE
    B. You better watch out, Sandra Bullock and George Clooney.
    C. Like Sandra Bullock and George Clooney.
    D. Sandra Bullock and George Clooney gave great performances in the film.

28. **F.** NO CHANGE
    G. show. Sorry
    H. show, sorry.
    J. show? sorry

29. How could the writer revise Paragraph 6 to fit with the structure of the overall article?
    A. Replace it with a list of other books that should not be adapted as plays.
    B. Add details about the faculty advisors, Ms. Cullen and Mr. Rodriguez.
    C. Add more details about what the writer thought of each play.
    D. Move the entire paragraph before Paragraph 3.

30. Which of the following would make an appropriate concluding paragraph for the article?
    F. Because some of the plays were bad, they should cancel next year's festival.
    G. Even the plays I didn't enjoy took a lot of hard work, and I hope that next year's playwrights are already firing up their laptops and writing away.
    H. Therefore, I will not be attending next year's festival.
    J. I can't wait to see what book Andrea Medeiros will be adapting next.

PASSAGE III

How Much Sleep Is Enough

[1]

How much sleep does a person <u>really</u> need? This has been debated numerous times
<u> </u>
 31
among <u>the years.</u> <u>If someone is interested in learning how much sleep is right for him</u>
 32 33
<u>or her, you should listen to the experts in the field.</u> Experts have concluded that how
 33
much sleep a person needs depends on the person's age first and foremost, but also on

how healthy <u>they are</u> in general.
 34

[2]

What happens when you sleep? During the first stage of sleep (a.k.a. the transitional

phase), your eyes move slowly underneath your eyelids, your muscles slow down, and

you can be awakened easily. During the second stage (a.k.a. light sleep), you are truly

asleep, and your body's processes slow down as your body temperature goes down as

well. In the third stage, <u>deep sleep,</u> your brain activity slows so much that if you're woken
 35
up, it can take some time to feel fully alert. The next stage is R.E.M. (Rapid Eye Movement

sleep, a.k.a. dream sleep), where your blood pressure and heart rate increase while you

dream. Also while you dream, your eyes move quickly <u>under your eyelids hence the name.</u>
 36

[3]

For teenagers, experts typically recommend 8–10 hours of sleep per night. Surveys

have shown that only about 15% of teens report getting 8.5 hours or more of sleep on

school nights. <u>This is a problem, being that the lack of sleep affects daily activities like</u>
 37
<u>driving safely, learning new information.</u> Lack of sleep can also lead to behavioral
 37
problems and <u>increased illness, colds, flu, etc.</u>
 38

CONTINUE

[4]

For adults, the recommended sleep period is 7–9 hours. Only, like, 52% of adults

                                                                                        39

report getting that amount of sleep on the regular. Results of this reduced sleep (or

                                                          39

"sleep debt" as it is sometimes called) can include an increased risk of serious diseases

like diabetes or heart disease, as well as decreased productivity during the day...

                                                                                        40

[5]

For older adults, the experts recommend 6–8 hours of sleep. In this group, 42% of

                                                                                        41

people surveyed say they do not get this much sleep. Just like in the other age groups,

                                                          41

this lack of sleep can weaken the immune system. It can also leave people tired and

disoriented throughout the day.

[6]

No matter what age a person is, the numbers make it clear that sleep health is very

much a public health issue. Developed good sleep habits should be a priority for

                                              42

everyone, not to mention an important part of any long-term health plan.

---

31. A. NO CHANGE
  B. truly
  C. very
  D. real

32. F. NO CHANGE
  G. in the years
  H. over the years
  J. around the years

33. A. NO CHANGE
  B. If someone is interested in learning how much sleep is right for him or her, he or she should listen to the experts in the field.
  C. If you are interested in learning how much sleep is right for someone, she should listen to the experts in the field.
  D. If he is interested in learning how much sleep is right for him, we should listen to the experts in the field.

34. F. NO CHANGE
  G. they is
  H. he or she are
  J. he or she is

---

35. **A.** NO CHANGE
    B. (a.k.a. deep sleep)
    C. also known as deep sleep
    D. so-called deep sleep

36. **F.** NO CHANGE
    G. under your eyelids_hence the name.
    H. under your eyelids…hence the name.
    J. under your eyelids, hence the name.

37. **A.** NO CHANGE
    B. The problem being that the lack of sleep affects daily activities like driving safety and learning new information.
    C. The lack of sleep is problematic because it affects daily activities like driving safely and learning new information.
    D. It being problematic, the lack of sleep affects daily activities like driving safely and learning new information.

38. **F.** NO CHANGE
    G. increased illness (colds, flu, etc.).
    H. increased illness/colds /flu/etc.
    J. increased (illness, colds, flu, etc.).

39. **A.** NO CHANGE
    B. Only about 52% of adults report getting that amount of sleep on the regular.
    C. Only about 52% of adults regularly report getting that amount of sleep.
    D. Only about 52% of adults report getting that amount of sleep regularly.

40. **F.** NO CHANGE
    G. day.
    H. day
    J. day;

41. **A.** NO CHANGE
    B. 42% of people say they do not get this much sleep
    C. 58% of people were surveyed and do get this much sleep.
    D. 58% of people surveyed get this amount of sleep.

42. **F.** NO CHANGE
    G. Developing
    H. To have developed
    J. To develop

Questions 43–45 deal with the passage as a whole.

43. Which of the following details would be relevant if added to the passage?

    A. Details about different people's dreams during R.E.M. sleep
    B. age ranges for teenagers, adults, and older adults
    C. The number of people surveyed
    D. Details about the health conditions caused by lack of sleep

44. Which paragraph could be deleted to better convey the theme of the essay?

    F. Paragraph 2
    G. Paragraph 3
    H. Paragraph 4
    J. Paragraph 6

CONTINUE

45. The writer wants to add another paragraph of supporting information. Which of the following would fit best in the essay?

    A. A more detailed analysis of R.E.M. sleep

    B. A discussion of which bedtimes doctors recommend

    C. Information about the amount of sleep that children need

    D. A list of famous doctors who treat sleep deprivation

PASSAGE IV

Swimming with Sharks

[1]

It was a beautiful Sunday morning, not yet 9:00 a.m. in the morning. I scarcely had
        46   47
been in the water for about ten minutes when I saw the fins jumping out in the surf.
47
Dark triangles surfaced briefly before disappearing back under the waves. My first

thought: sharks! There were sharks right off the coast of Southern Point Beach. [48] [49]

[2]

The beach was crowded with people, so my first thought was to save everyone.
                                                       50
"Shark?" I yelled at the top of my voice. The lifeguard, who was texting, didn't look up
  51
from his phone. People around me heard, though. Parents pulled their kids out of the

water; kids screamed. It was chaos. Pure chaos. So much chaos.
                                         52

[3]

Eventually, the lifeguard noticed the noise and looked up. Blew the whistle, then
                                                   53
waved everyone out of the water. By then I had made it back to my blanket. There were
  53
four young men playing volleyball nearby. I could still see those deadly fins lurking,
                                                     54
coming dangerously close to a paddle boarder who was still out on the water. Worried,
  54
I trotted over to the lifeguard to let him know. Surely, he had noticed he was in danger. [56]
                                                55

[4]

Before I could reach the lifeguard stand, he lowered his binoculars and hopped

down to the sand. "Everyone back in the water," the lifeguard shouted. "It's safe."

[5]

Safe? I asked him "how he could possibly let people back into the water with the

———————————————————————

57

sharks just off the shore." Had he not seen the movie *Jaws*?

——————————   ————————

57   58

[6]

"You mean the dolphins?" he replied. "Those are dolphin fins. They're out here every

day. There haven't been any sharks around here in at least 50 years." After he explained

——

59

46. **F.** NO CHANGE
    G. Sunday morning, beautiful, not yet 9:00.
    H. It was a beautiful Sunday morning, not yet 9:00 a.m.
    J. It was a beautiful Sunday morning, not yet 9:00.

47. **A.** NO CHANGE
    B. had scarcely been
    C. scarcely been
    D. had been scarcely

48. Which of the following would be an effective opening sentence choice for Paragraph 1?

    F. Let me tell you about an initially wonderful experience that turned out to be just life changing.
    G. Let me tell you about an initially scary experience that turned out to be just an awkward mishap.
    H. Let me tell you about an initially awkward experience that turned out to be just terrifying.
    J. Let me tell you about an initially boring experience that turned out to be just a humdrum event.

CONTINUE

49. Which of the following details could the writer add to Paragraph 1?

    A. The number of fins the writer saw in the water

    B. How long the writer had been at the beach

    C. A description of the kinds of wildlife found at Southern Point Beach

    D. The number of shark attacks in the United States last year

50. **F.** NO CHANGE
    G. my third thought
    H. my next thought
    J. the first thought

51. **A.** NO CHANGE
    B. "Shark;"
    C. 'Shark'
    D. "Shark!"

52. **F.** NO CHANGE
    G. It was pure chaos.
    H. was so much, pure, and chaos.
    J. Pure chaos, and so much.

53. **A.** NO CHANGE
    B. I blew the whistle, and waved everyone out of the water.
    C. The lifeguard blew his whistle, then waved everyone out of the water.
    D. They blew the whistle, then waved everyone out of the water.

54. **F.** NO CHANGE
    G. lurking, though coming dangerously close
    H. lurking
    J. lurking, or coming dangerously close

55. **A.** NO CHANGE
    B. the lifeguard
    C. I
    D. the paddle boarder

56. Which of the following sentences should be deleted from Paragraph 3?

    F. Eventually, the lifeguard noticed the noise and looked up.

    G. There were four young men playing volleyball nearby.

    H. Worried, I trotted over to the lifeguard to let him know.

    J. Surely, he had noticed he was in danger.

57. **A.** NO CHANGE

    B. how he could possibly let people back into the water with the sharks just off the shore.

    C. how he could possibly "let people back into the water with the sharks just off the shore."

    D. how he could "possibly let people back into the water with the sharks just off the shore."

58. **F.** NO CHANGE
    G. the movie *Jaws*?
    H. *Jaws the movie?*
    J. *Jaws, the movie!*

59. **A.** NO CHANGE
    B. Their
    C. They're
    D. Theirs

60. The writer wants to add a paragraph about sharks in general. Where should he place it?

    F.   After Paragraph 1
    G. After Paragraph 3
    H. Before Paragraph 5
    J.   He should not add another paragraph.

this, I felt pretty foolish. I walked back to my towel, but I could see the lifeguard shoot annoyed looks at me as other beachgoers peppered him with questions about the "sharks."

[7]

So to recap, my big adventure of swimming with the sea's deadliest creatures was really just an embarrassing mistake. At least now I know where I can go to watch friendly dolphins frolicking in the surf!

PASSAGE V

The Disappearing and Reappearing Brontosaurus

[1]

[1] For much of the twentieth century, the Brontosaurus was the dinosaur most people thought of when they heard the word "dinosaur." [2] With four tree-trunk-sized
                                                            61
legs, a long neck, and a long tail, the word *Brontosaurus* liberally translates to "thunder
                               61   62
lizard." [3] "Thunder lizard" was often used as a common nickname for dinosaurs in general. [4] However, even as the Brontosaurus became popular, experts insisted that no such dinosaur ever existed. [63]

[2]

In fact, paleontologists claimed that what we thought of as a "Brontosaurus" was really misassembled skeleton dating back to 1877. They believed that Yale University
                    64

CONTINUE

paleontologist O.C. Marsh had incorrectly put a Camarosaurus skull on an Apatosaurus body and proclaimed it a new kind of dinosaur. That being said, as "new" as dinosaurs
<u>65</u>
could be, millions of years after its extinction.
<u>66</u>

[3]

Other paleontologists they were skeptical from the start, given how closely the
<u>67</u>
Brontosaurus resembled the Apatosaurus. By 1903, the mistake was noticed by scientists. Yet it was not until the 1970s that the mistake was officially corrected in a museum. One was the first to attach a Camarosaurus skulls to the Apatosaurus body. 69
<u>68</u>

[4]

By then, the Brontosaurus was part of pop culture. It was featured in cartoons like *The Flintstones* and movies like *King Kong*. Decades later, the Brontosaurus would be one
<u>70</u>
of the dinosaurs in the 1993 movie *Jurassic Park* many years after scientists stopped
<u>70</u>
recognizing the Brontosaurus as a genus of dinosaur.
<u>70</u>

[5]

Twist! Now many scientists believe the Brontosaurus may have existed after all. This
<u>71</u>
is in contrast to some scientists' thoughts on the existence of aliens. A 2015 study revealed that after a careful review of fossils in museums around the world, there were enough differences between the Brontosaurus and the Apatosaurus to conclude that the two were different dinosaurs. Personally, I think this was a long time in coming. The Brontosaurus is back, and now it has a scientific consensus behind it. 72 73 74

---

61. **A.** NO CHANGE
     B. With its four tree-trunk-sized legs, a long neck, and a long tail, the word
     C. With four tree-trunk-sized legs, a long neck, and a long tail, the dinosaur was named appropriately.
     D. With four tree-trunk-sized legs, a long neck, and a long tail, the thunder lizard's name

62. **F.** NO CHANGE
     G. laterally
     H. legibly
     J. literally

63. Which of the following sentences could the writer delete from Paragraph 1 without affecting the flow of the topic paragraph?

    A. None; each sentence is absolutely crucial to the paragraph.

    B. Sentence 1

    C. Sentence 3

    D. Sentence 4

64. F. NO CHANGE

    G. really a misassembled skeleton

    H. a misassembled skeleton really

    J. a really misassembled skeleton

65. A. NO CHANGE

    B. That is, as "new" as dinosaurs

    C. That being said, insofar as dinosaurs

    D. Or rather, it was as "new" as dinosaurs

66. F. NO CHANGE

    G. they

    H. their

    J. his

67. A. NO CHANGE

    B. Other paleontologists were skeptical from the start,

    C. Skeptical from the start,

    D. The other paleontologists, they were skeptical from the start,

68. F. NO CHANGE

    G. a Camarosaurus skulls to Apatosaurus bodies.

    H. an Apatosaurus skull to the Camarosaurus body.

    J. an Apatosaurus skull to the Apatosaurus body.

69. Which of the following support details would be relevant in Paragraph 3?

    A. Details about how the Camarosaurus looked

    B. The names of paleontologists who were skeptical of the Brontosaurus

    C. That the museum who finally switched the skeletons back was the Carnegie Museum in Pittsburgh

    D. A direct quote from O.C. Marsh

70. F. NO CHANGE

    G. The movie *Jurassic Park* recognized the Brontosaurus even after decades of scientists not recognizing the Brontosaurus as a genus of dinosaur.

    H. Decades later, the 1993 movie *Jurassic Park* would include the Brontosaurus, even so many years after scientists stopped recognizing the Brontosaurus as a genus of dinosaur.

    J. Even after scientists stopped recognizing the Brontosaurus as a genus of dinosaur, the Brontosaurus would still become a star of the 1993 movie *Jurassic Park*.

71. A. NO CHANGE

    B. However, there is a recent twist to the story.

    C. There is a twist!

    D. The twists and turns of this story have arrived.

CONTINUE

72. Which sentence in Paragraph 5 fits least with the author's overall intended purpose?

    F. Now many scientists believe the Brontosaurus may have existed after all.

    G. This is in contrast to some scientists' thoughts on the existence of aliens.

    H. A 2015 study revealed that after a careful review of fossils in museums around the world, there were enough differences between the Brontosaurus and the Apatosaurus to conclude that the two were different dinosaurs.

    J. The Brontosaurus is back, and now it has a scientific consensus behind it.

73. Which sentence in Paragraph 5 does not fit with the tone and voice of the essay?

    A. Now many scientists believe the Brontosaurus may have existed after all.

    B. A 2015 study revealed that after a careful review of fossils in museums around the world, there were enough differences between the Brontosaurus and the Apatosaurus to conclude that the two were different dinosaurs.

    C. Personally, I think this was a long time in coming.

    D. The Brontosaurus is back, and now it has a scientific consensus behind it.

74. Which of the following would be an appropriate closing sentence for the essay?

    F. Perhaps now there will be enough room in the paleontology community for both the "thunder lizard" and the Apatosaurus.

    G. But did the Tyrannosaurus Rex really exist?

    H. And that's the story of the Brontosaurus.

    J. Somebody phone the museums!

> **Question 75 asks about the passage as a whole.**

75. The writer wants to add information about the Apatosaurus and how it was similar to the Brontosaurus. Where would this information fit in the essay?

    A. At the beginning of Paragraph 2

    B. At the end of Paragraph 2

    C. At the beginning of Paragraph 3

    D. At the end of Paragraph 4

STOP

MATHEMATICS TEST

60 MINUTES—60 QUESTIONS

DIRECTIONS: For each of the following items, solve each problem, choose the correct answer, and then fill in the corresponding circle on the answer sheet.

If you encounter problems that take too much time to solve, move on. Solve as many problems as you can; then return to the others in the time remaining for the test.

You may use a calculator on this test for any problems you choose, but some of the problems may best be solved without the use of a calculator.

Note: Unless otherwise stated, assume the following:

1. Illustrative figures are NOT necessarily drawn to scale.
2. Geometric figures lie in a plane.
3. The word *line* indicates a straight line.
4. The word *average* indicates arithmetic mean.

1. If $f(x) = -3x^3 + x - 1$, compute $f(-2)$.

   A. −27
   B. 15
   C. 25
   D. 21
   E. −11

2. What is the complete solution set for $3|x+5|-12=0$?

   F. {1, 9}
   G. {−7, 17}
   H. {−1, −9}
   J. {4, −14}
   K. {−17, 7}

3. Which of the points listed below is furthest from point P?

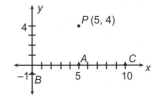

   A. A
   B. B
   C. C
   D. D
   E. E

CONTINUE

4. Which of the following could be the graph of $f(x) = -4(x + 2)^2 - 1$?

F.

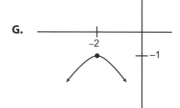

G.

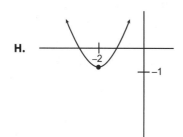

H.

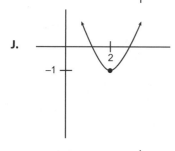

J.

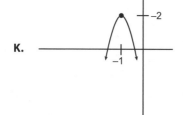

K.

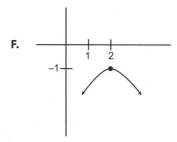

5. Consider the diagram shown:

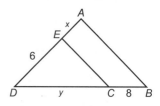

Assume that *AB* is parallel to *EC*. Express *y* in terms of *x*.

A. $y = \dfrac{48}{x}$

B. $y = 48x$

C. $y = \dfrac{x}{48}$

D. $y = \dfrac{6}{x}$

E. $y = 6x$

6. Consider the diagram shown:

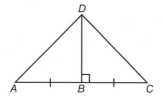

Which of the following properties can be used to prove the congruence of triangles *ABD* and *CBD*?

F. SSA Property
G. AAS Property
H. ASA Property
J. SSS Property
K. SAS Property

7. Which of the following is NOT a meaningful quantity?

A. $3\begin{bmatrix} 1 \\ 2 \\ -1 \end{bmatrix}$

B. $4\begin{bmatrix} -1 & 2 & 0 \\ 0 & 3 & 1 \\ -1 & 3 & 4 \end{bmatrix}$

C. $\begin{bmatrix} 2 & 4 \end{bmatrix} + \begin{bmatrix} -1 \\ 2 \end{bmatrix}$

D. $\begin{bmatrix} -2 & 3 & 1 & -1 \end{bmatrix} - 4\begin{bmatrix} 0 & 9 & -1 & 2 \end{bmatrix}$

E. $\det\begin{bmatrix} 3 & 21 \\ 1 & 3 \end{bmatrix}$

8. Maureen spent $\dfrac{2}{5}$ of her time this week studying for final exams. If she had 26 hours to devote to completing all activities, including studying, what amount of time did she spend studying?

F. 13 hours
G. 11 hours, 48 minutes
H. 9 hours, 30 minutes
J. 10 hours, 24 minutes
K. 15 hours, 36 minutes

9. What is the value of the expression $\dfrac{b^c - a^c}{ab}$ if $a = 2$, $b = -3$, and $c = 3$?

A. $\dfrac{1}{6}$

B. $5\dfrac{5}{6}$

C. 5

D. $3\dfrac{1}{6}$

E. $2\dfrac{5}{6}$

10. Which of the following expressions is equivalent to $\dfrac{z^a \cdot \left(z^2\right)^b}{z^{b-a}}$?

F. z^b
G. z^3
H. z^{a+b}
J. z^{2a+3b}
K. z^{2a+b}

11. What is the complete solution set for the equation $60x - 18 - 50x^2$?

A. $\left\{\dfrac{5}{3}\right\}$

B. $\left\{\dfrac{3}{5}\right\}$

C. $\left\{\dfrac{5}{3}, -\dfrac{5}{3}\right\}$

D. $\left\{3, \dfrac{1}{5}\right\}$

E. $\left\{\dfrac{3}{5}, -\dfrac{3}{5}\right\}$

12. Which of the following expressions is equivalent to

$$\sqrt{w^3 xy} \cdot 3\sqrt{wx^2}\,?$$

F. $3w^4x^3y$
G. $w^2x\sqrt{3xy}$
H. $xw\sqrt{3y}$
J. $3w^2x\sqrt{xy}$
K. $3w\sqrt{xy}$

13. Which of the following lines is perpendicular to $3x - 5y = -2$?

   A. $y = x - \dfrac{5}{3}$

   B. $3y + 5 = 5x$

   C. $3y - 5x = 0$

   D. $\dfrac{3}{5}x - y = 3$

   E. $y + \dfrac{5}{3}x = -2$

14. Which of the following is equal to

   $$\dfrac{3}{4(x-1)} - \dfrac{2}{4x-1}?$$

   F. $\dfrac{1}{4(x-1)}$

   G. $\dfrac{1}{4x-1}$

   H. $\dfrac{4x+5}{4(x-1)(4x-1)}$

   J. $\dfrac{x+5}{(x-1)(4x-1)}$

   K. $\dfrac{5}{-4(x-1)}$

15. Round 1,354,689,301 to the nearest million.

   A. 1,354,000,000
   B. 1,350,000,000
   C. 1,354,700,000
   D. 1,355,000,000
   E. 1,354,600,000

16. Which of the following statements is true regarding the relationship of the graphs of f and g?

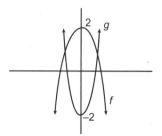

   F. $f(x) \le g(x)$ for all real numbers x.
   G. The equation $f(x) - g(x) = 0$ has no solutions.
   H. There is no x-value for which both $f(x) = 2$ and $g(x) = -2$ are satisfied simultaneously.
   J. The graphs of $f(x)$ and $g(x)$ are increasing and decreasing on opposite intervals.
   K. The graph of $g(x)$ is the reflection of the graph of $f(x)$ over the x-axis.

17. Consider the diagram shown:

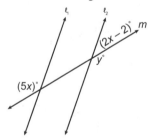

   If the lines l_1 and l_2 are parallel, what must be the value of y?

   A. 26
   B. 50
   C. 40
   D. 130
   E. 90

18. Consider the line segment PQ shown. If a translation is performed on PQ so that the image of P is the point $(-1, -1)$, what is the image of Q under this translation?

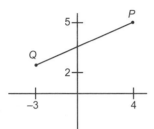

F. $(3, 2)$
G. $(-8, -4)$
H. $(-3, -2)$
J. $(2, -4)$
K. $(-8, 8)$

19. If $f(\theta) = 3 \cos (2\theta)$, what is $f\left(\dfrac{\pi}{2}\right)$?

A. 0
B. 1
C. -1
D. 3
E. -3

20. Which of the following is equal to $\dfrac{\sqrt{48}}{\sqrt{60}}$?

F. $\dfrac{\sqrt{10}}{5}$

G. $\dfrac{2\sqrt{5}}{5}$

H. $\sqrt{10}$

J. $\dfrac{\sqrt{5}}{2}$

K. $\dfrac{\sqrt{12}}{12}$

21. The number of books that 75 sixth-graders read during the summer months is listed in the following table:

Number of Books Read	Number of Students Who Read This Number of Books
0	2
1	8
2	11
3	21
4	15
5	8
6	2
7	5
8	1
9	2

What is the mode number of books read?

A. 3
B. 4
C. 8
D. 5
E. 21

22. Compute: $\dfrac{(4-5)^2}{4^2 - 5^2}$.

F. 1

G. -1

H. $\dfrac{1}{25}$

J. $-\dfrac{1}{9}$

K. $-\dfrac{1}{2}$

CONTINUE

23. Compute: $(-2|1 - 4|)^2$

    A. 100

    B. 6

    C. −6

    D. 36

    E. −36

24. What is the complete solution set for the equation $6x^2 + 3 = 11x$?

    F. $\left\{ \dfrac{2\sqrt{3}}{3}, -\dfrac{2\sqrt{3}}{3} \right\}$

    G. $\left\{ 3, \dfrac{2}{3} \right\}$

    H. $\left\{ -3, -\dfrac{2}{3} \right\}$

    J. $\left\{ \dfrac{1}{3}, \dfrac{3}{2} \right\}$

    K. $\left\{ -\dfrac{1}{3}, -\dfrac{3}{2} \right\}$

25. You have twice as many dimes as nickels and four more quarters than nickels. If the total amount of money that you have is $3.50, how many dimes do you have?

    A. 9

    B. 5

    C. 10

    D. 14

    E. 15

26. If $4m - 3n = -4$ and $2m - 2n = 5$, what is the value of $\dfrac{m}{n}$?

    F. 161

    G. $-\dfrac{23}{2}$

    H. −14

    J. $\dfrac{23}{28}$

    K. $\dfrac{28}{23}$

27. Which of the following is equivalent to $-2(3 + 4i) - (2i - 3)$?

    A. $-9 + 2i$

    B. $-9 - 10i$

    C. $-13i$

    D. $30i$

    E. $-3 - 10i$

28. For which of the following inequalities is the solution set shown?

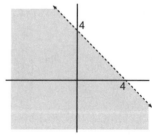

    F. $y \le 4 - x$

    G. $x + y < 4$

    H. $x + y > 4$

    J. $y - x < 4$

    K. $y \ge 4 + x$

29. Which of the equations describes the graph shown?

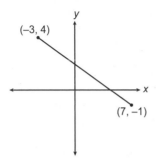

(−3, 4)

(7, −1)

A. $y = -x + 5$
B. $2y + x = 5$
C. $2y = -x + 8$
D. $2x + y = -2$
E. $7x + 8y = 11$

30. The length of a rectangle is 1 foot less than twice the width. If the area of the rectangle is 3 square feet, what is its perimeter?

F. 4 feet
G. 7 feet
H. 3.5 feet
J. 3 feet
K. 1.5 feet

31. If a triangle has sides of length 5 cm and 9 cm, which of the following cannot be the length of the third side?

A. 10 cm
B. 9 cm
C. 5 cm
D. 3 cm
E. 12 cm

32. Find y in the diagram shown:

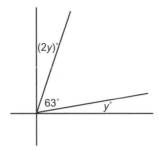

$(2y)°$

$63°$

$y°$

F. 14.5
G. 30
H. 27
J. 18
K. 9

33. Consider a circle with center (4, −3). What is the largest diameter possible so that the circle remains in quadrant IV and is at worst tangent to the x- or y-axis?

A. 3 units
B. 4 units
C. 6 units
D. 8 units
E. 10 units

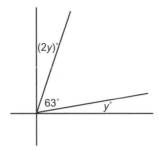

CONTINUE

34. Suppose a function $p(x)$ satisfies the following conditions:

- $p(-1) = 0$
- $x - 2$ and $x + 4$ are both factors of $p(x)$.
- $p(x)$ is a third degree polynomial.

Which of these could be the graph of $p(x)$?

F.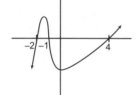

G.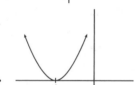

H.

J.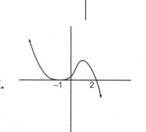

K.

35. Fifty tickets are being sold for a potluck raffle. There are 5 cash prizes, 14 door prizes, and 20 two-dollar coupons toward an ice cream sundae. What is the probability of winning either a door prize or no prize?

A. 0.14
B. 0.78
C. 0.22
D. 0.5
E. 0.25

36. Compute $3\dfrac{3}{7} \div 1\dfrac{5}{14}$.

F. $3\dfrac{6}{5}$

G. 2

H. $2\dfrac{10}{19}$

J. $\dfrac{19}{48}$

K. $4\dfrac{32}{49}$

37. If a right triangle has vertices $(0, 3)$, $(0, 0)$, and $(9, 0)$, what is the length of its hypotenuse?

A. $3\sqrt{10}$
B. 3
C. 9
D. $2\sqrt{3}$
E. 90

38. What is the midpoint of the line segment with endpoints $(a, -b)$ and $(b, -a)$, where a and b are real numbers?

F. $\left(-\dfrac{a+b}{2}, \dfrac{a+b}{2}\right)$

G. $(a+b, -a-b)$

H. $\left(\dfrac{a+b}{2}, -\dfrac{a+b}{2}\right)$

J. $(0, 0)$

K. $(-a-b, a+b)$

39. Which of the following is the largest set of values of a for which the quadratic equation $x^2 + ax + 4 = 0$ has two distinct real solutions?

A. $\{a : a > 0\}$

B. $\{a : a > 16\}$

C. $\{a : a < -4 \text{ or } a > 4\}$

D. $\{a : -4 < a < 4\}$

E. $\{a : a = 4 \text{ or } a = -4\}$

40. Which of the following is equivalent to $3(1 - 5w)^2$?

F. $75w^2 - 30w + 3$

G. $75w^2 - 15w + 3$

H. $3 - 75w^2$

J. $25w^2 - 10w + 3$

K. $15w^2 - 30w + 3$

41. Consider the following sequence:

$-8,$ _____ , _____ , $7, 12 \ldots$

If this sequence is arithmetic, what are the two missing terms?

A. $-1, 5$

B. $-3, 2$

C. $-4, 0$

D. $-2, 3$

E. $-2, 4$

42. Consider the graph shown.

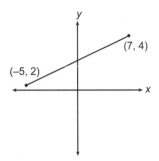

Which of the following lines is perpendicular to the line pictured?

F. $6x + 6y = 1$

G. $y = -6$

H. $6y = x + 1$

J. $y = x - 6$

K. $y + 6x = -1$

43. The graph of which of the following is an ellipse centered at the origin and longer in the x-direction than in the y-direction?

A. $\dfrac{x^2}{8} + \dfrac{y^2}{10} = 1s$

B. $x^2 = 3y^2$

C. $\dfrac{x^2}{4} + y^2 = 1$

D. $x + 5y^2 = 2$

E. $\dfrac{x^2}{8} - \dfrac{y^2}{2} = 1$

CONTINUE

44. What is the volume of a sphere with diameter $\sqrt{2}$ inches?

F. $\dfrac{\pi\sqrt{2}}{3}$ cubic inches

G. $\dfrac{8\pi\sqrt{2}}{3}$ cubic inches

H. $\dfrac{\pi\sqrt{2}}{4}$ cubic inches

J. $\dfrac{2\pi}{3}$ cubic inches

K. $2\pi\sqrt{2}$ cubic inches

45. What is the area of the parallel-ogram *WXYZ*?

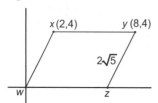

A. $12\sqrt{5}$ square units
B. 12 square units
C. 36 square units
D. 24 square units
E. 20 square units

46. Which of the following is equiv-alent to 0.0000108?

F. 1.08×10^{-4}
G. 1.08×10^{4}
H. 1.08×10^{5}
J. 1.08×10^{-5}
K. 10.8×10^{-5}

47. Miranda has four types of fruit, five types of cereal, and two beverages from which to choose for her breakfast. If she chooses one from each of these three categories, how many different combinations can she form?

A. 11
B. 10
C. 40
D. 8
E. 20

48. What is 225% of $\dfrac{3}{4}$?

F. $16\dfrac{7}{8}$

G. 3

H. $\dfrac{1}{3}$

J. $1\dfrac{11}{16}$

K. $1\dfrac{1}{2}$

49. If $f(x) = 2 + \dfrac{1}{x}$ and $g(x) = 2 - \dfrac{1}{x^2}$, which of the following equals $\dfrac{g(x)}{f(x)}$?

A. $\dfrac{2x^2 - 1}{2x^2 + x}$

B. $-x$

C. $-\dfrac{1}{x}$

D. $\dfrac{2x^2 - 1}{2x + 1}$

E. $\dfrac{2x^2 + x}{2x^2 - 1}$

50. Suppose a right circular cone has base radius R and height H. If the radius is divided by 3 and the height is quadrupled, what fraction of the volume of the original cone is the volume of the newly formed cone?

   F. $\dfrac{4}{27}$

   G. $\dfrac{4}{3}$

   H. $\dfrac{16}{3}$

   J. 4

   K. $\dfrac{4}{9}$

51. If you were to arrange the following numbers in order from least to greatest, which of them would be in third place?

   A. 40.3×10^2
   B. 4.03×10^{-2}
   C. 0.00403×10^{-1}
   D. 4.03×10^{-1}
   E. 0.403×10^1

52. Which of the following is the solution set for $|3x - 2| \le 13$?

   F.

   G.

   H.

   J.

   K.

53. What is the period of the function
$$f(x) = -2\sin\left(3x + \frac{\pi}{2}\right) + \pi \ ?$$

   A. $\dfrac{2\pi}{3}$

   B. $\dfrac{\pi}{6}$

   C. $\dfrac{\pi}{2}$

   D. π

   E. -2

54. What is the surface area of the rectangular box shown?

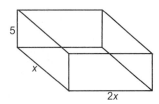

   F. $10x^2$
   G. $4x^2 + 20x$
   H. $2x^2 + 15x$
   J. $4x^2 + 30x$
   K. $2x^2 + 30x$

CONTINUE

55. What is the solution set for the given nonlinear system?

$$\begin{cases} y > x^2 - 1 \\ y \le 1 - x^2 \end{cases}$$

A.

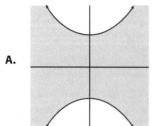

B.

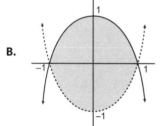

C.

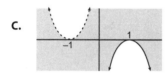

D.

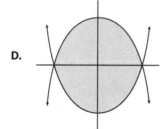

E.

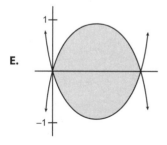

56. A quantity X is directly proportional to Y and inversely proportional to Z^2. For which of the following equations is this true?

F. $XYZ^2 = k$

G. $X = \dfrac{kZ^2}{Y}$

H. $X = k(Y + Z^2)$

J. $X = \dfrac{kY}{Z^2}$

K. $X = kYZ^2$

57. Suppose a quadrilateral $ABCD$ is such that angles ABC and BCD are both acute, and AD is parallel to BC. Which of the following shapes represents $ABCD$?

A. Trapezoid
B. Square
C. Parallelogram
D. Rhombus
E. Rectangle

58. Solve the quadratic inequality $6x^2 + 7x - 3 \ge 0$.

F. $\left\{ x : -\dfrac{3}{2} \le x \le \dfrac{1}{3} \right\}$

G. $\left\{ x : x < -\dfrac{1}{3} \text{ or } x > \dfrac{3}{2} \right\}$

H. $\left\{ x : x \le -\dfrac{3}{2} \text{ or } x \ge \dfrac{1}{3} \right\}$

J. $\left\{ x : x < -\dfrac{3}{2} \text{ or } x > \dfrac{1}{3} \right\}$

K. $\left\{ x : x \le -\dfrac{1}{3} \text{ or } x \ge \dfrac{3}{2} \right\}$

59. What is the area of the shaded sector?

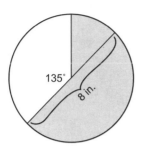

135°

8 in.

A. 10π square inches
B. 6π square inches
C. 24π square inches
D. 16π square inches
E. 8π square inches

60. To which of the following equations are both $\dfrac{5\pi}{4}$ and $\dfrac{7\pi}{4}$ solutions?

F. $\sin\theta + \cos\theta = 0$
G. $\sin\theta - \cos\theta = 0$
H. $\sin\theta + \dfrac{\sqrt{2}}{2} = 0$
J. $\cos\theta - \dfrac{\sqrt{2}}{2} = 0$
K. $\cos\theta + \dfrac{\sqrt{2}}{2} = 0$

Ⓧ
STOP

READING TEST

35 Minutes—40 Questions

> **DIRECTIONS:** There are four passages in this test. Each passage is followed by several questions. Read each passage, select the best answer to each related question, and fill in the corresponding circle on the answer sheet. You may look back at the passages as often as you need.

Passage I

PROSE FICTION: Passage A is an excerpt from *The Canterville Ghost* by Oscar Wilde. Passage B is an excerpt from *The Turn of the Screw* by Henry James.

Passage A

by Oscar Wilde

When Mr. Hiram B. Otis, the American Minister, bought Canterville Chase, every one told him he was doing a very foolish thing, as there was no doubt at all that the place was haunted. Indeed, Lord Canterville himself, who was a man of the most punctilious honour, had felt it his duty to mention the fact to Mr. Otis when they came to
5 discuss terms.

"We have not cared to live in the place ourselves," said Lord Canterville, "since my grandaunt, the Dowager Duchess of Bolton, was frightened into a fit, from which she never really recovered, by two skeleton hands being placed on her shoulders as she was dressing for dinner, and I feel bound to tell you, Mr. Otis, that the ghost has been seen
10 by several living members of my family, as well as by the rector of the parish, the Rev. Augustus Dampier, who is a Fellow of King's College, Cambridge. After the unfortunate accident to the Duchess, none of our younger servants would stay with us, and Lady Canterville often got very little sleep at night, in consequence of the mysterious noises that came from the corridor and the library."

15 "My Lord," answered the Minister, "I will take the furniture and the ghost at a valuation. I have come from a modern country, where we have everything that money can buy; and with all our spry young fellows painting the Old World red, and carrying off your best actors and prima-donnas, I reckon that if there were such a thing as a ghost in Europe, we'd have it at home in a very short time in one of our public museums, or
20 on the road as a show."

"I fear that the ghost exists," said Lord Canterville, smiling, "though it may have resisted the overtures of your enterprising impresarios. It has been well known for three centuries, since 1584 in fact, and always makes its appearance before the death of any member of our family."

CONTINUE

25   "Well, so does the family doctor for that matter, Lord Canterville. But there is no such thing, sir, as a ghost, and I guess the laws of Nature are not going to be suspended for the British aristocracy."

     "You are certainly very natural in America," answered Lord Canterville, who did not quite understand Mr. Otis's last observation, "and if you don't mind a ghost in the house,
30 it is all right. Only you must remember I warned you."

Passage B

by Henry James

     The story had held us, round the fire, sufficiently breathless, but except the obvious remark that it was gruesome, as, on Christmas Eve in an old house, a strange tale should essentially be, I remember no comment uttered till somebody happened to say that it was the only case he had met in which such a visitation had fallen on a child. The case,
5 I may mention, was that of an apparition in just such an old house as had gathered us for the occasion—an appearance, of a dreadful kind, to a little boy sleeping in the room with his mother and waking her up in the terror of it; waking her not to dissipate his dread and soothe him to sleep again, but to encounter also, herself, before she had succeeded in doing so, the same sight that had shaken him. It was this observation that
10 drew from Douglas—not immediately, but later in the evening—a reply that had the interesting consequence to which I call attention. Someone else told a story not particularly effective, which I saw he was not following. This I took for a sign that he had himself something to produce and that we should only have to wait. We waited in fact till two nights later; but that same evening, before we scattered, he brought out what was in
15 his mind.

     "I quite agree—in regard to Griffin's ghost, or whatever it was—that its appearing first to the little boy, at so tender an age, adds a particular touch. But it's not the first occurrence of its charming kind that I know to have involved a child. If the child gives the effect another turn of the screw, what do you say to TWO children—?"

20   "We say, of course," somebody exclaimed, "that they give two turns! Also that we want to hear about them."

     I can see Douglas there before the fire, to which he had got up to present his back, looking down at his interlocutor with his hands in his pockets. "Nobody but me, till now, has ever heard. It's quite too horrible." This, naturally, was declared by several voices to
25 give the thing the utmost price, and our friend, with quiet art, prepared his triumph by turning his eyes over the rest of us and going on: "It's beyond everything. Nothing at all that I know touches it."

     "For sheer terror?" I remember asking.

     He seemed to say it was not so simple as that; to be really at a loss how to qualify it.
30 He passed his hand over his eyes, made a little wincing grimace.

     "For dreadful—dreadfulness!"

"Oh, how delicious!" cried one of the women.

He took no notice of her; he looked at me, but as if, instead of me, he saw what he spoke of. "For general uncanny ugliness and horror and pain."

35   "Well then," I said, "just sit right down and begin."

He turned round to the fire, gave a kick to a log, watched it an instant. Then as he faced us again: "I can't begin. I shall have to send to town." There was a unanimous groan at this, and much reproach; after which, in his preoccupied way, he explained. "The story's written. It's in a locked drawer—it has not been out for years. I could write to my
40   man and enclose the key; he could send down the packet as he finds it." It was to me in particular that he appeared to propound this—appeared almost to appeal for aid not to hesitate. He had broken a thickness of ice, the formation of many a winter; had had his reasons for a long silence. The others resented postponement, but it was just his scruples that charmed me. I adjured him to write by the first post and to agree with us
45   for an early hearing; then I asked him if the experience in question had been his own. To this his answer was prompt. "Oh, thank God, no!"

"And is the record yours? You took the thing down?"

"Nothing but the impression. I took that HERE"—he tapped his heart. "I've never lost it."

Questions 1–3 ask about Passage A.

1. As it is used in line 22, the word *overtures* means:

A. signals.
B. prefaces.
C. forewords.
D. calls.

2. Why exactly does everyone say Hiram B. Otis's purchase of Canterville Chase is foolish?

F. It contains a dangerous ghost.
G. It has a number of monsters.
H. It is haunted by a ghost.
J. It is being destroyed by a ghost.

3. The Dowager Duchess of Bolton is Lord Canterville's:

A. daughter.
B. wife.
C. grandaunt.
D. sister.

Questions 4–6 ask about Passage B.

4. In Paragraph 7, a woman reacts to Douglas's story with:

F. delight.
G. dread.
H. hunger.
J. terror.

5. It is reasonable to infer from the passage that the author mentions Christmas Eve (line 2) because:

A. it is unusual to tell tales of ghosts on Christmas Eve.
B. Douglas is about to tell a story about spreading the holiday spirit.
C. it is traditional to tell gruesome tales on Christmas Eve.
D. Douglas tells only gruesome tales on Christmas Eve.

6. Which of the following most accurately describes how Douglas feels about telling stories?

   F. Telling gruesome stories makes him uncomfortable.
   G. He builds suspense by making his audience wait to hear his stories.
   H. He insists on telling stories with great accuracy.
   J. Telling stories brings out his mischievous and comedic side.

Questions 7–10 ask about both passages.

7. Both passages are mainly about people who:

   A. die mysterious deaths and become ghosts.
   B. are informing others about the existence of ghosts.
   C. discover ghosts that are haunting old houses.
   D. find that their holiday celebrations are ruined by ghosts.

8. In what way are Passage A and Passage B DIFFERENT?

   F. Passage A includes the appearance of a ghost, and Passage B merely features a discussion about ghosts.
   G. Passage A mentions a child who is disturbed by a ghost, and Passage B only mentions that adults have seen a ghost.
   H. Passage A revolves around ghost stories being told for entertainment, while the character in Passage B relates the ghost tale as a matter of honor and duty.
   J. Passage A contains a character who does not believe ghosts exist, and everyone in Passage B seems to believe in ghosts.

9. Considering how Lord Canterville is portrayed in Passage A and Douglas is portrayed in Passage B, they would both most accurately be described as:

   A. believers in strange phenomena.
   B. serious men of science.
   C. jokers with wicked senses of humor.
   D. deeply troubled individuals.

10. In what way are the ghosts in Passage A and Passage B DIFFERENT?

   F. The ghost in Passage A appears as a skeleton; the ghost in Passage B does not.
   G. The ghost in passage A is frightening; the ghost in Passage B is not.
   H. The ghost in passage A wants revenge; the ghost in Passage B does not.
   J. The ghost in Passage A is an adult; the ghost in Passage B is a child.

PASSAGE II

SOCIAL STUDIES: This passage is an excerpt from *Susan B. Anthony: Rebel, Crusader, Humanitarian* by Alma Lutz.

"If Sally Ann knows more about weaving than Elijah," reasoned eleven-year-old Susan with her father, "then why don't you make her overseer?"

"It would never do," replied Daniel Anthony as a matter of course. "It would never do to have a woman overseer in the mill."

5   This answer did not satisfy Susan and she often thought about it. To enter the mill, to stand quietly and look about, was the best kind of entertainment, for she was fascinated by the whir of the looms, by the nimble fingers of the weavers, and by the general air of efficiency. Admiringly she watched Sally Ann Hyatt, the tall capable weaver from Vermont. When the yarn on the beam was tangled or there was something wrong with
10 the machinery, Elijah, the overseer, always called out to Sally Ann, "I'll tend your loom, if you'll look after this." Sally Ann never failed to locate the trouble or to untangle the yarn. Yet she was never made overseer, and this continued to puzzle Susan.

The manufacture of cotton was a new industry, developing with great promise in the United States, when Susan B. Anthony was born on February 15, 1820, in the wide
15 valley at the foot of Mt. Greylock, near Adams, Massachusetts. Enterprising young men like her father, Daniel Anthony, saw a potential cotton mill by the side of every rushing brook, and young women, eager to earn the first money they could call their own, were leaving the farms, for a few months at least, to work in the mills. Cotton cloth was the new sensation and the demand for it was steadily growing. Brides were proud to display
20 a few cotton sheets instead of commonplace homespun linen.

CONTINUE

When Susan was two years old, her father built a cotton factory of twenty-six looms beside the brook which ran through Grandfather Read's meadow, hauling the cotton forty miles by wagon from Troy, New York. The millworkers, most of them young girls from Vermont, boarded, as was the custom, in the home of the millowner; Susan's mother,
25 Lucy Read Anthony, although she had three small daughters to care for, Guelma, Susan, and Hannah, boarded eleven of the millworkers with only the help of a thirteen-year-old girl who worked for her after school hours. Lucy Anthony cooked their meals on the hearth of the big kitchen fireplace, and in the large brick oven beside it baked crisp brown loaves of bread. In addition, washing, ironing, mending, and spinning filled her
30 days. But she was capable and strong and was doing only what all women in this new country were expected to do. She taught her young daughters to help her, and Susan, even before she was six, was very useful; by the time she was ten she could cook a good meal and pack a dinner pail.

Hard work and skill were respected as Susan grew up in the rapidly expanding
35 young republic which less than fifty years before had been founded and fought for. Settlers, steadily pushing westward, had built new states out of the wilderness, adding ten to the original thirteen. Everywhere the leaven of democracy was working and men were putting into practice many of the principles so boldly stated in the Declaration of Independence, claiming for themselves equal rights and opportunities. The new states
40 entered the Union with none of the traditional property and religious limitations on the franchise, but with manhood suffrage and all voters eligible for office. The older states soon fell into line, Massachusetts in 1820 removing property qualifications for voters. Before long, throughout the United States, all free white men were enfranchised, leaving only women, Negroes, and Indians without the full rights of citizenship.

45 Although women freeholders had voted in some of the colonies and in New Jersey as late as 1807, just as in England in the fifteenth franchise had gradually found its way into the statutes, and women's rights as citizens were ignored, in spite of the contribution they had made to the defense and development of the new nation. However, European travelers, among them De Tocqueville, recognized that the survival of the New World
50 experiment in government and the prosperity and strength of the people were due in large measure to the superiority of American women. A few women had urged their claims: Abigail Adams asked her husband, a member of the Continental Congress, "to remember the ladies" in the "new code of laws"; and Hannah Lee Corbin of Virginia pleaded with her brother, Richard Henry Lee, to make good the principle of "no taxation
55 without representation" by enfranchising widows with property.

11. According to the passage, which of the following does NOT accurately describe the manufacture of cotton in 1820s America?

A. It was an industry without opportunities for women.
B. It was a developing industry.
C. It was a promising industry.
D. It was an industry that satisfied a common demand.

12. Susan B. Anthony's grandfather's cotton factory:

I. was forty miles from Troy, New York.
II. had twenty-six looms.
III. was located by a brook.

F. I only
G. II only
H. III only
J. I, II, and II

13. According to the passage, people living in Massachusetts in 1820 could vote even if they:

A. were women.
B. did not own property.
C. were not white.
D. were not citizens of the United States.

14. The services Lucy Read Anthony provided for her boarders included:

I. the making of clothing.
II. the cooking of meals.
III. the care of clothing.

F. I only
G. II only
H. I and II only
J. I and III only

15. The passage implies that Susan B. Anthony will one day:

A. appear on a one-dollar coin.
B. fight for women's right to vote.
C. own her own cotton mill.
D. become president of the United States.

16. As it is used in line 40, the word *union* refers to:

F. the United States.
G. an organization for workers.
H. a marital relationship.
J. an emblem on a flag.

17. The author would most likely agree with which of the following statements regarding the United States in 1820?

A. It did not treat all of its citizens fairly.
B. It was an ideal time to be an American.
C. It was a time of tremendous prosperity.
D. It was ruled by hatred and ignorance.

CONTINUE

18. The passage implies all of the following about Susan B. Anthony EXCEPT:

F. she was very good at doing domestic chores at a young age.

G. she possessed qualities that were admired during her time.

H. she was interested in women's rights at an early age.

J. she secretly longed to work in her father's cotton factory.

19. In a cotton mill, which of the following seems to play the most significant role?

A. Its yarn supplier

B. Its location in a valley

C. Its staff of young brides

D. Its position by a waterway

20. Hannah Lee Corbin made a plea for:

F. laws to account for women.

G. property-owning widows' right to vote.

H. the superiority of women over men.

J. a woman's right to own property.

PASSAGE III

HUMANITIES: This is an excerpt from *Plays, Acting and Music: A Book Of Theory* by Arthur Symons.

After seeing a ballet, a farce, and the fragment of an opera performed by the marionettes at the Costanzi Theatre in Rome, I am inclined to ask myself why we require the intervention of any less perfect medium between the meaning of a piece, as the author conceived it, and that other meaning which it derives from our reception of it. The living
5 actor, even when he condescends to subordinate himself to the requirements of pantomime, has always what he is proud to call his temperament; in other words, so much personal caprice, which for the most part means wilful misunderstanding; and in seeing his acting you have to consider this intrusive little personality of his as well as the author's. The marionette may be relied upon. He will respond to an indication without reserve
10 or revolt; an error on his part (we are all human) will certainly be the fault of the author; he can be trained to perfection. As he is painted, so will he smile; as the wires lift or lower his hands, so will his gestures be; and he will dance when his legs are set in motion.

Seen at a distance, the puppets cease to be an amusing piece of mechanism, imitating real people; there is no difference. I protest that the Knight who came in with his
15 plumed hat, his shining sword, and flung back his long cloak with so fine a sweep of the arm, was exactly the same to me as if he had been a living actor, dressed in the same clothes, and imitating the gesture of a knight; and that the contrast of what was real, as we say, under the fiction appears to me less ironical in the former than in the latter. We have to allow, you will admit, at least as much to the beneficent heightening of travesty,
20 if we have ever seen the living actor in the morning, not yet shaved, standing at the bar, his hat on one side, his mouth spreading in that abandonment to laughter which has become from the necessity of his profession, a natural trick; oh, much more, I think, than

if we merely come upon an always decorative, never an obtrusive, costumed figure, leaning against the wall, nonchalantly enough, in a corner of the coulisses.

25   To sharpen our sense of what is illusive in the illusion of the puppets, let us sit not too far from the stage. Choosing our place carefully, we shall have the satisfaction of always seeing the wires at their work, while I think we shall lose nothing of what is most savoury in the feast of the illusion. There is not indeed the appeal to the senses of the first row of the stalls at a ballet of living dancers. But is not that a trifle too obvious
30 sentiment for the true artist in artificial things? Why leave the ball-room? It is not nature that one looks for on the stage in this kind of spectacle, and our excitement in watching it should remain purely intellectual. If you prefer that other kind of illusion, go a little further away, and, I assure you, you will find it quite easy to fall in love with a marionette. I have seen the most adorable heads, with real hair too, among the wooden dancers of
35 a theatre of puppets; faces which might easily, with but a little of that good-will which goes to all falling in love, seem the answer to a particular dream, making all other faces in the world but spoilt copies of this inspired piece of painted wood.

    But the illusion, to a more scrupulous taste, will consist simply in that complication of view which allows us to see wood and wire imitating an imitation, and which delights
40 us less when seen at what is called the proper distance, where the two are indistin-guishable, than when seen from just the point where all that is crudely mechanical hides the comedy of what is, absolutely, a deception. Losing, as we do, something of the particularity of these painted faces, we are able to enjoy all the better what it is certainly important we should appreciate, if we are truly to appreciate our puppets. This is nothing
45 less than a fantastic, yet a direct, return to the masks of the Greeks: that learned artifice by which tragedy and comedy were assisted in speaking to the world with the universal voice, by this deliberate generalising of emotion. It will be a lesson to some of our modern notions; and it may be instructive for us to consider that we could not give a play of Ibsen's to marionettes, but that we could give them the "Agamemnon."

50   Above all, for we need it above all, let the marionettes remind us that the art of the theatre should be beautiful first, and then indeed what you will afterwards. Gesture on the stage is the equivalent of rhythm in verse, and it can convey, as a perfect rhythm should, not a little of the inner meaning of words, a meaning perhaps more latent in things. Does not gesture indeed make emotion, more certainly and more immediately
55 than emotion makes gesture? You may feel that you may suppress emotion; but assume a smile, lifted eyebrows, a clenched fist, and it is impossible for you not to assume along with the gesture, if but for a moment, the emotion to which that gesture corresponds. In our marionettes, then, we get personified gesture, and the gesture, like all other forms of emotion, generalised. The appeal in what seems to you these childish manoeuvres is
60 to a finer, because to a more intimately poetic, sense of things than the merely rational-istic appeal of very modern plays. If at times we laugh, it is with wonder at seeing humanity so gay, heroic, and untiring. There is the romantic suggestion of magic in this beauty.

CONTINUE

21. According to the passage, the author believes that a performer's gestures can convey:

    I. emotions.
    II. rhythms.
    III. rationality.

    A. I only
    B. I and II only
    C. II and III only
    D. I, II, and III

22. It can be inferred from the passage that:

    F. the author believes human performers to be superior performers to marionettes.
    G. the quality of a performance is solely based on where a viewer is sitting in the audience.
    H. marionettes will one day replace human performers completely.
    J. what the author suggests about marionettes also applies to human performers.

23. According to the information in the fourth paragraph, the author of this passage would most likely describe which of the following as being an attribute of a theatrical mask?

    A. It eliminates the need for emotion.
    B. It emphasizes the performer's voice.
    C. It protects the performer's identity.
    D. It makes the performer look like a marionette.

24. According to the passage, attending a performance at the Constanzi Theatre in Rome was significant to the author because it made him:

    F. realize how entertaining marionettes are.
    G. think about the qualities of human performers.
    H. decide never to attend the theatre again.
    J. consider a career as a puppeteer.

25. As it is used in line 3, the word *piece* most nearly means:

    A. segment.
    B. calm.
    C. item.
    D. performance.

26. According to the passage, which of the following was part of the costume of the marionette knight the author mentions seeing perform in the passage?

    I. A theatrical mask
    II. A plumed hat
    III. A shining cloak

    F. I only
    G. II only
    H. I and III only
    J. I, II, and III

27. Which of the following quotations best expresses the main point of the fifth paragraph?

A. "Above all, for we need it above all, let the marionettes remind us that the art of the theatre should be beautiful first, and then indeed what you will afterwards."

B. "Gesture on the stage is the equivalent of rhythm in verse, and it can convey, as a perfect rhythm should, not a little of the inner meaning of words, a meaning perhaps more latent in things."

C. "You may feel that you may suppress emotion; but assume a smile, lifted eyebrows, a clenched fist, and it is impossible for you not to assume along with the gesture, if but for a moment, the emotion to which that gesture corresponds."

D. "In our marionettes, then, we get personified gesture, and the gesture, like all other forms of emotion, generalised."

28. Which of the following descriptions most accurately and completely represents this passage?

F. An exploration of the essence of stage performance

G. A critique of poor acting choices

H. A celebration of the art of puppetry

J. A debate about marionettes versus human performers

29. The passage states that it is important for audience members to:

A. avoid seeing the marionette's strings by sitting far away from the stage.

B. avoid going to performances with unnatural acting.

C. never sit anywhere but the front row of a theater.

D. choose their seats according to the particular experiences they want to have.

30. Based on the information in the passage, one could infer that a play by Ibsen is different from *Agamemnon* because:

F. *Agamemnon* is more lyrical than Ibsen's plays.

G. *Agamemnon* is more emotional than Ibsen's plays.

H. *Agamemnon* is more fantastical than Ibsen's plays.

J. *Agamemnon* is more objective than Ibsen's plays.

CONTINUE

PASSAGE IV

NATURAL SCIENCES: This is an excerpt from *The Science of Human Nature* by William Henry Pyle.

Science is knowledge; it is what we know. But mere knowledge is not science. For a bit of knowledge to become a part of science, its relation to other bits of knowledge must be found. In botany, for example, bits of knowledge about plants do not make a science of botany. To have a science of botany, we must not only know about leaves,
5   roots, flowers, seeds, etc., but we must know the relations of these parts and of all the parts of a plant to one another. In other words, in science, we must not only *know*, we must not only have *knowledge*, but we must know the significance of the knowledge, must know its *meaning*. This is only another way of saying that we must have knowledge and know its relation to other knowledge.

10 A scientist is one who has learned to organize his knowledge. The main difference between a scientist and one who is not a scientist is that the scientist sees the significance of facts, while the non-scientific man sees facts as more or less unrelated things. As one comes to hunt for causes and inquire into the significance of things, one becomes a scientist. A thing or an event always points beyond itself to something else. This something
15 else is what goes before it or comes after it,—is its cause or its effect. This causal relationship that exists between events enables a scientist to prophesy. By carefully determining what always precedes a certain event, a certain type of happening, a scientist is able to predict the event. All that is necessary to be able to predict an event is to have a clear knowledge of its true causes. Whenever, beyond any doubt, these causes are found
20 to be present, the scientist knows the event will follow. Of course, all that he really *knows* is that such results have always followed similar causes in the past. But he has come to have faith in the uniformity and regularity of nature. The chemist does not find sulphur, or oxygen, or any other element acting one way one day under a certain set of conditions, and acting another way the next day under exactly the same conditions. Nor does the
25 physicist find the laws of mechanics holding good one day and not the next.

The scientist, therefore, in his thinking brings order out of chaos in the world. If we do not know the causes and relations of things and events, the world seems a very mixed-up, chaotic place, where anything and everything is happening. But as we come to know causes and relations, the world turns out to be a very orderly and systematic place. It is a
30 lawful world; it is not a world of chance. Everything is related to everything else.

Now, the non-scientific mind sees things as more or less unrelated. The far-reaching causal relations are only imperfectly seen by it, while the scientific mind not only sees things, but inquires into their causes and effects or consequences. The non-scientific man, walking over the top of a mountain and noticing a stone there, is likely to see in it
35 only a stone and think nothing of how it came to be there; but the scientific man sees quite an interesting bit of history in the stone. He reads in the stone that millions of years ago the place where the rock now lies was under the sea. Many marine animals left their remains in the mud underneath the sea. The mud was afterward converted into rock. Later, the shrinking and warping earth-crust lifted the rock far above the level
40 of the sea, and it may now be found at the top of the mountain. The one bit of rock tells

its story to one who inquires into its causes. The scientific man, then, sees more significance, more meaning, in things and events than does the non-scientific man.

45 Each science has its own particular field. Zoölogy undertakes to answer every reasonable question about animals; botany, about plants; physics, about motion and forces; chemistry, about the composition of matter; astronomy, about the heavenly bodies, etc. The world has many aspects. Each science undertakes to describe and explain some particular aspect. To understand all the aspects of the world, we must study all the sciences.

31. This passage asserts that all scientific facts in the world:

 A. occur by chance.
 B. disprove each other.
 C. are related to each other.
 D. belong in a single category.

32. This passage states that a rock might teach us something about animals because:

 F. that rock may contain bite marks that convey information about the animal that partially ate it.
 G. many marine animals build undersea homes out of rocks found on the bottom of the sea.
 H. the remains of marine animals can often be found preserved in rocks later found outside the sea.
 J. geology is the study of rocks and zoology is the study of animals and both are important sciences.

33. The main point of the third paragraph is that the world:

 A. is understood through science.
 B. follows orderly rules.
 C. is extremely chaotic.
 D. often seems chaotic.

34. The word *field* in the final paragraph refers to the fact that:

 F. botanists do most of their work outdoors.
 G. there are several scientific categories.
 H. studying science can be as physical as playing a sport.
 J. scientists must be prepared to answer many questions.

35. As it is defined in the passage, the scientist:

 I. organizes knowledge.
 II. sees facts as unrelated.
 III. hunts for causes.

 A. I only
 B. only
 C. I and III
 D. I, II, and III

36. It can be reasonably deduced from the passage that physics:

 F. has absolutely nothing to do with zoölogy.
 G. is essentially the study of composition.
 H. is impossible to understand by non-scientists.
 J. may reveal vital information about astronomy.

CONTINUE

37. The word *reads* in line 36 refers to the fact that stones:

    A. may contain observable information.

    B. often contain markings that look like words.

    C. are full of known symbols.

    D. can be seen very easily.

38. This passage states that chemical elements include:

    I. sulphur.

    II. oxygen.

    III. stones.

    F. I only

    G. II only

    H. I and II

    J. I, II, and III

39. You could reasonably conclude from lines 15–18 that in some ways, a scientist is similar to a:

    A. non-scientist.

    B. fortune teller.

    C. mechanic.

    D. event planner.

40. According to the passage, in which order did the following events occur?

    I. The rock lifted above sea level.

    II. The earth's crust shrank.

    III. Mud was converted into rock.

    F. I, II, III

    G. III, II, I

    H. II, I, III

    J. I, III, II

Ⓧ
STOP

SCIENCE TEST

35 Minutes—40 Questions

> **DIRECTIONS:** There are seven passages in this test. Each passage is followed by several questions. Read each passage, select the best answer to each related question, and fill in the corresponding circle on the answer sheet. You may look back at the passages as often as you need.

PASSAGE I

There are a number of theories of personality, but only a few are based on biological evidence. Two such theories of personality based on biology are presented below.

Reinforcement Sensitivity Theory

Psychologist Jeffrey Alan Gray proposed the Reinforcement Sensitivity Theory of personality in 1970. This theory focused on the relationship between personality and sensitivity to reinforcement. Gray's theory proposes that there are three brain systems, each of which responds in a different manner to stimuli that reward or punish. The behavioral activation system (BAS) includes the parts of the brain involved in controlling arousal, namely the thalamus, striatum, and cerebral cortex. This system responds to reward cues and is accordingly known as the reward system. When people have more active BAS, they tend to be more impulsive and behaviorally outgoing upon approaching a goal. The behavioral inhibition system (BIS), which includes the brain stem and the neocortical projections to the frontal lobe of the brain, acts in the opposite way. BIS responds to punishment and non-rewarding stimuli, and people with more active BIS are more prone to experience negative emotions like fear, anxiety, and sadness. The third system is the fight/flight/freeze system (FFFS), also called the threat system, which regulates reactions of fight vs. flight and rage vs. panic. This system is sensitive to new, punishing stimuli.

In 1848, a 25-year-old named Phineas Gage survived a grisly accident, in which an iron rod was propelled through his skull, damaging his frontal cortex. His corresponding personality changes, namely in social cognition and decision making, served as evidence that the damaged portion of his brain was responsible for those particular traits. Experiments on primates in the 1870s confirmed similar personality traits upon damage to the frontal lobe.

Genetic Approach to Personality

The genetic approach to personality suggests that personality traits are determined by a complex combination of genes, not a single gene. Most of the evidence linking genetics and the environment to personality is based on studies with genetically

CONTINUE

identical twins. The Minnesota Study of Twins Reared Apart examined 350 pairs of twins, both fraternal and identical, from 1979 to 1999. This study found that identical twins raised together have very similar personalities, but also that identical twins raised apart also had very similar personalities. This finding indicates that some aspects of personality are controlled by genetics, and that some personality traits are heritable. Other twin studies have shown that there are higher correlations of personality traits in identical twins than in fraternal twins, which supports this link between genetics and personality. Still, the studies all indicate that while identical twins have similar personality traits, they also have distinct personalities overall, indicating that genetics alone do not determine personality. Another study that looked at twins in five different countries found 50% of personality traits in common among identical twins and 20% of traits in common for fraternal twins.

Recent studies in genetics and personality have focused on single nucleotide polymorphisms (SNPs), which are specific, small repeating sections of genes found in certain versions of the gene, usually noncoding regions more than coding regions. Well-studied SNPs include the APOE4 genetic polymorphism, which has been found to be linked to increased risk for Alzheimer's disease, and the GG variant of the oxytocin receptor gene rs53576, which has been found to be associated with intimacy and social bonds. Other SNPs related to dopamine are related to Parkinson's disease, attention deficit hyperactivity disorder (ADHD), and drug addiction.

1. According to the Reinforcement Sensitivity Theory, a student's level of nervousness before an exam for which he has not prepared can most nearly be attributed to a more active:

   A. SNPs.
   B. BAS.
   C. BIS.
   D. FFFS.

2. Single nucleotide polymorphisms occur in an organism's:

   F. proteins.
   G. DNA.
   H. sugars.
   J. lipids.

3. A similarity between the two viewpoints is that both:

   A. include a fight/flight/freeze personality component.
   B. use evidence from twin studies as support.
   C. attribute personality differences between siblings to SNPs.
   D. point to human biology as the basis for personality rather than environment.

4. Which viewpoint, if any, directly predicts sources for personality disorders?

    F. The Reinforcement Sensitivity Theory only
    G. The Genetic Approach to Personality only
    H. Both the Reinforcement Sensitivity Theory and the Genetic Approach to Personality
    J. Neither the Reinforcement Sensitivity Theory nor the Genetic Approach to Personality

5. A hypothetical genetic disorder causes a defect in the striatum of the forebrain. This genetic disorder is accompanied by a personality disorder. This evidence supports:

    A. the Reinforcement Sensitivity Theory only.
    B. the Genetic Approach to Personality only.
    C. both the Reinforcement Sensitivity Theory and the Genetic Approach to Personality.
    D. neither the Reinforcement Sensitivity Theory nor the Genetic Approach to Personality.

6. The case of Phineas Gage supports the Reinforcement Sensitivity Theory because:

    F. the victim's SNPs corresponded with the genetic disorder whose symptoms match the victim's personality changes.
    G. the victim experienced extrinsically induced DNA mutations that affected his personality in expected ways.
    H. the victim's regions of brain damage corresponded with personality changes proposed to be caused by those regions.
    J. the changes in the victim's personality corresponded with the resulting hormone imbalance due to his injuries.

CONTINUE

7. According to the two viewpoints, what is the significance of the environment with respect to personality?

A. The first viewpoint proposes that the environment does not affect personality, while the second viewpoint proposes that human personality is based on biological responses to the environment.

B. The first viewpoint proposes that human personality is based on biological responses to the environment, while the second viewpoint proposes that the environment does not affect personality.

C. The first viewpoint proposes that the environment plays a role in personality separate from biology, while the second viewpoint proposes that human personality is based on biological responses to the environment.

D. The first viewpoint proposes that human personality is based on biological responses to the environment, while the second viewpoint proposes that the environment plays a role in personality separate from biology.

PASSAGE II

A student noticed that at room temperature, she could not dissolve nearly as much sodium chloride (NaCl) or potassium chloride (KCl) in 100 mL of water as she could lead (II) nitrate ($Pb(NO_3)_2$). The student decided to test the solubility of these three salts at different temperatures. For each trial, the student measured out 100 mL of water and 100 g of the salt of interest. She then added salt to the water, stirring constantly, until the solution was completely saturated and no more salt would dissolve in the water. To determine the mass added, she measured the mass of salt remaining from her original 100 g stock and subtracted the new mass from the original mass. This mass difference represents the mass of salt that she could dissolve in 100 g of water. The student proceeded to perform this protocol for three salts at five different temperatures ranging from 0°C to 40°C. She entered the data into a table, as shown:

Table 1

Salts	Salt Solubility (g salt per 100 mL water) at Various Temperatures				
	0°C	10°C	20°C	30°C	40°C
NaCl	34.2	34.6	35.0	35.4	35.8
KCl	27.0	29.9	32.8	35.7	38.6
$Pb(NO_3)_2$	36.9	46.1	55.3	64.5	73.7

8. A constant in all trials in this experiment is the:

   F. temperature.
   G. type of salt.
   H. volume of water.
   J. mass of salt dissolved in the water.

9. Which salt exhibited the lowest solubility at 30°C?

   A. NaCl
   B. KCl
   C. $Pb(NO_3)_2$
   D. All three salts exhibited identical solubility.

10. At approximately which temperature do sodium chloride and potassium chloride have the same solubility?

   F. 0°C
   G. 17°C
   H. 28°C
   J. 35°C

CONTINUE

11. If the solubility of KCl is plotted as a function of temperature, which of the following best represents how this graph would look?

A.

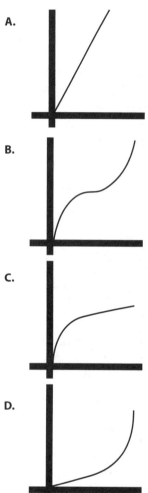

B.

C.

D.

12. Based on the collected data, what mass of $Pb(NO_3)_2$ would you expect to be able to dissolve in 100mL of water at 60°C?

F. 36.9 g
G. 73.7 g
H. 82.9 g
J. 92.1 g

13. What can be concluded about the effect of temperature on salt solubility?

A. Increasing the temperature increases the solubility of KCl and $Pb(NO_3)_2$ but decreases the solubility of NaCl.
B. Decreasing the temperature increases the solubility of KCl and $Pb(NO_3)_2$ but decreases the solubility of NaCl.
C. Increasing the temperature increases the solubility of KCl, NaCl, and $Pb(NO_3)_2$.
D. Decreasing the temperature increases the solubility of KCl, NaCl, and $Pb(NO_3)_2$.

PASSAGE III

A crystal is a solid whose molecules are arranged in an ordered, repeating pattern extending in all three spatial dimensions. In nature, crystalline solids usually form when molten materials cool and solidify. A key stage of the crystallization process is crystal growth. When a "seed" crystal is provided, crystal growth spreads outward from this site. As the crystal grows, an arranged system called a crystal lattice begins to form. Perfect crystals grow rather slowly, but real crystals grow more quickly because they contain defects that provided growth points, which catalyze further crystal formation.

After visiting a local underground cavern, a group of students became interested in crystal formation after seeing the stalactites and stalagmites. They decided to test the effect of pressure on crystal growth rate by using potassium ferricyanide, a compound that is red in color. The students prepared a single 70-mL solution of potassium ferricyanide in water at 99°C, keeping it well mixed to ensure even salt dispersion in the solution. They split this volume into two equal 35-mL portions, pouring the portions into separate flasks. Each flask is sealed with a rubber stopper and hooked up to pressure pumps that control the pressure inside the flask. There is also a pressure gauge that provides a pressure reading, allowing the students to make sure that the pressure remains constant. Flask #1 is kept at a pressure of 1 atm, which is normal atmospheric pressure, while Flask #2 is kept at a pressure of 9 atm. Both flasks were then cooled down to room temperature, and the salts came out of the solution for crystal growth to begin. The students used a caliper to measure crystal size over the course of three days. The students then measured the percent increase in crystal size and graphed their results below:

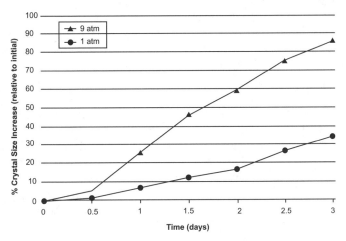

Figure 1

CONTINUE

14. The dependent variable in this experiment is:

    F. temperature.
    G. pressure.
    H. crystal size.
    J. time.

15. The purpose of preparing one solution for both trials rather than two separate solutions of equal concentration was to:

    A. equilibrate the solutions to their appropriate tested pressures in each trial.
    B. ensure that the concentration of starting salt "seed" is equal for both trials.
    C. serve as a temperature control for the experiment.
    D. provide a second trial for the crystals grown at 1 atmosphere.

16. The initial salt solution was prepared at 99°C because:

    F. potassium ferricyanide crystals can grow only at the higher temperature.
    G. potassium ferricyanide will dissolve in solution at the higher temperature.
    H. the higher temperature is required to maintain the 1 atmosphere and 9 atmosphere pressures.
    J. the water in the solution will evaporate to increase the concentration of the solution.

17. By approximately what percentage did the size of the crystals increase at a pressure of 9 atmospheres after 2.0 days?

    A. 8%
    B. 18%
    C. 25%
    D. 59%

18. One way to improve the reliability of the results in this experiment would be to:

    F. increase the number of trials at each tested pressure.
    G. perform the experiment at 99°C rather than room temperature.
    H. perform the experiment using smaller solution volumes and flasks.
    J. use different starting "seed" solution concentrations for each pressure trial.

19. Which of the following conclusions can be drawn from this experiment?

    A. Potassium ferricyanide crystals grow more rapidly than other crystal types.
    B. Potassium ferricyanide crystals grow more slowly than other crystal types.
    C. Potassium ferricyanide crystals grow more rapidly at low pressure than at high pressure.
    D. Potassium ferricyanide crystals grow more rapidly at high pressure than at low pressure.

PASSAGE IV

A manufacturer hopes to promote its new brand of fertilizer, PlantBoost, by claiming that it significantly boosts the growth rate of plants, more than any other fertilizers currently on the market. However, the manufacturer needs experimental evidence to support this claim, so its research and development team decides to test the effect of the fertilizer on the growth rate of pea plants. The researchers choose six identical pea plant seeds and plant them in pots in the same kind of soil at the same depth. Two plants were given no fertilizer, two plants were treated with PlantBoost, and two plants were treated with the current leading fertilizer brand, PlantGro. The plants were treated identically with sunlight and water in a greenhouse, and the plant heights were measured over the course of four days. The results are shown below:

Table 1						
	Plant Height (cm)					
Time (days)	Untreated— Trial 1	Untreated— Trial 2	PlantBoost— Trial 1	PlantBoost— Trial 2	PlantGro— Trial 1	PlantGro— Trial 1
0	0	0	0	0	0	0
1	0.3	0.2	1.2	1.2	1.4	1.4
2	1.0	1.0	2.4	2.5	3.1	3.2
3	4.5	4.6	5.1	5.4	6.3	6.6
4	7.6	7.6	10.4	10.6	13.0	13.6

20. What was the average height of the pea plants treated with PlantGro after 4 days?

F. 0 cm
G. 7.6 cm
H. 10.5 cm
J. 13.3 cm

21. The trials with the untreated plants serve as:

A. dependent variables.
B. independent variables.
C. negative controls.
D. positive controls.

22. Which of the following is a constant in this experiment?

F. The fertilizer brand
G. The soil type
H. The plant height
J. The number of leaves per plant

CONTINUE

23. Which of the following graphs most accurately displays the average plant height as a function of time for the pea plants treated with PlantBoost?

A.

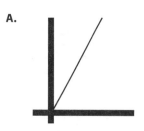

B.

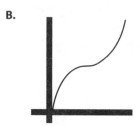

C.

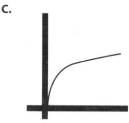

D.

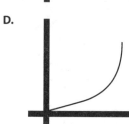

24. The most precise time point for the plants treated with PlantBoost occurred after:

F. 1 day.
G. 2 days.
H. 3 days.
J. 4 days.

25. Based on the data, can the manufacturer claim that Plant-Boost is the best fertilizer on the market?

A. Yes, because the plants treated with PlantBoost grew more quickly than those that were untreated or those that were treated with PlantGro.

B. No, because the plants treated with PlantBoost grew more quickly than the untreated plants but equally as quickly as those treated with PlantGro.

C. No, because the plants treated with PlantBoost grew more quickly than the untreated plants but not as quickly as those treated with PlantGro.

D. No, because the plants treated with PlantBoost did not grow as quickly as either the untreated plants or those treated with PlantGro.

A group of scientists wanted to study protein-protein interactions among proteins found in the capsid of human cytomegalovirus (HCMV), the largest human herpes virus. Based on potential binding domains, the scientists narrowed down their list to six pairs of proteins to test for protein-protein interactions. To determine if two proteins in each pair interact, the scientists decide to use the yeast two-hybrid assay. In this assay, one protein per pair is fused to a DNA-binding domain (BD) and the other protein is fused to an activating domain (AD). These two fusion proteins are inserted into yeast cells. The DNA-binding domain will bind near *lacZ*, the reporter gene. If the two proteins of interest bind to each other, the interaction will bring the activating domain close to RNA polymerase, causing expression of the *lacZ* gene. The general setup is shown in the figure below:

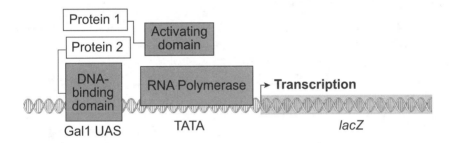

Figure 1

Yeast cells that express *lacZ* produce an enzyme that causes them to turn blue (shaded in the diagram below) when they are grown on special plates called X-gal plates, while yeast cells that lack interacting proteins will remain colorless. The scientists made fusion proteins, as described, for the protein pairs of interest. Their results are shown below:

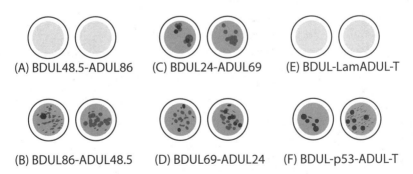

(A) BDUL48.5-ADUL86   (C) BDUL24-ADUL69   (E) BDUL-LamADUL-T

(B) BDUL86-ADUL48.5   (D) BDUL69-ADUL24   (F) BDUL-p53-ADUL-T

Figure 2

CONTINUE

26. Which of the following scientific questions is posed in this experiment?

    F. Which HCMV proteins interact with X-gal?
    G. Which HCMV protein pairs produce a blue color in solution?
    H. Which HCMV protein pairs interact with one another?
    J. Which HCMV protein pairs are expressed by genes located close to one another in the genome?

27. A positive control in this experiment would be to repeat the yeast two-hybrid assays by testing two proteins that are known to:

    A. bind to one another and growing yeast on X-gal plates.
    B. *not* bind to one another and growing yeast on X-gal plates.
    C. bind to one another and growing yeast on normal plates.
    D. *not* bind to one another and growing yeast on normal plates.

28. Based on the results, how many of the six tested protein pairs appear to interact with one another?

    F. 0
    G. 2
    H. 4
    J. 6

29. If you wanted to test other proteins using this same system, which of the following proteins would most likely cause problems in this experiment?

    A. Proteins that are relatively small in size
    B. Proteins with very specific binding partners
    C. Proteins that are toxic to yeast
    D. Proteins that are very well-characterized

30. Relative to yeast cells in a yeast two-hybrid assay that produce an intense blue color for two proteins of interest, yeast cells that produce a lighter blue color likely represent:

    F. very specific or strong protein-protein interactions.
    G. nonspecific or short-lived protein-protein interactions.
    H. interactions between the proteins of interest and DNA itself.
    J. interactions between the proteins of interest and RNA.

PASSAGE VI

An electromagnet is a type of magnet in which the magnetic field is produced by an electric current. A magnetic field can be created using coils of wire wrapped around a ferromagnetic material.

A group of students wanted to test the effects of voltage and number of coils on the strength of an electromagnet. The students first built an electromagnet by attaching wires to the two ends of a 9-volt battery. The students then wrapped the wire around an iron nail, a ferromagnetic material, to form the coils.

The basic setup is shown below. The arrows represent the direction of the current.

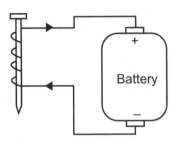

Figure 1

The students tested the strength of the electromagnet by counting the number of metal screws the electromagnet can pick up. The students varied the number of coils around the nail, and then they repeated the experiment using a 4.5-volt battery in place of the 9-volt battery. The same nail and wire were used throughout all experiments. The students recorded their results as shown below.

	Table 1	
	Number of Metal Screws Picked Up	
Number of Coils	9-Volt Battery	4.5-Volt Battery
0 (no nail)	0	0
5	3	2
10	6	4
20	24	16

CONTINUE

31. The purpose of the control with no nail (0 coils) is to:

A. confirm that there is a current running through the wire due to the battery.
B. show that current and voltage are directly proportional to one another.
C. demonstrate that the presence of the nail in the coils creates the magnetic field.
D. establish that the nail is essential for the creation of an electric field.

32. Approximately how many metal screws would you expect the setup to pick up if there were 15 coils and a 4.5-volt battery used?

F. 1
G. 3
H. 6
J. 16

33. The dependent variable in this experiment is the:

A. number of screws picked up.
B. voltage of the battery.
C. direction of the electric current.
D. number of coils around the nail.

34. Based on the data collected, increasing the number of coils around the nail in the tested setup causes:

F. a linear decrease in magnetic field strength.
G. an exponential decrease in magnetic field strength.
H. a linear increase in magnetic field strength.
J. an exponential increase in magnetic field strength.

35. What conclusion can be drawn about the effect of battery voltage on magnetic field strength?

A. As battery voltage increases, magnetic field strength increases.
B. As battery voltage increases, magnetic field strength increases and then decreases.
C. As battery voltage increases, magnetic field strength stays constant.
D. As battery voltage increases, magnetic field strength decreases.

PASSAGE VII

Parallax refers to an object's perceived path of motion upon observation from two different perspectives. A simple example of parallax occurs when you look at an object with your right eye closed, and then you look the same object with your left eye closed; the object appears to have moved, but in reality, the distance between your eyes has caused each eye to perceive the object differently from its unique position.

Parallax is widely used in astronomy, based on Earth's orbit around the sun, to measure distances between stars. If you look at the same stars when Earth is at different places in its orbit around the sun, the closer stars will appear to change position relative to the more distant stars. This allows for the determination of distances between Earth and specific nearby stars. The parallax method is shown below.

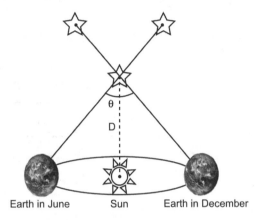

Figure 1

A group of three students wanted to test this method on a smaller scale. The students used the setup below, setting up their observation points a distance *D* of 2 m away from a tree, on which they tied a horizontal meter stick. Their goal was to use the tree location to examine the apparent movement of a traffic cone from two different observation points.

Figure 2

CONTINUE

Each of the three students sat at Observation Point 1 and looked directly at the traffic cone. They then recorded the number of centimeters on the meter stick that lined up with the traffic cone from that vantage point. They then repeated the same process at Observation Point 2. To analyze the data, the students subtracted their measurements from each observation point to determine the distance the traffic cone appeared to move, and they averaged these numbers. The process was then repeated at $D = 4$ m and $D = 6$ m. Their results are shown in the following table.

Table 1

D (m)	Distance of Apparent Cone Movement (cm)			
	Student 1	Student 2	Student 3	Average
2	201	200	202	201.0
4	159	159	161	159.7
6	146	140	139	141.7

The students then plotted the average distances moved as a function of distance D.

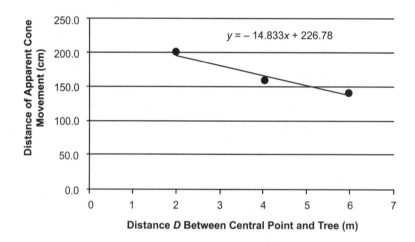

Figure 1

36. As distance D increases, how are the distances R_1 and R_2 affected?

    F. Both R_1 and R_2 increase.
    G. Both R_1 and R_2 decrease.
    H. R_1 increases, and R_2 decreases.
    J. R_1 decreases, and R_2 increases.

37. If the experiment were repeated at $D = 8$ m, estimate the observed distance of apparent cone movement.

    A. 0 cm
    B. 100 cm
    C. 120 cm
    D. 240 cm

38. Which of the three distances provided the least precise trial set?

    F. $D = 2$
    G. $D = 4$
    H. $D = 6$
    J. All three distances gave trials that were equally precise.

39. The x-intercept of the graph represents:

    A. the positive control for this experiment.
    B. the distance between the central point and the cone.
    C. the distance between the central point and the tree for which there is no apparent cone movement between the observation points.
    D. the distance between each observation point and the central point at which the tree is located.

40. What conclusion can be drawn from the students' experiment?

    F. Increasing the distance between the central point and the tree exponentially increases the distance of apparent cone movement.
    G. Increasing the distance between the central point and the tree exponentially decreases the distance of apparent cone movement.
    H. Increasing the distance between the central point and the tree linearly increases the distance of apparent cone movement.
    J. Increasing the distance between the central point and the tree linearly decreases the distance of apparent cone movement.

            Ⓧ
           STOP

WRITING TEST

40 Minutes

> **DIRECTIONS:** This is a test of your writing skills. You have forty (40) minutes to write an essay in English. Be sure to carefully read the issue and three perspectives presented before planning and writing your essay so you understand clearly the task you are being asked to do. Your essay will be graded on the evidence it provides of your ability to analyze the issue; evaluate and analyze the perspectives; state and develop a personal perspective; and describe the relationship between the given perspectives and your own, while effectively using organization, logic, and language according to the conventions of standard written English.

YEAR-ROUND SCHOOL?

In recent years, a great deal of concern has focused on whether or not the current generation of children and young adults—in school and recently graduating—are as well-educated as their counterparts from other developed nations and whether or not they can compete on a global stage in an increasingly hyper-connected world. One idea policymakers have considered to address these concerns is the notion of having students attend school year-round, with the goal of helping students to focus, learn, and retain material covered in classrooms, better positioning them for success in an increasingly competitive world after graduation. But will year-round school just add to the information and activity overload that so many young people face today? The question of whether or not the United States should move to a year-round educational system remains a hot-button issue, and, given its importance and implications for current and future generations both in and out of the classroom, it is worth examining in an effort to determine how best to move forward.

Read and carefully consider these perspectives. Each suggests a particular way of thinking about whether or not the United States should move to a year-round school model.

PERSPECTIVE ONE

The school year for all students should be extended to a year-round model. Doing so would be in the best interests of current and future students, the United States, and the world in which the students will grow to become productive citizens. American students currently receive an insufficient education compared to other modern nations around the world; as a result, they are woefully unprepared to lead the United States through the current century and beyond, or compete on a global level with emerging graduates from other countries. Today's educational system has set the bar too low for a country that seeks to lead and innovate and remain at the vanguard of advancement in science, technology, engineering, and medicine. Adopting a year-round educational model will reassert the importance and value of education, help students focus and retain material learned, and keep at bay dangerous and pernicious distractions that serve to undermine both the efforts of the classroom and the very future of the nation.

PERSPECTIVE TWO

Students already spend too much time in the classroom; moving to a year-round educational model would be nothing short of an expensive mistake. The traditional model of school, with carefully designed and implemented breaks and vacations, has served the United States well for many decades and has educated generations of productive, high-achieving women and men who have gone on to lead the nation—up through to the dawning of the twenty-first century and technological era. There's no reason to abandon a model that has proven successful. Furthermore, the expense of extending the school year would prove to be a great financial burden on a system that already suffers from limited resources. Yes, the United States is facing unprecedented challenges in the area of education, but simply increasing the number of hours that students spend in the classroom won't fix the problems.

The importance of properly educating young minds in order to prepare them well for the challenges of this young century, and to be competitive on a global scale, warrants new and innovative solutions for improving the system. The notion of shifting to a year-round model is a compelling one, but it is not without its challenges, including how such a program would be funded. Therefore, such a program would likely best be started on a small, local scale, where alternative sources of funding and resources may be easier to marshal. Perhaps voluntary pilot programs, with willing and eager students and parents, can be implemented and tracked for success. If proven successful, perhaps it can slowly expand and be adopted by additional communities, cities, and states and can garner the results everyone hopes to achieve—better educated generations of citizens to help lead the world in the right direction.

Essay Task

Write a cohesive, logical essay in which you consider multiple perspectives on the issue of year-round schooling in the United States. In your essay, be sure to:

- examine and assess the perspectives given.
- declare and explain your own perspective on the issue.
- discuss the relationship between your perspective and those given.

Your perspective may be in full or partial agreement, or in total disagreement, with any of the others. Whatever the case, support your ideas with logical reasoning and detailed, persuasive examples.

Plan and Write Your Essay

Use the first minutes of your time to generate ideas and plan your essay. Consider the following as you compose your essay:
What are the strengths and weaknesses of the three perspectives provided?

- Identify the insights they present and what they fail to consider.
- Ascertain why a given perspective might persuade or fail to persuade.

How can you apply your own experience, knowledge, and values?

- Express your perspective on the issue, identifying the perspective's strengths and weaknesses.
- Formulate a plan to support your perspective in your essay.

ENGLISH

1. B	16. H	31. A	46. J	61. C
2. G	17. B	32. H	47. B	62. J
3. D	18. J	33. B	48. G	63. C
4. H	19. D	34. J	49. A	64. G
5. C	20. G	35. B	50. H	65. D
6. G	21. A	36. J	51. D	66. H
7. C	22. J	37. C	52. G	67. B
8. F	23. C	38. G	53. C	68. J
9. B	24. J	39. D	54. F	69. C
10. H	25. B	40. G	55. D	70. J
11. D	26. H	41. D	56. G	71. B
12. H	27. A	42. G	57. B	72. G
13. B	28. G	43. B	58. G	73. C
14. J	29. C	44. F	59. A	74. F
15. B	30. G	45. C	60. J	75. B

1. **The correct answer is B.** The underlined text (choice A) is inappropriate as an introductory sentence to the passage, as it repeats the same statement twice in different words. Choice B is correct because it offers two separate but related thoughts. It is also a good choice because it opens up into the theme of the passage; it is clear to the reader that the writer will discuss those fitness tracker options. Choice C is incorrect because the short, declarative sentence is confusing (how does the writer know what the reader is doing?) and does very little to establish a theme for the passage. Choice D is incorrect because it establishes a theme that's not supported by the rest of the passage—that shopping for fitness trackers is hard.

2. **The correct answer is G.** As it's written, this sentence is an incomplete thought and a fragment, so choice F is incorrect. Choice G is correct because it is a complete sentence and clarifies how the trackers and apps can help with eating and exercise. Choice H is incorrect because it incorrectly doubles up on the subject (*the data* and *it*). Choice J is incorrect because it is confusing and doesn't explain how the data lead to better exercise and eating.

3. **The correct answer is D.** The new sentence should help give background on what fitness trackers are before the essay transitions to talking about different trackers. Choice A is incorrect because the topic of the essay is not about gyms, or exercise in general. Choice B is

incorrect because the writer goes into detail about specific functions of trackers in the next few paragraphs, and this information does not really fit in the first paragraph. Choice C is incorrect because this is not a personal essay about the writer's own experiences. Choice D is correct because it tells the reader more about what trackers do, so that the supporting info in the next several paragraphs makes sense.

4. **The correct answer is H.** *Frequent* (choice F) is an adjective, but because it describes the verb *considered*, you need an adverb. *Hardly* (choice G) is an adverb, but it means the opposite of what the writer is trying to say. Choice H is correct because it takes the same root word (which works in the context of the sentence), but turns the adjective into an adverb. Choice J is incorrect because it turns the adjective into a verb.

5. **The correct answer is C.** As written (choice A), the text is incorrect because it has two independent clauses joined by a comma. This creates a comma splice. Choice B is incorrect because *although* is a word used to show that one statement is happening despite the other statement. In reality, these two statements are connected, not competing. Choice C is correct because it uses the coordinating conjunction *so* to link the two clauses. Choice D is incorrect because it is still a comma splice, but also adds the adverb *why* to create a subordinate clause that

makes no sense within the context of the sentence.

6. **The correct answer is G.** The sentence is incorrect because it offers a list of items incorrectly set off by a comma. One way the writer could fix this is by using a colon and then listing the items. Another way, which choice G uses, is getting rid of the introductory text "the following situations." The sentence is smoother if the writer deletes that and edits it down to "wear it in the pool, the shower, or the rain." Choice H is incorrect because "the following" suggests a list of examples, so you don't need *like*. Choice J is incorrect because it breaks up the list of examples into small fragments.

7. **The correct answer is C.** The underlined text needs to be a verb, and, *syncs* (choice C), meaning "to connect," fits well into the sentence. Choice F (*sinks*) is a homonym of *syncs*, and thus incorrect. Choice B is incorrect because it could be a noun or a verb, but the meaning of the verb ("to transmit") doesn't fit with the rest of the sentence. Choice D is incorrect because it's entirely the wrong verb. The writer gives no indication that fitness trackers are musical.

8. **The correct answer is F.** The underlined text should agree in pronoun and verb tense with the rest of the given noun (*drawback*). Choice F is singular and present, so it fits. Choice G is incorrect because it is plural. Choice H is incorrect because it is singular but past tense. Choice J is incorrect

because it is singular but future tense.

9.   **The correct answer is B.** The phrase is both a fragment and unclear in meaning. The writer doesn't indicate why the price would be a drawback. Choice B does this, while turning the fragment into a full sentence with the transitional adverb *also*. Choice C is incorrect because there should be a comma after *also*, and because this sentence contradicts what the author is trying to say. If the tracker is not expensive, why would this sentence be connected to the "drawback"? Choice D is incorrect because it doesn't provide any support for why the price is a drawback.

10.   **The correct answer is H.** The verb phrase is incorrect as is because it is missing a helping verb to show time and tense. The writer is suggesting that the Fitness Buddy will be plugged in in the future, so the correct option is choice H, which inserts the future *to be* to indicate that this is an action that hasn't yet happened. Choice G is incorrect because it is still missing a form of the helping verb *to be*. Choice J is incorrect because it is missing the modal (or modifying) verb *needs*.

11.   **The correct answer is D.** Despite the appearance of a common question word (*what*) in the sentence, the author is not posing a question, so a question mark is not appropriate end punctuation. Instead, this sentence requires a period to end it (choice D). A

semicolon (choice B) or comma (choice C) are not appropriate types of end punctuation.

12.   **The correct answer is H.** Choice H uses the appropriate coordinating conjunction for this sentence. Coordinating conjunctions are typically used to connect words, ideas, and phrases within sentences. There are seven common coordinating conjunctions, each having its own purpose and meaning given the context of the sentence it is being used in: *for*, *and*, *nor*, *but*, *or*, *yet*, and *so* (use the acronym FANBOYS to help remember them). Choice H uses the appropriate conjunction *so* for this sentence, which is commonly used when showing a consequence or result (here, the result of the Fitness Buddy not being very water-tight is that it shouldn't be used in the water). Choice F uses the conjunction *or*, which is more appropriately used when offering an alternative idea or choice. Choice G uses the conjunction *for*, which is commonly used when providing a purpose or reason for something, like a decision. Choice J uses the coordinating conjunction *nor*, which is commonly used when presenting an alternative thought.

13.   **The correct answer is B.** *Newer* is a comparative adjective, which suggests a comparison between only two. Because there are more than two trackers on the market (the writer has already told the reader that there are "many options"), the best option is the superlative *newest* (choice B).

Choice C is incorrect because it tells the reader nothing about how the VivaLife tracker compares to the rest of the market. Choice D is incorrect because *news* is a noun and unrelated to the topic.

14. **The correct answer is J.** The word used here should be a contraction of *it* and *is*. There should be an apostrophe + *s* because the pronoun and verb are singular. Choice J is the only option that matches this. Choice F is incorrect because *its* is a possessive pronoun, not a contraction. Choice G is incorrect because the apostrophe is in the wrong place. Choice H is incorrect because it uses a plural verb.

15. **The correct answer is B.** Choice A is incorrect because it mentions a new tracker in the paragraph talking about the VivaLife tracker. Choice B is correct because it sums up the comparisons the writer has been making between the VivaLife and both the MyFit and the Fitness Buddy. Choice C is incorrect because additional information about the MyFit should likely go in Paragraph 2. Choice D is incorrect because specific pricing information has not been given for any of the other trackers, so it would be inconsistent to include it just for the VivaLife.

16. **The correct answer is H.** The first way to solve any *me/I/myself* issue is to sound out the sentence in your head. Which one *sounds right*? In this case, you need to figure out which is the correct pronoun. Because "And ___" is the

subject of the sentence, you need a subject pronoun. That's *I* (choice H). Choice F is incorrect because *me* is an object pronoun and belongs as the object in a sentence. (Example: "He gave the orange to me.") Choice G is incorrect because it uses the wrong pronoun altogether. From the rest of the passage, you know the writer is giving his own perspective on the plays, not anyone else's. Choice J is incorrect because *myself* is a reflexive pronoun, meaning it's used to refer back to the subject of the sentence, not act as the subject itself.

17. **The correct answer is B.** *Has* is a helping verb, and it needs to agree with the noun/subject of the sentence. In this case, the subject *I* is first-person singular and the verb *attended* is past tense, so the helping verb should match both of those elements. Choice B is correct because *have* is the correct verb form for first-person singular statements. Choice A is incorrect because *has* can be singular, but it's in the present tense, and you already know that the festival happened in the past. Choice C is incorrect because it's future tense. Choice D is incorrect because it has the third-person singular verb form and also inserts another verb (*been*) in front of the main verb *attended*.

18. **The correct answer is J.** This sentence is incorrect for two reasons: it uses the same phrase ("their own shows") for two of the list items when one time would

do, and it also is not parallel in structure. To make the sentence stronger, the writer should give equal weight and construction to each item. These verbs act as adjectives, which means they should be present participle phrases ending in –ing. Choice J is correct because it uses "their own shows" once to apply to all of the verbs and correctly turns the verbs into participle phrases. Choice G changes the verbs, but it is incorrect because it removes all other context (Writing what, producing what, staging what?). Choice H is incorrect because it uses the infinitive form of each verb ("write, produce, and stage") instead of the participle phrase.

19. **The correct answer is D.** The first clause of this sentence is a dependent clause that acts as an adjective for the subject of the main clause ("the festival"). As a dependent clause, it needs a noun ("Ms. Campbell and Mr. Rodriguez") and a verb. *Sponsorship* is a noun, so this is incorrect. Choice B is a verb, but it is present-tense, when you already know that the festival has already happened. Choice C is incorrect because it too is a noun. That leaves choice D, which is a verb in the past tense.

20. **The correct answer is G.** In this sentence the adverb (*actually*) is misplaced. When there is more than one verb (in this case *has* and *been*, the adverb should go after the helping verb (*has*). Choice G does this correctly. Choice H is incorrect because it removes the helping verb. Choice J is incorrect

because it puts the adverb before both verbs, so it is unclear which one is supposed to be modified.

21. **The correct answer is A.** This sentence sets up the structure of the piece (a series of observations about the plays in the festival) and also connects to the main topic of the next two paragraphs: that the writer liked some of the plays. While choice B vaguely introduces the topic (the plays that were not bad), it is incorrect because it doesn't set up a strong comparison. The writer is comparing plays he liked to plays he didn't, so it's important to make that distinction as clear as possible. Choice C is incorrect because it states a fact that is totally unrelated to the rest of the paragraph. Choice D is incorrect because the statement may very well be true, but the writer does not offer any support for it, and it doesn't establish the main topic of the paragraph. It doesn't fit in with the surrounding text.

22. **The correct answer is J.** The adjective phrase "last year" tells you when the noun (*performance*) happened, so choice J is correct. Choices F and H are incorrect because both of these placements make it look like "last year" is describing the possessive pronoun *his*. Choice G is incorrect because this places the phrase right after another adjective, so there's confusion over what is modifying what.

23. **The correct answer is C.** The full noun ("Garfield Drama Club") is a specific proper noun, so it is likely

to be singular. *Clubs'* is incorrect because the apostrophe placement suggests that *Club* is plural. Choice B is incorrect because it adds an apostrophe + *s* while also keeping *Clubs* plural. Choice C is correct because it puts the apostrophe between the singular *Club* and the singular possessive *s*. Choice D is incorrect because it removes the possessive apostrophe altogether and pluralizes *Club*.

24. **The correct answer is J.** Because *In which* is a prepositional phrase, it should consist of preposition + regular noun (or pronoun). Choice J is correct because it has the preposition (*in*) and the pronoun (*it*). Choices F and G are incorrect because *what* and *that* are relative pronouns, not regular ones. Relative pronouns are typically used to introduce a dependent clause, when in this sentence the related clause is independent. Choice H is incorrect because *what* is a relative pronoun that stands in for the phrase "the thing which…" It doesn't stand in for a noun, which the pronoun in this phrase should. The pronoun in the underlined clause stands in for *show* in the previous sentence.

25. **The correct answer is B.** When the adverb *also* is placed in the middle of a sentence, it goes before the verb. In this case, that verb is *starred*. Choice B does this correctly. Choice A is incorrect because it places the adverb after the verb. Choice C is incorrect because it uses an adverb phrase that means the same thing as *also* in the same wrong spot in the

sentence. Choice D is incorrect because although *too* is an adverb like *also*, it should be placed at the end of the clause. A more correct way to use *too* in this sentence would be: "Mirabelli wrote this play and starred in it too, as an astronaut who lost contact with his ship."

26. **The correct answer is H.** While the reader knows that *Gravity* is a title of some kind, the reader may not know that it's a movie. It would also be helpful because the writer later mentions the stars of the movie, Sandra Bullock and George Clooney. Choice H is correct because it gives context on what *Gravity* is without sidetracking from the main point of the paragraph. Choice F is incorrect because the writer has already given a basic idea of the plot (it's similar to Joey Mirabelli's play), so there is no need to add a tangent about that. Choice G is incorrect because the writer is making a specific comparison, not comparing the play to a number of space movies. Choice J is incorrect because it is unnecessary information; he is reviewing plays in this article, not movies.

27. **The correct answer is A.** The sentence is fine as is. It fits with the personal, somewhat informal tone of the rest of the article, and it adds depth to the comparison between *Gravity* and Joey Mirabelli's play. Choice B is incorrect because it is vague on the connection between George Clooney, Sandra Bullock, and any of the content in Paragraph 4.

Choice C is incorrect because it's a sentence fragment and also unclear. Choice D is incorrect because it may be the author's opinion, but it doesn't fit well with the author's attempt to compare Joey Mirabelli and Sandra Bullock/George Clooney.

28. **The correct answer is G.** Proper end punctuation for a sentence is essential to help convey intended meaning and clarity. Using a comma to end a sentence is grammatically incorrect and can create a long and awkward run-on sentence. Choice G corrects the problem by inserting a period after *show*. Choice H makes the mistake of lowercasing *sorry* and leaving the run-on sentence uncorrected. Choice J makes incorrect use of a question mark, and incorrectly lowercases *sorry*, which begins the next sentence.

29. **The correct answer is C.** Paragraph 6 is problematic because the writer has made a point of discussing individual plays he liked or didn't like. Taking a number of other plays in the festival and just listing them without giving any information about them feels rushed and changes the overall flow of the writing. Choice C would put this list more in line with the theme of the article (the writer's opinions of the festival). Choice A is incorrect because it's just a continuation of the last sentence of Paragraph 5 and doesn't connect to the overall topic/theme of the article. Choice B is incorrect because the faculty advisors were only mentioned once (in Paragraph 2), and they

have little to do with the writer's opinions. Choice D is incorrect because this paragraph (as it stands) would be out of place before the writer even talks about the plays he liked and didn't like.

30. **The correct answer is G.** This sentence sums up the theme of the article by mentioning both the plays he liked and didn't like and wraps up the topic by mentioning next year's festival. Choice F is incorrect because throughout the article, there is no information given about the writer's opinion of the festival itself—just his opinions of the individual plays. This would not be an appropriate conclusion for the information he has written. Choice H is incorrect because it contradicts the first sentence of the paragraph. If the festival were successful, why would he not attend next year's? There is not enough supporting information given as to why he would come to that conclusion. Choice J is incorrect because the reference is specific to a single paragraph (Paragraph 5) and has little to do with the article as a whole.

31. **The correct answer is A.** The sentence needs an adverb that modifies the verb *need*. Choice A matches that, so the underlined text is correct as is. Choice B is incorrect because it means the same as the existing word, so there is no need to change. Choice C is incorrect because although *very* is an adverb, it cannot modify verbs. Choice D is incorrect because *real* is an adjective, not an adverb.

Answer Keys and Explanations

32. The correct answer is H. This question calls for you to identify the correct preposition—in this case, a preposition of time. *Among* and *in* are prepositions of place, so choices F and G are incorrect. *Over* is a preposition of time, so choice H is correct. *Around* is a preposition that shows direction, so choice J is incorrect.

33. The correct answer is B. A common error in sentence construction is an abrupt and incorrect shift in perspective (first, second, or third person). As written (choice A), this sentence shifts from the third person (*someone*) to the second person (*you*). Choice B fixes this mistake, using the third person *he* or *she*, which is aligned with the third person *someone*. Choice C makes an incorrect shift from the second person (*you*) to the third person (*she*). Choice D makes an incorrect shift from the third person (*he*) to the first person (*we*).

34. The correct answer is J. This is a question about pronoun and verb agreement. The pronoun stands in for *person*, so it needs to be singular. You also need to make sure that the verb is singular as well. Choice J has a singular pronoun ("he *or* she," not "he *and* she") and a singular verb, so it is the correct choice. Choice F is incorrect because it pluralizes the pronoun and the verb. Choice G is incorrect because it has a singular verb, but a plural pronoun. Choice H is incorrect because it has singular pronouns, but a plural verb.

35. The correct answer is B. This is a case where you need to look at the rest of the paragraph. How is the author presenting similar information? Throughout Paragraph 2, the writer has set a pattern of describing the stages with "a.k.a. ___" in parentheses. The abbreviation "a.k.a." is a well-known abbreviation, so it doesn't necessarily need to be spelled out. Choice B is correct because it matches the sentence to similar ones in the paragraph. Choice A is incorrect because it does not match the other parenthetical phrases. Choice C is incorrect because it spells out the abbreviation, when the others are abbreviated. Consistency is key. Choice D is incorrect because it's inconsistent and also uses a slightly different phrasing for "a.k.a."

36. The correct answer is J. You need to find the correct punctuation to set off the restrictive clause "hence the name." Choice F is incorrect because it has no punctuation and incorrectly pushes the clauses of the sentence together. Choice G is incorrect because an under-score is not appropriate punctu-ation in a sentence. Choice H is incorrect because an ellipsis indicates text that has been left out, not just a pause in the sentence. Choice J is correct because the comma is appro-priate to join the clauses.

37. The correct answer is C. As written, the biggest issue is the phrase "being that" in the middle of the sentence. This is a non-standard conjunction that creates awkward construction, so choice A is incorrect. "Being that" or "being as" is typically used informally to mean *because*, so you should use that conjunction instead. To make the sentence less awkward, it's best to rework it down to the most basic elements. Choice B is incorrect because it too includes "being that," and it's also a sentence fragment. Choice C is correct because it creates two clear clauses joined by the conjunction *because*: "The lack of sleep is problematic" and "because it affects daily activities like driving safely and learning new information." Choice D is incorrect because "it being" puts the sentence in the same boat as the other incorrect choices.

38. **The correct answer is G.** The problem with the underlined text is that it is either redundant, because the writer uses "colds, flu, etc." in addition to *illness*, or poorly punctuated because she meant to use "colds, flu, etc." as examples of illnesses. This needs to be clarified. Choice G is correct because it sets "colds, flu, etc." in parentheses so that the phrase modifies *illness*. Choice H is incorrect because in formal writing, slashes should not be used to show items in a list. Choice J is incorrect because it puts the opening parenthesis before *illness*, making it look like the phrase "illness, colds, flu, etc." describes the verb *increased*.

39. **The correct answer is D.** As written, the sentence is too informal and slangy for formal writing. The rest of the passage is serious and neutral in tone, and

choice A does not fit with that. Choice B is incorrect because it still uses the phrase "on the regular," which is slang. Choice C is incorrect because *regularly* is incorrectly placed so that it appears to describe *report*, not *getting*. Choice D is correct because it keeps the tone of the sentence neutral, while still presenting the same information.

40. **The correct answer is G.** Ellipses are commonly used to indicate missing text at the beginning, middle, or end of quoted material, or to add a dramatic pause or tension to a sentence in a piece of writing. In this straightforward sentence, ellipses are not an appropriate choice as end punctuation. Choice G fixes this issue by using a period, which is the appropriate end punctuation for this sentence. Using no punctuation (choice H) or a semicolon (choice J) are not appropriate choices for punctuating the end of a sentence.

41. **The correct answer is D.** The issue here is inconsistency in the way the writer presented the information throughout the rest of the passage. For teenagers and adults, she reported the results as the percentage of people who did get the amount of recommended sleep. In Paragraph 3, she changes the way she presents the results for older adults and gives the percentage for people who do *not* get that amount of sleep. For consistency, it's best to keep the information presented the same way for each group, so choice D is correct. Choice A is incorrect

because it is inconsistent with the presentation of the same data throughout the essay. Choice B is incorrect because, it changes the meaning of the sentence. Choice C is incorrect because, although it corrects the percentage to match the same criteria as the other groups', it incorrectly suggests that 58% of all people were surveyed.

42. **The correct answer is G.** The underlined verb is a gerund phrase that acts in the place of a noun, as a subject for the sentence. Gerunds end in *-ing,* and only choice G matches this.

43. **The correct answer is B.** Choice A is incorrect because dream details do not connect to the overall theme of the essay (how much sleep people need and the consequences if they do not meet that need). Choice B is correct because the ages of each group surveyed would give helpful information to the reader. Choice C is incorrect because the writer uses percentages to get the point across about how many people are not getting enough sleep, so it is not necessary to give the actual numbers. Choice D is incorrect because the health conditions are not especially relevant to the main question of "how much sleep do we need?"

44. **The correct answer is F.** Paragraph 2 contains information about sleep itself, but it doesn't really relate to the stated main topic of the essay, which is determining how much sleep people actually need. It could be deleted to tighten the essay around that theme. Paragraph 3 shouldn't be deleted because it provides supporting information about how much sleep teenagers need, so choice G is incorrect. Paragraph 4 shouldn't be deleted because it provides supporting information about how much sleep adults need, so choice H is incorrect. Paragraph 6 is the concluding paragraph, in which the writer ties back to the theme of sleep needs, so it should not be deleted. Choice J is incorrect.

45. **The correct answer is C.** Information about the amount of sleep that children need fits in with the pattern of describing how much sleep is needed by people of other age groups, so choice C is correct. Choice A is incorrect because the description of R.E.M. sleep is not very relevant to the topic of sleep amounts. Choices B and D are incorrect because the essay does not focus on how sleep deprivation is treated.

46. **The correct answer is J.** In the underlined sentence, the writer tells you three times that the story takes place in the morning ("morning," "9:00 a.m.," and "in the morning." He needs to mention this only once, so choice F is incorrect and choice J is correct. Choice G is incorrect because it turns the sentence into a fragment with no verbs. Choice H is incorrect because it still includes both "morning" and "a.m."

47. **The correct answer is B.** The adverb *scarcely* should go as close

as possible to the verb it is modifying. In the underlined text, *scarcely* is awkwardly inserted before the helping verb, not the action verb. Choice B is correct because it works with *been* to show time. Choice C is incorrect because it takes out the helping verb *had*. Choice D is incorrect because it misplaces *scarcely* after the verbs.

48. **The correct answer is G.** Choosing the most effective introductory sentence for this paragraph requires an understanding of the chain of events in the passage. The false shark sighting was initially scary, but once the author found at they were actually dolphins, it became just an awkward mishap (choice G). There's nothing in the passage that would indicate that the experience was wonderful and life changing (choice F), or boring and humdrum (choice J). Choice H is actually the reverse of how the series of events occurred—it was initially scary but ended awkwardly.

49. **The correct answer is A.** The writer is trying to tell a colorful story, so he should add as many details as possible to make the scene vivid for the reader. The number of fins in the water (choice A) would give the reader a sense of the size of the problem— was it two shark fins or ten? Choice B is incorrect because the writer has already given the time of day he saw the fins. Knowing how long he was at the beach before that is not especially necessary. Choice C is incorrect

because the story is specifically about the creatures he saw on this Sunday morning at the beach, not any other kinds of animals normally found on the beach. Choice D is incorrect because talking about shark attacks elsewhere distracts from the story the writer is trying to tell.

50. **The correct answer is H.** In Paragraph 1, the writer has already said that his first thought was that the fins were sharks. So his thought to "save everyone" was at least second, not first (choice F). Choice H is correct because it doesn't pin the writer down to exact numbering of his thoughts during the moment. Choice G is incorrect because if this was his third thought, it makes the sequence of events confusing—what was the second thought? The writer doesn't say. Choice J is incorrect because it has the confusing second use of *first*, but also removes the possessive pronoun that tells you the thoughts are his and not someone else's.

51. **The correct answer is D.** Proper punctuation in a sentence is essential for conveying the author's intended meaning. When one feels that he or she is in a dangerous situation, a pitched, emotionally charged response is appropriate and often necessary to convey this state. In such an instance, an exclamation point (choice D) is the most effective way to convey a dramatic exclamation, and it is the correct choice for this sentence. As written (choice A), the question

mark takes away from the declarative exclamation that the author is looking to convey. A semicolon (choice B) is not appropriate punctuation within this short, punchy quote. Single quotes (choice C) are used when referencing a quote within a quote, which is not the case here.

52. **The correct answer is G.** In this sentence, there is a lot of unnecessary repetition. Choice G is correct because it refines the three sentences (or sentence fragments) into a single strong, coherent statement. Choice F is incorrect because two out of the three statements are fragments, and none of them says anything different or additional about the chaos. Choice H is incorrect because it sets the three elements as a list. Choice J is incorrect because it is a fragment that lacks a verb to make it a complete thought.

53. **The correct answer is C.** The underlined text is incorrect because it is an unclear fragment. The writer doesn't make it clear who blew the whistle, so there is no subject. Choice B is incorrect because, based on the context, it is much likelier that the lifeguard (choice C) and not the writer (choice B) blew the whistle. Choice D is incorrect because the pronoun *they* does not agree in number for the context, and it is still unclear as to who is actually blowing the whistle.

54. **The correct answer is F.** The sentence as written has two parts: a main clause ("I could still see

those deadly fins lurking") and a subordinate clause that gives more detail ("coming dangerously close to a paddle boarder who was still out on the water"). These are connected appropriately, so choice F is correct. Choice G is incorrect because the conjunction *though* suggests that the fins are coming dangerously close *despite* the lurking, which doesn't make much sense. Choice H is incorrect because "lurking to a paddle boarder . . ." does not make sense. Choice J is incorrect because it sets up the two clauses as a choice between one and the other.

55. **The correct answer is D.** The pronoun *he* is too vague, so choice A is incorrect. Choice B is incorrect because the lifeguard is on the beach, out of danger. Choice C is incorrect because the writer is not worried about himself; he is worried about the sharks getting close to the paddle boarder (choice D). Choice D is correct.

56. **The correct answer is G.** Paragraph 3 is about the writer observing the lifeguard and the sharks. The detail about the men playing volleyball (choice G) is out of place and does not add to the drama of the story. Choices F and H are incorrect because they are part of the sequence of events. Choice J is incorrect because it explains why the writer is worried.

57. **The correct answer is B.** The writer is paraphrasing what he asked the lifeguard. It is not a direct quote, so there should not be any quotation marks at all.

Choice B eliminates the quotation marks, so it is correct. Choices A, C, and D are all incorrect because they have quotation marks that make the statement look like a direct quote.

58. **The correct answer is G.** Careful use of punctuation here can help avoid a significant confusion regarding the title of the movie being referenced (*Jaws*). As written (choice F), italicizing the question mark along with the movie title leads readers to believe that the name of the movie is *Jaws?*, which is incorrect. Choice G corrects the error by removing the italics from the question mark. Choice H incorrectly leads readers to think that the title of the movie is *Jaws the movie?* and choice J incorrectly leads readers to think that the title of the movie is *Jaws, the movie!*

59. **The correct answer is A.** *There* (choice A) is a pronoun used as the subject of the sentence. Choice A uses it correctly. Choices B and D are incorrect because *their* is a possessive pronoun, not a standard pronoun. Choice C is incorrect because *they're* is a contraction of noun and verb, not a pronoun.

60. **The correct answer is J.** This essay is a personal story about a specific event. General information about sharks distracts from the sequence of events and does not have a place within the existing story. Choice J is correct, and the new paragraph would not fit well after Paragraph 1 (choice

F), after Paragraph 3 (choice G), or before Paragraph 5 (choice H).

61. **The correct answer is C.** This sentence is made awkward by a misplaced modifier. *Word* is the subject of the sentence, but the adjective phrase that starts the sentence ("With four tree-trunk-sized legs, a long neck, and a long tail") refers to the dinosaur itself. The best way to untangle this is to make sure the introductory clause refers to the noun/subject. Choice B is incorrect because it inserts the possessive *its*, but still leaves the phrase incorrectly describing *word*. Choice C is correct because it changes the subject of the sentence, with *dinosaur* replacing *word*. It also breaks up the two sentences to avoid confusion and wordiness. Choice D is incorrect for two reasons: it fails to fix the modifier confusion, and it also uses the phrase "thunder lizard" before the writer defines it in the next sentence.

62. **The correct answer is J.** The underlined word is meant to show that the Brontosaurus's name translates exactly to "thunder lizard." Choice F is incorrect because *liberally* means "freely." Choice G is incorrect because *laterally* means "sideways." Choice H is incorrect because *legibly* means "clearly." Choice J is correct because *literally* means "exactly."

63. **The correct answer is C.** The detail about how the phrase "thunder lizard" relates to dinosaurs in general is not especially relevant to the discussion of the Brontosaurus in

particular. The first paragraph sets the tone and structure for the rest of the essay, so it is important to make sure that all the sentences relate to the overall topic. Choice A is incorrect because the sentence about thunder lizards is too general to keep in the essay. Choice B is incorrect because it tells the reader essential back-ground about how the Brontosaurus has been perceived over the years. Choice D is incorrect because it sets up the main topic of the essay: the question of whether the Brontosaurus ever actually existed.

64. **The correct answer is G.** The underlined text is missing an article to tell the reader about how many skeletons there were. Choice G is correct because it uses the article *a* to indicate that there was one skeleton to start. Choice H is incorrect because it adds the article, but misplaces the adverb *really*. Choice J is incorrect because although it too adds the article *a*, it misplaces the adverb *really*. In this case, it changes the meaning of the modifier from *truly* to *very*.

65. **The correct answer is D.** The underlined text represents the first part of a sentence fragment. It needs to be revised so that it is a complete thought. Choice B is incorrect because it still leads to a sentence fragment. Choice C is incorrect because it does not resolve the sentence fragment and also adds the word *insofar*, which makes the sentence wordier. Choice D creates a

subject (*it*) and a predicate ("was as 'new' as dinosaurs could be"), so it is correct.

66. **The correct answer is H.** The underlined text should be a possessive pronoun that relates back to the plural noun *dinosaurs*. Choice F is incorrect because it is a singular possessive pronoun. Choice G is incorrect because it is a simple pronoun, not possessive. Choice H is correct because *their* is a plural possessive pronoun. Choice J is incorrect because it is a singular possessive pronoun.

67. **The correct answer is B.** The sentence has two competing subjects that refer to the same people, so it is incorrect and should be revised down to one. Choice B is correct because it removes the unnecessary pronoun *they*. Choice C is incorrect because it turns the sentence into a fragment. Choice D is incorrect because it creates an unnecessary adjective phrase and keeps the extra pronoun *they*.

68. **The correct answer is J.** The underlined text (choice F) includes a plural noun and a singular noun. Because of "a/an," you know that there is one skull and one body, so the text should match. Choice J correctly has a singular skull and a singular body. Choice G is incorrect because it makes both nouns plural. Choice H is incorrect because it swaps the Apatosaurus and the Camarosaurus, when you know from Paragraph 2 that O.C. Marsh had created the Brontosaurus by attaching an Apatosaurus skull to a Camarosaurus body.

69. **The correct answer is C.** The main point of Paragraph 3 is how the controversy finally led to the Brontosaurus being removed from at least one museum. The writer uses one specific museum as an example, so it would be appropriate to include the name of that museum (choice C). Choice A is incorrect because the Camarosaurus's appearance has nothing to do with the topic of the paragraph. Choice B is incorrect because the writer is trying to emphasize that there was a general call to take back the Brontosaurus's status, so individual paleontologists' names would not really do much to support the main topic. Choice D is incorrect because O.C. Marsh was part of Paragraph 2 and not part of the 1970s changes outlined in Paragraph 3.

70. **The correct answer is J.** As written, this sentence is very wordy and unclear. Choices G and H are also very long and wordy. Choice J is correct because it reduces the sentence to two clear parts: the modifying clause "even after scientists stopped recognizing the Brontosaurus as a genus of dinosaur, the Brontosaurus would still become a star of the 1993 movie *Jurassic Park*."

71. **The correct answer is B.** *Twist!* is not an effective transition, especially with the informative tone of the essay. Choice B uses a transition word (*however*) and completes the thought by stating that the story has changed. Choice C is incorrect because it

has the same abrupt exclamation as *Twist!* with no context or transition. Choice D is incorrect because it is even more vague than choice B.

72. **The correct answer is G.** A thorough understanding of the intent, focus, and purpose of the passage will help you discern between essential sentences and sentences that are a poor fit. This passage focuses on the Brontosaurus and how scientists' beliefs regarding this dinosaur have evolved over time. Choices F, H, and J are clearly related to this topic. Choice G, which makes a contrast with scientists' thoughts on the existence of aliens, fits least with the overall intended purpose of the passage.

73. **The correct answer is C.** The rest of the essay has a neutral, informative voice. It is odd that the writer would suddenly insert her opinion at the very end, so choice C is correct. Choices A, B, and D are all in the same neutral voice as the rest of the passage, with similar sentence structure and word choices.

74. **The correct answer is F.** Choice F is a good closing sentence because it calls back to previous elements in the essay, like the "thunder lizard" name and the main topic of the dispute over the dinosaurs. Choice G is incorrect because it introduces yet another dinosaur with no context. Choice H is incorrect because it is too simple and does little to connect to the information that came before it in the essay. Choice J is

incorrect because the jokey tone
does not really fit with the rest of
the essay.

75. **The correct answer is B.** Because
the writer mentions the
Apatosaurus for the first time in
Paragraph 2, it could be appropriate to insert more information
at the end of that paragraph to
emphasize how O.C. Marsh could
have made the mistake. Choice A
is incorrect because Paragraph 2
starts with a direct transition from
Paragraph 1, and that should stay
as is. Choice C is incorrect because
the writer has already moved
away from the actual dinosaur
skeletons and characteristics.
Choice D is incorrect because
Paragraph 4's topic is the
Brontosaurus's role in pop culture.

MATHEMATICS

1. D	**13.** E	**25.** C	**37.** A	**49.** A
2. H	**14.** H	**26.** J	**38.** H	**50.** K
3. B	**15.** D	**27.** E	**39.** C	**51.** D
4. G	**16.** J	**28.** G	**40.** F	**52.** K
5. A	**17.** D	**29.** B	**41.** B	**53.** A
6. K	**18.** G	**30.** G	**42.** K	**54.** J
7. C	**19.** E	**31.** D	**43.** C	**55.** B
8. J	**20.** G	**32.** K	**44.** F	**56.** J
9. B	**21.** A	**33.** C	**45.** D	**57.** A
10. K	**22.** J	**34.** J	**46.** J	**58.** H
11. B	**23.** D	**35.** D	**47.** C	**59.** A
12. J	**24.** J	**36.** H	**48.** J	**60.** H

1. **The correct answer is D.** Substitute –2 in for x and simplify using the order of operations:

$$f(-2) = -3(-2)^3 + (-2) - 1 =$$
$$-3(-8) - 2 - 1 = 24 - 2 - 1 = 21$$

Choice A is incorrect because $-3(-2)^3 = 24$, not –24. Choice B is incorrect because $(-2)^3 = -8$, not –6; do not multiply base and exponent to compute a power. Choice C is incorrect because when substituting in –2 for x, you seemingly dropped the negative on the middle term. Choice E is incorrect because you dropped the –3 in the term $-3x^3$.

2. **The correct answer is H.** Observe that:

$$3|x+5| - 12 = 0$$
$$3|x+5| = 12$$
$$|x+5| = 4$$
$$x+5 = 4 \text{ or } x+5 = -4$$
$$x = -1 \text{ or } x = -9$$

So, the solution set is {–1, –9}. Choice F is incorrect because the signs are both incorrect. Choice G is incorrect because once you add 12 to both sides, you must then divide both sides by 3. Choice J is incorrect because once you add 12 to both sides, you must divide by 3, not subtract 3 from both sides. Choice K is incorrect because you ignored the 3 completely.

3. **The correct answer is B.** Use the distance formula to compute each of these distances—do not eyeball them!

$$d(A,P) = \sqrt{(5-5)^2 + (4-0)^2} = \sqrt{16}$$
$$d(B,P) = \sqrt{(5-0)^2 + (4-(-1))^2} = \sqrt{50}$$
$$d(C,P) = \sqrt{(10-5)^2 + (0-4)^2} = \sqrt{41}$$
$$d(D,P) = \sqrt{(5-1)^2 + (4-9)^2} = \sqrt{41}$$
$$d(E,P) = \sqrt{(9-5)^2 + (9-4)^2} = \sqrt{41}$$

So point B is furthest away.

Answer Keys and Explanations

4. **The correct answer is G.** The vertex is at (−2, −1), and the parabola opens down because the coefficient of x^2 is negative. The only graph that satisfies these two conditions is the one in choice G. Choice F is incorrect because the vertex is wrong. Choice H is incorrect because the parabola should open down. Choice J is incorrect because the vertex is wrong and the parabola should open down. Choice K is incorrect because the vertex is wrong.

5. **The correct answer is A.** By the AA theorem, we know that triangles EDC and ADB are similar. So, corresponding sides are in proportion. As such, we know that $\dfrac{6+x}{6} = \dfrac{8+y}{y}$.

Solving for y yields:

$$\frac{6+x}{6} = \frac{8+y}{y}$$
$$y(6+x) = 6(8+y)$$
$$6y + xy = 48 + 6y$$
$$xy = 48$$
$$y = \frac{48}{x}$$

Choice B is incorrect because you should be dividing 48 by x, not multiplying by it. Choice C is incorrect because this is the reciprocal of the correct relationship. Choice D is incorrect because the numerator is wrong, which is the likely result of an arithmetic error. Choice E is incorrect because you should be dividing by x, not multiplying by it, and the 6 is wrong, which is the likely result of an arithmetic error.

6. **The correct answer is K.** Observe that BD is congruent to itself, angle ABD is congruent to angle CBD, and AB is congruent to BC. Since the angle is the included angle, we conclude that triangles ABD and CBD are congruent using the SAS Property. Choice F is incorrect because in this property, the angle is not the one between the two given sides. Choice G is incorrect because we are not told that two pairs of angles are congruent. Choice H is incorrect because we are not told that two pairs of angles are congruent. Choice J is incorrect because we are not told that all three pairs of sides are congruent.

7. **The correct answer is C.** You can only add matrices that have the exact same number of rows and columns, which these do not. Choice A is incorrect because you can multiply any matrix by a scalar. Choice B is incorrect because you can multiply any matrix by a scalar. Choice D is incorrect because you can subtract matrices that have the same number of rows and columns. Choice E is incorrect because you can compute the determinant of any square matrix.

8. **The correct answer is J.** Let x be the amount of time she spent studying. Set up the following proportion and solve for x:

$$\frac{2}{5} = \frac{x}{26}$$
$$5x = 52$$
$$x = 10\frac{2}{5} = 10 \text{ hours, 24 minutes}$$

$\frac{2}{5}$ of an hour equals

$$\left(\frac{2}{5}\right)(60) = 24 \text{ minutes.}$$

Choice F is incorrect because this is exactly $\frac{1}{2}$ of the time she has to spend, not $\frac{2}{5}$ of it.

Choice G is incorrect because this constitutes more than $\frac{2}{5}$ of 26 hours. Choice H is incorrect because this constitutes less than $\frac{2}{5}$ of 26 hours. Choice K is incorrect because this is the time she spent not studying.

9. **The correct answer is B.** Substitute in the values of a, b, and c, and simplify the resulting expression using the order of operations:

$$\frac{b^c - a^c}{ab} = \frac{(-3)^3 - 2^3}{2(-3)} = \frac{-27 - 8}{-6}$$

$$= \frac{35}{6} = 5\frac{5}{6}$$

Choice A is incorrect because when you simplify the expression, you do not get −1. Choice C is incorrect because you cannot cancel a and b in this manner; you can only cancel like *factors*, not *terms*. Choice D is incorrect because $(-3)^3 = -27$, not 27. Choice E is incorrect because when computing powers, you do not multiply base times exponent.

10. **The correct answer is K.** Use the exponent rules to simplify as follows:

$$\frac{z^a \cdot \left(z^2\right)^b}{z^{b-a}} = z^a \cdot z^{2b} \cdot z^{-b} \cdot z^a =$$

$$\left(z^a \cdot z^a\right) \cdot \left(z^{2b} \cdot z^{-b}\right) =$$

$$z^{2a} \cdot z^b = z^{2a+b}$$

Choice F is incorrect because you did not treat the "*a* powers" of *z* correctly; specifically,

$$\frac{z^a}{z^{-a}} = z^{2a}, \text{ not } z^0 = 1. \text{ Choice G is}$$

incorrect because you incorrectly canceled a and b when simplifying the powers. Choice H is incorrect because you did not handle the term z^{-a} in the denominator correctly. Choice J is incorrect because you did not handle the "*b* powers" of *z* correctly; you should subtract the exponents when dividing.

11. **The correct answer is B.** Write the terms in decreasing order (according to degree), factor out a common factor of −2, factor the trinomial, and set the factor equal to zero and solve for *x*:

$$60x - 18 - 50x^2 = 0$$

$$2\left(25x^2 - 30x + 9\right) = 0$$

$$2(5x - 3)^2 = 0$$

$$5x - 3 = 0$$

$$x = \frac{3}{5}$$

So the complete solution set is $\left\{\frac{3}{5}\right\}$. Choice A is incorrect because this is the reciprocal of the correct answer. Choice C is incorrect because you factored incorrectly, and when solving the equations obtained by setting each factor equal to zero, you did not divide by the coefficient of x, but rather the constant term on the right side. Choice D is incorrect because neither of these values is a solution, which suggests a problem with factoring. Choice E is incorrect because is not a solution; you factored incorrectly.

12. **The correct answer is J.** Applying properties of radicals yields

$$\sqrt{w^3xy} \cdot 3\sqrt{wx^2} = 3\sqrt{w^3xy \cdot wx^2} =$$
$$3\sqrt{w^4x^3y} = 3w^2x\sqrt{xy}.$$

You disregarded the square root signs throughout the calculation. The 3 should be outside the radical sign. Choice H is incorrect because the powers of x and w are wrong, and the 3 should be outside the radical sign. Choice K is incorrect because the power of w is wrong.

13. **The correct answer is E.** We must determine the slope of the given line. To do so, solve for y:

$$y = \frac{3}{5}x + \frac{2}{5}.$$ So, the slope is $\frac{3}{5}$.

So, any line that has slope $-\frac{5}{3}$ is perpendicular to this one. The line in choice E can be written as

$$y = -\frac{5}{3}x - 2,$$ which has slope $-\frac{5}{3}$.

So, it is perpendicular to the given line. Choice A is incorrect because

the y-intercept is $-\frac{5}{3}$, but the slope is 1. Choice B is incorrect because the slope is $\frac{5}{3}$, not $-\frac{5}{3}$. Choice C is incorrect because the slope is $\frac{5}{3}$, not $-\frac{5}{3}$. Choice D is incorrect because the slope is $\frac{3}{5}$, so it is actually parallel to the given line.

14. **The correct answer is H.** The least common denominator is $4(x-1)(4x-1)$. Multiply the first fraction by $4x-1$ and the second by $4(x-1)$, and simplify:

$$\frac{3}{4(x-1)} - \frac{2}{4x-1}$$
$$= \frac{3 \cdot (4x-1)}{4(x-1)(4x-1)} - \frac{2 \cdot 4(x-1)}{4(x-1)(4x-1)}$$
$$= \frac{3 \cdot (4x-1) - 2 \cdot 4(x-1)}{4(x-1)(4x-1)}$$
$$= \frac{12x-3-8(x-1)}{4(x-1)(4x-1)}$$
$$= \frac{12x-3-8x+8}{4(x-1)(4x-1)}$$
$$= \frac{4x+5}{4(x-1)(4x-1)}$$

Choices F and G are incorrect because these two fractions have different denominators, so you cannot simply subtract the numerators and put that difference over one of the denominators. Choice J is incorrect because you cannot cancel terms as follows in a fraction:

$$\frac{4x+5}{4(x-1)(4x-1)} \neq \frac{\cancel{4}x+5}{\cancel{4}(x-1)(4x-1)}$$

Choice K is incorrect because you cannot cancel terms as follows in a fraction:

$$\frac{4x+5}{4(x-1)(4x-1)} \neq \frac{\cancel{4x}+5}{4(x-1)(\cancel{4x}-1)}$$

15. **The correct answer is D.** The digit in the millions place is 4. It must be rounded up to 5 because the digit to its immediate right, 6, is greater than 5. Choice A is incorrect because the 4 should have been rounded up to 5 since the value to its immediate right is greater than 5. Choice B is incorrect because you rounded to the ten millions place, not the millions place. Choice C is incorrect because you rounded to the hundred thousands place, not the millions place. Choice E is incorrect because you rounded to the hundred thousands place, not the millions place, and did so incorrectly.

16. **The correct answer is J.** Observe that the graph of $f(x)$ is increasing (that is, rising from left to right) for negative x and decreasing (that is, falling from left to right) for positive x. The graph of $g(x)$ is doing the exact opposite on those intervals. So, choice J is correct. Choice F is incorrect because this would mean the graph of $f(x)$ is always below the graph of $g(x)$, but it is not. Choice G is incorrect because there are two points of intersection of the two graphs and the x-values of these points are solutions to this equation. Choice H is incorrect because the value $x = 0$ satisfies both equations. Choice K is incorrect because in such case,

the graphs would have the same x-intercepts, and they do not.

17. **The correct answer is D.** Since l_1 and l_2 are parallel, the angles marked as $2x - 2$ and $5x$ are supplementary. So, $2x - 2 + 5x = 180$. Solving for x yields $7x = 182$, and so $x = 26$. Thus, $5x = 130$. Since the angle vertical to the one marked $5x$ is also the corresponding angle to the one marked y, and vertical angles and corresponding angles are congruent, we conclude that $y = 130$. Choice A is incorrect because this is x, not y. Choice B is incorrect because this is the supplement to y. Choice C is incorrect because y and $2x - 2$ are supplementary, not complementary. Choice E is incorrect because the line m is not perpendicular to line l_2.

18. **The correct answer is G.** Since the image of $P(4, 5)$ under this translation is $(-1, -1)$, all points on the segment PQ must be moved 5 units to the left and 6 units down. Doing this to $Q(-3, 2)$ results in the point $(-8, -4)$. This is the image of Q. Choice F is incorrect because this is the reflection of Q over the y-axis. Choice H is incorrect because this is the reflection of Q over the x-axis. Choice J is incorrect because you shifted Q to the right 5 units instead of left 5 units. Choice K is incorrect because you shifted Q up 6 units instead of down 6 units.

Answer Keys and Explanations

19. The correct answer is E.

$$f\left(\frac{\pi}{2}\right) = 3\cos\left(2 \cdot \frac{\pi}{2}\right) =$$
$$3\cos(\pi) = 3(-1) = -3.$$

Choice A is incorrect because $\cos\pi = -1$, not 0. Choice B is incorrect because you forgot to multiply by 3, and $\cos\pi = -1$, not 1. Choice C is incorrect because you forgot to multiply by 3. Choice D is incorrect because $\cos\pi = -1$, not 1.

20. The correct answer is G. Use the radical properties to simplify:

$$\frac{\sqrt{48}}{\sqrt{60}} = \sqrt{\frac{48}{60}} = \sqrt{\frac{4}{5}} = \frac{\sqrt{4}}{\sqrt{5}} = \frac{2}{\sqrt{5}} =$$
$$\frac{2}{\sqrt{5}} \cdot \frac{\sqrt{5}}{\sqrt{5}} = \frac{2\sqrt{5}}{5}$$

Choice F is incorrect because you simplified incorrectly; note that $\frac{2}{\sqrt{5}} \neq \frac{\sqrt{2}}{\sqrt{5}}$. Choice H is incorrect because $\sqrt{10} = \sqrt{2} \cdot \sqrt{5}$, not $\frac{2}{\sqrt{5}}$. Choice J is incorrect because this is the reciprocal of the correct answer. Choice K is incorrect because $\frac{\sqrt{a}}{\sqrt{b}} \neq \frac{1}{\sqrt{b-a}}$.

21. The correct answer is A. The mode of a data set is the most frequently occurring data value. In this case, the most frequently occurring number of books read is 3. Choice B is incorrect because this is the *second* most frequently occurring number of books read. Choice C is incorrect because this is the most *in*frequently occurring number of books read. Choice D is

incorrect because this is the middle value of the data set, but it is not the mode. Choice E is incorrect because this is the frequency of the most commonly occurring member of the data set, but the mode is the member of the data set itself, which would be 3.

22. The correct answer is J. Observe that $(4-5)^2 = (-1)^2 = 1$ and $4^2 - 5^2 = 16 - 25 = -9$.

So $\frac{(4-5)^2}{4^2-5^2} = \frac{1}{-9} = -\frac{1}{9}$. Choice F is incorrect because the numerator and denominator are not equal; in general, $(a-b)^2 \neq a^2 - b^2$. Choice G is incorrect because you cannot cancel a 4 and 5 in top and bottom of the fraction like this; you can only cancel like terms. Choice H is incorrect because $-5^2 = -1 \times 5^2$, which is -25; this is not the same as $(-5)^2$, which equals 25. Choice K is incorrect because when computing powers, you do not multiply base times exponent.

23. The correct answer is D. Observe that $|1-4| = |-3| = 3$ and so $-2|1-4| = -2(3) = -6$. So, squaring this value yields 36. Choice A is incorrect because $|1-4| \neq |1| + |4|$. Choice B is incorrect because the value of the expression inside the parentheses is -6 and you forgot to square it. Choice C is incorrect because you forgot to square this quantity. Choice E is incorrect because when squaring -6, you also square the -1.

24. **The correct answer is J.** Bring all terms to the left side of the equation, factor the expression, set each factor equal to zero, and solve for x:

$$6x^2 + 3 = 11x$$
$$6x^2 - 11x + 3 = 0$$
$$(2x - 3)(3x - 1) = 0$$
$$2x - 3 = 0 \text{ or } 3x - 1 = 0$$
$$x = \frac{3}{2} \text{ or } x = \frac{1}{3}$$

So, the solution set is $\left\{\frac{1}{3}, \frac{3}{2}\right\}$.

Choice F is incorrect because you must first take all of the terms to the left side of the equation before trying to solve the equation. Choice G is incorrect because these are the reciprocals of the correct solutions. Choice H is incorrect because these are the reciprocal of the correct solutions, but with the incorrect signs. Choice K is incorrect because both signs are incorrect.

25. **The correct answer is C.** Let x be the number of nickels. Then, there are $2x$ dimes and $x + 4$ quarters. Multiplying each of these quantities by the monetary value of each type, adding them together and setting the sum equal to $3.50 yields the equation $0.05x + 0.10(2x) + 0.25(x + 4) = 3.50$. Solve for x as follows:

$$0.05x + 0.10(2x) + 0.25(x + 4) = 3.50$$
$$0.5x + 1 = 3.50$$
$$0.5x = 2.50$$
$$x = 5$$

So, you have $2(5) = 10$ dimes. Choice A is incorrect because this is the number of quarters you have. Choice B is incorrect because this is the number of nickels you have. Choice D is incorrect because this is the combination of nickels and quarters that you have. Choice E is incorrect because this is the combination of nickels and dimes that you have.

26. **The correct answer is J.** Multiply the second equation by –2, and then add the resulting equation to the first one in order to eliminate m and solve for n:

$$4m - 3n = -4$$
$$\underline{-4m + 4n = -10}$$
$$n = -14$$

Now, plug this value of n back into one of the original two equations, say the first one, to solve for m:

$$4m - 3(-14) = -4$$
$$4m = -46$$
$$m = -\frac{23}{2}$$

So $\dfrac{m}{n} = \dfrac{-\frac{23}{2}}{-14} = \dfrac{23}{28}$. Choice F is incorrect because you multiplied m and n instead of dividing m by n. Choice G is incorrect because this is just the value of m. Choice H is incorrect because this is just the value of n. Choice K is incorrect because this is the reciprocal of the correct answer.

Answer Keys and Explanations

27. **The correct answer is E.** Use the distributive property first, and then combine like terms:

$$-2(3+4i)-(2i-3)=$$
$$-6-8i-2i+3=-3-10i$$

Choice A is incorrect because you did not distribute the −2 and −1 through both terms of the binomial each time. Choice B is incorrect because you did not distribute the −1 through both terms of the second binomial. Choice C is incorrect because you cannot combine the terms −3 and −10i because they do not have the same variable part. Choice D is incorrect because you are not supposed to multiply −3 and −10i when you have −3 − 10i.

28. **The correct answer is G.** First, we need the equation of the line. Since the points (0, 4) and (4, 0) are on the line, the slope is

$$m=\frac{4-0}{0-4}=-1.$$ Since the

y-intercept is 4, the equation of the line in slope-intercept form is $y=-x+4$. Since the region is shaded below the line and the line is dashed, the inequality sign we use is < to get the inequality $y<-x+4y$. Adding x to both sides yields the equivalent inequality $x+y<4$. Choice F is incorrect because the inequality sign should not include *equals* because the line is dashed. Choice H is incorrect because the inequality sign should be reversed since the region is shaded below. Choice J is incorrect because the slope of the

pictured line is −1, not 1. Choice K is incorrect because the slope is incorrect and the inequality sign is incorrect.

29. **The correct answer is B.** First, determine the slope:

$$m=\frac{4-(-1)}{-3-7}=-\frac{5}{10}=-\frac{1}{2}.$$ Using

the point (−3, 4), the equation in point-slope form is

$$y-4=-\frac{1}{2}(x+3),$$ which is

equivalent to $y=-\frac{1}{2}x+\frac{5}{2}$, or

$2y+x=5$. Choice A is incorrect because you dropped the coefficient on y. Choice C is incorrect because you mistakenly used (−3, 4) as the y-intercept. Choice D is incorrect because you computed the slope as run over rise, not rise over run. Choice E is incorrect because you computed the slope incorrectly; don't subtract the coordinates of the single points, but rather subtract the y-coordinates and then divide that difference by the difference in the x-coordinates.

30. **The correct answer is G.** Let w be the width of this rectangle. Then, its length is $2w-1$. Since the area is 3 square feet, we have the equation $w(2w-1)=3$. Solve this equation as follows:

$$w(2w-1)=3$$
$$2w^2-w-3=0$$
$$(2w-3)(w+1)=0$$
$$w=\frac{3}{2},-1$$

Since width cannot be negative, we conclude that $w = \dfrac{3}{2}$ feet. Hence, the length is

$2\left(\dfrac{3}{2}\right) - 1 = 2$ feet. And so, the

perimeter is $2\left(\dfrac{3}{2}\right) + 2(2) =$

7 feet. Choice F is incorrect because you used 1 for w, which suggests that you factored the area equation incorrectly. Choice H is incorrect because you need to double both the width and length when computing the perimeter. Choice J is incorrect because this is twice the width only; you need to add twice the length to this to get the perimeter. Choice K is incorrect because this is just the width.

31. **The correct answer is D.** The sum of any two sides of a triangle must be strictly larger than the length of the third side. Note that given that two sides are 5 and 9, the third one cannot be 3 since 3 + 5 is not larger than 9. The third side can have a length strictly larger than 4 and less than 14. All other choices fall within this range.

32. **The correct answer is K.** The sum of the measures of the three labeled angles must be 90 degrees. This yields the equation $y + 2y + 63 = 90$, so that $3y = 27$ and so, $y = 9$. Choice F is incorrect because the sum of 2y and 63 is not 90, but rather the sum of all three marked angles is 90. Choice G is incorrect because the angles marked y and 2y are not

complementary. Choice H is incorrect because this is the sum of y and 2y. Choice J is incorrect because this is 2y, not y.

33. **The correct answer is C.** Consider the diagram shown:

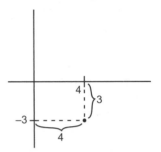

A radius of 3 units would make the circle tangent to the x-axis. Any larger, and the circle would at least extend into quadrant I. So, the maximum *diameter* is 6 units. Choice A is incorrect because this is the maximum *radius*, not diameter. Choice B is incorrect because a *radius* of 4 units would make the circle tangent to the y-axis, but would allow it to extend into quadrant I; a *diameter* of 4 units is too small. Choice D is incorrect because a *radius* of 4 units would make the circle tangent to the y-axis, but would allow it to extend into quadrant I. Choice E is incorrect because such a circle would extend into both quadrants I and III.

34. **The correct answer is J.** First, note from bullets 1 and 2 that the function has three x-intercepts, namely when $x = -1$, 2, and −4. By bullet 3, there are no more x-intercepts because the degree is 3. The only graph for which these

observations are all true is the one in choice J. Choice F is incorrect because the graph should have x-intercepts at 2 and –4, not at –2 and 4. Choice G is incorrect because the graph cannot also cross at $x = 5$ because it is a third degree polynomial and bullets 1 and 2, together, already give three x-intercepts. Choice H is incorrect because the graph should cross the x-axis at 2 and –4. Choice K is incorrect because the graph must cross the x-axis at –4 because $x + 4$ is a factor of the function.

35. **The correct answer is D.**
First, note that there are 50 – (5 + 14 + 20) = 11 people who will receive no prize. So, the probability of getting either a door prize or no prize is $14 + \dfrac{11}{50} = \dfrac{25}{50} = .5.$

Choice A is incorrect because 14 is simply the number of door prizes; you did not account for the number who will receive no prize, and you did not divide by the total number of tickets. Choice B is incorrect because this is the probability of winning *something*. Choice C is incorrect because this is the probability of winning *nothing*. Choice E is incorrect because you did not divide 25 by 50 (the total number of tickets).

36. **The correct answer is H.** First, convert both mixed numbers to improper fractions:

$$3\dfrac{3}{7} = \dfrac{24}{7}; \ 1\dfrac{5}{14} = \dfrac{19}{14}.$$

Now, divide:

$$3\dfrac{3}{7} \div 1\dfrac{5}{14} =$$
$$\dfrac{24}{7} \div \dfrac{19}{14} =$$
$$\dfrac{24}{7} \times \dfrac{14}{19} =$$
$$\dfrac{48}{19} = 2\dfrac{10}{19}.$$

Choice F is incorrect because you divided the whole parts and fractional parts separately; you must convert both mixed numbers to improper fractions. Choice G is incorrect because this is just an estimate. Choice J is incorrect because this is the reciprocal of the correct quotient. Choice K is incorrect because you multiplied instead of divided.

37. **The correct answer is A.** This is equivalent to asking for the distance between the points (0, 3) and (9, 0). Using the distance formula, calculate:

$$\sqrt{(3-0)^2 + (0-9)^2} = \sqrt{9+81} =$$
$$\sqrt{90} = 3\sqrt{10}.$$

Choice B is incorrect because this is the length of the shortest side; the hypotenuse is the length of the longest side. Choice C is incorrect because this is the length of the longer of the two legs, not the hypotenuse. Choice D is incorrect because you forgot to square each of the differences inside the radicand. Choice E is incorrect because you forgot to take the square root.

38. The correct answer is H. To form the midpoint of a line segment, average the *x*- and *y*-coordinates separately and form the point with *x*- and *y*-coordinates equal to these averages. Choice F is incorrect because you interchanged the *x*- and *y*-coordinates. Choice G is incorrect because you need to divide each of the coordinates by 2 since each one is an average. Choice J is incorrect because you added the *x*-coordinate of one point to the *y*-coordinate of the other point each time, but you should be averaging the *x*- and *y*-coordinates. Choice K is incorrect because you need to divide each of the coordinates by 2 since each one is an average, and when forming the actual midpoint, you interchanged the *x*- and *y*-coordinates.

39. The correct answer is C. Using the quadratic formula, the solutions of the given equation are:

$$x = \frac{-a \pm \sqrt{a^2 - 4(1)(4)}}{2(1)} = \frac{-a \pm \sqrt{a^2 - 16}}{2}$$

This expression will produce two distinct real solutions only if the radicand is strictly positive. So, we must solve the quadratic inequality $a^2 - 16 > 0$. The left side factors as $(a - 4)(a + 4) > 0$, so the left side is zero when $a = 4$ or -4. Now, put those numbers on a number line and choose a value in each interval to test

the sign of the left side, as shown:

Thus, the largest set of values for a for which the equation has two distinct real solutions is $\{a : a < -4 \text{ or } a > 4\}$. Choice A is incorrect because the values between 0 and 4 must be excluded. Choice B is incorrect because you forgot to square *a* in the radicand when using the quadratic formula. Choice D is incorrect because the equation has complex conjugate solutions when *a* belongs to this set. Choice E is incorrect because the equation has exactly one repeated real solution if *a* is either of these values.

40. The correct answer is F. FOIL the binomial squared first, and then distribute the 3:

$$3(1 - 5w)^2 =$$
$$3(1 - 10w + 25w^2) =$$
$$3 - 30w + 75w^2 =$$
$$75w^2 - 30w + 3$$

Choice G is incorrect because you did not double the middle term when squaring the binomial. Choice H is incorrect because you did not square the binomial correctly; specifically, $(a - b)^2 \neq a^2 - b^2$. Choice J is incorrect because you did not distribute the 3 through all terms of the squared binomial. Choice K is incorrect because you did not compute $(5w)^2$ correctly; you forgot to square the 5.

Answer Keys and Explanations

41. The correct answer is B. Since the sequence is arithmetic, the same number is added to a term to get the next one in the list. Since you add 5 to 7 to get from 7 to 12, we must do so to –8 to get that the second term is –3 and then again to –3 to get that the third term is 2. Choice A is incorrect because there is no common difference between the first and second term, and the second and third term, which cannot be the case if the sequence is arithmetic. Choice C is incorrect because the difference between consecutive terms is 5, not 4. Choice D is incorrect because you got the negative signs reversed on the terms. Choice E is incorrect because the difference between consecutive terms is 5, not 6.

42. The correct answer is K. Determine the slope of the graphed line. Observe that it is $m = \frac{4-2}{7+5} = \frac{1}{6}$. So, any line with slope –6 must be perpendicular to this one. Choice F is incorrect because the slope of this line is –1, not –6. Choice G is incorrect because this line is horizontal while the given one has a positive slope, and is slanted upward from left to right. Horizontal lines are only perpendicular to vertical ones. Choice H is incorrect because this line is parallel to the given one since its slope is the same as the slope of the graphed line. Choice J is incorrect because while the y-intercept is –6, the slope is not. And, for a line to be

perpendicular to the graphed one, its slope must be –6.

43. The correct answer is C. The standard form of an ellipse centered at the origin that is longer in the x-direction than in the y-direction is $\frac{x^2}{a^2} + \frac{y^2}{b^2} = 1$, where $a^2 > b^2$. The only equation that has this form is the one in choice C. Choice A is incorrect because this ellipse is longer in the y-direction. Choice B is incorrect because the graph of this equation would be two intersecting lines passing through the origin. Choice D is incorrect because the graph of this would be a parabola opening to the left. Choice E is incorrect because the graph of this would be a hyperbola because of the minus sign.

44. The correct answer is F. The volume of a sphere with radius r is $\frac{4}{3}\pi r^3$. Here, the diameter is $\sqrt{2}$ inches, so the radius is $\frac{1}{2}\sqrt{2}$ inches. So, the volume is

$$\frac{4}{3}\pi\left(\frac{1}{2}\sqrt{2}\right)^3 = \frac{4}{3}\pi \cdot \frac{2\sqrt{2}}{8} = \frac{\pi\sqrt{2}}{3}$$

cubic inches. Choice G is incorrect because you used the diameter instead of the radius. Choice H is incorrect because you forgot to multiply by $\frac{4}{3}$. Choice J is incorrect because you squared the radius, but it should be cubed. Choice K is incorrect because you used the diameter instead of the radius and you forgot to multiply by $\frac{4}{3}$.

45. The correct answer is D. You must determine the height and the base, and they must be perpendicular to each other. Using the base as the line segment XY, its length is 6 units. Now, to get the height, drop a perpendicular from the point Y down to the x-axis. This forms a right triangle, and the length of this vertical segment just formed is 4 units. So, the area of the parallelogram is base *times* height, which is 24 square units. Choice A is incorrect because $2\sqrt{5}$ is not the height of the parallelogram; it must be perpendicular to the base. Choice B is incorrect because you incorrectly multi-plied by $\frac{1}{2}$ when computing the area. Choice C is incorrect because the area is not the square of the base; that only works for a square. Choice E is incorrect because the area is not the square of the width; that only works for a square.

46. The correct answer is J. You must move the decimal point five places to the left to get the decimal into the proper form, and this amounts to multiplying 1.08 by 10^{-5}. Choice F is incorrect because this involves the incorrect power of 10; don't just count the zeros, but rather move one place beyond the first nonzero digit. Choice G is incorrect because the power of 10 should be negative. Choice H is incorrect because the power of 10 should be negative.

Choice K is incorrect because the power of 10 should be −6 if you use this form of the decimal.

47. The correct answer is C. Multiply the number of options available in each category to get the number of combinations: $5(4)(2) = 40$ combinations. Choice A is incorrect because you multiply the number of options available in each category, not add them. Choice B is incorrect because you did not include the types of fruit in forming the combinations. Choice D is incorrect because you did not include the types of cereal in forming the combinations. Choice E is incorrect because you did not include the types of beverages in forming the combinations.

48. The correct answer is J. Observe that $225\% = 2.25 = 2\frac{1}{4} = \frac{9}{4}$. So, 225% of $\frac{3}{4}$ is $\frac{9}{4} \cdot \frac{3}{4} = \frac{27}{16} = 1\frac{11}{16}$. Choice F is incorrect because $225\% = 2.25$, not 22.5. Choice G is incorrect because you should multiply 2.25 by $\frac{3}{4}$, not add them. Choice H is incorrect because you multiplied $\frac{3}{4}$ by $\frac{4}{9}$, which is the reciprocal of 225%. Choice K is incorrect because this is 200% of $\frac{3}{4}$, not 225%.

49. The correct answer is A.

Observe that:

$$\frac{g(x)}{f(x)} = \frac{2 - \dfrac{1}{x^2}}{2 + \dfrac{1}{x}} = \frac{\dfrac{2x^2 - 1}{x^2}}{\dfrac{2x + 1}{x}}$$

$$= \frac{2x^2 - 1}{x^2} \cdot \frac{x}{2x + 1}$$

$$= \frac{2x^2 - 1}{x(2x + 1)}$$

$$= \frac{2x^2 - 1}{2x^2 + x}$$

Choices B and C are incorrect because you cannot cancel like *terms* in the top and bottom of a fraction; you can only cancel like *factors*. Choice D is incorrect because you forgot a factor of *x* in the denominator. Choice E is incorrect because this is the reciprocal of the correct quotient.

50. The correct answer is K. The radius of the new cone is $\dfrac{R}{3}$ and the height is $4H$. Therefore, the volume is

$$\frac{1}{3}\pi\left(\frac{R}{3}\right)^2 (4H) = \frac{4}{9}\left(\frac{1}{3}\pi R^2 H\right).$$

So, the volume of the newly formed cone is $\dfrac{4}{9}$ the volume of the original cone. Choice F is incorrect because you incorporated the factor of $\dfrac{1}{3}$ that is part of the volume formula of the original cone into the fraction of this volume that the volume of the newly formed cone comprises. Choice G is incorrect because you

forgot to square the $\dfrac{1}{3}$ in the radius portion $\dfrac{R}{3}$ when computing the volume of the newly formed cone. Choice H is incorrect because you squared the height instead of the radius when computing the volume. Choice J is incorrect because you ignored the multiple of $\dfrac{1}{3}$ on the radius.

51. The correct answer is D. Express each of these as decimals and put them in order:

$$40.3 \times 10^2 = 4,030 \ 5^{\text{th}}$$
$$4.03 \times 10^{-2} = 0.0403 \ 2^{\text{nd}}$$
$$0.00403 \times 10^{-1} = 0.000403 \ 1^{\text{s}}$$
$$4.03 \times 10^{-1} = 0.4030 \ 3^{\text{rd}}$$
$$0.403 \times 10^1 = 4.03 \ 4^{\text{th}}$$

Choice D is in third place.

52. The correct answer is K. The given absolute value inequality is equivalent to the double inequality $-13 \le 3x - 2 \le 13$. Solve this inequality by adding 2 to all parts of the inequality and dividing all parts by 3:

$$-13 \le 3x - 2 \le 13$$
$$-11 \le 3x \le 15$$
$$-\frac{11}{3} \le x \le 5$$

This is illustrated by the region in choice K. Choice F is incorrect because the signs of the endpoints are incorrect and there should be closed circles, not open circles, on the number line at the endpoints. Choice G is incorrect because the signs of the endpoints are incorrect. Choice H is incorrect because you forgot about the left side of the inequality; remember, the absolute value inequality is equivalent to the double inequality $-13 \le 3x - 2 \le 13$. Choice J is incorrect because this is the solution to the inequality $|3x - 2| > 13$.

53. **The correct answer is A.** The period of a function of the form $G(x) = A\sin(Bx + C) + D$ is $\frac{2\pi}{B}$. For the given function, $B = 3$, and so the period is $\frac{2\pi}{3}$. Choice B is incorrect because this is the phase shift. Choice C is incorrect because this is part of the phase shift. Choice D is incorrect because this is the vertical shift. Choice E is incorrect because this is the amplitude.

54. **The correct answer is J.** The surface area of a rectangular box is the sum of the areas of its six faces, all of which are rectangular. Each pair of parallel faces are congruent, and so we simply need to find the area of three different faces (front, side, and bottom) and multiply each by 2:

$2(5x) + 2(x \times 2x) + 2(5 \times 2x) =$
$10x + 4x^2 + 20x = 4x^2 + 30x$

Choice F is incorrect because this is the volume of the box, not its surface area. Choice G is incorrect because you neglected to include the faces whose area is $5x$. Choice H is incorrect because you only counted one of each face.

Choice K is incorrect because you forgot to include the top.

55. **The correct answer is B.** The graph of $y = 1 - x^2$ should be solid, the graph of $y = x^2 - 1$ should be dashed, and the region between them should be shaded. This is pictured in the region in choice B. Choice A is incorrect because the graphs are both incorrect; the graph of $y = 1 - x^2$ opens downward with vertex at $(0, 1)$ and the graph of $y = x^2 - 1$ opens upward with a vertex of $(0, -1)$. Choice C is incorrect because the vertices of both graphs are off; the graph of $y = 1 - x^2$ opens downward with vertex at $(0, 1)$ and the graph of $y = x^2 - 1$ opens upward with a vertex of $(0, -1)$. Choice D is incorrect because the graph of $y = x^2 - 1$ should be dashed. Choice E is incorrect because the graph of $y = x^2 - 1$ should be dashed and neither parabola should be translated to the right.

56. **The correct answer is J.** Using the definition of directly and indirectly proportional immediately yields the relationship $X = \frac{kY}{Z^2}$. Choice F is incorrect because this means X is inversely proportional to both Y and Z^2. Choice G is incorrect because the placement of Y and Z^2 in the fraction should both be switched. Choice H is incorrect because this makes X directly proportional to the sum of Y and Z^2. Choice K is incorrect because this makes X directly proportional to Z^2, not inversely proportional.

57. **The correct answer is A.** We are only given that one pair of opposite sides is parallel, whereas all other choices require *both* pairs of opposite sides be parallel. Moreover, adjacent angles in all other of the listed quadrilaterals are supplementary, which is impossible here since the two adjacent base angles ABC and BCD are acute. Choice B is incorrect because all angles in a square are right angles, and this quadrilateral has two acute angles. Choice C is incorrect because both pairs of opposite sides in a parallelogram must be parallel. Moreover, adjacent angles in a parallelogram are supplementary, which is impossible here since the two adjacent base angles ABC and BCD are acute. Choice D is incorrect because both pairs of opposite sides in a rhombus must be parallel. Moreover, adjacent angles in a rhombus are supplementary, which is impossible here since the two adjacent base angles ABC and BCD are acute. Choice E is incorrect because all angles in a rectangle are right angles, and this quadrilateral has two acute angles.

58. **The correct answer is H.** First, factor the left side and determine the x-values that make it equal to zero:

$$6x^2 + 7x - 3 \geq 0$$
$$(2x + 3)(3x - 1) \geq 0$$

The values of x that make the left side zero are $-\frac{3}{2}$ and $\frac{1}{3}$. Put these on a number line and test points in each interval to assess the sign of the left side, as shown:

So, the solution set is

$$\left\{ x : x \leq -\frac{3}{2} \text{ or } x \geq \frac{1}{3} \right\}, \text{ where}$$

we have included the values that make the left side 0 because the inequality sign includes equals. Choice F is incorrect because this is the solution set for the inequality $6x^2 + 7x - 3 \leq 0$. Choice G is incorrect because the signs of the zeros are both incorrect, and they should be included in the solution set since the inequality sign includes equals. Choice J is incorrect because the zeros should be included in the solution set since the inequality sign includes equals. Choice K is incorrect because the signs of the zeros are incorrect.

59. **The correct answer is A.** The area of a sector with central angle θ (expressed in degrees) in a circle of radius r is $\left(\dfrac{\theta}{360}\right) \cdot \pi r^2$. Here, the radius is $r = \dfrac{1}{2}(8 \text{ in.}) = 4$ in. and $\theta = 360 - 135 = 225$. So, the area is $\left(\dfrac{225}{360}\right) \cdot \pi(4 \text{ in.})^2 = 10\pi$ square inches. Choice B is incorrect because this is the area of the unshaded sector. Choice C is incorrect because you used the diameter in place of the radius. Choice D is incorrect because this is the area of the whole circle. Choice E is incorrect because this is the circumference of the whole circle.

60. **The correct answer is H.** Note that the equation $\sin\theta + \dfrac{\sqrt{2}}{2} = 0$ is equivalent to $\sin\theta = -\dfrac{\sqrt{2}}{2}$. This is satisfied when the terminal side of θ is in quadrant III or IV and a multiple of $\dfrac{\pi}{4}$. So, $\theta = \dfrac{5\pi}{4}, \dfrac{7\pi}{4}$ are both solutions of this equation. Choice F is incorrect because $\dfrac{5\pi}{4}$ is not a solution of this equation. Choice G is incorrect because $\dfrac{7\pi}{4}$ is not a solution of this equation. Choice J is incorrect because $\dfrac{7\pi}{4}$ is not a solution of this equation. Choice K is incorrect because $\dfrac{5\pi}{4}$ is not a solution of this equation.

READING

1. D	**9.** A	**17.** A	**25.** D	**33.** B
2. H	**10.** F	**18.** J	**26.** G	**34.** G
3. C	**11.** A	**19.** D	**27.** B	**35.** C
4. F	**12.** J	**20.** G	**28.** F	**36.** J
5. C	**13.** B	**21.** A	**29.** D	**37.** A
6. H	**14.** G	**22.** J	**30.** G	**38.** H
7. B	**15.** B	**23.** B	**31.** C	**39.** B
8. J	**16.** F	**24.** G	**32.** H	**40.** G

1. **The correct answer is D.** Each answer choice is a synonym of *overtures,* but only one makes sense if used in place of the word in this particular passage. *Signals* (choice A) is too vague. There is another answer choice that more specifically indicates what *overtures* means in this context. *Prefaces* (choice B) and *openings* (choice C) suggest the beginnings of stories or pieces of music, and not something that a person might communicate to a ghost, which is how *overtures* is used in the passage. However, *calls* does imply such communication, so choice D is the best answer.

2. **The correct answer is H.** Sometimes, the simplest answer is the best answer, and that is the case with this question. The passage does not indicate that the ghost in Canterville Chase is dangerous (choice F) or destructive (choice J), nor does it indicate that there are more supernatural creatures or monsters in the dwelling than a single ghost, which eliminates choice G. The simple fact that Canterville Chase is haunted has caused everyone to tell Hiram B. Otis that "he was doing a very foolish thing" according to the first paragraph of the passage. Therefore, choice H is the best answer.

3. **The correct answer is C.** In the second paragraph, Lord Canterville describes the Dowager Duchess of Bolton as his "grandaunt." This confirms choice C and eliminates choices A, B, and D.

4. **The correct answer is F.** Although the narrator asks if Douglas's story is beyond "sheer terror," and Douglas replies that his story is beyond "dreadfulness," Paragraph 7 simply states: "'Oh, how delicious!' cried one of the women." Douglas's story may be one that would inspire dread (choice G) or terror (choice J), but the exclamation "Oh, how delicious" suggests delight, and it is not unusual for someone to enjoy hearing a terrifying or dreadful story, so choice F is the best answer. In this exclamation, the word *delicious* is not intended to suggest delicious food, so choice H is not the best answer.

5. **The correct answer is C.** The first sentence of the passage reads, "The story had held us, round the fire, sufficiently breathless, but except the obvious remark that it was gruesome, as, on Christmas Eve in an old house, a strange tale should essentially be…" The suggestion that a "strange tale" told on Christmas Eve "should essentially be *gruesome* implies a tradition of telling such stories on the holiday, and in fact, this is a tradition in Britain where this story takes place. So even if you are not familiar with the tradition of telling gruesome stories on Christmas Eve, you should have deduced that this is a tradition where this particular story is set based on clues in the passage. This means that choice C is the best answer. These clues contradict choice A, even if it is unusual to tell tales about ghosts on Christmas Eve in the United States. If you continue reading the passage beyond the opening sentence, you will discover that Douglas does not "tell a story about spreading the holiday spirit" and eliminate choice B. Whether or not Douglas tells only gruesome tales on Christmas Eve is never implied in the passage, so choice D is not the best answer.

6. **The correct answer is H.** The key to answering this question is in the tenth paragraph when Douglas refuses to tell his story about the ghost right away. The paragraph reveals that he does not do so because telling gruesome stories makes him feel uncomfortable (choice F), that he is delaying telling the story to build suspense (choice G), or that he is delaying it to be mischievous or comedic (choice J). In fact, he delays telling the story because it is written down and locked in a drawer. He wants that written story before telling it, which suggests that he does not just want to improvise the tale or read it without preparation, and that indicates that accuracy is important to Douglas when he is telling a tale. These clues all support the conclusion in choice H.

7. **The correct answer is B.** This question asks you to identify the main idea that both passages have in common. You can eliminate choice A since it does not describe the main idea of either passage; although both passages are about ghosts, neither passage explains how the people those ghosts once were died. Choice C may seem like a good answer, but no ghosts are actually discovered in these particular passages; there are only people explaining to others about the existence of particular ghosts. Therefore, choice B is the best answer. Only Passage B mentions a holiday, Christmas Eve, and that holiday is not ruined by ghosts, so choice D does not describe the main idea of either passage.

8. **The correct answer is J.** This question asks you to spot a key difference between the two passages. You can eliminate choice F because ghosts do not actually appear in either passage, they are only discussed. Choice G

mixes up the passages; it is Passage B in which a child is disturbed by a ghost, not Passage A. Passage A contains the character relating the ghost story as a matter of honor, not Passage B, so Choice H is incorrect. However, only Passage A contains a character who makes it clear that he does not believe in ghosts, so choice J is the best answer.

9. **The correct answer is A.** Ghosts are not something one sees every day. In fact, there is no proof at all that such things exist, so they can be categorized as "strange phenomena." Since Lord Canterville and Douglas both profess to believe in ghosts, choice A is the best answer. Men of science do not tend to believe in strange phenomena of which there is not proof, so choice B is not the best answer. While it is possible that Lord Canterville and Douglas are joking around by pretending to believe in ghosts, these passages provide no evidence of this conclusion, so choice C is not the best answer. Although it is highly unlikely that ghosts exist in the real world, they may exist in fictional stories such as Passages A and B, so it might not be accurate to conclude that their belief in ghosts means Lord Canterville and Douglas are deeply troubled. Choice D is not the best answer choice.

10. **The correct answer is F.** In Passage A, Lord Canterville tells the story of how the Dowager Duchess of Bolton is frightened by a ghost who places "two skeleton hands" on her shoulders. There is

no mention of skeletons in Passage B. Therefore, choice F is the best answer. The ghosts in both passages frighten people— in Passage A, the ghost frightens the dowager and in Passage B it frightens a child—so choice G is incorrect. There is no mention of the ghosts' motivations in either passage, so choice H is not the best answer. In Passage B, the ghost frightens a child, but the ghost is not a child, so choice J is wrong.

11. **The correct answer is A.** After reading the fourth paragraph, you should have been able to eliminate choices B and C since the manufacture of cotton is explicitly described as "developing with great promise." Choice D is a little trickier since the paragraph does not state that manufacture of cotton "satisfied a common demand" explicitly. However, it does state that "Cotton cloth was the new sensation and the demand for it was steadily growing," which certainly implies that choice D is true and should therefore be eliminated. That just leaves choice A, and since women did have opportunities to work in cotton mills, according to the passage, it is untrue, which means that choice A is the correct answer.

12. **The correct answer is J.** According to the fourth paragraph, "When Susan was two years old, her father built a cotton factory of twenty-six looms beside the brook which ran through Grandfather Read's meadow, hauling the cotton forty miles by

wagon from Troy, New York." This one sentence confirms the truth of all three statements in this question, and so the correct answer must account for all three statements. Only choice J does this. Choices F, G, and H each omit two essential statements.

13. **The correct answer is B.** The answer to this question can be found toward the end of the sixth paragraph when the author states, "The older states soon fell into line, Massachusetts in 1820 removing property qualifications for voters." This statement supports choice B. The author then goes on to state that "Before long, throughout the United States, all free white men were enfranchised, leaving only women, Negroes, and Indians without the full rights of citizenship." "Negroes" is an antiquated way of referring to African Americans, and "Indians" is an antiquated way of referring to Native Americans, and this statement suggests that neither group of people had the right to vote in 1820 by indicating that they were "without the full rights of citizenship." It also states that women were denied those rights. This eliminates choices A and C. Although people who were not white men were denied "the full rights of citizenship" at that time, this does not mean that they were not citizens of the United States. They just did not enjoy the privileges that white men did in a racist and sexist society, so choice D is not the best answer.

14. **The correct answer is G.** Although the fifth paragraph states that Lucy Read Anthony washed, ironed, and mended—which are all ways of caring for clothing—and that she spun—which is a way of spinning thread into cloth to make clothing—it does not suggest that she necessarily performed these duties for her boarders. It only states that she cooked their food. Therefore, Statement II is the only true one, and choice G is the only correct answer. Choices F and J only account for untrue statements, and choice H pairs a true statement with an untrue one.

15. **The correct answer is B.** This question requires you to think about how seemingly unrelated ideas in the passage connect with each other. The first five paragraphs are mostly about Susan B. Anthony as a young girl. The sixth paragraph changes to the topic of women not having the right to vote in much of 1820s America. The fact that both topics appear in the same passage indicates that they relate to each other in some way, and a logical conclusion is that Susan B. Anthony will one day join the fight to get women the right to vote throughout the country. Therefore, choice B is the best answer. While it is true that Susan B. Anthony would one day appear on a one-dollar coin, there is nothing to suggest this in the passage. Your answers should always be based on evidence actually presented in the given passage and not on outside knowledge, so choice A is not the

best answer. There is also nothing to suggest that she would one day own her own cotton mill (choice C) or become president of the United States (choice D), both of which are things that never happened.

16. **The correct answer is F.** Although each answer choice is a definition of *union*, only one describes how that word is used in line 40. One clue is that the line refers to how states joined the Union. States would not join an organization for workers (choice G) or a marital relationship (choice H). It also does not make sense for states to join an emblem on a flag (choice J). It only makes sense for states to join the flourishing United States, so choice F is the only answer that makes sense.

17. **The correct answer is A.** Women, African Americans, and Native Americans did not have the right to vote everywhere in the United States in 1820. The author also points out that women did not have this essential right "in spite of the contribution they had made to the defense and development of the new nation." This implies that she believes women deserved that right, so it is logical to conclude that she believed that the denial of that right was unfair. Choice A is really the only logical conclusion. The unfairness of the denial of women and other citizen's rights to vote contradicts choice B. The author only discusses one industry in the passage, the cotton industry, so there is not enough evidence to reach the conclusion in choice C.

Although the author likely believed that all citizens were not treated fairly in the 1820s United States, choice D is an extreme conclusion that suggests a level of anger and passion not present in this fairly unemotional passage.

18. **The correct answer is J.** Cooking and packing dinner pails are domestic chores, and the fifth paragraph states that Susan B. Anthony was very good at these tasks by the age of ten, so choice F is not the best answer. The first sentence of the sixth paragraph supports the conclusion in choice G, and since this question asks you to find the unsupported conclusion, this answer choice is incorrect. The beginning of the passage supports the conclusion in choice H since Susan B. Anthony often thought about the unfair treatment Sally Ann received just because she was a woman. Only choice J reaches a conclusion unsupported by evidence in the passage.

19. **The correct answer is D.** Remember that all conclusions must be based on evidence present in the given passage. Although its yarn supplier probably plays a significant role in the success of a cotton mill, there is no evidence to support this conclusion in the passage. Although Daniel Anthony's cotton mill was located in a valley, the author does not suggest that this fact had any effect on the mill, so choice B is not the best answer. Choice C is simply incorrect; cotton mills catered to young brides by spinning the cotton

cloth needed for their sheets. There is no indication that young brides comprised the staffs of mills. However, a cotton mill did need a waterway to provide its power in 1820, and this is implied by Anthony's seeing of "a potential cotton mill by the side of every rushing brook." Choice D is the best answer.

20. **The correct answer is G.** The answer to this question can be found in the very last sentence of the passage when the author states, "Hannah Lee Corbin of Virginia pleaded with her brother, Richard Henry Lee, to make good the principle of 'no taxation without representation' by enfranchising widows with property." This statement supports choice G. According to the final paragraph, choice F applies to Abigail Adams, not Hannah Lee Corbin. That paragraph implies that De Tocqueville may have had the opinion expressed in choice H, but once again, this does not apply to Hannah Lee Corbin. Choice J is not a theme explored in this passage; widows could already own property at the time of Corbin's plea.

21. **The correct answer is A.** The answer to this question can be found in the final paragraph of the passage, and that paragraph focuses on how performer's gestures convey emotions on the stage. The author compares stage gestures to rhythms in verse, but does not imply that performers use gestures to convey rhythms, so any answer choice containing

Statement II is incorrect, and choices B, C, and D all include Statement II. Furthermore, the author merely refers to "rationalistic appeal of very modern plays" and makes no suggestion that a performer's gestures convey rationality, which means statement III is also false. Choices B, C, and D can all be eliminated for containing Statement II alone, while choices C and D make the additional error of including untrue Statement III, and choice C fails to include the one true statement. Once again that true statement is Statement I, and since choice A only includes that statement, it is the correct answer.

22. **The correct answer is J.** Throughout the passage, the author discusses marionettes' acting and ability to translate a playwright's work. Most of what he says can also apply to human performers, and subtle comparisons to human actors throughout the passage indicate that this is his intention. However, even if this intention is too subtle to detect, choice J still reveals itself as the correct answer by process of elimination. If anything, the author suggests the opposite of choice F. Choice G exaggerates the main idea of the third paragraph. Choice H is unrealistic. By eliminating those answer choices, choice J is left as the most logical selection.

23. **The correct answer is B.** In the fourth paragraph, the author writes, "This is nothing less than a fantastic, yet a direct, return to the masks of the Greeks: that learned

artifice by which tragedy and comedy were assisted in speaking to the world with the universal voice, by this deliberate generalising of emotion." This statement suggests the way such masks force performers to express emotion with their voices since they do not have use of their facial expressions, which supports choice B and eliminates choice A, since the statement implies that emotion is important whether a performer is or isn't wearing a mask. Protecting a performer's identity may be an attribute of a mask, but there is nothing in the passage to imply the author believes such a thing to be important. The same is true of choice D since the passage never implies that making a performer look like a marionette is a valuable attribute.

24. **The correct answer is G.** Although the author seems very engrossed in the marionettes' performance at the Constanzi Theatre in Rome, the conclusion in choice F is not really one expressed in the passage. Rather, seeing the marionettes' performance at the theater made him develop theories on the gestures and emotions of human performers, which he shares throughout the passage. Choice G is the best answer. Choice H and J are simply not implied in the passage in any way.

25. **The correct answer is D.** First of all, you should eliminate choice B since *calm* is a synonym of *peace*, not *piece*. This leaves choices A, C, and D, all of which are synonyms

of *piece*, but only one of which is a synonym for the word as it is used in this particular line. In this context, piece refers to such things as "a ballet, a farce, and the fragment of an opera." These are types of performances, so choice D is the best answer. You may have been confused by the author's use of the word *fragment*, which is a synonym for *segment*, but since he uses *piece* to refer to more than just that word, choice A is not the best answer. Choice C is too vague; choice D is a much more specific answer.

26. **The correct answer is G.** Of the three statements, the author mentions only that the marionette was wearing a plumed hat in the second paragraph. Although the marionette is wearing a cloak, the author describes it as *long*, not *shining*, which is the word he uses to describe the marionette's sword. The author does not mention theatrical masks until the fourth paragraph, and he does not indicate that the knight marionette wore one. Therefore, the correct answer should contain only Statement II, and that answer is choice G. Choice F includes only a single untrue statement, while choice H includes two. Choice J includes the true statement, but it also includes the two untrue ones, so it is incorrect as well.

27. **The correct answer is B.** Although the fifth paragraph begins with a comment on the importance of beauty in theatrical art (choice A), this is not the quotation that expresses the main point of the paragraph, which is

mainly about how gestures on stage are used for expression. Choice B states this idea better than any other answer choice. Choices C and D support that idea; they do not summarize it.

28. **The correct answer is F.** Throughout the passage, the author uses his experiences seeing human and puppet performers to theorize about the essence of stage performance. Choice F best expresses this idea. Although the author refers to some poor acting choices in the passage, such as performers' tendency to overemphasize their own personalities in their performances, this is hardly the most important idea in the passage, so choice G is incorrect. Although the author does write complimentary things about marionettes in this passage, celebrating puppetry is not its main purpose, so choice H is not the best answer. There needs to be at least two people to debate any issue. You can eliminate choice J since a single author wrote this passage.

29. **The correct answer is D.** This question can be answered by reading the third paragraph carefully. Although the author recommends sitting close to the stage in the beginning of the paragraph, he then says that you should sit further away if you prefer the illusion of naturalness. Therefore, choice D is the best answer and you can eliminate choices A and C, which both indicate that there is one particular spot in the theater

audience members should sit. In the paragraph, the author presents unnaturalness in theater as a positive thing, so choice B is not the best answer.

30. **The correct answer is G.** In the fourth paragraph, the author writes of how emotional plays are best suited to the expressionless faces of marionettes before stating that *Agamemnon* would be better suited to marionettes than a play by Ibsen would. Therefore, you can conclude that *Agamemnon* is more emotional than Ibsen's plays (choice G). That conclusion also contradicts choice J. There is no indication of which play is more lyrical (choice F), and though the presence of marionettes may make a performance seem more fantastical (choice H), this distinction is not indicated in the passage.

31. **The correct answer is C.** The author provides the answer to this question at the end of the third paragraph when he writes that "It is a lawful world; it is not a world of chance. Everything is related to everything else." This statement supports choice C and contradicts choices A and B, both of which you can eliminate. While the author asserts that all scientific facts in the world are related to each other, he does not say that they all belong in the same category. In fact, he mentions several of the various categories in the final paragraph of the passage ("Each science has its own particular field. Zoölogy undertakes to answer every reasonable question about animals; botany,

about plants; physics, about motion and forces; chemistry, about the composition of matter; astronomy, about the heavenly bodies, etc."). Therefore, choice D is incorrect.

32. **The correct answer is H.** The answer to this question appears in the fourth paragraph when the author explains, "Many marine animals left their remains in the mud underneath the sea. The mud was afterward converted into rock. Later, the shrinking and warping earth-crust lifted the rock far above the level of the sea, and it may now be found at the top of the mountain." This supports choice H. There is no information in the passage that supports the conclusions in choices F or G. Choice J may be true in and of itself, but it does not explain how rocks can teach us about animals.

33. **The correct answer is B.** The third paragraph is mainly about how the world may seem chaotic but is actually very orderly. Choice B summarizes this idea well. You can eliminate choice C since it contradicts the paragraph's main idea. Choice A may be true, but it is too general to summarize the third paragraph effectively. It is not the very best answer. Choice D describes a single detail in the third paragraph, but it does not summarize the paragraph's overall idea well.

34. **The correct answer is G.** The word *field* has a number of meanings, and each answer choice in this question refers to one of those meanings. Choice A takes *field* to mean a wide outdoor space, but a careful reading of the final paragraph reveals that this is not how the author is using *field*. The fact that the paragraph refers to a number of sciences, not just botany, is a clue that choice F probably isn't the best answer. It is also a clue that choice G is probably the best answer. The paragraph never discusses the physicality of studying science, so choice H does not make much sense. Choice J may be true in and of itself, but the fact that the next sentence after the one that uses the word *field* discusses scientific categories and not scientific questions indicates that choice J is not the correct answer but choice G is correct.

35. **The correct answer is C.** Read the opening sentences of the second paragraph: "A scientist is one who has learned to organize his knowledge. The main difference between a scientist and one who is not a scientist is that the scientist sees the significance of facts, while the non-scientific man sees facts as more or less unrelated things. As one comes to hunt for causes and inquire into the significance of things, one becomes a scientist." This information supports Statements I and III and shows that Statement II refers to a non-scientific man and not a scientist. Therefore, the correct answer choice must include Statements I and III and omit Statement II. Only choice C does this. Choice A omits a true statement. Choice B includes only the untrue statement. Choice D

includes both true statements, but it also includes the untrue one.

36. **The correct answer is J.** The author explains that all categories of science are related to each other, so it is logical to conclude that the category of physics may teach us vital information about astronomy. Choice J is the most logical answer. The fact that the sciences are all related contradicts the conclusion in choice F. Although all sciences are related to each other, they each have their own essential purpose, and the final paragraph reveals that the essential purpose of physics is the study of motion and forces while the essential purpose of chemistry is the study of the composition of matter, so choice G is not the best answer. Choice H is an extreme assumption. One does not have to be a professional scientist to understand physics. If that were true, the subject would not be taught in high schools all over the world!

37. **The correct answer is A.** The word *read* has several meanings, and each answer choice refers to one of these meanings. However, only one choice is correct. When a scientist reads a stone, he or she is not actually reading words and symbols like the ones you would read in a book, which eliminates choices B and C. If you are capable of reading something, you can see it easily, but this is not how the word is used in line 36 either, so choice D is incorrect too. Rather, *reads* refers to the fact that scientists may understand information by observing the properties of stones. Therefore, the best answer is choice A.

38. **The correct answer is H.** The three statements all refer to things mentioned in the passage, but only two are chemical elements according to the second paragraph, when the author states that "The chemist does not find sulphur, or oxygen, or any other element acting one way one day under a certain set of conditions." Stones are not mentioned until the fourth paragraph, and they are not referred to as chemical elements. Therefore, the correct answer will include Statements I and II and omit Statement III. Only choice H does this, so it is the correct answer. Choices F and G each omit one of the true statements. Choice J pairs the true statement with the untrue one.

39. **The correct answer is B.** Lines 15–18 refer to how a scientist makes a "prophesy" or a "prediction." These are things that fictional fortune tellers do when looking into their crystal balls or reading a person's palms, so choice B is the best answer. The passage points out several differences between non-scientific people and scientists but never indicates how they might be similar, so choice A is not the best answer. At the end of the paragraph that includes lines 15–18, the author mentions "the laws of mechanics" but not in any way that indicates a similarity between scientists and mechanics, so choice C is not the best answer either. An event planner (choice D) is someone

who plans parties professionally, so even though lines 15–18 mention how scientists study events, they do not make scientists seem similar to event planners. Furthermore, the passage never suggests that scientists can plan events; they can only understand and predict events.

40. **The correct answer is G.** This question refers to the fourth paragraph's explanation of how a sea rock might end up atop a mountain. That paragraph reveals that mud is first converted into rock, and then the shrinking of the earth's crust lifts that rock far above the level of the sea. This order of events supports choice G. Choices F, H, and J all present the events out of order.

SCIENCE

1. C	**9.** A	**17.** D	**25.** C	**33.** A
2. G	**10.** H	**18.** F	**26.** H	**34.** J
3. D	**11.** A	**19.** D	**27.** A	**35.** A
4. G	**12.** J	**20.** J	**28.** H	**36.** F
5. C	**13.** C	**21.** C	**29.** C	**37.** B
6. H	**14.** H	**22.** G	**30.** G	**38.** H
7. D	**15.** B	**23.** D	**31.** C	**39.** C
8. H	**16.** G	**24.** F	**32.** H	**40.** J

1. **The correct answer is C.** A more active BIS contributes to anxiety and nervousness due to a negative stimulus, in this case an exam for which the student has not prepared. Choice A is incorrect because SNPs are relevant to the second viewpoint, not the first viewpoint. Choice B is incorrect because a more active BAS contributes to impulsiveness and behavior leading to a positive stimulus or end goal. Choice D is incorrect because an exam is not a new or unexpected stimulus that would require a fight/flight/freeze response.

2. **The correct answer is G.** According to the second viewpoint, single nucleotide polymorphisms (SNPs) are small, specific, repeating sequences in genes, which are made up of DNA. Choice F is incorrect because SNPs usually occur in noncoding regions of genes, which means they are not expressed in proteins. Choices H and J are incorrect because sugars and lipids are not at all relevant here.

3. **The correct answer is D.** Both viewpoints indicate that human biology is the basis for personality; the introduction before the passages states this outright, but one can draw the same conclusion from the viewpoints themselves because the first viewpoint discusses the nervous system and the second viewpoint discusses genetics. Choice A is incorrect because the fight/flight/freeze personality component is discussed only in the first viewpoint. Choice B is incorrect because twin studies are discussed only in the second viewpoint. Choice C is incorrect because SNPs are mentioned only in the second viewpoint, though not specifically in the manner described by this choice.

4. **The correct answer is G.** The genetic approach specifically seeks sources for personality disorders in genes, while the Reinforcement Sensitivity Theory focuses more on types of behaviors rather than specific

personality disorders. Choices F and H are incorrect because they indicate that the Reinforcement Sensitivity Theory seeks such sources, while choice J is incorrect because it indicates that the genetic approach does not address this.

5. **The correct answer is C.** This disorder involves a genetic defect that effectively causes a defect in the nervous system, which in turn causes a personality disorder. Therefore, this disorder is consistent with both viewpoints. Choices A and B are incorrect because they each indicate that only one viewpoint is consistent with this hypothetical piece of data. Choice D is incorrect because it indicates that the hypothetical piece of data supports neither viewpoint.

6. **The correct answer is H.** Choices F and G are incorrect because they do not accurately describe the case of Phineas Gage and also would support the genetic approach to personality rather than the Reinforcement Sensitivity Theory. Choice J is incorrect because, while hormone imbalances may be relevant to the activities of the nervous system, this was not the case in Phineas Gage, according to the first passage.

7. **The correct answer is D.** The first viewpoint is based on reward/punishment responses to the environment, while the second viewpoint concedes that the environment affects personality where genetics do not. Choices A

and B are incorrect because each indicates that one of the viewpoints discounts the significance of environment on personality, which is untrue. Choice C is incorrect because it swaps the roles of the environment in each viewpoint.

8. **The correct answer is H.** The temperature and type of salt are independent variables altered by the student, so choices F and G are incorrect. Choice J is incorrect because the salt mass is the dependent variable since it is the measurement the student is using as the solubility in this experiment. Since 100 mL of water is used in every trial in this experiment, the water volume is the constant in all trials.

9. **The correct answer is A.** According to the table, the solubility of NaCl, KCl, and $Pb(NO_3)_2$ at 30°C were 35.4 g, 35.7 g, and 64.5 g salt per 100 mL water. The lowest number of the bunch is 35.4 g, which corresponds with NaCl, so NaCl exhibited the lowest solubility at 30°C.

10. **The correct answer is H.** Choice F, the only answer choice directly represented on the data table, is incorrect because the data show that NaCl and KCl have different solubilities at 0°C. Based on the data, the solubility of both salts increases with temperature, but the rate of increase is higher for KCl than NaCl. Therefore, even though KCl has a lower solubility than NaCl at lower temperatures, it has a higher solubility than NaCl

at higher temperatures. Based on the data table, the solubility of KCl is lower than that of NaCl up to 20°C, and then higher than that of NaCl over 30°C. Therefore, the correct answer must be between 20°C and 30°C. Choice H is the only one that falls in this range.

11. **The correct answer is A.** KCl, as well as the other two salts, exhibits a linear increase in solubility as a function of temperature. For KCl, the solubility increases by 2.9 g salt per 100 mL water for every 10°C change in temperature. This constant increase in solubility relative to temperature indicates a linear increase, and choice A is the only graph that displays a linear increase.

12. **The correct answer is J.** The data show a linear change in $Pb(NO_3)_2$ solubility as a function of temperature, and based on the provided data, there is an increase in solubility of 9.2 g salt per 100 mL water with every 10°C increase in temperature. The highest temperature provided on the table is 73.7 g at 40°C. To get to 60°C, two consecutive 10°C temperature increases are needed, so 9.2 g must be added twice to 73.7 g to get the mass of $Pb(NO_3)_2$ that will dissolve in 100 mL of water at 60°C: 73.7 + (2)(9.2) = 92.1 g.

13. **The correct answer is C.** According to the data in the table, all three salts exhibit increases in solubility as temperature increases. Choice A is incorrect because even though NaCl

exhibits a smaller increase in solubility with temperature than the other salts, it is still an increase and not a decrease. Choice B is incorrect because the trend is incorrect with regard to KCl and $Pb(NO_3)_2$. Choice D is incorrect because it describes a trend that is completely opposite to what the data actually show.

14. **The correct answer is H.** Choice F is incorrect because temperature is not a variable in this experiment. Choice G is incorrect because pressure is an independent variable controlled by the students. Choice J is incorrect because time is also an independent variable. Since crystal size is the variable that is being measured, crystal size is the dependent variable.

15. **The correct answer is B.** Choice A is incorrect because the solution preparation is unrelated to pressure equilibration. Choice C is incorrect because temperature is not a tested variable in this experiment, so no temperature control would be required here. Choice D is incorrect because these two trials are not repeated trials because they were performed at two different pressures. Choice B is correct because using the same starting solution guarantees that both trials will use the same starting "seed" concentration.

16. **The correct answer is G.** Choice F is incorrect because the crystals only grew when the flasks were cooled down to room temperature, according to the

passage. Choice H is incorrect because the pressures were maintained at room temperature, so the 99°C temperature was not required to keep these pressures constant. Choice J is incorrect because water evaporation would disturb the carefully controlled salt concentration; plus, the boiling point of water is 100°C. Since cooling down the solutions results in crystal formation, the higher temperature is required to keep the ferricyanide dissolved in solution until after the solution has been aliquoted for use in the two trials.

17. **The correct answer is D.** On the graph, the line marked with triangles represents the 9-atmosphere trial, while the line marked with circles represents the 1-atmosphere trial. The question is asking about the 9-atmosphere trial, so if we look at the triangle-marked line at the 2.0-day mark on the x-axis, the corresponding percent size increase is 59.

18. **The correct answer is F.** Increasing the number of trials in an experiment always increases reliability because you are collecting more data, making it easier to see trends and recognize outliers. Choice G is incorrect because performing the experiment at the high temperature will keep the salt dissolved in solution, preventing crystal growth. Choice H is incorrect because using smaller volumes will only make crystal size measurements more difficult and less reliable. Choice J is incorrect because starting at

different "seed" solution concentrations will make it more difficult to compare the separate trials.

19. **The correct answer is D.** Choices A and B are incorrect because potassium ferricyanide was the only tested crystal, so no comparisons can be made with other crystal types. Choice C is incorrect because the 9-atmosphere line increased more rapidly over time than the 1-atmosphere line, and this trend is also the reason why choice D is correct.

20. **The correct answer is J.** According to the data table, the heights of the PlantGro-treated plants were 13.0 and 13.6 cm. The average of these two heights is 13.3 cm.

21. **The correct answer is C.** Choice A is incorrect because plant height is the dependent variable. Choice B is incorrect because fertilizer brand is the independent variable. Choice D is incorrect because a positive control here would be a group treated with a known fertilizer; the trials with PlantGro most closely represent positive controls. The untreated plants represent negative controls because they represent the group that is unaffected by the altered independent variable, which in this case is the fertilizer brand.

22. **The correct answer is G.** Choice F is incorrect because fertilizer brand is the independent variable. Choice H is incorrect because plant height is the dependent variable. Choice J is incorrect; this is irrelevant to the experiment. The soil type is a constant because

every trial in the experiment uses the same kind of soil.

23. **The correct answer is D.** Choice A is incorrect because the increase in plant height is not constant per unit time. Choice B is incorrect because there is no period of subdued growth midway through the growth period. Choice C is incorrect because the growth rate does not increase more rapidly at the beginning of the growth period than toward the end. Choice D is correct because over the given time period, the growth rate is exponential for the plants treated with PlantBoost because the plant height nearly doubles each day.

24. **The correct answer is F.** Precision refers to how close the trials are to one another. Since the trials gave identical heights after 1 day for the plants treated with PlantBoost, this is the most precise time point for the PlantBoost-treated plants. At the other time points, the heights were not identical and were therefore less precise.

25. **The correct answer is C.** Based on the data, the plants treated with PlantBoost grew more quickly than the untreated plants, but they did not grow as quickly as the plants treated with PlantGro, so the PlantBoost manufacturer cannot claim that its fertilizer is the best fertilizer on the market.

26. **The correct answer is H.** Choice F is incorrect because, as the passage indicates, the enzyme produced by *lacZ* interacts with X-gal, not the HCMV proteins. Choice G is incorrect because it is

the interaction of *lacZ*'s protein with X-gal that produces the blue color, not the HCMV protein pairs themselves. Choice J is incorrect because this experiment is unrelated to HCMV gene locations. This experiment tests protein-protein interactions, as described by choice H.

27. **The correct answer is A.** Choices C and D are incorrect because growing yeast on normal plates is not useful in the yeast two-hybrid assay because it gives no indication of whether or not the proteins of interest actually interact. Choice B is incorrect because it describes a negative control. Choice A correctly describes a positive control for this experiment; this should result in blue yeast cells.

28. **The correct answer is H.** Of the six protein pairs, four of the protein-protein interactions produce a shaded tint, while two remain colorless. This means that four of the six tested protein pairs appear to interact with one another.

29. **The correct answer is C.** Choice A is incorrect because small proteins might actually be beneficial since they are unlikely to sterically block RNA polymerase or other transcription factors. Choice B is incorrect because proteins with very specific binding partners are actually ideal for an experiment that looks for protein-protein binding interactions. Choice D is incorrect because proteins that are very well-characterized will have more information available

Answer Keys and Explanations

and could be easier to use. The correct answer is C; this experiment relies on yeast viability, and if proteins are toxic to yeast, there is no chance that the experiment will work because the proteins will simply kill the yeast.

30. **The correct answer is G.** Choice F is incorrect because very strong and specific interactions will exhibit a more intense blue color because these interactions happen often and produce a large amount of *lacZ*, causing the blue color. Choices H and J are incorrect because the test tells nothing about direct interactions between the proteins of interest and nucleic acids. Choice G is correct because if the two tested proteins interact nonspecifically or transiently, the two proteins of interest will not stay bound and less *lacZ* will be produced, giving a blue color that is less intense than that produced by two proteins that interact strongly and/or specifically.

31. **The correct answer is C.** With no nail, there is no magnetic field, and consequently, no metal screws are picked up. Choice A is incorrect because this trial does nothing to prove that current is flowing through the wires. Choice B is incorrect because there is no measurement of current, so the trial demonstrates nothing about the relationship between current and voltage. Choice D is incorrect because it is a magnetic field, not an electric field, that is created when the nail is present, and attraction of the nail to metal

screws demonstrates that there is a magnetic field, not an electric field.

32. **The correct answer is H.** Based on the data for the 4.5-volt battery, the number of screws picked up increases as the number of coils increases; 15 coils falls between 10 and 20 coils, both of which were tested for the 4.5-volt battery. With 10 coils and the 4.5-volt battery, the electromagnet picked up 4 screws. With 20 coils and the 4.5-volt battery, the electromagnet picked up 16 screws. Therefore, for 15 coils, the number of screws should be between 4 and 16. Choice H is the only number that falls within this range.

33. **The correct answer is A.** This is the number that is being measured, so it is the dependent variable. Choice B is incorrect because the battery voltage is an independent variable. Choice C is incorrect because the direction of the current is a constant for all trials. Choice D is incorrect because the number of coils is an additional independent variable tested.

34. **The correct answer is J.** Choices F and G are incorrect because increasing the number of coils around the nail increases the magnetic field strength. Choice H is incorrect because the increase is not constant, so it is not linear. Rather, it is exponential, so choice J is correct.

35. **The correct answer is A.** For each tested number of coils, more screws were picked up by the nail hooked up to the 9-volt battery than the 4.5-volt battery. Therefore, increasing the battery voltage increases the number of screws picked up, which is an indication of a stronger magnetic field.

36. **The correct answer is F.** Based on the figure showing the experiment setup, increasing D increases the distance between the tree and central point, effectively increasing the distance between each observation point and the tree.

37. **The correct answer is B.** Based on the table, every 2-m increase in D results in approximately a 40 cm decrease in the distance of apparent cone movement. Therefore, at $D = 8$ m, the distance of apparent cone movement would be expected to be approximately 40 cm less than that at $D = 6$ m. The relationship is linear, as the graph shows. Since 140 – 40 is equal to 100, the correct answer should be close to 100 cm. Therefore, the correct answer is choice B.

38. **The correct answer is H.** The least precise trial set would be the one in which the measured values are furthest apart, and in this experiment, the trial set that provides the set of numbers that strays the most is the set of data for $D = 6$ m.

39. **The correct answer is C.** Choice A is incorrect because there really is no positive control in this experiment; this experiment is merely looking for patterns in a widely used astronomical technique. Choice B is incorrect because the independent variable, distance D, represents the distance between the central point and the tree. Choice D is incorrect because this describes the significance of the y-axis.

40. **The correct answer is J.** Choices F and G are incorrect because they indicate an exponential change, when the graph clearly exhibits a linear change. Choices H and J both correctly point to a linear relationship between the variables, but choice H is incorrect because it describes the opposite trend than what is observed in the graph. Choice J is correct because the distance of apparent cone movement decrease as the distance increases between central point and the tree, according to the data.

Sample Essay: Score 1

Ideas and Analysis:	Score = 1
Development and Support:	Score = 1
Organization:	Score = 1
Language Use and Conventions:	Score = 1

> Most people rather go to school less than they already go to school it would be better if we got to spend more time out of class and do more fun things. Kids get bored and crazy. Spending too long in one place. Kids these days would rather spend time talking to their friends playing games or sports on their computer and phones than sitting and lerning lesons that he don't even really need to now. If everybody got spend less time in the class they can be happy and be better in the mood to do what thre parents tell them to do and do chores around the house and when they get old enuff get ready to get good jobs and have a family. Kids distracted. They shuld start to get lesons from at home so they can lern on there own time and be able to have more fun then they are able to do. Maybe now that everybody lern things on there computers and phones they don't even need to go back to classes anymore.

Scoring Explanation

Ideas and Analysis: Score = 1

This essay demonstrates a minimal level of investment and effort toward analyzing the relative merits and challenges of the United States adopting a year-round school model. Instead of addressing the essay task directly, the author makes a weak plea for reducing the amount of time students spend in the classroom ("most people rather go to school less than they already go to school it would be better if we got to spend more time out of class and do more fun things"). As a result, the written response provided falls far from the mark and fails to provide a cogent perspective on the essay prompt.

Development and Support: Score = 1

This written response suffers from inadequate focus, direction, and development, resulting in an essay that fails to respond to the essay task at hand. Instead of focusing the essay on addressing the pros and cons of year-round schooling, the essay veers off on a tangent; we are informed via a loose set of meandering thoughts that the author feels as if students already spend too much time in school, and perhaps technology has made classrooms obsolete ("maybe now that everybody lern things on there computers and phones they don't even need to go back to classes anymore"). We can extrapolate from this that the author is likely not an advocate of year-round schooling, but overall this essay fails to provide a direct and convincing perspective that would merit a higher score.

Answer Keys and Explanations

Organization: Score = 1

This essay demonstrates a haphazard and poorly conceived level of construction—the written response is comprised of just one paragraph that fails to adhere to the principles of sound essay organization and structure. There is no discernible introduction, body, or conclusion, and it's a challenge to determine the author's central thesis, other than an assertion that students should spend more time outside of the classroom ("kids shuld start to get lesons from at home so they can lern on there own time"). The end result is an essay that lacks depth, clarity of ideas and purpose, and authority.

Language Use and Conventions: Score = 1

It's evident that this written argument represents an inadequate level of care or skill regarding appropriate language use and principles. There are numerous errors in spelling (*lerning, lesons,* etc.), punctuation (lack of appropriate comma use, etc.), and sentence structure (fragments and run-ons); the result is a poorly conceived essay that is challenging to comprehend and fails to adequately support a clear perspective on the essay prompt.

SAMPLE ESSAY: SCORE 6

Ideas and Analysis:	Score = 6
Development and Support:	Score = 6
Organization:	Score = 6
Language Use and Conventions:	Score = 6

It can be argued that a society can make no greater investment than in educating its citizens. In addition to advancing knowledge and truth, it sparks new ideas and innovation, moves the wheels and engines of nations forward, and helps promote a more aware and enlightened people. It not only advances the nation itself; in today's interconnected world, it helps move the whole world forward. Therefore, exploring ways to improve the systems for how hungry and eager young minds get educated is of primary importance, and no idea is too big, too bold, or too audacious to consider in pursuit of the goal of improving education. Is adopting a year-round education model the answer for the United States? Will it lead to improvements in an imperfect system that should always strive to be better? As with many things, it must be tested to be proven. As with important things, it's worth testing if it could make the educational system better. As with things worth doing properly, it should be handled with the careful thought and planning it deserves.

It's true that some students likely struggle to retain material they've learned, and renew their abilities to focus, when long interruptions, vacations, and holidays occur. A year-round school model could theoretically help to overcome this obstacle, and help keep young minds, sharp, disciplined, and ready to achieve. Rolling out a widespread, all-encompassing, year-round school model across the United States is too ambitious and unrealistic a strategy; furthermore, in a system that's already beleaguered by a lack of sufficient funds, attempting to fund such a model would pose logistical and financial challenges that may undermine the program before it could even start. A pilot program would be the best approach. A community that could absorb the added costs of adopting a year-round model, perhaps with private funding helping to shoulder the expense, would be a good place to test this program. Local businesses, corporations, and citizens might be eager to provide support, and it should be comprised of student and parent volunteers. Careful analysis and tracking of students in the program at every level needs to occur in an effort to determine program results. Clearly, this would take several years and a great deal of effort, mobilization, and support to implement properly. But, as mentioned, there is little more important to ensuring the future well-being and prosperity of a nation than to make sure its minds are properly educated. However, policymakers in education must remain aware that there is more to life than school, and that adopting a year-round school model must also leave time for pursuits beyond the classroom. Time away from school is essential, and allows students the opportunity to digest and reflect upon the material learned, to engage in other interests and extracurricular activities, and to enter the classroom rested and renewed, able to tackle new academic goals.

Furthermore, testing a year-round educational model shouldn't close the United States off from exploring other ways of improving its educational system. After all, it's the quality—not just the quantity—of education received that will really make a difference. Beyond testing a year-round model, hopefully, discussing this issue further will highlight the need for systemic reform in general. The challenge of educating America's students is tougher than ever—in addition to a scarcity of resources to properly fund the nation's educational system, as technology becomes increasingly more mobile, students have a growing world of distracting entertainment and communication options on their cell phones and in their pockets; students' ability to focus on schoolwork becomes tougher as their attention is more atomized, and engaging them on a deep level and holding their attention is more difficult than ever before.

Policymakers and teachers need to think of new and creative ways to educate upcoming techno-centric generations of students, who interact differently, engage with the world differently, and learn differently. Extra hours in school may prove helpful, but until real reform is made, true and lasting progress in education may prove elusive. For many, the classroom is the first place where they encounter, engage with, and learn about the world outside of their homes. The world is changing and rapidly evolving in new and exciting ways—shouldn't the nation's classrooms make every effort to try to keep up?

Scoring Explanation

Ideas and Analysis: Score = 6

This written response provides an excellent level of analysis and insight into the essay topic. The author provides strong coverage of the merits and disadvantages of both sides of the debate regarding the adoption of a year-round school model in the United States, while simultaneously offering a clear and engaging perspective ("exploring ways to improve the systems for how hungry and eager young minds get educated is of primary importance, and no idea is too big, too bold, or too audacious to consider in pursuit of the goal of improving education"). The author takes an impressive approach to addressing the essay prompt by highlighting the notion that a year-round school model shouldn't be seen as a "cure-all" to the challenges that America's educational system faces; rather, it is one idea worth exploring and should not inhibit other ideas or initiatives for improvement ("beyond testing a year-round model, hopefully, discussing this issue further highlights the need for systemic reform in general."). The resulting essay is a confident piece of writing full of compelling thoughts that hits the mark.

Development and Support: Score = 6

It's evident from this well-developed written response that the author has strong thoughts regarding the importance of education in advancing society and makes an impassioned, earnest plea to address the challenges that America's educational system currently faces. The author carefully considers both sides of the debate while building toward his or her own perspective, and wisely frames the issue against a current techno-centric backdrop ("The challenge of educating America's students is tougher than ever—in addition to a scarcity of resources to properly fund the nation's educational system, as technology becomes increasingly more mobile, students have a growing world of distracting entertainment and communication options in their pockets"), thereby ensuring that today's challenges are represented and bolstering support for a cogent set of ideas.

Organization: Score = 6

The author does a commendable job of engaging with the audience and developing a memorable essay with a clear point of view on an important topic, first by highlighting the importance of the issue ("it can be argued that a society can make no greater investment than in educating its citizens"), then by offering a strong perspective that weighs both sides of the debate regarding a year-round school model, and finally by keeping the conversation open for new ideas ("Policymakers and teachers need to think of new and creative ways to educate upcoming techno-centric generations of students, who interact differently, engage with the world differently, and learn differently"). The author ends this well-organized piece of writing with a compelling plea to keep this issue elevated above a mere academic exercise, and to work on implementing bold ideas to improve education in the United States ("The world is changing and rapidly evolving in new and exciting ways—shouldn't the nation's classrooms make every effort to try to keep up?").

Language Use and Conventions: Score = 6

Clearly, the author has a firm grasp of the core principles of grammar and conventions of argumentative writing and is capable of deploying them in this well-executed essay. The author makes strong choices regarding sentence structure and transitions and utilizes a richly varied vocabulary throughout this written piece. Overall, the essay is polished and largely free of errors, and the author's deft hand and ability result in an effective and passionate work that does an exemplary job of supporting his or her perspective.

DIAGNOSTIC TEST ASSESSMENT GRID

Now that you've completed the diagnostic test and read through the answer explanations, you can use your results to target your studying. The following tables will direct you to the chapters where you will find the help you need to focus on problem subject areas. Find the numbers of the questions on the diagnostic test that gave you trouble and highlight or circle them below. The chapters with the most markings are your ideal starting points on your preparation journey.

English Test (Chapter 3)	
Usage/Mechanics	
Question Type	**Question Numbers**
Grammar and Usage	4, 8, 10, 12, 13, 16, 17, 19, 24, 31, 32, 33, 34, 40, 42, 47, 59, 64, 66, 68
Punctuation	6, 11, 14, 23, 28, 36, 38, 51, 57, 58
Sentence Structure	2, 5, 9, 18, 20, 25, 37, 52, 54, 61, 65, 67, 70
Rhetorical Skills	
Question Type	**Question Numbers**
Organization	3, 21, 22, 48, 50, 60, 75
Style	1, 7, 27, 35, 39, 46, 53, 55, 62, 71, 73
Strategy	15, 26, 29, 30, 41, 43, 44, 45, 49, 56, 63, 69, 72, 74

Question types to focus on:

Grammar and Usage	☐	**Organization**	☐
Punctuation	☐	**Style**	☐
Sentence Structure	☐	**Strategy**	☐

Mathematics Test (Chapter 4)

Pre-Algebra and Elementary Algebra

Question Type	Topic	Question Numbers
Pre-Algebra		
	Absolute Value	23
	Concept of Exponents	22
	Data Interpretation	21
	Elementary Counting Techniques and Simple Probability	35, 47
	Linear Equations in One Variable	25
	Operations Using Fractions	36
	Ordering Numbers by Value	51
	Percent	48
	Proportion	8
	Scientific Notation	46
	Square Roots	20
Elementary Algebra		
	Evaluation of Algebraic Expressions Through Substitution	1, 9, 26
	Understanding Algebraic Operations	2, 7, 37, 38, 57
	Properties of Exponents	10, 40
	Solution of Quadratic Equations by Factoring	11, 24
	Square Roots	12

Mathematics Test (Chapter 4)

Intermediate Algebra and Coordinate Geometry

Question Type	Topic	Question Numbers
Intermediate Algebra		
	Absolute Value Equations	52
	Complex Numbers	27
	Functions	49, 56
	Quadratic Inequalities	58
	Sequences and Patterns	41
	Understanding the Quadratic Formula	39
Coordinate Geometry		
	Graphing Inequalities	28, 55
	Relations Between Equations and Graphs, Including Other Curves	43
	Relations Between Equations and Graphs, Including Circles	33
	Relations Between Equations and Graphs, Including Points	3, 29
	Relations Between Equations and Graphs, Including Polynomials	4, 15, 16, 34
	Slope	13, 14, 42
Plane Geometry		
	Application of geometry to three dimensions	54
	Concept of proof and proof techniques	6
	Properties and relations of plane figures, including angles	17, 22

Mathematics Test (Chapter 4)		
Intermediate Algebra and Coordinate Geometry		
	Properties and relations of plane figures, including circles	59
	Properties and relations of plane figures, including parallelograms	45
	Properties and relations of plane figures, including rectangles	30
	Properties and relations of plane figures, including triangles	5, 31, 50
	Transformations	18
	Volume	44
Trigonometry		
	Graphing Trigonometric Functions	53
	Solving Trigonometric Equations	19
	Use of Trigonometric Identities	60

Question types to focus on:

Pre-Algebra   ☐

Topics: _____

_____

_____

_____

Coordinate Geometry   ☐

Topics: _____

_____

_____

_____

Elementary Algebra   ☐

Topics: _____

_____

_____

_____

Plane Geometry   ☐

Topics: _____

_____

_____

_____

Intermediate Algebra   ☐

Topics: _____

_____

_____

_____

Trigonometry   ☐

Topics: _____

_____

_____

_____

Reading Test (Chapter 5)	
Social Studies/Natural Sciences Passages	
Question Type	**Question Numbers**
Detail	12, 13, 14, 20, 31, 38, 40
Inference	11, 15, 17, 18, 19, 32, 35, 36, 39
Vocabulary	16, 34, 37
Main Idea	33
Literary Narrative/Prose Fiction and Humanities Passages	
Question Type	**Question Numbers**
Detail	3, 8, 10, 24, 26, 29
Inference	2, 4, 5, 6, 9, 21, 22, 23, 30
Vocabulary	1, 25
Main Idea	7, 27, 28

Question types to focus on:

Social Studies/Natural Sciences Passages		Literary Narrative/Prose Fiction and Humanities Passages	
Detail	☐	Detail	☐
Inference	☐	Inference	☐
Vocabulary	☐	Vocabulary	☐
Main Idea	☐	Main Idea	☐

Science Test (Chapter 6)

Data Representation

Question Type	Question Numbers
Inferences	9, 10, 12, 13, 37, 38, 40
Looking Up Answers	31, 33, 39
Spotting Trends	11, 32, 34, 35, 36

Research Summaries

Question Type	Question Numbers
Inferences	16, 19, 25, 26, 29, 30
Looking Up Answers	17, 20, 28
Scientific Method	14, 15, 18, 21, 22, 24, 27
Spotting Trends	23

Conflicting Viewpoints

Question Type	Question Numbers
Inferences	3, 4, 8
Compare/Contrast	1, 2, 5, 6, 7

Question types to focus on:

Data Representation		Research Summaries		Conflicting Viewpoints	
Inferences	☐	Inferences	☐	Inferences	☐
Looking Up Answers	☐	Looking Up Answers	☐	Compare/Contrast	☐
Spotting Trends	☐	Scientific Method	☐		
		Spotting Trends	☐		

A Word About the Writing Test

If you took the writing test and found that your essay did not compare well to the level 6 essay sample, don't worry. Chapter 7, "The ACT® Writing Test," has the information you need to strengthen your writing skills. It also includes a full essay grading rubric, which tells you what the graders are looking for in a high-quality essay. Use the rubric as you would use the grids to help you focus on the areas in which you need to improve.

DIAGNOSTIC TEST CONCLUSION

Taking the diagnostic test should have given you more insight into the ACT: what it feels like to take such a long test, how you perform on a timed exam, and where you now need to focus your energy in the time leading up to your test day.

Here are some questions to keep in mind as you move on to the preparation part of your ACT study plan:

How did I do under timed conditions?

Did you find yourself rushing to answer the final questions in every test section? Did one particular section give you more problems than others? Take note of how timing affected you in this test, and see if you can make small changes to your test-taking approach. For example, maybe you spent too much time reading the passages in the Reading test and then didn't actually have time to answer all the questions. The good news? This book offers tips on how to efficiently and quickly answer ACT test questions.

Did I just not know how to answer questions in a particular section?

Maybe you sailed through the Mathematics test but could barely get through a Science test passage. Or maybe the Reading test was a breeze, but you can't for the life of you remember anything about trigonometry. Now that you have a better understanding of your strengths and weaknesses as they relate to the ACT, you can customize your study plan.

Did I make careless mistakes or second-guess myself?

Well, first of all, you're not alone. Testing is *hard*—you're under timed conditions and you want to do very well. The best part about taking on a plan of study with this book is that when you are done, you will be *prepared*. First, you will know the test inside and out. This is a very important bit of knowledge, as you won't even have to stop to read directions or familiarize yourself with the test come exam day—you will be ready to go! Second, you will have a better understanding not only of the different topics tested on the ACT, but also how the exam presents them (the language it uses and how it asks questions). The key to excelling on the ACT is to speak the language of the test maker, and that's what we're here to help you do.

No matter what challenges you faced on the diagnostic test, this book is designed to help you overcome them—fast. Stay focused, commit the time, and take your practice tests—if you do that, you are sure to get the score you want on the ACT.

CHAPTER 3
THE ACT® ENGLISH TEST

OVERVIEW

- Test Overview
- Usage/Mechanics Questions
- Practice: Usage/Mechanics Questions
- Rhetorical Skills Questions
- Analyzing Passages for Rhetorical Issues
- Practice: Rhetorical Skills Questions
- Summing It Up

Although you might not have a lot of time between now and test day, that doesn't mean that you can't prepare effectively! This chapter provides a clear overview of the ACT English test and the two major areas tested: **Usage/Mechanics** and **Rhetorical Skills**; quick coverage of the topics that are tested in each section; effective tips, strategies, and advice for building your skills when you're short on time; and helpful test-like practice to get you ready for test day fast. Let's get started!

TEST OVERVIEW

The ACT English test is always the first one you'll see on test day. It is a multiple-choice test that assesses your overall ability and skill level in the following six aspects of effective writing:

- Grammar and usage
- Organization
- Strategy
- Punctuation
- Sentence structure
- Style

The English test contains five essays or passages, accompanied by 14–16 multiple-choice questions each. Each passage will be numbered throughout, many with corresponding underlined words, phrases, or sentences. The numbers in the passage correspond to the multiple-choice questions that follow.

The questions may ask you to determine whether an underlined word or phrase is grammatically correct or to make decisions about a paragraph or the passage as a whole in one of the six aspects of effective writing.

Pace Yourself!

The ACT English test is a fast-moving section, with 75 questions to answer in 45 minutes. *Keep these numbers in mind as you make your way through the test!*

You'll have about 90 seconds to read each passage and 30 seconds per question in order to stay on a good test-taking pace. You need to be ready to read, digest, and answer questions pretty quickly. What's the best plan for getting ready? Use the passages and questions in this book to build a good test-taking pace before test day!

Your score on the English test will be made up of your subscores in Usage/Mechanics and Rhetorical Skills and is based on the number of correct answers you select. Your score on this section of the exam will range from 1 to 36 (the best possible score), and your overall ACT composite score will be the average of your scores on the four tests (English, Math, Reading, and Science).

As mentioned, the ACT English test assesses two general areas:

1. **Usage/Mechanics** includes grammar usage, punctuation, and sentence structure.

2. **Rhetorical Skills** includes organization, strategy, and style questions.

Let's look at each area in greater detail and develop a solid plan for test day success!

USAGE/MECHANICS QUESTIONS

On the ACT, Usage/Mechanics errors may really jump out at you. For example, a sentence that asks a question but ends in an exclamation point ("Is that your sock!") just looks wrong. Of course, you'll need to know a little more than "find the sentences that look wrong" to answer Usage/Mechanics questions correctly. The good news is that you've probably learned most of the rules discussed in this chapter already.

But let's not get ahead of ourselves. First of all, we should probably define the terms *usage* and *mechanics*. **Usage** refers to the way words are used in a sentence. Obviously, you'll want to make sure they're used correctly to select the best answers on the ACT. **Mechanics** refers to the more technical components of sentences, such as punctuation, which will be the first topic in this chapter.

PUNCTUATION QUESTIONS

On the ACT English exam, 10–15 percent of the Usage/Mechanics questions will test your ability to recognize the correct way to use all sorts of punctuation, including periods, commas, semicolons, apostrophes, and more.

Let's tackle a sample punctuation question. Read the following paragraph and answer the question that follows.

· ·

<u>I really love going to carnivals?</u> Even before I enter a carnival, a smile hits my face from
<u style="text-align:center">1</u>
the smell of the delicious foods and snacks that I know will be there. I love all the

colorful lights and sounds of the rides and attractions. The only thing I don't like

about carnivals is the fact that I know they all eventually have to end.

1. **A.**   NO CHANGE
    B.   I really love going to carnivals!
    C.   I really love going to carnivals,
    D.   I really love going to carnivals

The correct answer is B. This question is a good example of how incorrect or inappropriate punctuation—in this case end punctuation—can really set the wrong tone for a piece of writing. Ending the opening sentence in a question mark (choice A) sets the completely wrong tone; here, we are left to wonder if the author really doesn't know if he or she loves carnivals, and it casts all of the claims made in the subsequent sentences in doubt. Using an exclamation mark transforms the opening sentence into a bold assertion of the author's positive feelings about carnivals. Choices C and D incorrectly leave off end punctuation from the opening sentence.

· ·

There are quite a few different kinds of punctuation, each with its own purpose. We'll review the types that most commonly appear on the ACT English test.

End-of-Sentence Punctuation

Every sentence must eventually come to an end, which means that the one form of punctuation you will *always* see in every complete sentence is **end-of-sentence punctuation**.

These are probably the very first punctuation marks you learned about:

- **The period (.):** good for ending most declarative sentences
- **The exclamation point (!):** used for ending exclamations, which indicate extreme excitement
- **The question mark (?):** absolutely necessary for ending questions

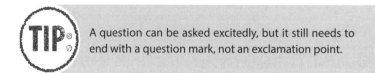

TIP A question can be asked excitedly, but it still needs to end with a question mark, not an exclamation point.

End-of-sentence marks are usually pretty straightforward. You probably already know that you shouldn't end a question with a period or an exclamation with a question mark.

These marks become slightly trickier when **quotation marks** are added to the punctuation mix. End-of-sentence punctuation usually belongs *inside* the quotation marks:

> *Zakia asked, "Where did you last see my cell phone?"*

The only exception occurs when the quotation marks indicate a title, and placing end-of-sentence punctuation within the marks might give the false impression that the mark is part of the title.

> *Have you read the new article, "The Last Alien Invasion"?*

Commas

Let's continue with one of the most common forms of punctuation—and the one that's most often misused. Some writers use **commas** like salt—they sprinkle them all over their sentences. And just as sprinkling around too much salt will make your food taste pretty bad, sprinkling around too many commas without rhyme or reason will make sentences pretty bad, too.

Here's an example of a sentence with way too many commas:

> *I like, to dance, whenever I'm at a birthday party, celebration, or any event, with a live band, or a DJ.*

While there is the odd situation in which the use of a comma is up to the writer, there are almost always very definite rules for comma use. Let's look at some of the most important ones.

Introductory or Transitional Words and Phrases

Commas should be used to offset **introductory words or phrases** from the words that follow.

Here are some examples:

> *Suddenly, I realized I was locked out of the house.*

> *At that moment, the entire room began to shake.*

> *My alarm never went off. Therefore, I missed my job interview.*

Compound Sentences

Compound sentences consist of two independent clauses, which means that both parts of the sentence would be complete sentences on their own. Each independent clause in a compound sentence with a conjunction needs a comma to separate it.

For example:

> *Chandra is going to see that new movie at the theater, but Mason is going to watch it on demand.*

Chandra is going to see that new movie at the theater is the first independent clause. *Mason is going to watch it on demand* is the second. The conjunction is *but* and a comma is used to separate those clauses correctly.

 Commas are *not* needed to separate the dependent clauses in complex and compound-complex sentences.

Non-Restrictive Phrases

A **non-restrictive phrase** is not essential to the meaning of the sentence and should be separated with one comma if it comes at the beginning or end of the sentence and two commas if it is placed in the middle.

Read this sentence:

> *My pants, which I bought at the mall, are too tight.*

This sentence would still make sense without the phrase *which I bought at the mall*. It would read *My pants are too tight*, which is a perfectly fine sentence. That means the phrase is non-restrictive and should be enclosed in commas like it is in the sentence above. However, if that phrase were restrictive—essential to the meaning of the sentence—no commas would be needed. (Example: *The pants I bought at the mall are too tight.*)

Series

A comma should separate each item in a series or list.

For example:

> *I keep my cell phone, tablet, pens, and wallet in my desk drawer.*

In this sentence, a comma also precedes the conjunction *and*, although this is not a hard and fast rule. Some writers prefer not to use that extra comma. So, the following sentence is also technically correct:

> *I keep my cell phone, tablet, pens and wallet in my desk drawer.*

The decision to place a comma before the conjunction in a series of items is up to the writer. Passages on the ACT use the comma before the conjunction, but you will not be expected to answer questions about such situations without concrete rules.

Appositives

An **appositive** is a phrase that describes a noun. An appositive contains a noun or pronoun and often one or more modifiers and appears directly before or after the noun it describes. Appositives need to be separated with commas.

For example:

> *My car, a real piece of garbage, keeps breaking down on the highway.*

In this sentence, the appositive is *a real piece of garbage*, and commas are used to separate it correctly.

Quotations

When quoting a complete phrase that someone said, **quotation marks** are needed and one or more commas are required to separate it from the rest of the sentence. See how the commas are used in these examples:

> *Buddy said, "That sandwich made me feel sick."*

> *"That sandwich made me feel sick," Buddy said.*

> *"That sandwich," Buddy began, "made me feel sick."*

However, if that quotation includes end-of-sentence punctuation, a comma is not needed at the end of it.

For example:

> **Incorrect:** *"That sandwich made me feel sick!," Buddy said.*

> **Correct:** *"That sandwich made me feel sick!" Buddy said.*

Now answer this quick exercise question. Keep in mind that all questions on the ACT will relate to a larger passage and not a standalone statement like this one.

. . . .

This novel which Herman Melville wrote, is packed with action and adventure.
                                                        2

2.   **F.**   NO CHANGE
    G.   This novel, which Herman Melville wrote,
    H.   This novel which Herman Melville wrote
    J.   This novel, which Herman Melville wrote

The correct answer is choice G. The phrase "which Herman Melville wrote" is an appositive, so it must be separated with commas from the rest of the sentence.

. . . .

Apostrophes

Apostrophes are most often used to indicate that a word is a contraction or to show possession in a sentence.

The correct use of apostrophes in **contractions** mostly depends on placing the apostrophe in the right place within a word:

> **Incorrect:** *Do'nt*

> **Correct:** *Don't*

You'll also need to recognize when a word that looks like a contraction is not a contraction:

> *it's* (a contraction of *it is*)

> *its* (the possessive form of *it*)

Using apostrophes in possessive words is a little trickier. For the most part, the apostrophe will be placed before the letter *-s*.

For example:

> *Madison's keys*

> *the dog's bone*

> *the car's headlights*

> *the sun's beams*

However, if the possessive word ends with an *s*, the apostrophe belongs after the -*s*.

For example:

> *the glasses' lenses*
>
> *the two kittens' guardian*
>
> *the states' laws*

This rule is different when a specifically named person is doing the possessing. For people whose names end in *s*, an apostrophe and an extra *s* is required.

For example:

> *Mavis's hair*
>
> *Augustus's shoes*
>
> *Venus's lunch*
>
> *Charles's smile*

When more than one noun is doing the possessing, only the last noun in the pair or list needs an apostrophe.

For example:

> *my father and mother's favorite restaurant*
>
> *the bedspread and the curtains' pattern*
>
> *Cherie and Gladys's address*
>
> *the bass and drums' sounds*

Colons

Colons are typically used to introduce a list or series of examples:

> *My pack contains everything I need for school: books, pens, a calculator, and a lunch bag.*

Colons are also used to offset and emphasize an example:

> *That book taught me the most important lesson of all: true friendship never dies.*

They can also be placed after a salutation in a letter:

> *To whom it may concern:*

Colons are also used to separate a title from a subtitle in a piece of work like a book or movie:

> *Green Peas: The Movie*

However, colons should *not* be used to separate objects and verbs or prepositions and objects:

> **Incorrect:** *My opinion is: irrelevant.*

> **Incorrect:** *Gluten is found in: bread, pasta, and many other basic foods.*

Semicolons

Semicolons can be used in place of conjunctions in compound sentences, joining the independent clauses just as *and, or, but,* or *because* would:

For example:

> *I spent the day reorganizing my bedroom; it was a complete mess.*

Semicolons are also used in lists that contain items with commas to keep all those commas from becoming confusing.

For example:

> *This meal contains only the freshest ingredients: tomatoes and onions, which I bought at the farmer's market; basil, which I grew in a pot in the kitchen; and peppers, which I grew in the backyard garden.*

 Don't forget that colons and semicolons are not interchangeable. Each punctuation mark has its own function.

Dashes

Much like commas, **dashes** tend to get overused and misused. A big problem with dashes is that they're almost never *absolutely necessary* according to the rules of mechanics, so a lot of writers just aren't sure what to do with them. You're about to become one of the lucky ones who know when to use them.

Like the colon, a dash can be used to offset and emphasize a single example:

> *In trying times, I knew I could always turn to the one individual who understood me—my dog, Blinky.*

Two dashes can also be used to separate an example or examples in the middle of a sentence:

> *Everything came tumbling from the top shelf—boxes, hats, and games—during the earthquake.*

Dashes are also useful for indicating a pause or interruption in dialogue:

> Marcus asked, "Can I borrow your—"

> "Sure! Whatever! Take what you want!" Paulette enthused before Marcus could complete his question.

Parentheses

Sometimes, a few extra details are needed to make a sentence as informative as it can be—but those details aren't always easy to cram into the natural flow of the sentence. In such cases, parentheses are in order. **Parentheses** are often used to enclose additional examples that tend to be a little less relevant to a sentence than the ones you'd place between dashes.

For example:

> Mrs. Gale (my brother's Earth science teacher when he was in high school) is going to be teaching biology next quarter.

 Watch out for sentences that overuse parentheses. They clutter sentences with too much nonessential information. You may be expected to delete unnecessary parenthetical information on the ACT.

GRAMMAR AND USAGE QUESTIONS

About 15–20 percent of the questions you'll encounter on the ACT English test will involve grammar and usage issues, which require you to understand how words work with each other and in the context of the passage as a whole. This includes the following:

- Do subjects and verbs agree?
- Do pronouns and their antecedents or modifiers and the words they modify agree?
- Does the writer use idioms correctly?

Let's tackle a sample grammar and usage question. Read the following paragraph and answer the question that follows.

. . . .

Making a safe and durable tree house takes a bit more time and effort than finding a usable tree, buying supplies from the hardware store, and nailing together a few pieces of wood. Every detail must be carefully planned and considered—from the location to the building plans and the eventual construction. A good tree house follows a clear blueprint, makes use of the proper tools and materials based on how it will be used, and leaves no room for sloppy guesswork. However, a well-constructed tree house is worth the effort, and <u>they can be</u> enjoyed for many years.

3

3. **A.** NO CHANGE
  B. she can be
  C. it can be
  D. he can be

The correct answer is C. As mentioned, usage/mechanics issues can be more subtle and difficult to spot, especially when you're reading quickly. At first glance, the sentence as written (choice A) may *seem* perfectly ok. However, upon closer inspection there's a problem with the author's pronoun choice. The author uses a plural pronoun (*they*) to refer to a singular noun (*a well-constructed tree house*), which is grammatically incorrect. Switching to a singular, gender-neutral pronoun (*it*) corrects the problem. Choices B and D also deploy singular pronouns but incorrectly use gender-specific pronouns (*she* and *he*), which aren't appropriate for referring to a tree house.

· ·

For some, answering grammar and usage questions can be a bit more complicated than answering punctuation questions—but knowing the rules is the key to success on test day.

 While incorrect punctuation won't necessarily make a sentence sound wrong, poor grammar almost certainly will. So, thinking about how sentences sound can help you select the best answers to grammar and usage questions.

Now let's do a quick review of the most essential grammar and usage concepts and rules—the ones that you'll need to know and use on test day.

NOUNS

The subject of any sentence is always a **noun: the person, place,** or **thing** performing the action that the sentence describes. Some grammar and usage questions on the ACT will likely involve a sentence's subject, often in terms of how it agrees with verbs or pronouns.

Before we discuss how nouns interact with other words, let's look at some specific noun forms.

Plural Nouns

The nice thing about nouns is that they really only have two general forms: singular and plural.

- The **singular** form is the most basic: *cat, dog, otter, lampshade, avocado,* and *eyebrow*—these are all nouns in their most basic singular form.

- Making a singular noun **plural** is often as simple as adding the letter *s* to the end (for example: *cat–cats*). Plural nouns only get tricky when they are irregular—hard-and-fast rules for creating irregular plural nouns are often tough to apply to a language as complicated as English. We can't simply say that you're *always* safe adding -*es* to the end of all nouns that end in -*o* to make them plural. For example, the plural of *avocado* is *avocados*.

While you cannot be expected to memorize every single irregular noun for the ACT, it's a good idea to familiarize yourself with some of the most common. Review the nouns in this table:

Common Irregular Plural Nouns		
Noun Ends With	**Creating the Plural Form**	**Examples**
-*f*	change *f* to *v* and add –*es*	**singular:** calf / **singular:** elf / **singular:** half / **singular:** leaf / **singular:** shelf / **singular:** thief / **singular:** wolf	**plural:** calves / **plural:** elves / **plural:** halves / **plural:** leaves / **plural:** shelves / **plural:** thieves / **plural:** wolves
-*fe*	change *f* to *v* and add –*s*	**singular:** knife / **singular:** life / **singular:** wife	**plural:** knives / **plural:** lives / **plural:** wives
-*is*	change to –*es*	**singular:** axis / **singular:** analysis / **singular:** parenthesis	**plural:** axes / **plural:** analyses / **plural:** parentheses
-*o*	add –*es*	**singular:** echo / **singular:** hero / **singular:** potato / **singular:** tomato	**plural:** echoes / **plural:** heroes / **plural:** potatoes / **plural:** tomatoes

Common Irregular Plural Nouns		
Noun Ends With	**Creating the Plural Form**	**Examples**
-ous	change to *-ice*	**singular:** louse	**plural:** lice
		singular: mouse	**plural:** mice
-s	add *-es*	**singular:** class	**plural:** classes
		singular: boss	**plural:** bosses
-us	change to *-i*	**singular:** alumnus	**plural:** alumni
		singular: fungus	**plural:** fungi

There are a few other variations of irregular plural nouns that do not involve changing the last letter or two of the singular form. Fortunately, most of these should be very familiar to you.

Nouns that require *-oo-* to be changed to *-ee-* for their plural form:

singular: foot	**plural:** feet
singular: goose	**plural:** geese
singular: tooth	**plural:** teeth

Nouns that require the addition or substitution of *-en* for their plural form:

singular: child	**plural:** children
singular: man	**plural:** men
singular: ox	**plural:** oxen
singular: woman	**plural:** women

Finally, there are nouns that require no change whatsoever to become plural:

singular: deer	**plural:** deer
singular: fish	**plural:** fish
singular: offspring	**plural:** offspring
singular: series	**plural:** series
singular: sheep	**plural:** sheep
singular: species	**plural:** species

Collective Nouns

Collective nouns are interesting because they have some of the flavor of plural nouns since they seem to describe more than one thing.

For example:

- a bunch of students in a *class*
- a group of sailors in a *navy*
- several fish in a *school*

However, while the individual nouns in these collections are plural (*students*, *sailors*, *fish*), the collections themselves are singular (*class*, *navy*, *school*). This means that these collective nouns must be treated as singular nouns. This will be particularly important when we deal with subject-verb agreement and noun-pronoun agreement in the next section.

Familiarize yourself with some common collective nouns. All of these nouns are singular, not plural:

army	audience	band	board	class
committee	company	corporation	council	department
faculty	family	firm	flock	group
herd	jury	majority	navy	public
school	senate	society	team	unit

AGREEMENT

When words in a sentence agree, things tend to go smoothly. When they don't, there can be trouble. You can ensure that the elements in sentences don't clash by recognizing when they are, and aren't, in agreement.

Subjects and **verbs** need to agree in terms of number. The same is true of **pronouns** and **antecedents**, which also need to agree in terms of gender.

Subject/Verb Agreement

Every complete sentence has a **subject** and a **verb.**

- The subject is the noun doing the action.
- The verb is the action that the subject is doing.

Simple, right? Actually, it can be—a sentence with just a subject and a verb can be really simple.

For example:

The dog growls.

That sentence has only three words, but it's still a complete sentence because it has a subject and a verb. Just as important, the subject and verb agree: the singular subject *dog* agrees with the singular verb *growls*. (That's right: the verb is singular even though it ends with the letter -*s*.)

Determining whether or not subjects and verbs are in agreement can get a little more complicated in sentences with compound subjects.

For example:

The dog and the bear growl.

Neither *dog* nor *bear* ends with an *s*, so they may not look plural, but they work together as a compound subject when joined with a conjunction (*and*). This means that they require a plural verb and, as you may have guessed, the plural verb does not end in an extra -*s*. The compound subject and verb are in agreement in this example.

However, if the conjunction were *or* or *nor*, a singular verb would be required.

For example:

Neither the dog nor the bear growls.

Once again, the compound subject and verb are in agreement.

 Subject-verb agreement can get confusing when there is a word or phrase between the subject and verb. Make sure you have identified the *entire* subject and verb correctly before figuring out whether or not they agree.

When dealing with collective nouns, the agreement rule depends on what the collective noun is doing. If every member of the collective noun is doing the exact same thing, it is operating as a single unit and the verb should be singular.

For example:

*The jury **deliberates** late into the night.*

However, if each member of that collective noun is considered as an individual, those members should be specified and a plural verb is required:

*The jury **have** different perspectives on the evidence presented.*

To avoid the awkward-sounding construction using the plural form, writers often will include the word *members* in the sentence:

*The jury members **have** different perspectives on the evidence presented.*

*The members of the jury **have** different perspectives on the evidence presented.*

Pronoun/Antecedent Agreement

Pronouns and **antecedents** also need to play nice. A pronoun replaces a specific noun. Its antecedent is the noun the pronoun replaces. Since it would sound kind of clumsy to say *Luisa drives Luisa's car*, most writers would replace the second *Luisa* with a pronoun:

> *Luisa drives her car.*

Much better, right? In this sentence, *Luisa* is the antecedent and the pronoun is *her*, a female pronoun. Both are in agreement in this sentence. It is also singular, which is appropriate since Luisa is only one woman.

Now, if the sentence read *Luisa drives his car*, it would lack pronoun-antecedent agreement in terms of gender (unless, of course, if Luisa was borrowing some guy's car). If it read *Luisa drives their car*, it would sound as if Luisa was driving a car owned by two or more people other than herself.

However, *their* would be necessary in a sentence with a **compound antecedent.** For example, maybe Luisa co-owns her car with a friend named Ginnie. Then the sentence should read, *Luisa and Ginnie drive their car.* Compound antecedents are a bit more complicated when the conjunction is *or* or *nor* instead of *and*. In such cases, you will select your pronoun based on which antecedent it is nearest.

For example:

> *Neither my wife nor my daughters brought **their** luggage out to the car yet.*

> *Neither my daughters nor my wife brought **her** luggage out to the car yet.*

Both of these sentences are written correctly. Since the plural antecedent *daughters* is closer to the pronoun in sentence 1, the plural pronoun *their* is required.

Since the singular antecedent *wife* is closer to the pronoun in sentence 2, the singular pronoun *her* is required.

Now, if your antecedent is a collective noun, selecting the right pronoun depends on what the collective noun is doing and how it is doing it. If every member of the collective noun is doing the exact same thing as a single unit, the singular pronoun is needed.

For example:

> *The soccer team played **its** game magnificently.*

In this example, everyone on the team is playing the same game, and the singular pronoun *its* is used correctly. However, if all of the members of that collective noun are doing their own thing, a plural pronoun is in order.

For example:

> *The soccer team played **their** individual positions magnificently.*

This example describes how the members of the team handled their individual positions (goalkeeper, defenders, midfielders, forwards), and it uses the plural pronoun *their* correctly.

Selecting Pronouns

Selecting appropriate pronouns, given the context of the sentences they will appear in, is another challenge you'll likely face on the ACT English test.

Perspective will be a factor when figuring out the best way to use pronouns on test day. Let's look at a few essential rules:

- A **first-person pronoun** (*I, me, we, us*) is necessary when a writer is referring to her- or himself.

- A **second-person pronoun** (*you*) is needed when the writer is addressing the reader.

- A **third-person pronoun** (*she, he, her, him, they, them*) is needed when the pronoun refers to a third person who is neither writing nor reading the passage.

Choosing the right pronoun can be tricky in sentences that pair them with nouns. Is *Ricky and I went to the game* or *Ricky and me went to the game* correct?

In such cases, try removing the noun and saying the sentence with just the pronoun (*I went to the game; me went to the game*). Chances are the wrong pronoun will now sound wrong.

Relative Pronouns

The **relative pronouns** *who, whom, whose,* and *that* all refer to people; the relative pronouns *that* and *which* refer to things.

Relative clauses are like adjectives: they exist to describe. Restrictive relative clauses cannot stand on their own. You can recognize a relative clause from the presence of a relative pronoun.

The relative clauses in the following sentences are underlined:

> *Mr. Marshall, who used to live next door to me, is the head manager at my new job.*

> *The person to whom you want to speak is not at home.*

> *Florida, which is where I went on vacation last year, is located at the bottom of the United States.*

> *The truck that is parked across the street belongs to Francois.*

Reflexive Pronouns

When a subject needs a pronoun to refer to itself, a reflexive pronoun fits the bill. In fact, *itself* is a **reflexive pronoun,** as is any pronoun that ends with *-self* or *-selves*.

- There are **five singular reflexive pronouns**: *myself, yourself, himself, herself, itself*

- There are **three plural reflexive pronouns**: (*ourselves, yourselves, themselves*).

Interrogative Pronouns

To interrogate is to question, and **interrogative pronouns** are used to ask questions.

- There are **five main interrogative pronouns**: *whose, who*, and *whom* refer to people exclusively; *what* refers to things exclusively; and *which* can refer to people or things.

- The addition of the suffix *-ever* also creates five less common interrogative pronouns: *whatever, whichever, whoever, whomever,* and *whosever.*

 A common confusion regarding interrogative pronouns is when to use *who* and when to use *whom.*

- *Who* is used as the subject of a question (example: *Who called at 3 a.m. last night?*).
- *Whom* is used as the object of a question (example: *To whom am I speaking?*).

Possessive Pronouns

Apostrophes are used when indicating that a noun possesses something. More often than not, you can just add an apostrophe and an *-s* to the end of a word to make it possessive.

For example:

> *That guitar is Jimi's.*

> *There is a goldfish in Jess's bathtub.*

The extra *-s* is not necessary with a possessive noun that already ends in *-s* but is not someone's name.

For example:

> *The lions' cubs played in the grass.*

> *Those books' covers are falling apart.*

Pronouns, however, usually have their very own forms to show possession. Since pronouns such as *his, her, its, my, mine, yours, their,* and *theirs* already show possession, they don't need an apostrophe or an extra *-s*.

For example:

> The game is **mine.**
>
> **Their** friend is coming to the beach with us.
>
> **Her** father is coaching the team.
>
> The cat licked **its** paws.

The only pronouns that need that apostrophe and extra *-s* are *anybody, anyone, everybody, everyone, no one,* and *nobody*.

For example:

> **Anybody's** guess is as good as mine.
>
> **Everybody's** weekend will be spent studying.

 Remember that *it's* is *not* the possessive form of *it*; it is a contraction of *it is*.

Verb Tense

Verbs are words that refer to action, and their **tense** indicates *when* that action happened.

- Is the action happening now? If so, then the verb is in the **present tense**.
- Did the action already happen? If so, then the verb is in the **past tense**.
- Are you still waiting for the action to happen? If so, then the verb is in the **future tense**.

Past, present, and future are the most basic points in time. However, there are quite a few more than three verb tenses. Let's take a quick look at possible verb tenses:

- **Simple present tense** indicates an action happening now: *I am here.*
- **Present progressive tense** indicates an action happening now that will continue into the future: *I am walking.*
- **Present perfect progressive tense** indicates an unfinished action: *I have been studying all day.*
- **Present perfect simple tense** indicates an action that occurred in the past but continues to be relevant: *I have eaten artichokes.*

- **Past perfect simple tense** indicates an action that occurred in the past but is now complete: *When I woke up this morning, I realized that it had rained last night.*

- **Past simple tense** indicates an action that happened already: *I was asleep.*

- **Past progressive tense** pairs a past tense verb with a continuous verb ending in -*ing*: *I was dreaming.*

- **Past perfect progressive tense** reflects on an ongoing action from the past: *By the 1990s, hip-hop had been a popular form of music for several years.*

- **Future simple tense** indicates an action that will happen later: *I will be home by 5:00.*

- **Future progressive tense** indicates an action that will happen later and continue: *I will be working all day tomorrow.*

- **Future perfect simple tense** indicates the completion of an action that will happen later: *I will have finished cleaning the house by noon today.*

- **Future perfect progressive tense** indicates an incomplete action that will happen later: *I will have been cooking for 3 hours by the time my guests arrive.*

Adjectives and Adverbs

As we've already established, the only *completely essential* elements of a sentence are its subject and verb.

For example:

> *The dog barks.*

Once again, this is a complete sentence. Is it a particularly *interesting* sentence though? Writing a sentence with nothing but a subject and a verb is like making soup with nothing but water and tomatoes. Where are the other flavors, the words that give a sentence some unique and memorable character?

In a sentence, **adjectives** (words that describe nouns) and **adverbs** (words that describe verbs) add some extra sentence flavor. Think of them as the spices of a sentence.

Let's add some spice to our previous example:

> *The furious dog barks uncontrollably.*

Now there's a sentence that paints a picture! The adjective *furious* shows that the dog is *not* barking playfully. The adverb *uncontrollably* shows that the dog is really worked up and probably won't be calming down anytime soon.

In this section, we'll take a look at the different forms of adjectives and adverbs you will have to know before taking the ACT.

Comparative and Superlative Adjectives

Big! Bigger! Biggest! Adjectives and adverbs change form when they are used to make a comparison.

The **comparative** form is used when comparing two things.

> **comparative adjectives:**
>
> *This street is <u>wider</u> than the last one.*
>
> *I feel <u>more limber</u> than I did before I stretched.*

> **comparative adverbs:**
>
> *This week seemed to go by <u>more quickly</u> than last week did.*
>
> *I am taking my studies <u>more seriously</u> than I ever have before.*

The **superlative** form is used when comparing three or more things.

> **superlative adjectives:**
>
> *This is the <u>strangest</u> book I own.*
>
> *Alshad is the <u>politest</u> boy in my class.*

> **superlative adverbs:**
>
> *Out of everyone in the office, Peri works the <u>hardest</u>.*
>
> *This is the <u>quickest</u> I have ever run.*

As you may have noticed, simply adding *-er* to the end of comparative adjectives and *-est* to the end of superlative adjectives is not always enough. Once again, there are a number of exceptions you need to understand to use comparative and superlative adjectives correctly. Review the following:

Case	Adjective	Comparative	Superlative
One- and two-syllable adjectives ending in -e do not need an extra -e.	*close* *large* *simple*	*closer* *larger* *simpler*	*closest* *largest* *simplest*
One-syllable adjectives ending in a consonant need to have that consonant doubled.	*big* *sad* *thin*	*bigger* *sadder* *thinner*	*biggest* *saddest* *thinnest*
One- and two-syllable adjectives ending in -y change that -y to an -i.	*dry* *heavy* *tiny*	*drier* *heavier* *tinier*	*driest* *heaviest* *tiniest*
Certain adjectives with two or more syllables remain the same but need the addition of *more* for comparatives and *most* for superlatives.	*beautiful* *complete* *important*	*more beautiful* *more complete* *more important*	*most beautiful* *most complete* *most important*
Irregular adjectives require their own special alterations in the comparative and superlative forms.	*bad* *far* *good* *many*	*worse* *farther* *better* *more*	*worst* *farthest* *best* *most*

For comparative adverbs, adding *more* is usually enough, and superlative adverbs usually only need *most*.

For example:

> *I sang more quietly than Enid did.*

> *The car runs most smoothly on paved roads.*

As you may have guessed, there are exceptions to this rule, but don't worry, because there aren't as many exceptions for adverbs as there are for adjectives. Basically, any adverb that does not end in -*ly* should be treated the same way you would treat it if it were being used to modify a noun instead of a verb .

Adverb	Comparative	Superlative
bad	worse	worst
far	farther	farthest
fast	faster	fastest
good	better	best
hard	harder	hardest
little	less	least
long	longer	longest
loud	louder	loudest
many	more	most
quick	quicker	quickest
soon	sooner	soonest

One thing you need to make sure of when taking the ACT is that comparatives and superlatives are actually being used to make a comparison.

You may have seen an advertisement that boasts, *Our product is better!* Well, your product is better than what? Obviously, the implication is that the product is better than other similar products, but the comparison is not correct and complete if that information is not stated directly, as follows:

> *Our product is better than other similar products!*

This may not be the catchiest slogan in the world, but it is a complete comparison. Remember that incomplete comparisons are incorrect when you're reading English passages on the ACT.

Idioms

For some students, **idioms** can be confusing because they use words to mean something other than their literal meanings.

For example, if you were to *pull the wool over someone's eyes*, you probably would not *literally* grab a wool scarf and pull it over that person's eyes. However, you may *deceive* them, which is the idiomatic meaning of *pull the wool over someone's eyes*. See what we mean? Idioms can be tricky.

Idiom questions on the ACT often require you to identify mistakes in their wording. So, even if you don't know what the idiom *bite off more than you can chew* means, you may still have heard it before, and you should be able to recognize that *bite off more than you can see* is not a correctly composed idiom (you may also deduce that biting with your eyes is both difficult and uncomfortable).

Here are some other common idioms:

Idiom	Meaning
Actions speak louder than words.	What one does is more important than what one says.
Back to the drawing board!	Time to start all over again!
Barking up the wrong tree	Drawing the wrong conclusion
Beat around the bush	Avoid the topic
Bite off more than you can chew	To take on too large a task
Costs an arm and a leg	Very expensive
Cry over spilt milk	Complain about something that cannot be changed
Feel under the weather	Feel ill
Is on the ball	Is very competent
Hit the sack	Go to bed
Kill two birds with one stone	Accomplish two tasks with a single action
Let sleeping dogs lie	Do not provoke a potentially unpleasant situation
Let the cat out of the bag	Reveal a secret
Piece of cake	Easy
Take with a grain of salt	Not take something too seriously
The whole nine yards	Everything

TIP — A good way to become familiar with a wide variety of idioms is to read a lot. Writers love to use idioms!

Prepositional Phrases

As the old lesson goes, a **preposition** is anywhere a mouse can go: *over, under, sideways, down, in, out, at, from, above, to, inside, outside, before, after, forward, toward*, etc.

Prepositions indicate time and direction and are pretty straightforward. **Prepositional phrases**, however, are a bit less straightforward. In fact, they're very similar to idioms in that they cannot be explained with simple rules—you just have to get familiar with them and decide what works best.

A prepositional phrase combines a preposition with one or more words. For example, *at home* is a common prepositional phrase. Technically, there is nothing grammatically wrong with saying *in home* (*I didn't go to the park last weekend; I was in home*); however, it simply isn't common to say *I was in home*, and you'll need to be aware of the most commonly used prepositional phrases on the ACT.

Here are a few common prepositional phrases you should remember:

among friends	at school	in the family	in the yard
around the corner	at work	in the grass	in your mind
at home	at the beach	in the room	on the lawn
at the office	in my heart	in the tree	on the road
at play	in the doorway	in the window	on the roof

SENTENCE STRUCTURE QUESTIONS

Sentence structure questions are the most common usage/mechanics questions on the ACT English test: 20–25 percent of usage/mechanics questions will test your ability to understand the relationships between and among clauses, the placement of modifiers, and the shifts in construction. You'll have to spot and possibly fix fragments, run-ons, and more.

Let's tackle a sample sentence structure question. Read the following paragraph and answer the question that follows.

· ·

Do you know the history of one of America's favorite things to chew? Bubblegum was invented in 1928 by Walter Diemer, an employee for a well-known chewing gum company in Philadelphia. The recipe that Diemer tinkered with was more stretchable and less sticky than its chewing gum counterpart the bubblegum was pink in color, which was Diemer's favorite color. Today, bubblegum comes in a wide array of colors and flavors and is a multibillion-dollar-a-year treat that children and adults around the world enjoy.

4. **F.** NO CHANGE

G. The recipe that Diemer tinkered with was more stretchable and less sticky. Than its chewing gum counterpart the bubblegum was pink in color, which was Diemer's favorite color.

H. The recipe that Diemer tinkered, with was more stretchable, and less sticky, than its chewing gum counterpart, the bubblegum was pink in color, which was, Diemer's favorite color.

J. The recipe that Diemer tinkered with was more stretchable and less sticky than its chewing gum counterpart. The bubblegum was pink in color, which was Diemer's favorite color.

The correct answer is J. Even if the underlined sentence wasn't underlined, you might've noticed while reading it that something is wrong. As written (choice F), it's awkward and attempts to combine two distinct ideas into one overly long and convoluted sentence. That's because we're dealing with two independent clauses, complete thoughts that would work much better as separate sentences. Choice J fixes the problem—it creates two complete and independent sentences that are much easier to read. Choice G attempts to fix the problem but fails to do so—it breaks the clauses at the incorrect point and creates a second sentence that is awkward and confusing (what is the comparison that "Than its chewing gum counterpart" is referring to?). Choice H fails to fix the problem as well; instead, it introduces a bunch of incorrectly placed commas that only serve to make the problem worse.

· ·

Clauses

Just as you can't have a sentence without a subject and verb that express a complete thought, you can't have a sentence without clauses.

We'll let you in on a little secret: A subject and verb that express a complete thought *is* a clause. It's an independent clause, because it can stand on its own.

- **Independent clause**: *The dog barks.*

A clause that has its own subject and verb but can't stand on its own is a dependent or subordinate clause.

- **Subordinate clause**: *when the mail carrier arrives*

A subordinate clause needs to be paired with an independent clause to be part of a complete sentence.

> *The dog barks when the mail carrier arrives.*

There are four different sentence structures. Notice that each one always includes at least one independent clause.

1. A **simple sentence** has only one independent clause :

   - *The dog barks.*

2. A **compound sentence** has two independent clauses joined with a conjunction or semicolon:

   - *The dog barks and the cat meows.*

   - *The dog barks; the cat meows.*

3. A **complex sentence** has one independent clause and at least one subordinate clause:

   - *The dog barks when the mail carrier arrives.*

4. A **compound-complex** sentence has at least two independent clauses and at least one subordinate clause:

   - *When the mail carrier arrives, the dog barks and the cat meows.*

A semicolon is the only punctuation that can join clauses without a conjunction. Using only a comma is known as a **comma splice**— and it is wrong.

Conjunctions

You may have noticed the important role that conjunctions play in various sentence structures. When a conjunction joins independent clauses of equal importance, it is known as a **coordinating conjunction.**

For example:

> *The movie was very good, but the book was terrible.*

In this compound sentence, *but* is the coordinating conjunction. If you divide the sentence before and after the coordinating conjunction, you will still have two independent clauses of equal importance:

For example:

> *The movie was very good.*

> *The book was terrible.*

If a conjunction joins a subordinate clause to an independent clause, it is known as a **subordinating conjunction.**

> The movie that I didn't want to see was actually very good.

In this sentence, the subordinate clause is *that I didn't want to see*, which is not a complete sentence on its own. The subordinating conjunction is *that*.

Here are some other coordinating and subordinating conjunctions:

Coordinating Conjunctions	
and	or
but	so
for	yet
nor	

Subordinating Conjunctions	
after	until
although	when
as	whenever
because	whereas
before	wherever
even though	whether
if	which
since	while
that	who
though	why
unless	

Fragments and Run-ons

Two of the most common sentence structure errors are **fragments** and **run-ons.**

A **fragment** is a piece of a sentence that is not complete on its own.

For example:

> Bouncing on the waves.

What was bouncing on the waves? We'll never know. This sentence needs a subject:

> The little boat is bouncing on the waves.

That's more like it! The subject-verb pair *The little boat* and *is bouncing* rescued this sentence from the fragment heap.

Sometimes, writers purposely use fragments and run-on sentences to achieve a particular effect. However, as far as the ACT English test is concerned, fragments and run-on sentences are *always* wrong.

Run-on sentences are the opposite of fragments, but they are just as incorrect. They are full of words, but their lack of coherent structure keeps them from expressing ideas clearly.

For example:

> The sea is rough and stormy, the little boat bounces helplessly on the waves.

This run-on sentence needs a conjunction to join the two independent clauses (that comma splice does not do the job on its own). The good news is that the sentence can be repaired easily:

> The sea is rough and stormy, and the little boat bounces helplessly on the waves.

Now it's a clearly expressed thought!

Modifiers

Modifiers such as adjectives and adverbs and descriptive phrases and clauses need to be placed correctly in sentences. Otherwise, you can end up with some *very* bewildering thoughts.

The two most common modifier issues are misplaced modifiers and dangling modifiers. Let's examine them more closely.

A **misplaced modifier** creates confusion because it's not placed next to the word it's supposed to modify.

For example:

> I tiptoed across the floor because I didn't want to wake the people sleeping in the room below mine carefully.

In this sentence, the modifier *carefully* is not where it should be. In fact, its placement makes it seem as though *the people* were sleeping carefully. How do you sleep carefully? You have to be conscious and careful about where information is placed in sentences.

The adverb *carefully* would be put to better use modifying *tiptoed*:

> I tiptoed carefully across the floor because I didn't want to wake the people sleeping in the room below mine.

Excellent! In this sentence, the modifier *carefully* is no longer misplaced.

Dangling modifiers are often more confusing than misplaced ones. They don't modify anything at all. Take a look at this sentence:

> *Worrying about the time, rushed through breakfast.*

The modifier in this sentence is *Worrying about the time*. There's a problem: We don't know exactly who was worrying about the time. This sentence's lack of a subject leaves the modifier dangling without anything to modify. Someone needs to add a subject to give the modifier something to do, as follows:

> *Worrying about the time, Greta rushed through breakfast.*

The addition of the subject *Greta* gives the phrase *worrying about the time* something to modify.

 On the ACT, make sure you choose the right noun to give the modifier something to modify. You will make the best selection by reading the passage very carefully.

Parallel Structure

Sentences with correct **parallel structure** have all of their parts moving cohesively and in the same tense and direction. You can't place a word or phrase that's going backward into the past alongside one that's moving into the future. **Parallel structure** crumbles when groups of words combine different types of phrases, clauses, and parts of speech.

For example:

> *Tomorrow morning I will brush my teeth, eat breakfast, and went to school.*

This sentence begins by describing things that are going to happen in the future—*tomorrow* to be precise. Everything is smooth until that final phrase: *went to school*. It's written in the *past tense*, which violates the parallel structure of a sentence that is otherwise written in the *future tense*. Let's take a look at a revised version of the sentence:

> *Tomorrow morning I will brush my teeth, eat breakfast, and go to school.*

This version corrects the parallel structure by putting the phrase *went to school* into the future tense (*go to school*), where it belongs.

 A sentence does not need to be written entirely in the same tense to be correct. It just needs to be structured correctly.

For example: The sentence *I ate an apple yesterday, and I am going to eat an orange tonight* does not violate parallel structure.

Correlative Conjunctions

You must be mindful of parallel structure when dealing with **correlative conjunctions**. These are conjunctions that work in pairs: *either... or, neither... nor*, and *not only... but also*. Mixing correlative conjunctions is another way to violate parallel structure.

For example:

> *Neither the pants or the shirt suit my taste in clothing.*

Oops! *Neither* indicates a negative and *or* indicates a positive. So, what does this sentence mean? Do the pants and shirt suit the writer's very particular tastes or don't they? We'll only know if the parallel structure is repaired:

> *Either the pants or the shirt suit my taste in clothing.*

Oh, he likes the pants *and* the shirt. Good to know!

You now have a solid set of test-taking tools in your arsenal—practice using them alongside your critical eye and freshly honed skills to succeed on the ACT English test.

Make the most of your time between now and test day to practice and review the core Rhetorical Skills and Usage/Mechanics concepts covered in this chapter, and you'll set yourself up for success on the ACT!

PRACTICE: USAGE/MECHANICS QUESTIONS

Now it's time to put your usage/mechanics skills to the test! Read and carefully analyze the following full-length ACT English passage. The 10 questions that follow it are designed to test your understanding of the passage, as well as your ability to recognize and use appropriate English usage/mechanics skills.

Use the proven tips, strategies, and advice you've gotten so far in this chapter—alongside the wealth of knowledge you've acquired in your academic career—to answer them.

The detailed answer explanations that follow each question provide a complete breakdown and discussion for arriving at the correct answers. We strongly recommend that you review them carefully to help you understand why the incorrect answer choices are incorrect, why you may have selected them, and how to avoid making the same errors on the actual ACT. Use this information to help refine and direct your study time between now and test day—regardless of how limited it may be.

The Stethoscope: Listen Up!

[1]

It may seem like a relatively low-tech innovation <u>today the</u> invention of the
<u></u>
                                    1
stethoscope was a significant medical advancement in the nineteenth century. To

some, the stethoscope may be a simplistic and easy-to-ignore tool used by doctors,

but it actually helped usher in a new and improved level of healthcare and diagnostic

capability. Although the stethoscope has evolved and become more sophisticated

over the years since it was first created, this instantly recognizable symbol of

healthcare remains a fundamental and indispensable part of every <u>doctor list</u> of
                                                                      2
essential instruments. Let's take a <u>closer. Look</u> at this helpful tool.
                                         3

[2]

The rubber and steel stethoscope that we recognize today actually started out

looking quite a bit different when it was originally created. The original instrument,

created in 1816 by French physician René Laennec, was a much cruder monaural

wooden tube that more closely resembled an ear trumpet than the stethoscope we

all know. It wasn't until many years later, in 1829, that the first version of the binaural

stethoscope that resembles the instrument still in use today was created. Since

<u>her creation</u> through today, the stethoscope has served a wide array of important
    4
uses, including listening to sounds from the hearts, lungs, and intestines of patients,

<u>and check</u> internal sounds for healthy and productive blood flow through the veins
    5
and arteries. It even serves as a diagnostic tool for malfunctioning machinery and

equipment.

[3]

Although most of us likely conjure a similar mental image when we think of

stethoscopes, there <u>will be</u> several different types of these instruments, each of
                        6
which has been tinkered with, tweaked, and refined over the years to enhance

effectiveness and usability. Among the various types of available stethoscopes are

the acoustic stethoscope, the model we most commonly associate when we think of these instruments; the electronic stethoscope, or stethophone, which utilizes electronic amplification technology to make body sounds louder; the recording stethoscope, which allows for direct audio output into external recording devices (such as computers) for enhanced diagnostic capability; and the fetal stethoscope, or
                    ―――――――
                       7
fetoscope, used to listen to body sounds of fetuses in pregnant women. Here's some interesting trivia regarding the stethoscope—the first model that could work in conjunction with a smart phone, and the first usable 3-D printed stethoscope, were
                                                                      ――――
                                                                        8
both introduced in 2015?
――――――――――――――
        8

[4]

Some experts in the field of healthcare has proclaimed that more modern
                                            ――――――――――――
                                                   9
medical innovations, including portable ultrasonography units, have rendered the stethoscope virtually obsolete. She argues that once newer listening technology
                                      ―――――――
                                         10
becomes cheaper and more readily available, the need for stethoscopes will continue to decrease until they are simply no longer needed. Although the stethoscope may not be around forever, as medicine and technology continue to work together toward revolutionizing and evolving the field of healthcare, the fact that the stetho-scope was once an innovative and game-changing medical instrument that helped save lives will always be difficult to dispute. Only time will tell what the future of the stethoscope will be.

1. **A.** NO CHANGE
   B. today—the
   C. today, but the
   D. today, or the

The correct answer is C. As written (choice A), the sentence is an awkward run-on, with two independent clauses set together with no punctuation. The two clauses are in desperate need of some punctuation and a coordinating conjunction to properly join them, which choice C does: *It may seem like a relatively low-tech innovation today, but the invention of the stethoscope was a significant medical advancement in the nineteenth century.* The choice of a proper coordinating conjunction, given the context of the sentence, is crucial—choice D uses an inappropriate coordinating conjunction (*or*) and is incorrect. How can you tell it's incorrect? Just plug it into the sentence and you'll see that it only adds to the confusion: *It may seem like a relatively low-tech innovation today,* *or the invention of the stethoscope was a significant medical advancement in the nineteenth century.* Choice B attempts to deploy a much needed break in the sentence with an em-dash, which is often a good way to create a needed pause within a sentence, but places it in an inappropriate spot and is therefore incorrect.

2. **F.** NO CHANGE
    G. "doctors list"
    H. doctor's list
    J. doctors-list

The correct answer is H. The underlined portion of the sentence refers to possession—namely, the list of essential instruments that every doctor has. Apostrophes are used to connote possession in a sentence, and in this instance *doctor's list* (choice H) is the correct answer. As written (choice F), the sentence is unclear regarding who owns the list of essential instruments and is incorrect. Choice G incorrectly adds quotation marks to the sentence. Quotation marks are typically used for dialogue, to indicate a book or article title, or when quoting a complete phrase that someone said. Choice J incorrectly uses a hyphen, which is not appropriate in this sentence.

3. **A.** NO CHANGE
    B. , closer look
    C. closer; Look
    D. closer look

The correct answer is D. When end punctuation is used incorrectly, it could potentially create sentence fragments, which is what happened in this instance. As written (choice A), the incorrect use of a period creates a sentence fragment: *Let's take a closer.* Removing the period and creating one complete sentence (choice D) fixes the issue. Choice B incorrectly inserts a comma, and choice C incorrectly inserts a semicolon into the sentence, both of which lead to grammatically incorrect sentences.

4. **F.** NO CHANGE
    G. his creation
    H. our creation
    J. its creation

The correct answer is J. The underlined portion of the sentence as written (choice F) highlights a common problem—pronoun/antecedent agreement. In order to select an appropriate pronoun, the noun which it will replace must be identified first. In this sentence, that noun is *stethoscope*, and the proper pronoun to replace it is the gender-neutral *its* (choice J). The masculine, gender-specific *his* (choice G) and the plural pronoun *our* (choice H) are both incorrect in this context.

5. **A.** NO CHANGE
    B. and checking
    C. and will check
    D. and checked

The correct answer is B. In order for a sentence to be grammatically correct, it must demonstrate proper parallel structure. Sentences with correct parallel structure have all of their parts moving cohesively and in the same tense and direction, including verbs. As written (choice A), the underlined verb *check* is in the wrong tense and isn't parallel with the verb *listening*. Revising it to *checking* (choice B) fixes the parallel problem. The future tense *will check* (choice C), and the past tense *checked* (choice D) are also incorrect given the context of the sentence.

6. **F.** NO CHANGE
    G. used to be
    H. are
    J. were

The correct answer is H. In its current form (choice F), the sentence uses the wrong verb tense. The future tense *will be* is inappropriate for instruments that already exist. Using the past tense (choices G and J) is incorrect for a similar reason, as the different types of stethoscopes still exist and are not relics of the past. Choice H fixes the verb tense problem; since the different types of instruments in the sentence are still in existence, using the present tense *are* is the correct choice.

7. **A.** NO CHANGE
    B. such as "computers"
    C. such as—computers—
    D. such as; computers;

The correct answer is A. The sentence as written (choice A) reflects the correct and appropriate use of parentheses; parentheses are often used to provide additional information or examples, as is the case in this sentence. Here, *computers* is provided as an example of an external recording device that recording stethoscopes can be used with. When providing an example, using quotation marks (choice B), em-dashes (choice C), or semicolons (choice D) are incorrect choices.

8. **F.** NO CHANGE
    G. were both introduced in 2015
    H. were both introduced in 2015.
    J. were both introduced in 2015;

The correct answer is H. Based on the available answer choices, you can quickly discern that this is an end punctuation question. Is the sentence correct as written? Is a question mark appropriate here? The answer to both of these questions is no; this isn't a question, so a question mark (choice F) is incorrect. Choice G leaves off any form of end punctuation, which is *always* incorrect for any sentence. Choice H correctly uses a period for this straightforward, declarative sentence. Choice J uses a semicolon; semicolons are used to separate independent but related independent clauses, not as end punctuation for a sentence.

9. **A.** NO CHANGE
   B. have proclaimed
   C. having proclaimed
   D. haven't proclaimed

The correct answer is B. Proper subject/verb agreement is an essential component of appropriate sentence structure. In this sentence, the plural *experts* needs a plural verb form, *have* (choice B). As written (choice A), the singular *has* is not in agreement with the plural subject (*experts*). The continuous verb form *having* (choice C) is inappropriate here, as the experts have already completed the action of proclaiming. Negating the action by inserting the word *haven't* (choice D) completely changes the meaning of the sentence and is incorrect here.

10. **F.** NO CHANGE
    G. He argues
    H. They argue
    J. It argues

The correct answer is H. Careful selection of the appropriate pronoun to replace an antecedent in a sentence is a critical skill for effective writing. The underlined pronoun in question is meant to replace the plural *experts* and requires a plural pronoun. As written (choice F), the feminine singular *she* is incorrect. The masculine singular *he* (choice G) and the gender-neutral singular *it* (choice J) are also incorrect. *They* (choice H) is the correct pronoun to replace *experts*, and *argues* needs to become *argue* to agree with the plural pronoun. Both words can be inserted into the sentence to check: *They argue that once newer listening technology becomes cheaper and more readily available, the need for stethoscopes will continue to decrease until they are simply no longer needed.*

• •

RHETORICAL SKILLS QUESTIONS

Rhetorical skills questions test your ability to comprehend a written passage and make decisions regarding the author's use of **strategy, organization,** and **style.**

Your job on test day will be to determine if the author made appropriate rhetorical choices within the context of the passage and to decide if the alternative options provided in the answer choices for each question enhance and improve the writing and make it more effective.

Why are rhetorical skills such a key part of the ACT test? Along with usage/mechanics, they are core skills for crafting effective, compelling, and persuasive pieces of writing and are important skills to have throughout your academic career and later on when you begin your professional career.

NOTE: Rhetorical skills and usage/mechanics questions appear *together* within the reading passages you'll encounter on test day. One of the challenges on the ACT is to recognize which type of question you're facing and which strategies you should use to arrive at the correct answers.

Practice and review *before* test day is the best strategy for getting good at identifying each question type and using the appropriate tools to get the right answers.

It should be clear why you should devote some time in your limited study schedule to building your skills in this area—especially if you've used the study plan strategy in Chapter 1 and have determined that English is one of your weaker subjects.

Compared to questions involving usage and mechanics, rhetorical skills issues can be a bit of a challenge to identify quickly in a piece of writing because the issues may not always be as immediately obvious as punctuation or spelling errors, for example.

Issues of **style, strategy,** and **organization** are often more subtle and require a deeper level of reading comprehension. Factor in the pressure of the ticking clock on test day, and you'll quickly understand why it's in your best interest to come equipped with a proven set of test-taking strategies and plenty of advance practice.

Take a look at the following brief paragraph:

> Ansel Adams is a world-famous twentieth-century photographer, whose work celebrated the romantic idealism of the American West. His lush black-and-white photo landscapes captured the majestic beauty of nature and natural landscapes. Today, people often use their cell phones to take photos. Adams was also a proactive environmentalist and an ardent believer in preserving nature whenever possible.

Grammatically speaking, there's nothing wrong with this paragraph. The punctuation is in the right place. The sentences are all well-constructed. However, upon closer analysis, there is something wrong with it. A sentence about cell phone photography in a paragraph devoted to highlighting a famous artist is ill-placed and reflects ineffective writing strategy. In fact, it's downright distracting!

This is the kind of subtle error you will have to recognize when answering rhetorical skills questions on the ACT.

Obviously, all rhetorical skills questions do not deal with off-topic details. Rhetorical skills questions focus on:

- Improving the overall **clarity** and **effectiveness** of a piece of writing

- Making sure that the **tone** and **mood** of a piece of writing are consistent and appropriate

- Ensuring that the piece reflects effective **organization** and structure

- Making sure that the piece is free from **off-topic** and **redundant details**

- Ensuring that **transitions** between ideas are strong

- Making sure that **wordiness** is avoided

 A key point to remember for test day: *Every decision you make on the ACT English test should accomplish the following goal: improve the quality and effectiveness of the written passages.*

On test day, and in the practice you'll find in this book, you'll see various portions of underlined text within the passages provided, as well as questions that will refer to rhetorical issues related to the underlined text.

You'll be tasked with making decisions about **adding, deleting, moving,** and **revising** words, sentences, and phrases within the passage, with the goal being to improve the **readability, appropriateness,** and **effectiveness** of the author's work.

Context Is Key!

Understanding passage **context** is crucial for making correct decisions on the ACT English test, ranging from grammar and word choices to the appropriateness of sentences and passage organization and construction.

Before choosing what may seem like an obvious answer choice, make sure you *fully* comprehend the context of each question as well as the author's perspective—it will be time well spent!

Let's move forward and take a look at each question type and strategies that you can quickly acquire for attacking them!

STYLE QUESTIONS

About 15–20 percent of questions you'll see on the ACT English test will assess issues of style, including word choice; the appropriateness of an author's tone and style; the effectiveness of different sentence elements; and avoiding ambiguous and redundant words, phrases, and sentences.

Here's an example of a style question that you may encounter on the ACT and how to effectively attack it:

Is it a good decision to require that all public school students in the United

States wear uniforms? There are strong voices both for and against this controversial

issue. Proponents of requiring students to wear uniforms to school argue that having students wear uniforms will make them more serious, committed, and engaged in the overall learning process. Supporters of the idea of having all public school
5
students wear uniforms claim that this will rob students of creative and individual self-expression and create unhappiness and cynicism among the student population.

5. **A.** NO CHANGE
   B. Endorsers
   C. Critics
   D. Thinkers

Attacking the question: This question is designed to assess your ability to decide if an author's word choice is appropriate given the context. The underlined word, *supporters*, would be appropriate to use only to describe individuals who endorse the specific issue at the heart of the paragraph—whether or not public school students should be required to wear uniforms to school. The sentence that contains the underlined word seems to be referring to individuals who *oppose* the idea, claiming, "that this will rob students of creative and individual self-expression and create unhappiness and cynicism among the student population." Therefore, using the word *supporters* (choice A) here is inappropriate. *Endorsers* (choice B) has the same problem, and *thinkers* (choice D) does not fit within the context of the sentence. *Critics* works well in the sentence—a critic of the initiative will likely have the opinion described here. **The correct answer is C.**

 ALERT: When tackling word choice questions, jump to the underlined word and the sentence it appears in—sometimes you can get a quick sense of what type of word is required here, as well as eliminate some obviously incorrect answer choices.

It's common for words that have the **direct opposite** meaning, as well as completely **off-topic** words, to appear among the answer choices. These can sometimes be quickly eliminated, leaving you with a clearer path to the correct answer.

TONE AND MOOD QUESTIONS

When you read a piece of writing, you should be able to determine how the writer *feels* about the topic and how the writer wants to make his or her readers feel.

Writers employ elements of tone and mood to create their intended effects:

- **Tone** refers to the author's attitude toward the subject she or he is discussing.

- **Mood** refers to the emotions that the piece of writing makes readers feel.

Sometimes, it's easy to recognize the intended tone of a piece; other times, the writer is subtler or purposefully deceptive. On the ACT test, rhetorical skills questions may ask you to identify the audience for a particular piece of writing or determine if the tone or mood of a passage is consistent.

You'll need to be able to recognize and fix logical inconsistencies on the ACT English test. To answer these types of questions, be sure to analyze the tone and mood of each passage and ask yourself the following questions:

- Does the writer seem to be in favor of a particular topic and then suddenly seem to take a negative stance without rhyme or reason?

- Does the writer seem to be establishing a cheerful mood and then suddenly things get dark for no logical reason?

WORDINESS QUESTIONS

Strong writing reflects a thorough understanding of **word economy**—making concise and effective points in as few words as possible. Unnecessary words, phrases, and sentences can turn a lean and mean piece of writing into a bloated, rambling, and confusing mess.

If a question on the ACT involves the option to delete text, this is often a signal that there are issues involving redundancy or wordiness to address. These types of questions are often posed at the sentence or paragraph level, and you may be able to answer them without having to analyze the entire passage—saving you time on test day.

On the ACT English test, you'll likely be tested on your ability to recognize and fix issues of **wordiness** and **redundancy** in the passages to improve the flow of sentences and improve the passages as a whole.

Don't delete necessary words!

Some tricky answer choices for wordiness questions may *seem* correct at first glance, because they correctly delete unnecessary words, but they are actually incorrect because they delete necessary words as well.

Correct answers will correct the wordiness *without* depriving the original sentence of key details and meaning.

Passive vs. Active Voice Questions

Another style judgment that writers must make is whether to use an active voice or a passive voice in their writing, as each has a distinct effect on a final written piece.

The **active voice** is typically employed in most forms of writing and demonstrates a clear and straightforward connection between the subject of a sentence and the action being performed. Sentences written in the active voice are typically less wordy and more emotionally powerful.

Sentences written in the **passive voice** typically describe the action of the sentence as indirectly happening to the subject. These sentences are often wordier, more meandering, and subtler.

On the ACT you may be asked to recognize the use of the passive voice as an ineffective option or be tasked with revising a sentence so that it employs an active voice.

Keep in mind that point of view is *not* being tested. When making decisions about an author's writing choices, your goal is *not* to revise the author's perspective or point of view to align it with yours.

Strategy Questions

Strategy questions on the ACT English test typically cover issues of **audience** and **purpose,** as well as the appropriate and relevant use of words, phrases, and sentences.

Let's quickly review some of the most widely used strategy question types on the ACT exam and how to effectively answer them.

Supporting Examples and Evidence Questions

As you already know, an effective piece of writing contains the following:

- A clear and compelling topic or central theme
- Supporting evidence designed to convince readers of the soundness of one's point of view.

On the ACT, you'll be tasked with making decisions on adding, revising, and deleting material and determining how this affects (strengthens or weakens) the overall effectiveness of the passages.

Here's an example of a strategy question that you may encounter on the ACT and how to effectively attack it:

[1] The rhinoceros is a large, herbivorous mammal that is native to Southern Asia and parts of Africa. [2] Rhinoceros are known for their massive size, thick hide, and large horn. [3] The antelope is another example of a horned herbivore. [4] The name *rhinoceros* is Latin for "nose horn." [5] The main species of rhino that have been classified by scientists include the white rhinoceros, black rhinoceros, Indian rhinoceros, Javan rhinoceros, and Sumatran rhinoceros.

6.   Which of the sentences provided should be deleted to enhance the overall focus and effectiveness of the paragraph?

   F.   Sentence 1
   G.   Sentence 2
   H.   Sentence 3
   J.   Sentence 4

Attacking the question: There's a quick strategy for addressing these sorts of "deletion" questions, a common type of question on the ACT:

   • Assess the **main idea** of the passage and the **focus** of the particular paragraph under analysis.

   • Look for the **connecting theme** between the answer choices and isolate the word, passage, phrase, sentence, or idea that *doesn't* quite fit with the others.

The correct answer is H. The first step is to identify the main idea of the paragraph, which is the rhinoceros. Next, let's look for a connecting theme among the answer choices. Choices F, G, and J all have a common connecting thread, providing readers with information pertaining to the central theme—the rhinoceros. Is there an answer choice that doesn't focus on the rhinoceros? Yes, and it is Sentence 3 that should be deleted—it takes the comment that rhinoceros have horns and goes off on a tangent involving another horned herbivore (*antelope*).

Check for a Stem

Strategy questions on the ACT English test often appear with a question stem, asking you to make a key decision about specific text, either currently within the passage or within the question and/or answer choices. A typical strategy question stem could be as follows:

Which of the following sentences should be deleted to reinforce the author's point of view that football is a violent sport?

Use this signal to help you quickly identify this question type and determine the best approach for getting the correct answer.

Pay attention to the precise location of details you are reviewing in a passage, which is typically provided in the question stem. This will provide you with crucial contextual cues for answering ACT English questions.

Off-Topic and Redundant Details Questions

Recognizing—and eradicating—irrelevant, tangential, or redundant information within a passage is a common question type on the ACT. Remember, your goal on the ACT English test is to improve the passages you'll encounter, which includes word economy and focus.

Bring your best editing eye on test day, and when you read each passage make note of anything that seems off, including redundant words and phrases and text that seems completely off-topic or just barely related to the central ideas of the passage.

Here's the bottom line: When you confront a tough question on the ACT English test, break it down, use your analytical skills, and hunt down the correct answer.

If you're reading a passage and something seems wrong to you, make note of it. Chances are it's *not* a coincidence and you'll come across it again when you're answering the questions.

Appropriate Expressions Questions

We'll say it again because it's important—*context is key*! When a writer is crafting a piece of writing, he or she has to think about the audience, which will help guide the appropriate presentation and tone. You shouldn't be using the same formal tone in a professional letter or technical academic journal article as you would in a casual e-mail or friendly letter.

You may be tasked with answering questions that test your ability to recognize appropriate and consistent writing, based on context.

You'll typically be given a piece of formal or informal writing and will need to determine the overall tone that's appropriate and whether or not there are parts of the writing or answer choices that are inappropriate given the context.

The following table contains examples of the kinds of formal and informal writing categories that you may encounter on test day.

Formal	Informal
Technical journal	Blog post
Academic paper	Entertainment magazine article
Newspaper article	Fictional story
Scientific study	Novel
Professional correspondence	Personal essay
Educational textbook	Post on social media site
Professional presentation	Friendly e-mail or tweet

Passages on the ACT won't *necessarily* announce the kinds of writing they are, but you'll be able to tell if they require formal or informal language based on how they're written.

ORGANIZATION QUESTIONS

Organization questions on the ACT English test will assess how well you can make decisions about effective **grouping, distribution,** and **arrangement of ideas** at the word, phrase, sentence, and paragraph levels.

Organization questions typically ask you to make passage- and paragraph-level decisions about appropriate sequencing of **opening, transitional,** and **closing sentences,** including **adding, deleting,** and **rearranging text** for maximum effectiveness.

Here's an example of an organization question that you may encounter on the ACT English test and how to effectively attack it:

[1] He's widely considered one of the most influential and respected Founding Fathers of America, even though he never became president. [2] Benjamin Franklin was born in 1705 to a family of modest means, but his natural talents and abilities helped him rise in prominence and influence. Franklin's skills were certainly not limited to politics—he was also a successful author, scientist, and inventor. [3] Among his most famous inventions were the Franklin Stove, bifocals, and the lightning rod. [4] What do you know about Benjamin Franklin?

7. Which of the sentences within the paragraph would be the most effective introductory sentence?

   A. Sentence 1
   B. Sentence 2
   C. Sentence 3
   D. Sentence 4

Attacking the question: Since we're being asked to determine which sentence would be the most effective introductory sentence, let's first determine what makes a good introductory sentence. A good introductory sentence clearly introduces and establishes the main idea or topic of a piece of writing and serves to capture the readers' attention, enticing them to continue reading. Which of the sentences in the answer choices best accomplishes this?

The correct answer is D. As written (choice A), readers may be initially confused, as we're not told whom the sentence is referring to. Choices B and C don't seem to introduce a topic; instead, they serve as informative sentences that are better suited within the body of the paragraph. Choice D effectively introduces the topic (Benjamin Franklin) and entices the reader to continue reading by posing a question.

When you're making decisions about sentence organization in a paragraph, keep in mind that a paragraph shouldn't begin with a pronoun—the noun it replaces should appear first. If you notice that the pronoun is preceding the noun it replaces, that may be a clue that something is out of order.

Recognizing Effective Opening Sentences

You've no doubt learned on school writing assignments that starting a piece of writing with a powerful, effective **opening sentence** is critical. The opening sentence sets the tone for all the other sentences that follow. It's also the sentence that most needs to hook the reader's interest. If you fail to capture a reader's attention early on, he or she may stop reading before reaching your key points!

On the ACT English test, you may be tasked with identifying effective opening sentences for the writing passages provided. Typically, you'll be given a series of possible intro- ductory sentences in a set of answer choices and will be asked to determine which is the most effective, given the context of the passage.

Here are a few quick tips for recognizing effective opening sentences:

- **They state the topic of the piece succinctly, confidently, and clearly.** (Example: Without question, Shakespeare was the finest playwright who has ever lived.)

- **They use exciting words to capture interest and attention.** (Example: Although William Shakespeare wrote his plays four hundred years ago, they still have the unbridled power to thrill and dazzle audiences today.)

- **They pose an intriguing or provocative question.** (Example: Who is generally considered to be the finest playwright who has ever lived?)

- **They use a point-counterpoint structure.** (Example: Most people think William Shakespeare is the finest playwright who has ever lived; however,... .)

- **They use a surprising fact or theory or a bit of interesting trivia.** (Example: William Shakespeare is generally regarded as the finest playwright who has ever lived, but there is a pervasive theory that he didn't actually write some of his most well-known plays.)

- **If appropriate, they try using a bit of humor.** (Example: If William Shakespeare is the great playwright everyone seems to think he is, why do I fall asleep every time I have to sit through one of his plays?)

- **They start with a poignant quote.** (Example: "The remarkable thing about Shakespeare is that he is really very good—in spite of all the people who say he is very good." –poet Robert Graves in "Sayings of the Week," The Observer, 1964)

Beware of the Answer-As-You-Go Approach!

When you're short on time, in preparing for the ACT or on test day, you may feel a strong urge to work as fast as possible and tackle each question quickly, sometimes without even reading the entire passages.

While this *can* be a good way to save time and work quickly through the exam, this strategy usually is more effective on usage and mechanics questions, where context is less relevant.

On rhetorical skills questions, the answer-as-you-go approach may backfire, particularly if there are carefully designed answer distracters that may *seem* correct—until you've read the passage and realize they were just cleverly designed traps.

Bottom line: Be careful!

Recognizing Effective Concluding Sentences

How you conclude a piece of writing is just as crucial as how you begin it. Remember, you want your writing to have two key impacts: *a great first impression* and *a memorable final impression*.

A great **conclusion** successfully ties up the ideas in a piece of writing and leaves a lasting impression. Not surprisingly, a strong closing should include many of the same elements of a strong introduction:

- Present a succinct, clear, and poignant wrap-up of core ideas.
- Reiterate key words or phrases from the passage.
- Consider a memorable quote or question that encapsulates your main point(s).
- Redefine an important idea or detail in the passage.
- Capture your perspective or point of view regarding the topic.

Recognizing Effective Transition Words and Phrases

An important factor in writing and organization is how ideas **connect** to each other. The right use of effective **transition words** and **phrases** in a piece of writing can make all the difference, and without them a compelling passage with powerful ideas could devolve into a rambling and incoherent mess that lacks authority.

Sometimes, writers use entire sentences to transition between ideas, as in the following example:

> People currently understand that the earth is spherical. However, this was not always the case. The common belief used to be that the earth was flat.

Notice how the transitional sentence helps connect the contrasting ideas (*people now know the earth is spherical; people once thought the earth was flat*) in an effective way.

Different transition words and phrases perform different functions, and your ability to recognize when transitions are being used correctly—and when they're not—will likely be put to the test on the ACT English test.

Use the following table for a quick review of transition words and phrases, which will help you to be able to quickly and effectively tackle questions involving transitions on test day.

Function	Transitional Words and Phrases
Introduction	*to begin, first of all, to start with*
An addition	*additionally, also, furthermore, in addition, moreover, secondly*
Clarification	*in other words, that is to say, to put it another way*
Passage of time	*afterwards, later, meanwhile, next, subsequently*
Examples	*for example, for instance, to demonstrate, specifically, to illustrate*
Cause	*because, since*
Effect	*as a result, consequently, therefore*
Comparison	*comparatively, in comparison, in similar fashion, likewise, similarly*
Contrast	*at the same time, however, in contrast, nevertheless, notwithstanding, on the contrary, yet*
Conclusion	*in conclusion, in short, to conclude, to sum up, to summarize, ultimately*

Organization for Clarity and Effect

No passage can simply rest on a powerful introduction, memorable conclusion, and strong transitions. For a piece of writing to be truly effective, every sentence and paragraph that follows needs to be on target and well organized.

Effectively tackling these sorts of questions begins even before you reach the questions.

While reading each passage, keep your "editor instincts" sharp. Note the type of organization it follows and get a sense of the structure and flow of the piece, which will help you identify any inconsistencies or illogical organization.

Here are some of the most common organizational formats:

- **Chronological:** information is organized by the time that the events occurred (can be forward or reverse).
- **Sequential:** often used when describing a process, information is organized by the order in which the steps or parts occur.
- **Order of importance:** information is organized by its relative value or importance (can be most to least important, or vice versa).

- **Compare and contrast:** often used when writing about two or more things, wherein one is discussed, then another to compare it with, and so on.

- **Cause and effect:** often used to describe a particular result and the events or reasons behind why that result occurred.

- **Issue/problem and solution:** in this type of organization, a central dilemma is discussed, followed by strategies for addressing/fixing the problem.

ANALYZING PASSAGES FOR RHETORICAL ISSUES

Let's look at some quick yet helpful strategies for effectively analyzing ACT English test passages and identifying rhetorical issues.

STRATEGY 1: ANALYZE THE PASSAGE TYPE

After you read each passage, take quick but careful note of what type of passage it is and what the main ideas are. Was it informational? Was it a persuasive piece? Does it present opposing sides of a controversial issue? Did it cover a significant event in history or a seminal figure? This process will help you identify—and remember—the main purpose of the passage, which will help you save time in the long run as you attack the questions.

STRATEGY 2: NOTE GENERAL ESSAY CONSTRUCTION AND ORGANIZATION

This step is especially useful for attacking rhetorical skills questions, which include issues of organization. Quickly note the general construction of the piece—this will really help you make determinations about proper placement and movement of new words, phrases, sentences, and paragraphs if the need arises in the questions that follow.

STRATEGY 3: NOTE ANY GLARING RHETORICAL ISSUES

Does something strange jump out at you while reading a passage? Is there information that's clearly missing, strangely worded, or glaringly out of place? If so, consider making a brief mental or written note about it. The passages you'll encounter on test day are carefully designed with meticulous attention to detail, so you can be sure that any glaring errors are intentional—and that you'll be tasked with fixing them when you start attacking the questions.

 *Don't* spend a great deal of time on these steps—remember, you need to maintain a fast and steady test-taking pace, and the last thing you want is to run out of time. However, it would be to your benefit to quickly go through these steps when attacking an English passage, regardless of what it's about, so you'll be well prepared to handle any type of rhetorical skills question that you may face.

PRACTICE: RHETORICAL SKILLS QUESTIONS

Now that you have a better understanding of the types of rhetorical skills questions that you'll encounter on the ACT English test, it's time to put your knowledge to work.

Read and carefully analyze this full-length, ACT-like English passage. The 10 questions that follow are designed to test your understanding of the passage, as well as your written rhetorical skills. Use the proven tips, strategies, and advice you've gotten so far in this chapter—alongside the wealth of knowledge you've acquired in your academic career—to answer them.

The detailed answer explanation that follows each question provides a complete breakdown and discussion for arriving at the correct answer. We strongly recommend that you review these explanations carefully to reinforce your correct decisions and see where you may have gone wrong. Use this information to help refine and direct your study time between now and test day—regardless of how limited it may be.

· ·

William Wegman: Weimaraners in Focus

[1]

[1] Weimaraners are tall, lanky dogs with silvery coats that are so distinctive they've earned the nickname "grey ghosts." It's hard to imagine a bigger fan of the breed than William Wegman. Wegman is an American-born artist and photographer who has dedicated a significant portion of his creative output to photographing these wonderful creatures in a variety of whimsical poses and outfits. He's a real example of an artist who has found a unique niche in popular culture and has used it to his advantage.

[2]

[1] William Wegman began his professional life as a classically trained painter, having earned both a bachelor of fine arts degree and a master of fine arts degree in painting in the 1960s. [2] As a result, he obtained his first Weimaraner while teaching
<u>   2</u>
at California State University. [3] It was a male puppy, who he named Man Ray, an homage to the famous twentieth-century visual artist and photographer. [4] Other famous dogs in popular culture include Lassie, Benji, and Rin Tin Tin. [5] It's safe to say

that with Man Ray—the dog, not the artist—Wegman's life-long fascination with the breed was fully cemented. 3

[3]

[1] Wegman quickly began his iconic and unforgettable artistic collaboration with Man Ray, whose distinctively deadpan countenance loomed large in a wide array of humorous photographs, videos, drawings, and other creative projects. [2] Wegman, currently in his 70s, lives in New York and Maine and is still an active presence in the art scene. 4 [3] The endearingly loyal Man Ray, as well as his owner, quickly garnered worldwide acclaim. [4] The duo continued to work together and delight the world until 1982, when Man Ray died. [5] The void that opened upon Man Ray's death did
5
not get filled until 1986, when Wegman received a new Weimaraner, a female who he
5
named Fay Ray, in homage to the famous *King Kong* actress. [6] Wegman and his new female companion carried on the tradition of celebrating the breed through artwork that has received both critical and popular acclaim. [7] Fay Ray's offspring, and their offspring as well, have even gotten into the act through the years.

[4]

[1] Among the honors that Wegman and his furry friends have earned over the years are pieces in the collections of the Whitney Museum of American Art, the Museum of Modern Art, the Los Angeles County Museum of Art, and the Smithsonian American Art Museum, television appearances on *Saturday Night Live*, *The Tonight Show*, and *Sesame Street*. [2] He continues to create work that celebrates and shares his love of Weimaraners. [3] It's a true testament to both the enduring legacy of Wegman's vision and the enduring beauty of the Weimaraner. 6 7

1. The writer wishes to open Paragraph 1 with a sentence that will set the theme and tone of the passage. Which of the following would most effectively accomplish this?

    A. Personally, I don't like dogs or pets of any kind.
    B. The bond between man and dog can endure the test of time.
    C. Here are a few reasons to consider attending art school.
    D. The history of Weimaraners is a fascinating tale of a wonderful breed.

The correct answer is B. This question asks you to make a decision about including additional supporting information in the passage. In particular, you're being tasked with adding an introductory sentence; introductory sentences should serve to grab the reader's attention and help set the theme and tone of the passage. The main idea of the passage is succinctly captured in choice B—this passage highlights the bond between William Wegman and his Weimaraners, and how it has endured the test of time. Choice A is a personal opinion about pets in general that does not fit in with the biographical nature of the passage. Choice C focuses on art school, which is just a small detail in Wegman's life and not the primary focus of the piece. Choice D reflects tangential information; although the passage focuses on this specific dog breed, it doesn't veer off on a discussion of their history.

2. **F.** NO CHANGE
    G. Therefore, he
    H. He
    J. They

The correct answer is H. This question is asking you to make a decision regarding the appropriate use of a transition word given the context of the sentences in question. Choice H is correct. As there is no causal link to highlight between these two sentences, no transition word is needed here. Using the phrase "as a result" (choice F) is inappropriate; this transitional phrase is used when information from the previous sentence directly links to a result in the following sentence, which is not the case here. Wegman obtaining Man Ray was not a result of Wegman having obtained college degrees, so it is an illogical transition. Choice G is similarly inappropriate. *Therefore* is used to demonstrate a causal link, which does not exist here. Although Choice J correctly avoids an unnecessary transition, it is an incorrect pronoun choice.

3. For the sake of unity and coherence, which of the following sentences does not belong in Paragraph 2?

    A. Sentence 1
    B. Sentence 2
    C. Sentence 3
    D. Sentence 4

The correct answer is D. This question is designed to gauge your ability to identify superfluous or inappropriate textual information within a piece of writing, in an effort to enhance the overall economy of the piece. This paragraph focuses primarily on the genesis of the bond between Wegman and Weimaraners, in particular his beloved Man Ray. Choice D lists the sentence among the answer choices that does not tie into this central idea; although it's a bit of interesting trivia, a list of other famous dogs does not support the main idea of the paragraph or passage and should be removed. Choice A provides appropriate contextual background regarding Wegman's professional career. Choices B and C provide key details of the beginning of Wegman's fascination with Weimaraners and his bond with Man Ray.

4.   What organizational strategy should the writer employ for Sentence 2 in Paragraph 3?

    F.   Move it to the beginning of Paragraph 2.
    G. Move it before Sentence 2 in Paragraph 2.
    H. Move it after Sentence 7 in Paragraph 3.
    J.   Move it before Sentence 2 in Paragraph 4.

The correct answer is J. This question is asking you to make a strategic contextual decision regarding information in the passage and where it best fits into the overall structure of the piece. The second sentence of Paragraph 3 focuses on Wegman's current status, which best fits into Paragraph 4. In particular, Sentence 2 of paragraph 4 discusses the fact that Wegman continues to produce artwork—the sentence in question would best fit before this one. Paragraph 2 focuses on Wegman's early professional years and the beginning of his relationship with Weimaraners, so choices F and G aren't appropriate choices. Paragraph 3 (choice C) highlights Wegman's success with Man Ray, and later Fay Ray, and wouldn't be the best place for this sentence.

5.   If the writer deleted the underlined portion of the sentence, the essay would primarily lose:

    A. a poignant reminder of the enduring bond between Wegman and Man Ray.
    B. a snapshot of Wegman's least productive professional period.
    C. coverage of Wegman's obsessive hunt for a new Weimaraner.
    D. the reason why Wegman decided to end his professional teaching career.

The correct answer is A. This question is designed to assess your understanding of the effect of deleting text from a written passage, which requires both a small-scale understanding of the text in question and a holistic-level understanding of the written piece. In this instance, deleting the underlined text would obscure the fact that Wegman felt a void in his life after Man Ray's death, and weaken the reader's perception of the enduring bond between Wegman and Man Ray, so choice A is correct. This underlined portion of text does not represent a snapshot of Wegman's least productive professional period (choice B), coverage of Wegman's obsessive hunt for a new Weimaraner (choice C), or a reason why Wegman decided to end his professional teaching career (choice D).

6. Which of the following could successfully be added to the essay's concluding sentence to support its primary purpose?

F. that both have been so successful at capturing the imagination and remaining on the pop culture radar for so long.

G. despite the fact that Wegman had hoped that he could incorporate other dog breeds into his artwork.

H. and Wegman hopes that new generations of artists embrace the Weimaraner and use them in their artistic creations.

J. although it became apparent to Wegman in his later years that Weimaraners can be moody and difficult to work with.

The correct answer is F. This question is asking you to help craft an effective concluding statement for the passage. An effective conclusion effectively ties up the central themes in the passage and, when particularly effective, leaves a lasting impression on readers. Choice F accurately captures the intended spirit of the passage, that Wegman's distinguished career and popularity, spanning decades, is a testament to both the enduring legacy of his vision and his bond with the Weimaraner. Choice G is incorrect, as the passage makes no mention of a desire on Wegman's part to incorporate other dog breeds into his artwork. Choice H is incorrect because the passage doesn't mention that Wegman hopes that new generations of artists embrace the Weimaraner and use them in their artistic creations. Choice J is incorrect because the passage doesn't mention that Wegman thought that Weimaraners can be moody and difficult to work with.

7. Which of the following sequences will make the flow of the paragraphs within the passage most logical?

A. NO CHANGE

B. 3, 4, 1, 2

C. 2, 1, 4, 3

D. 1, 2, 4, 3

The correct answer is A. This question is designed to gauge your ability to recognize effective passage organization—and recognize when there's an issue with organization in a given piece of writing. As written (choice A), the passage reflects effective organization. Paragraph 1 appropriately introduces the topic of the essay, namely William Wegman and Weimaraners. Paragraph 2 delves into Wegman's early professional years and the genesis of his bond with Weimaraners. Paragraph 3 covers his relationship with his favorite Weimaraners as well as his prolific artistic pursuits through the years. Paragraph 4 covers Wegman's later years and accolades. The organization reflected in the other answer choices (choices B, C, and D) either doesn't materially improve the essay or detracts from its effectiveness.

8. The writer wants to add the following information to the essay:

    William Wegman's first professional teaching experience was in the fine arts.

    This information would most logically be placed in which paragraph?

    F. Paragraph 1
    G. Paragraph 2
    H. Paragraph 3
    J. Paragraph 4

The correct answer is G. This question is asking you to assess the relevance and logical placement of new textual information within a provided passage. The sentence in question discusses Wegman's early professional teaching experience, which would fit quite well in Paragraph 2 (choice G), which covers Wegman's early professional experience in academia. Paragraph 1 (choice F) introduces the topic of the essay, William Wegman and Weimaraners. Paragraph 3 (choice H) covers Wegman's relationship with his favorite Weimaraners, as well as his prolific artistic pursuits through the years. Paragraph 4 (choice J) covers Wegman's later years and accolades.

9. Which of the following information, if added to the essay, would not serve to support the author's main theme?

    A. Some examples of Wegman's most commercially successful artistic works featuring Weimaraners.
    B. A description of how Wegman prepares for a photo shoot with his beloved dogs.
    C. Where Wegman first saw and obtained his beloved Man Ray.
    D. A review of other dog breeds that come from the same country that Weimaraners do.

The correct answer is D. This question requires you to recognize the central theme of the passage as well as what information could potentially serve to support it—and not support it. Choices A, B, and C would help to support the main purpose of the passage, which is to highlight William Wegman, his artwork, and his relationship with Weimaraners. Choice D would be tangential information at best and would not support the passage's main idea, so it is the correct answer choice.

10. Suppose the writer's primary purpose had been to describe how an individual can overcome adversity and achieve success. Does this passage accomplish that purpose?

F. Yes, because working with animals can be challenging, but Wegman had discovered a way to make this work for him and find success.

G. Yes, because Wegman never felt he had any artistic talent while growing up, but as an adult he was still able to become a successful artist.

H. No, because the essay does not describe a specific adversity that Wegman had overcome on his path to becoming a successful artist.

J. No, because the challenges that Wegman had faced early in his life were relatively easy to overcome along his path to success.

The correct answer is H. This question is designed to assess your ability to analyze a passage and determine if it effectively achieves a specific purpose. Does this essay describe how an individual can overcome adversity and achieve success? A careful analysis of the piece will uncover the fact that the essay does not describe a specific adversity that Wegman had overcome on his path to becoming a successful artist, so it clearly doesn't accomplish this purpose and choice H is correct. Choice J is incorrect because the passage does not cover any challenges that Wegman faced early in his life. Choices F and G are incorrect as well; as discussed, the passage does not accomplish the primary purpose highlighted in the question.

SUMMING IT UP

- **End-of-sentence punctuation** includes the period, the exclamation mark, and the question mark. When a sentence ends with quotation marks used to indicate dialogue, the end-of-sentence punctuation is placed *within* the quotation marks. If the quotation marks indicate a title and placing end-of-sentence punctuation within the marks might give the false impression that the mark is part of the title, the end-of-sentence punctuation is placed *after* the closing quotation marks.

- Remember the following punctuation and each mark's function:

  ○ **Commas** are used to separate introductory words and phrases, clauses in compound sentences, nonrestrictive phrases, items in series, appositives, and quotations.

  ○ **Apostrophes** are used to separate letters in contractions and indicate possession. When indicating possession, an apostrophe is usually followed by the letter -*s*. However, no extra -*s* is necessary if the possessing word ends in -*s* and is not someone's name.

  ○ **Colons** are used to introduce a list of items or offset an example.

  ○ **Dashes** are used to offset examples and indicate a pause or interruption in dialogue.

  ○ **Parentheses** often enclose tangential or bonus information that cannot be fit into a sentence naturally.

- Remember the parts of speech and their functions and relationships with other parts of speech:

    ○ **Plural nouns** do not always end with -s; there are several variations among plural nouns depending on the words' letters. **Collective nouns** are not plural nouns; they are singular.

    ○ **Subjects and verbs** are in agreement when they are in the same form. They both need to be either singular or plural and not a combination of both forms.

    ○ **Pronouns and antecedents**—the words for which the pronouns stand in—need to be in agreement. They need to agree in terms of number, gender, and person.

    ○ **Relative pronouns** signal relative clauses, which are used to describe nouns; **reflexive pronouns** refer back to their subjects; **interrogative pronouns** are used when asking a question; **possessive pronouns** show ownership.

    ○ **Comparative adjectives and adverbs** are used when comparing two things. They usually end in -er. **Superlative adjectives and adverbs** are used when comparing three or more things. They usually end in -est.

    ○ **Verb tense** indicates when the action the verb describes takes place.

- **Idioms** use words to mean something other than their literal meanings.

- **Prepositional phrases** combine a preposition with other words to indicate direction and time. Their particular word often depends on common usage.

- **Independent clauses** contain a subject and a verb and make sense on their own. Although they contain a subject and a verb, **subordinate clauses** cannot stand alone and must be linked to an independent clause to be correct.

- **Fragments** are partial sentences that lack either a subject or a verb.

- **Run-on sentences** are grammatically incorrect compound or complex sentences that fail to link their parts with the necessary conjunction or punctuation.

- **Modifiers** are words and phrases that describe. **Misplaced modifiers** are not placed next to the words they are supposed to modify. **Dangling modifiers** fail to modify any word at all.

- **Parallel structure** occurs when all groups of words in a sentence are written in the same tense and form. When such words are not in the same tense or form, the sentence is grammatically incorrect. Failing to pair correlative conjunctions correctly also violates parallel structure.

- Rhetorical Skills questions test your ability to analyze a written passage and make decisions regarding the author's deployment of **strategy, organization,** and **style.**

    ○ You'll be tasked with determining whether the authors made appropriate rhetorical choices within the context of the passages, as well as decide if the alternative options provided in the answer choices of each question serve to enhance and improve the writing.

- Rhetorical Skills questions focus on improving the overall clarity and effectiveness of a piece of writing, making sure that the tone and mood of a piece of writing are consistent and appropriate, that the piece reflects effective organization and is free from off-topic and redundant details, that transitions between ideas are strong, and that wordiness is avoided.
  - **Tone** refers to the author's attitude toward the subject she or he is discussing; **mood** refers to the emotions that the piece of writing makes readers feel.
  - The **active voice** demonstrates a clear and straightforward connection between the subject of a sentence and the action being performed; sentences written in the **passive voice** typically describe the action of the sentence as indirectly happening to the subject.
  - **Supporting examples** and **evidence** questions will test your ability to recognize and add clear and compelling supporting evidence to a passage, to convince readers of the soundness of one's point of view.
  - An effective **opening sentence** sets the tone for all the other sentences that follow. It's also the sentence that most needs to hook the reader's interest. A great **conclusion** serves to tie up the ideas in the writing and leaves a lasting impression.
- Follow the quick yet helpful steps for attacking ACT English passages:
  - Step 1: Analyze the passage type.
  - Step 2: Note general essay construction and organization.
  - Step 3: Note any glaring rhetorical issues.
- To attack Rhetorical Skills questions:
  - Break down and analyze the reading passages.
  - Identify each type of question you encounter.
  - Make sure you're fully aware of what you're being asked.
  - Be sure that when you select an answer you're taking into account the proper context. Noting the precise location of details you are reviewing in a passage will provide you with crucial contextual cues for answering a question.

CHAPTER 4:
THE ACT® MATHEMATICS TEST

OVERVIEW

- Test Overview
- Basic Arithmetic
- Exponents
- Scientific Notation
- Radicals
- Ratios, Proportions, and Percentages
- Linear Equations in One Variable
- Absolute Value
- Algebraic Expressions
- Elementary Counting Techniques
- Simple Probability and Descriptive Statistics
- Lines

- Rational Expressions
- Complex Numbers
- Quadratic Equations and the Quadratic Formula
- Linear Inequalities
- Systems of Linear Equations
- Basic Coordinate Geometry
- Functions
- Matrices
- Basic Elements of Geometry
- Right Triangle Trigonometry
- Summing It Up

TEST OVERVIEW

The second part of your ACT experience will be the ACT Mathematics test. This multiple-choice assessment gives you 60 minutes to answer 60 questions. That allots—you guessed it—an average of 1 minute to answer each question. If that sounds super-fast, well, it is—that's why it's essential to become familiar with all the terms and concepts you'll see on the test. Familiarity means you can read a question and dive right in, rather than stopping to figure out what exactly is it asking you to do.

The ACT Mathematics test assesses your ability in three major areas:

1. Pre-Algebra/Elementary Algebra (40% of the entire test)

2. Intermediate Algebra/Coordinate Geometry (30% of the entire test)

3. Plane Geometry/Trigonometry (30% of the entire test)

The skills tested are ones covered in high school courses, typically up to the beginning of 12th grade.

Unlike the other ACT sections, each math question is accompanied by 5 answer choices, not 4.

This chapter reviews the most common vocabulary, concepts, and procedures that come up on the ACT Mathematics test—we want to make sure you don't miss *any* question on test day because you're tripped up by an unfamiliar term. We'll make our way fast and furious through every major concept on the test, showing you the formulas, graphs, and images you'll need to know alongside test-like questions.

Though it's ASAP-style, this chapter is as comprehensive as can be—you'll just have to work extra hard in the time you have to review the math content we'll throw your way!

Remember, although you are allowed to use certain calculators on the ACT Mathematics test (see the Introduction for a complete list), a calculator is *not* required. You technically are able to answer every single test question *without* using a calculator.

BASIC ARITHMETIC

In order to perform almost any calculation, you must be familiar with the set of **whole numbers**: 1, 2, 3, 4, ... The following divisibility rules provide a way to determine if a number can divide evenly into another whole number.

Whole Number	A whole number *n* is divisible by the number in the left column if . . .
2	The number *n* ends in 0, 2, 4, 6, or 8.
3	The digit sum of *n* (i.e., the sum of all digits in the numeral *n*) is a multiple of 3.
4	The last two numbers of *n*, taken as a number in and of itself, is a multiple of 4.
5	The number *n* ends in 0 or 5.
6	The number *n* is divisible by both 2 and 3.
9	The digit sum of *n* is divisible by 9.
10	The number *n* ends in 0.

Keep these additional rules in mind any time you make calculations, big and small:

- A whole number is **even** if it is multiple of 2; it is **odd** if this is not the case.
- A whole number n greater than 1 whose only factors are the numbers 1 and n is called **prime**; if it has other factors, it is called **composite**.
- Every composite number can be written as a product of **prime** numbers; the product is called the prime **factorization** of the number, like $30 = 2 \times 3 \times 5$.

Try the following arithmetic question.

. . . .

What is the largest possible value for the product xy if $x + y = 18$ and x and y are both prime numbers?

- **A.** 17
- **B.** 81
- **C.** 65
- **D.** 77
- **E.** 80

The correct answer is D. Two pairs of prime numbers sum to 18: $7 + 11$, $5 + 13$. The largest resulting product is $7 \times 11 = 77$, so 77 is the largest possible value of xy if x and y are both prime numbers for which $x + y = 18$. For choice A, be careful—the number 1 is not considered to be prime. Choice B is incorrect because it is the result of using 9 and 9, but 9 is not prime. Choice C is incorrect because although it is the product of two primes, it is not the largest possible value. Choice E is the result of using 8 and 10, neither of which is prime.

. . . .

The set of **integers** is comprised of the whole numbers, their negatives, and zero. You must be careful with negative signs when performing arithmetic operations on integers.

Here are the rules to keep in mind when performing operations with negatives.

1. $-(-a) = a$, for any integer a.

2. $a - (-b) = a + b$, for any integers a, b.

3. Sums of positive integers are positive, and sums of negative integers are negative.

4. A product involving an even number of negative integers is positive.

5. A product involving an odd number of negative integers is negative.

FRACTIONS AND DECIMALS

A **fraction** (or **rational number**) is a quotient of whole numbers, denoted $\frac{a}{b}$, where $b \neq 0$.

- A fraction is **simplified** or in **reduced form** if the numerator and denominator do not share common factors.

- If $a \neq 0$, the **reciprocal** of $\frac{a}{b}$, can be computed by flipping the fraction to get $\frac{b}{a}$.

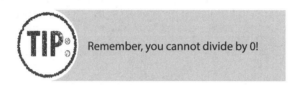 **TIP** Remember, you cannot divide by 0!

The rules of fraction arithmetic are as follows:

Arithmetic Operation	Rule (in symbols)	In words...
Sum/Difference	$\frac{a}{b} \pm \frac{c}{d} = \frac{ad \pm cb}{bd}$	First get a common denominator. Apply it to the fractions and then add the numerators.
Simplifying/Reducing	$\frac{a \cdot c}{b \cdot c} = \frac{a}{b}$	Cancel like factors in the numerator and denominator to reduce it to lowest terms.
Multiplying by –1	$-\frac{a}{b} = \frac{-a}{b} = \frac{a}{-b}$	When multiplying a fraction by –1, you can multiply either the top or bottom by –1, but NOT both.
Product	$\frac{a}{b} \cdot \frac{c}{d} = \frac{ac}{bd}$	When multiplying two fractions, simply multiply their numerators and denominators.

Arithmetic Operation	Rule (in symbols)	In words...
Quotient	$\dfrac{a}{b} \div \dfrac{c}{d} = \dfrac{a}{b} \cdot \dfrac{d}{c} = \dfrac{ad}{bc}$ $\dfrac{\frac{a}{b}}{\frac{c}{d}}$ means $\dfrac{a}{b} \div \dfrac{c}{d}$	When dividing two fractions, start by converting to a multiplication problem.

Sometimes, fractions will be written as **mixed numbers.** It is often easier to convert them to improper fractions in order to make calculations; for example, $7\dfrac{3}{4} = \dfrac{4 \cdot 7 + 3}{4} = \dfrac{31}{4}$.

Arithmetic involving **decimals** is the same as for integers, with the extra step of correctly positioning the decimal point. The same sign conversions for integers apply here. The following are some rules of thumb to apply when working with decimals:

- When *adding or subtracting decimals*, line up the decimal points and add or subtract as you would whole numbers, keeping the decimal point in the same position.

- When *multiplying* decimals, multiply the numbers as you would whole numbers. To determine the position of the decimal point, count the number of digits present after the decimal point in all numbers being multiplied, move that many steps from the right of the product, and place the decimal point.

A fraction can be converted into a decimal by dividing the numerator by the denominator. All such decimals must either terminate or repeat. Any decimal that neither repeats nor terminates is called **irrational.**

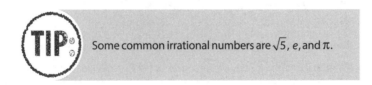

Some common irrational numbers are $\sqrt{5}$, e, and π.

Number Properties

The following properties apply for *all* real numbers *a, b,* and *c*:

Property	Rule (in symbols)	In words...
Associative	$(a+b)+c=a+(b+c)$ $(a \cdot b) \cdot c = a \cdot (b \cdot c)$	You can group the terms of a sum or a product in any manner you like.
Commutative	$a+b=b+a$ $a \cdot b = b \cdot a$	You can add or multiply real numbers in any order.
Distributive	$a \cdot (b \pm c) = a \cdot b \pm a \cdot c$	To multiply a sum or difference by a real number, multiply each term by the number and add/subtract the results.
FOIL	$(a+b) \cdot (c+d) =$ $a \cdot c + a \cdot d + b \cdot c + b \cdot d$	This follows from using the distributive property twice. The acronym FOIL means "First, Outer, Inner, Last" and signifies all combinations of terms to be multiplied.

Simplifying an arithmetic expression involving multiple types of numbers and operations requires the use of the **order of operations:**

- **Step 1:** Simplify all expressions contained within parentheses.
- **Step 2:** Simplify all expressions involving exponents.
- **Step 3:** Perform all multiplication and division as they arise from left to right.
- **Step 4:** Perform all addition and subtraction as they arise from left to right.

If there are multiple groupings, apply the same steps *within* each grouping.

EXPONENTS

If b and n are natural numbers, then $b^n = \underbrace{b \times \ldots \times b}_{n \text{ times}}$. Here, b is called the **base** and n is the **exponent.**

The following table features the rules you should know when working with exponents. Assume that the bases a and b are greater than 1 and that the exponents n and m are real numbers.

	Exponent Rule (in symbols)	Interpretation
1.	$a^0 = 1$	The result of raising any nonzero real number to the zero power is 1.
2.	$a^{-n} = \dfrac{1}{a^n}$ $a^n = \dfrac{1}{a^{-n}}$	A term in the numerator that is raised to a negative exponent is equivalent to a term in the denominator with the same base, but positive exponent, and vice versa.
3.	$a^n \cdot a^m = a^{n+m}$	When multiplying terms with the same base being raised to powers, just add the powers.
4.	$\dfrac{a^n}{a^m} = a^{n-m}$	When dividing terms with the same base being raised to powers, just subtract the powers.
5.	$\left(a^n\right)^m = a^{n \cdot m}$	When raising a term that is already raised to a power to another power, just multiply the powers.
6.	$(a \cdot b)^n = a^n \cdot b^n$	When raising a product to a power, apply the power to each term and multiply the results.
7.	$\left(\dfrac{a}{b}\right)^n = \dfrac{a^n}{b^n}$	When raising a quotient to a power, apply the power to each term and divide the results.

Try your hand at tackling an exponent problem.

. . . .

$(0.01)^{-4} =$

- **F.** 10^{-8}
- **G.** 10^{-6}
- **H.** 10^{-4}
- **J.** 10^4
- **K.** 10^8

The correct answer is K. The value in parentheses, 0.01, can be rewritten as 10^{-2} (since it is equivalent to $\frac{1}{100}$). Therefore, $(0.01)^{-4} = (10^{-2})^{-4} = 10^{(-2)(-4)} = 10^8$. Choice F is incorrect because 0.01 equals 10^{-2}, not 10^2. Choice G is incorrect because you added the exponents but should have multiplied them. Choice H is incorrect because the value in parentheses is 10^{-2}, not 10. Choice J is incorrect because the value in parentheses is 10^{-2}, not 10^{-1}.

. . . .

TIP Always look for new ways to rewrite numbers presented on the ACT, as in this sample question. A simple rewrite can save you lots of time when solving a problem.

SCIENTIFIC NOTATION

Decimals that have several digits before and/or after the decimal point are often expressed using **scientific notation.** This notation is simply a way of expressing the decimal as a product of another decimal comprised of a single digit to the left of the decimal point and an appropriate power of 10. For example,

$$14,201 = 1.4201 \times 10^4 \text{ and } 0.000052 = 5.2 \times 10^{-5}$$

RADICALS

The **square root** of a nonnegative real number a is another number b with a square of a: that is $b^2 = a$. In such case, we write $\sqrt{a} = b$. The following are useful properties of radicals to master before the exam.

	Radical Rule (in Symbols)	Interpretation
1.	$\left(\sqrt{a}\right)^2 = a$	Raising a square root to the second power gives back the original radicand.
2.	$\sqrt{a \cdot b} = \sqrt{a} \cdot \sqrt{b}$, for $a \geq 0$ and $b \geq 0$.	The square root of a product is the product of the square roots.
3.	$\sqrt{\dfrac{a}{b}} = \dfrac{\sqrt{a}}{\sqrt{b}}$, for $a \geq 0$ and $b \geq 0$.	The square root of a quotient is the quotient of the square roots.

If the terms of a sum or difference of radicals have the same radical parts, just add or subtract the coefficients:

$$2\sqrt{11}-5\sqrt{11}=(2-5)\sqrt{11}=-3\sqrt{11}$$

Beware: You can't treat the combination of two radical parts the same way. Here is an example of how to add radicals that have different radical parts that cannot be combined:

$$3\sqrt{13}+3\sqrt{3}-5\sqrt{13}=$$
$$(3-5)\sqrt{13}+3\sqrt{3}=$$
$$-2\sqrt{13}+3\sqrt{3}$$

Now, test your skill with the following question.

· ·

If x is a real number such that $x^3 = 122$, between which two consecutive integers does x lie on the number line?

    A.   2 and 3
    B.   3 and 4
    C.   4 and 5
    D.   5 and 6
    E.   6 and 7

The correct answer is C. The problem is asking you to find two consecutive integers, the first with a cube less than 122, and the second with a cube greater than 122. Use the answer choices to help you. The cubes of 2, 3, 4, 5, and 6 are, respectively: 8, 27, 64, 125, and 216. Since 122 falls between 64 and 125, you know that x is between 4 and 5, and you do not need to go any further. As such, the other choices are not possible.

· ·

RATIOS, PROPORTIONS, AND PERCENTAGES

A **ratio** is a comparison of one quantity x to another quantity y, expressed as a fraction $\dfrac{x}{y}$ or sometimes using the notation $x{:}y$ (read "x to y"). In words, this is interpreted as, "for every x of one type, there are y of the second type." The order in which the quantities appear in a ratio is important because we represent the ratio as a fraction.

A **proportion** is an equation relating two ratios. In symbols, a proportion is expressed by setting two fractions equal to each other, say $\dfrac{a}{b}=\dfrac{c}{d}$. Proportions arise when solving many different types of problems, including changing units of measure and similar triangles. Proportions are often formulated when one ratio is known and one of the two quantities in an equivalent ratio is unknown.

The word **percent** means per hundred. A percent is used to express the number of *parts* of a *whole*. For instance, 34 percent means "34 parts of 100," which can be expressed as the fraction $\frac{34}{100}$ and as the decimal 0.34. It is also denoted as 34%. These three representations are all equivalent.

- To convert from decimal form to percent form, simply move the decimal point two units to the right and affix the % sign.

- To convert from percent form to decimal form, move the decimal point two units to the left, insert a decimal point and drop the % sign.

Problems involving percentages can be whittled down to three varieties:

Problem Type	Method Used to Solve the Problem	Example
Compute x% of y.	Convert x% to a decimal and multiply by y.	**Q:** Compute 73% of 8. **A:** $0.73(8) = 5.84$
What percent of x is y?	Divide x by y.	**Q:** What percent of 150 is 90? **A:** $\frac{90}{150} = 0.60 = 60\%$
x is y% of what number z?	Convert y% to a decimal, multiply it by z, and set equal to x. Solve for z.	**Q:** 33 is 40% of what number z? **A:** Solve $0.40z = 33$ to get $z = 82.5$.

Solve the following percentage question.

. . . .

Mary answered 37 of the 42 questions on her job application exam correctly. What percent of the questions did Mary answer incorrectly?

F. $\dfrac{37}{42} \times 100\%$

G. $\dfrac{5}{42} \times 100\%$

H. $\dfrac{5}{42 \times 100}\%$

J. $\dfrac{37}{42 \times 100}\%$

K. $\dfrac{42}{100\%} \times 5$

The correct answer is G. If Mary answered 37 of the 42 questions correctly, then she answered $42 - 37 = 5$ incorrectly. By definition, the percent is equal to $\frac{\text{part}}{\text{whole}} \times 100\%$. So, Mary answered $\frac{5}{42} \times 100\%$ of the questions incorrectly, which is choice G. Choice F is the percentage of questions she answered *correctly*. Choices H and J are incorrect because the 100 should be in the numerator so you are taking a proportion of 100%. Choice J also is configuring the percentage she answered *correctly*. Choice K is incorrect because you need to interchange the 42 and 100% in this expression.

. . . .

LINEAR EQUATIONS IN ONE VARIABLE

Linear equations are equations in which the variable is raised to the first power, like $5x = 13$ and $4(y - 1) = 5$. The process of solving linear equations is as follows:

- **Step 1:** Simplify the equation by clearing fractions—multiply all terms by the least common denominator of all fractions appearing in the equation.

- **Step 2:** Use the order of operations and the distributive property of multiplication to simplify both sides of the equation.

- **Step 3:** Isolate the variable on one side. The basic rule to remember is *balancing* both sides of the equations. If you add or subtract a number from one side, you MUST do so to the other; if you divide or multiply one side by a number, you MUST do it to the other as well.

For example, if $3(1 - 2x) + 4(2x - 1) = -x$, what is the value of x^2?

First, you must solve the given equation:

$$3(1 - 2x) + 4(2x - 1) = -x$$
$$3 - 6x + 8x - 4 = -x$$
$$2x - 1 = -x$$
$$2x + x = 1$$
$$3x = 1$$
$$x = \frac{1}{3}$$

But that's not all!

Next, compute x^2 to get $\left(\frac{1}{3}\right)^2 = \frac{1}{9}$.

ALWAYS read, and then reread, the question stem to make sure you are answering the exact question asked. The ACT will feature several questions that ask you to solve a problem, and then perform an additional operation to reach the correct answer. Don't stop in the middle of a problem!

Sometimes, a linear equation can involve more than one letter and you can be asked to solve for one of them in terms of the others. The same exact procedure applies!

Put your knowledge to work solving this problem.

. . . .

If $8x - 5 = 14x - 17$, then $-3x^3 =$

    A. -8
    B. -18
    C. -24
    D. 2
    E. -216

The correct answer is C. First, solve the given equation for x:

$$8x - 5 = 14x - 17$$
$$-5 = 6x - 17$$
$$12 = 6x$$
$$2 = x$$

Now, evaluate $-3x^3$ at $x = 2$ to get $-3(2)^3 = -3(8) = -24$. So, choice C is the correct answer. Choice A is incorrect because you forgot to multiply by 3. When computing $(2)^3$, you multiplied the base times the exponent to get choice B, but this is not how you compute a power. Choice D is incorrect because this is the value of x, not $-3x^3$. For choice E, you cubed the -3 as well, but in the expression $-3x^3$, the -3 is not cubed.

. . . .

ABSOLUTE VALUE

For any real number a, we use the **absolute value** of a, denoted $|a|$, to measure the distance between a and 0. The definition is given in two parts:

$$|a| = \begin{cases} a, & \text{if } a \geq 0 \\ -a, & \text{if } a < 0 \end{cases}$$

For instance, $|9| = 9$ and $|-9| = -(-9) = 9$. This definition works for *any type* of real number. The following are some useful properties of absolute value to review before test day:

	Property (in Symbols)	Property (in Words)
1.	$|a| = b$ whenever $a = b$ or $a = -b$	Both b and $-b$ are $|b|$ units from the origin.
2.	$|a \cdot b| = |a| \cdot |b|$	The absolute value of a product is the product of the absolute values.
3.	$\left|\dfrac{a}{b}\right| = \dfrac{|a|}{|b|}$, whenever $b \neq 0$	The absolute value of a quotient is the quotient of the absolute values.
3.	When a and b, have opposite signs, $|a + b| \neq |a| + |b|$	When a and b have opposite signs, the absolute value of the sum of two numbers is not equal to the sum of the absolute values of those two numbers.

Here's another try at a test-like question.

. . . .

$-9 - |-9| =$

    F.   −9
    G.   −18
    H.   0
    J.   18
    K.   81

The correct answer is G. First, note that $|-9| = 9$. So, $-9 - |-9| = -9 - 9$. Now, just add these integers as usual to get −18. So, the correct is G. In choice F, you dropped one of the two terms from the expression. Choice H is incorrect because $-|-9| = -9$, not 9. In choice J, the sign is wrong. In choice K, you multiplied −9 and $-|-9|$ instead of adding them.

. . . .

ALGEBRAIC EXPRESSIONS

As we mentioned at the start of this chapter, knowing vocabulary is often half the battle when approaching ACT Mathematics questions. Don't miss out on solving a problem because you *do* know the math but *don't* understand what the question is asking.

Here are the terms you should know when working with expressions:

- A **variable** is an unknown quantity represented by a letter, like x, y, or z.
- A **constant** is a real number whose value does not change.
- A **term** is a variable or constant, or products of powers thereof.
- An **algebraic expression** is an arithmetic combination of terms, like $5x - 3yz$.
- If two terms have the same "variable part," they are called **like terms.**

When evaluating algebraic expressions for specific values of the variables, simply substitute the values in and simplify the arithmetic expression.

If $a = 4$, then compute $3a(a - 1)^2 + a \div 2$.

First, plug $a = 4$ into the expression:

$$3a(a-1)^2 + a \div 2 = 3(4)(4-1)^2 + 4 \div 2$$

This is just an arithmetic expression, so use the order of operations to simplify it:

$$
\begin{aligned}
3(4)(4-1)^2 + 4 \div 2 &= 3(4)(3)^2 + 4 \div 2 \\
&= 3(4)(9) + 4 \div 2 \\
&= 108 + 2 \\
&= 110
\end{aligned}
$$

Since variables represent real numbers, all of the rules (e.g., exponent rules, order of operations, etc.) and properties of arithmetic (e.g., commutative property, associative property, etc.) apply to algebraic expressions.

- To add (or subtract) like terms, we add (or subtract) the coefficients of the terms and keep the variable parts the same.

- To multiply or divide terms, use the exponent rules just as when simplifying arithmetic expressions. The FOIL method is used when multiplying two binomials. (Remember, $(a+b)^2 = a^2 + \boxed{2ab} + b^2$, not $a^2 + b^2$!)

For example:

$$(2x+3y)(x-5)=$$
$$2x(x)+2x(-5)+3y(x)+3y(-5)=$$
$$2x^2 - 10x + 3xy - 15y$$

Now put your skills to the test with the following question.

· ·

Which of the following is equivalent to $(-5x^2)^3$?

- **A.** $-5x^5$
- **B.** $-5x^6$
- **C.** $-125x^6$
- **D.** $25x^6$
- **E.** $-15x^6$

The correct answer is C. For this problem, it is important to remember the rules of exponents. When a product is raised to a power, each of the terms must be raised to that power. So, $(-5x^2)^3$ is equal to $(-5)^3 \times (x^2)^3$. When a power is raised to another power, you multiply the exponents. So $(-5)^3 \times (x^2)^3$ is equal to $(-5)^3 \times (x^6)$. Now evaluate: $(-5)^3 \times (x^6) = -125 \times (x^6) = -125x^6$.

Choice A is incorrect because $\left(a^b\right)^c \neq a^{b+c}$, and you must apply the exponent to the coefficient, −5, as well. Choice B is incorrect because you must apply the exponent to the coefficient, −5. Choice D is incorrect because the cube of −1 is −1. Choice E is incorrect because $(-5)^3 = (-5)(-5)(-5)$; you do not multiply the base times the exponent.

· ·

ELEMENTARY COUNTING TECHNIQUES

There are two common types of counting problems:

1. **Type I:** Determine the number of combinations that can be formed from *a* of quantity 1, *b* of quantity 2, *c* of quantity 3, etc. Assuming that order is not important and that all of the quantities are different, simply multiply *a*, *b*, *c*, etc., together.

2. **Type II:** Find the number of *ordered* arrangements of *n* objects. This is solved using factorials *n*!. (For instance, $5! = 5 \times 4 \times 3 \times 2 \times 1$.)

SIMPLE PROBABILITY AND DESCRIPTIVE STATISTICS

All experiments that involve uncertainty or chance (e.g., predicting the stock market or weather, guessing the percentage of votes a candidate will receive, or simply flipping a coin) involve probability.

An **outcome** is the result of a single trial of a probability experiment. The collection of all outcomes is the **sample space**, which is written as a set. For instance, if you roll a typical six-sided die and record the number of the face on which it comes to rest, the outcomes are the labels on the faces, namely $S = \{1, 2, 3, 4, 5, 6\}$. An **event** is a subset of the sample space and is usually described using one or more conditions. For instance, the event that "the die lands on an odd number" is the subset $E = \{1, 3, 5\}$.

Suppose *E* and *F* represent events of some probability experiment. The following table shows some common possibilities and what they mean:

Event	Description in words
E or F	All outcomes in E or in F or in both
E and F	All outcomes in common to E and F
Complement of E	All outcomes NOT in E

The **probability** of an event *A*, denoted by $P(A)$, is a number between 0 and 1, inclusive, that describes the percent chance that event *A* has of occurring. If *N* outcomes in the sample space are *equally likely*, then the probability of any *single outcome* occurring is $\frac{1}{N}$. More generally, if *A* is an event containing *k* elements, then

$$P(A) = \frac{\text{Number of outcomes in } A}{\text{Number of possible outcomes}} = \frac{k}{N}$$

Questions involving data usually take the form of interpreting some feature of a bar or line graph or computing the average (or mean) of a list of numbers in some applied context.

- To compute the **mean** of a list of numbers, simply add the numbers and divide by how many numbers you added.
- To find the **median**, arrange the numbers in increasing order; if there is an odd number of data values, the value in the middle position is the median, and if there is an even number of data values, the average of the values in the two middle positions is the median.

Sequences

There are two special types of sequences that might come up on the ACT Mathematics test, where a question may ask you to find a specific nth term: arithmetic sequences and geometric sequences.

1. An **arithmetic sequence** is a sequence whose terms are obtained by adding a fixed constant to the previous term. For instance, the sequence 8, 12, 16, 20, 24, ... is an arithmetic sequence because the constant 4 is added to one term to get the next term. However, the sequence 3, 6, 10, 15, 21, ... is not an arithmetic sequence because the *same* constant is not added to each term to get the next.

2. A **geometric sequence** is a sequence whose terms are obtained by multiplying the previous term by a fixed constant r. For instance, the sequence $\frac{1}{3}, \frac{1}{9}, \frac{1}{27}, \frac{1}{81}$, ... is a geometric sequence because each term is multiplied by $\frac{1}{3}$ to get the next term. However, the sequence 8, 4, 0, −4, −8, ... is not geometric because there is no single number you can multiply each term by to get the next term.

LINES

The equation of a line can be given in **standard form,** $Ax + By = C$, or **slope-intercept form,** $y = mx + b$, where A, B, C, m, and b are real numbers. In the slope-intercept form, b represents the y-intercept (meaning that the graph of the line crosses the y-axis at the point $(0, b)$) and m represents the slope of the line (which measures steepness of the line or the change in y-value per unit change in x-value).

If you have two points on the line, say (x_1, y_1) and (x_2, y_2), the slope is the "change in y over the change in x," which we write symbolically as:

$$m = \frac{y_1 - y_2}{x_1 - x_2} = \frac{y_2 - y_1}{x_2 - x_1}$$

- If m is positive, then the graph of the line rises from left to right.
- If m is negative, it falls from left to right.
- If $m = 0$, then the equation becomes $y = b$ and the graph is a horizontal line.
- The graph of the equation $x = a$ is a vertical line and said to have *undefined slope*.

If you have a point (x_1, y_1) on a line and you know its slope m, then the **point-slope form** for the equation of this line is $y - y_1 = m(x - x_1)$.

The following table summarizes some typical problem varieties and the best method of attack:

	Problem Type	Method of Attack
1.	Given a point and a slope (either written or by way of a graph), find the equation of the line.	Use point-slope formula immediately.
2.	Given two points on a line (either written or by way of a graph), determine the slope or the equation of the line.	First, find the slope of the line. Then, use point-slope formula to find its equation.
3.	Given a table of points that describe a linear relationship between variables x and y, determine the equation of the line.	First, use any two of the points to find the slope. Then, use any of the points from the table with the slope to find the equation of the line.

Two lines with equations $y = m_1 x + b_1$ and $y = m_2 x + b_2$ are **parallel** if the slopes are equal $(m_1 = m_2)$. They are **perpendicular** if the product of the slopes is -1 $(m_1 \cdot m_2 = -1)$.

Give this sample ACT-type question a try.

If line *l* is defined by the equation $3y - x = 8$, which of the following equations could define a line that is perpendicular to line *l*?

F. $y = -3x + 4$

G. $y = \dfrac{1}{3}x + 5$

H. $y = 3x - 8$

J. $3y = x + 6$

K. $-y = -3x + 1$

The correct answer is F. First, rewrite the equation for line *l* in slope-intercept form:

$$3y - x = 8$$
$$3y = x + 8$$
$$y = \frac{1}{3}x + \frac{8}{3}$$

So, the line *l* has a slope of $\dfrac{1}{3}$. The product of the slopes of perpendicular *l* lines is -1, so the slope of a line perpendicular to line *l* is -3. Only choice F satisfies this condition.

RATIONAL EXPRESSIONS

The arithmetic of fractions in which the numerator and/or denominator contains an algebraic expression is similar to what you have already seen—you simply add, subtract, multiply, and divide polynomials like you did before and cancel like factors in the top and bottom as you would when simplifying a fraction involving numbers.

ADDING/SUBTRACTING

Before you add or subtract, you must find a common denominator. The easiest way to do this is to simply multiply the denominators already present. Express both fractions using this denominator, and then combine and simplify:

$$\frac{1}{1+2x} - \frac{1}{1-2x} =$$
$$\frac{1-2x}{(1-2x)(1+2x)} - \frac{1+2x}{(1-2x)(1+2x)} = \frac{-4x}{(1-2x)(1+2x)}$$

Multiplying/Dividing

First, factor all expressions. If multiplying, cancel factors common to the top and bottom; if dividing, flip the fraction after the division sign, change the sign to a product, and then cancel factors common to the top and bottom:

$$\frac{2x^2+2x}{x^2-4} \bullet \frac{x+2}{x^2-1} =$$

$$\frac{2x\,\cancel{(x+1)}}{(x-2)\cancel{(x+2)}} \bullet \frac{\cancel{x+2}}{\cancel{(x+1)}(x-1)} = \frac{2x}{(x-2)(x-1)}$$

Radical Expressions

The radical rules can be used to simplify more complicated algebraic expressions involving radicals. For example:

$$\sqrt{32x^8y^2z^3} = \sqrt{2 \bullet 4 \bullet 4 \bullet \left(x^4\right)^2 \bullet \left(y^2\right) \bullet \left(z^2\right) \bullet z}$$

$$= \sqrt{2} \bullet \sqrt{4} \bullet \sqrt{4} \bullet \sqrt{\left(x^4\right)^2} \bullet \sqrt{y^2} \bullet \sqrt{z^2} \bullet \sqrt{z}$$

$$= \sqrt{2} \bullet 2 \bullet 2 \bullet \left(x^4\right) \bullet y \bullet z \bullet \sqrt{z}$$

$$= 4 \bullet x^4 \bullet y \bullet z \bullet \sqrt{2} \bullet \sqrt{z}$$

$$= 4 \bullet x^4 \bullet y \bullet z \bullet \sqrt{2z}$$

COMPLEX NUMBERS

A **complex number** is a number of the form $a + bi$, where a and b are both real numbers and $i^2 = -1$. For example:

$$\sqrt{81} - \sqrt{-125} =$$

$$9 - \sqrt{-1} \bullet \sqrt{125} =$$

$$9 - i \bullet 5\sqrt{5} = 9 - \left(5\sqrt{5}\right)i$$

The following are the basic rules of arithmetic involving complex numbers:

Definition (in Symbols)	Definition (in Words)
Sum/Difference $(a+bi)+(c+di)=(a+c)+(b+d)i$ $(a+bi)-(c+di)=(a-c)+(b-d)i$	When adding or subtracting complex numbers, add or subtract the real parts and the imaginary parts separately and form the complex number using those sums or differences.
Product $(a+bi)\cdot(c+di)=(ac-bd)+(bc+ad)i$	To multiply two complex numbers, apply the FOIL technique and use the fact that $i^2 = -1$.

QUADRATIC EQUATIONS AND THE QUADRATIC FORMULA

A **quadratic equation** is of the form $ax^2 + bx + c = 0$, where a, b, and c are real numbers and $a \neq 0$. You can solve a quadratic equation by using factoring or the quadratic formula.

The process of solving a quadratic equation by factoring is simple:

- First, put the equation into the standard form $ax^2 + bx + c = 0$.
- Next, if possible, factor the quadratic expression into a product of two factors.
- Once factored, set each factor equal to zero and solve for x.

Often, quadratic equations cannot be solved by factoring. In these cases, you should use the **quadratic formula.** The solutions of $ax^2 + bx + c = 0$ are given by the quadratic formula:

$$x = \frac{-b \pm \sqrt{b^2 - 4ac}}{2a}$$

The types of solutions of a quadratic equation depend solely on the sign of the radicand $b^2 - 4ac$:

$b^2 - 4ac > 0$	Two distinct real solutions
$b^2 - 4ac = 0$	One repeated real solution
$b^2 - 4ac < 0$	Two complex conjugate solutions

LINEAR INEQUALITIES

Linear inequalities are solved just like linear equations, with the one very important additional step of switching the inequality sign whenever both sides of the inequality are multiplied by a negative real number.

The solution set of an inequality is an interval on the number line. The following table shows different versions of inequalities and their number line equivalents:

Linear Inequality	Picture on Number Line
$x < a$	
$x \leq a$	
$x > a$	
$x \geq a$	
$a \leq x \leq b$	
$a < x < b$	
$-\infty < x < \infty$	

Here are some typical forms of questions involving inequalities you might see on the ACT Mathematics test, along with some suggestions about how to attack them:

	Problem Type	Method of Attack
1.	Solve a given inequality, and the choices are given symbolically in the forms in the above table.	Solve the inequality as you would a linear equation, being careful with the inequality sign. The final step will have the variable on one side and a number on the other.
2.	Solve a given inequality, and the choices are given graphically on the number line in the forms in the above table.	Solve the inequality as you would a linear equation, being careful with the inequality sign. Once you have the variable on one side and a number on the other, match that to the correct picture.

 TIP Double inequalities, such as $-4 < 8 - 3x < 20$, are solved similarly, but now "balance" refers to all three parts of the inequality, not just both sides of an equation.

ABSOLUTE VALUE EQUATIONS AND INEQUALITIES

You can solve absolute value equations and inequalities by writing them just as you would linear equations and inequalities *without* absolute values.

However, because there are two possible values for the contents inside absolute value bars, you have to take care when getting rid of the bars to write your equations or inequalities.

Take a look at the equations and inequalities that are equivalent to different absolute value expressions:

Absolute Value Equation/Inequality	Solution
$|x| = a$	$x = a$ or $x = -a$
$|x| \geq a$	$x \geq a$ or $x \leq -a$
$|x| > a$	$x > a$ or $x < -a$
$|x| \leq a$	$-a \leq x \leq a$
$|x| < a$	$-a < x < a$

Now apply what you learned to solve the following question.

. . . .

What is the solution set for the inequality $|3x - 2| > 6$?

A. $x < -\dfrac{4}{3}$

B. $x > \dfrac{8}{3}$

C. $-\dfrac{4}{3} < x < \dfrac{8}{3}$

D. $x < -\dfrac{8}{3}$ or $x > \dfrac{4}{3}$

E. $x > \dfrac{8}{3}$ or $x < -\dfrac{4}{3}$

The correct answer is E. First, rewrite the absolute value inequality as the two inequalities: $3x - 2 > 6$ or $3x - 2 < -6$. To solve these inequalities, add 2 to both sides to get $3x > 8$ or $3x < -4$. Now, divide by 3 to get $x > \dfrac{8}{3}$ or $x < -\dfrac{4}{3}$. So, the solution set is $x > \dfrac{8}{3}$ or $x < -\dfrac{4}{3}$. Choice A is incorrect because you ignored one of the two inequalities obtained when reformulating the absolute value inequality; you can also have $x > \dfrac{8}{3}$. In choice B, you ignored one of the two inequalities obtained when reformulating the absolute value inequality; you can also have $x < -\dfrac{4}{3}$. Choice C is incorrect because you incorrectly converted the absolute value inequality to a double inequality. In choice D, the signs of both fractions are incorrect.

. . . .

SYSTEMS OF LINEAR EQUATIONS

A **system of linear equations** is a pair of linear equations involving x and y that must be satisfied *at the same time*. To solve a system means to identify ordered pairs (x, y) that satisfy *both* equations—not just one, but both! There are only three possibilities that can occur:

Number of Solutions	Geometric Interpretation
0	The graphs of the lines in the system are parallel. Hence, there is no point that is on both lines simultaneously.
1	The graphs of the lines in the system intersect in a single point. The intersection point *is* the solution of the system.
Infinitely many	The graphs of the lines in the system are exactly the same. Every point on the line is a solution of the system.

There are two algebraic methods that you can use to solve a system: the **elimination method** and the **substitution method.**

ELIMINATION METHOD

The strategy behind this method is to multiply both equations by the right numbers so that when you add the left sides and the right sides, one of the variables drops out (or is eliminated). Then, you solve for that variable and plug the value you get back into either equation to find the value of the other variable. When complete, you have your ordered pair.

SUBSTITUTION METHOD

The strategy behind this method is to solve one of the equations for a variable (either x or y, whichever is slightly easier to isolate) and **substitute** that expression for the variable into the other equation (doing so results in an equation involving only one variable). Solve that equation, and then plug the value you get back into either equation to find the value of the other variable. When complete, you have your ordered pair.

If you are given a system and asked which of a list of choices is a solution, remember that the ordered pair must satisfy BOTH equations, not just one of them. Among the choices will be points that satisfy one of the equations, but not the other!

Use the following facts about lines to quickly ascertain the number of solutions in a given system of equations:

- A system has a **unique solution** if the slopes of the two lines are different.
- A system has **no solution** if the slopes of the two lines are equal.
- A system has **infinitely many solutions** if the two lines are constant multiples of each other.

BASIC COORDINATE GEOMETRY

The *xy*-coordinate plane is divided into four congruent **quadrants** numbered I, II, III, and IV counterclockwise as shown below, along with the signs of the coordinates of points in each quadrant:

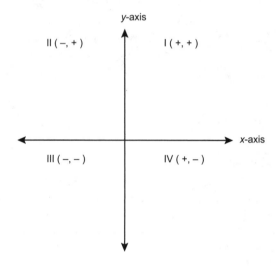

- The distance between two points $P(x_1, y_1)$ and $Q(x_2, y_2)$ is $\sqrt{(x_2 - x_1)^2 + (y_2 - y_1)^2}$.
- The midpoint of the line segment with endpoints $P(x_1, y_1)$ and $Q(x_2, y_2)$ is the point with coordinates $\left(\dfrac{x_1 + x_2}{2}, \dfrac{y_1 + y_2}{2} \right)$.

Get ready to use the distance formula to solve the following question.

· ·

What is the length of the line segment with endpoints (−1, 4) and (−2, −1)?

F. $\sqrt{26}$

G. $\sqrt{10}$

H. 10

J. 6

K. 26

The correct answer is F. Use the distance formula to find the length:

$$\sqrt{(-1-(-2))^2 + (4-(-1))^2} = \sqrt{(1)^2 + (5)^2} = \sqrt{26} \text{ units}$$

Choice G is incorrect because you computed the differences of the coordinates of single points rather than the x-coordinates of both points and the y-coordinates of both points. Choice H is incorrect because you computed the differences of the coordinates of single points rather than the x-coordinates of both points and the y-coordinates of both points and forgot the square root. Choice J is incorrect because you mistakenly calculated $\sqrt{a^2 + b^2} = a + b$; you cannot distribute the square root across a sum. Choice K is incorrect because you forgot to take the square root.

· ·

FUNCTIONS

A **function** is a rule that associates to each input x a corresponding y-value.

- Functions are denoted using letters, like f or g.

- When we want to emphasize the input-output defining relationship of a function, an expression of the form $y = f(x)$ (read "y equals f of x") is often used.

- Functions are often described using algebraic expressions, which can then be illustrated by a graph.

- The **domain** of a function is the set of all values of x that can be substituted into the expression and yield a meaningful output.

- The **range** of a function is the set of all possible y-values attained at some member of the domain.

Function questions on the ACT Mathematics test will often ask you to compute the value $f(x)$ for various inputs, for example:

If $f(x) = 2x^2 - x + 1$, compute $f(a + 2)$.

$$f(a+2) = 2(a+2)^2 - (a+2) + 1$$
$$= 2(a^2 + 4a + 4) - (a+2) + 1$$
$$= 2a^2 + 8a + 8 - a - 2 + 1$$
$$= 2a^2 + 7a + 7$$

 ALERT: A common mistake is to say $f(a + 2) = f(a) + f(2)$. You cannot distribute the function in this manner.)

The arithmetic operations on functions are defined in the same manner as arithmetic of real numbers.

For example, if f and g are functions, then:

- The sum function $(f + g)(x)$ is defined to be $f(x) + g(x)$.
- The difference function $(f - g)(x)$ is defined to be $f(x) - g(x)$.
- The product function $(f \cdot g)(x)$ is defined to be $f(x) \cdot g(x)$.
- The quotient function $\left(\dfrac{f}{g}\right)(x)$ is defined to be $\dfrac{f(x)}{g(x)}$.
- The composition of f and g, denoted by $(f \circ g)$, is defined to be $(f \circ g)(x) = f(g(x))$.

  (**Note:** In general, $(f \circ g) \neq (g \circ f)$. The order in which you compose two functions matters.)

POLYNOMIALS

A polynomial is a function of the form $f(x) = a_n x^n + a_{n-1} x^{n-1} + \ldots + a_1 x + a_0$, where $a_0, a_1, \ldots, a_n$ are real numbers, and n is a nonnegative integer. Such a polynomial has **degree n.**

The three main concepts for a polynomial $p(x)$ with which you should be familiar are **x-intercept, zero,** and **factor.** All are defined in the following table.

Term	Definition
x-intercept	A point $(a, 0)$ on the graph of $y = p(x)$. Then, $x = a$ is a solution of the equation $p(x) = 0$.
zero	A real number a such that $p(a) = 0$.
factor	An expression of the form $(x - a)$ in which a is a zero of $p(x)$.

Graphing Functions

The following are the graphs of some of the most common functions you will encounter on the ACT.

Function	Typical Graphs
Linear Functions $f(x) = mx + b$	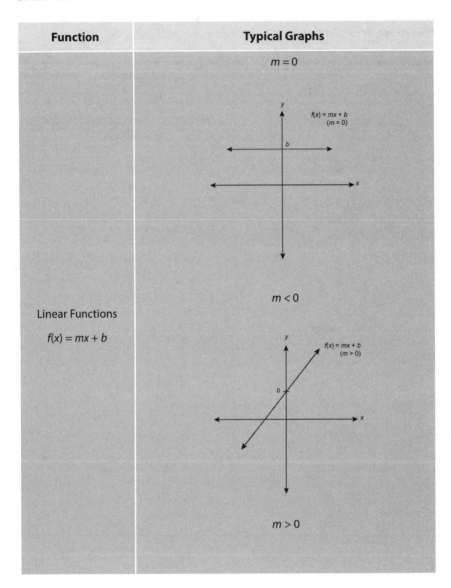

Function	Typical Graphs
Quadratic Functions $f(x) = a(x-h)^2 + k$	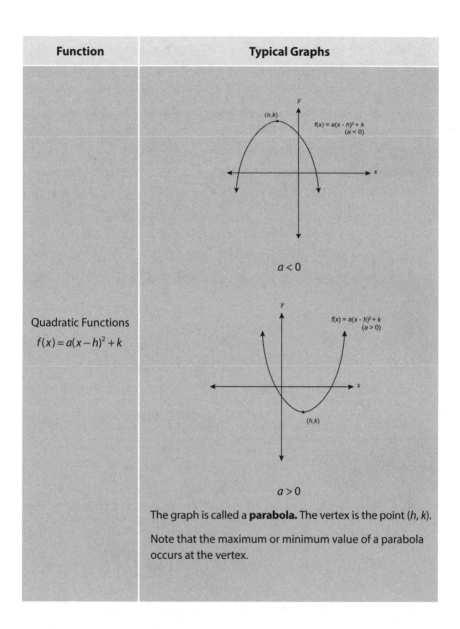

$a < 0$

$a > 0$

The graph is called a **parabola.** The vertex is the point (h, k).

Note that the maximum or minimum value of a parabola occurs at the vertex.

Function	Typical Graphs
Cubic Function $f(x) = x^3$	
Absolute Value Function $f(x) = \lvert x \rvert$	More generally, if h and k are positive numbers, then the graph of $g(x) = \lvert x - h \rvert + k$ is obtained by moving the shown graph to the right h units and up k units.
Square Root Function $f(x) = \sqrt{x}$	

The following are some main features of the graph of a function $y = f(x)$:

1. An *x*-intercept of *f* is a point of the form $(x, 0)$. You determine the *x*-intercepts of a function by solving the equation $f(x) = 0$.

2. A *y*-intercept of *f* is the point $(0, f(0))$.

3. The **minimum of *f*** is the smallest *y*-value in the range of *f*; it is the *y*-value of the lowest point on the graph of *f*.

4. The **maximum of *f*** is the largest *y*-value in the range of *f*; it is the *y*-value of the highest point on the graph of *f*.

5. *f* is *increasing* on an interval if its graph rises from left to right as you progress through the interval from left to right.

6. *f* is *decreasing* if its graph falls from left to right as you progress through the interval from left to right.

MATRICES

A **matrix** is an array of real numbers. If a matrix **A** has *r* rows and *c* columns, we say **A** is an $r \times c$ (read "*r* by *c*") matrix. A matrix is written by listing all of its entries in an array, enclosed by brackets.

Take a look at some examples:

$$\underbrace{\begin{bmatrix} a & b \\ c & d \end{bmatrix}}_{2\times 2 \text{ matrix}} \qquad \underbrace{\begin{bmatrix} 1 & -2 & 3 \\ 1 & 0 & 2 \\ 5 & 2 & 1 \end{bmatrix}}_{3\times 3 \text{ matrix}} \qquad \underbrace{\begin{bmatrix} 1 \\ 3 \\ 2 \\ 1 \end{bmatrix}}_{4\times 1 \text{ matrix}}$$

The basic arithmetic operations involving matrices are performed "componentwise." The following is a list of the basic operations on 2×2 matrices. All letters stand for real numbers.

Term/Operation	Definition
Equality: $\begin{bmatrix} a & b \\ c & d \end{bmatrix} = \begin{bmatrix} e & f \\ g & h \end{bmatrix}$	$\begin{bmatrix} a & b \\ c & d \end{bmatrix} = \begin{bmatrix} e & f \\ g & h \end{bmatrix}$ whenever $\underbrace{a = e,\ b = f,\ c = g,\ d = h}_{\text{corresponding entries are equal}}$

Term/Operation	Definition
Sum/Difference: $\begin{bmatrix} a & b \\ c & d \end{bmatrix} \pm \begin{bmatrix} e & f \\ g & h \end{bmatrix}$	$\begin{bmatrix} a & b \\ c & d \end{bmatrix} \pm \begin{bmatrix} e & f \\ g & h \end{bmatrix} = \begin{bmatrix} a\pm e & b\pm f \\ c\pm g & d\pm h \end{bmatrix}$ Add (subtract) corresponding entries to get the sum (difference).
Scalar Multiplication: $k\begin{bmatrix} a & b \\ c & d \end{bmatrix}$	$k\begin{bmatrix} a & b \\ c & d \end{bmatrix} = \begin{bmatrix} ka & kb \\ kc & kd \end{bmatrix}$ Multiply all entries by the constant k.

BASIC ELEMENTS OF GEOMETRY

Angles are classified according to their "size," or **measure;** the units in which this is expressed are **degrees** (and often **radians** when studying trigonometry). The notation $m(\angle A)$ is used to denote the measure of angle A.

The following table characterizes the angle types you will see on the exam:

Term	Definition
Acute Angle	An angle whose measure is between 0 and 90 degrees.
Right Angle	An angle whose measure is 90 degrees.
Obtuse Angle	An angle whose measure is between 90 and 180 degrees.
Straight Angle	An angle whose measure is 180 degrees.
Complementary Angles	Two angles whose measures sum to 90 degrees.
Supplementary Angles	Two angles whose measures sum to 180 degrees.
Congruent Angles	Two angles that have the same measure.

Other pairs of angles are important as well. Consider the following diagram:

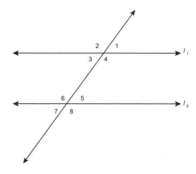

Term	Examples from Diagram
Corresponding Angles	$\angle 1$ and $\angle 5$, $\angle 3$ and $\angle 7$
Adjacent Angles	$\angle 1$ and $\angle 2$, $\angle 5$ and $\angle 6$
Vertical Angles	$\angle 1$ and $\angle 3$, $\angle 6$ and $\angle 8$
Alternate Interior Angles	$\angle 4$ and $\angle 6$, $\angle 3$ and $\angle 5$

- Vertical angles are *always* congruent!

- If the lines l_1 and l_2 are parallel, then corresponding angles are necessarily congruent, as are alternate interior angles.

TRIANGLES

Triangles are classified using their angles and sides, as follows:

Type	Defining Characteristic
Right	One of the angles is a right angle. (The other two, therefore, must be acute.)
Acute	All three angles are acute.
Obtuse	One of the angles is obtuse. (The other two, therefore, must be acute.)
Equilateral	All three sides have the same length; that is, all three sides are *congruent*.

Type	Defining Characteristic
Isosceles	At least two sides have the same length.
Scalene	All three sides have different lengths.

All triangles obey the Triangle Sum Rule and Triangle Inequality.

- The **Triangle Sum Rule** says that the sum of the measures of the three angles in any triangle must be 180°.

- The **Triangle Inequality** says that the sum of the lengths of any two sides of a triangle must be strictly larger than the length of the third side.

- The lengths of the sides of right triangles are related by the **Pythagorean theorem.** The sides with lengths a and b are called **legs,** and the side opposite the right angle is the **hypotenuse;** the hypotenuse is the longest side of a right triangle. The Pythagorean theorem says that $a^2 + b^2 = c^2$.

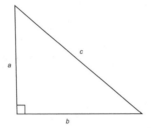

Two triangles ABC and DEF are **congruent** if all three corresponding pairs of angles are congruent AND all three corresponding sides are congruent. Two triangles ABC and DEF that are *not* congruent can still be proportional to each other if the ratios of the three pairs of corresponding sides are the same; that is, $\dfrac{AB}{DE} = \dfrac{BC}{EF} = \dfrac{AC}{DF} = k$, where k is a positive number. In such case, we say $\triangle ABC$ and $\triangle DEF$ are **similar.**

 Corresponding angles in two similar triangles must be congruent.

Test your skills on the following test-like question.

Which of the following lists of side lengths represent sides of a right triangle?

    A.   1, 3, 5

    B.   5, 6, 7

    C.   4, 7, 11

    D.   2, 2, 8

    E.   5, 12, 13

The correct answer is E. The sides of any right triangle are related by the Pythagorean theorem, which states that the sum of the squares of the legs is equal to the square of the hypotenuse. This is often written as $a^2 + b^2 = c^2$, where a and b are the legs and c is the hypotenuse (the longest of the three sides). Test each set of sides to see which satisfies the Pythagorean theorem and is therefore a right triangle. Observe for choice E, $\underbrace{5^2 + 12^2}_{=169} = \underbrace{13^2}_{=169}$. For all other choices, this relationship does not hold.

TIP: The sides in a right triangle measuring 3–4–5 or 5–12–13 (as in the sample question) or multiples thereof are examples of **Pythagorean triples**—recognizing them in a problem can make identifying a right triangle or calculating a missing side of a right triangle easier.

PERIMETER AND AREA

The **perimeter** of a region in the plane is the "distance around" and is computed by adding the lengths of all segments/curves forming its outer boundary. The standard units of measure of length are *inches, feet, yards,* etc.; the metric system is also commonly used (e.g., *centimeters, meters*, etc).

The **area** of a region in the plane is the number of *unit squares* needed to cover it. The standard units of measure of area are *square inches, square feet, square yards,* etc.; the metric system is also commonly used (e.g., *square centimeters, square meters*, etc.)

The area formula for a triangle with **base** b and **height** h, as illustrated below, is $A = \frac{1}{2}b \cdot h$.

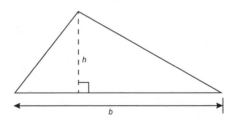

QUADRILATERALS

Quadrilaterals are four-sided figures in the plane in which each side is a line segment. The following are the common quadrilaterals—make sure you know the definitions so you don't get confused on test day.

Quadrilateral	Defining Characteristics
Square	Two pairs of parallel sides, all sides congruent, and a right angle
Rectangle	Two pairs of parallel sides and a right angle
Parallelogram	Two pairs of parallel sides
Rhombus	Two pairs of parallel sides and all four sides are congruent
Trapezoid	Exactly one pair of parallel sides
Isosceles Trapezoid	Exactly one pair of parallel sides and one pair of opposite sides are congruent

Two quadrilaterals of the same type are congruent if their corresponding sides are all congruent, and they are called similar if the four ratios of their corresponding sides are equal. Compute the perimeter of any quadrilateral by adding together the lengths of its four sides.

CIRCLES

The set of all points in the plane that are a given distance r from a fixed point P is a **circle.**

Circles will definitely come up on the ACT—here is the terminology you should know:

Term	Definition
Center	The point P equidistant from all points on the circle
Radius	The common distance r by which points on the circle lie from the center
Diameter	A line segment that passes through the center of the circle and has endpoints on the circle (its length is twice the radius)

Term	Definition
Central Angle	An angle formed between two radial segments
Arc	A portion of the circle lying between two points
Sector	The portion of the inside of a circle lying between two radial segments

The following are the usual perimeter and area formulas for circles.

Circumference of a circle	Since the diameter d is $2r$, there are two expressions you can use for this formula: $P = 2\pi r = \pi d$
Area of a circle	$A = \pi r^2$
Length of an arc of a circle	$P = \left(\dfrac{\theta}{180°} \right) \cdot \pi$
Area of a sector of a circle	$A = \left(\dfrac{\theta}{360°} \right) \cdot \pi r^2$

The equation of a circle with center (h, k) and radius r is $(x - h)^2 + (y - k)^2 = r^2$.

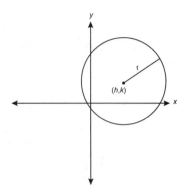

Try this test-like question about circles.

· ·

A circle exists such that its center is at $C(-4, -3)$ and has diameter 12. Which equation determines the circle described?

    F. $(x - 4)^2 + (y - 3)^2 = 12$

    G. $(x + 4)^2 + (y + 3)^2 = 6$

    H. $(x + 4)^2 + (y + 3)^2 = 36$

    J. $(x + 4)^2 + (y - 3)^2 = 144$

    K. $(x + 4)^2 + (y - 3)^2 = 6$

The correct answer is H. The general formula for a circle is $(x - h)^2 + (y - k)^2 = r^2$, where (h, k) is the center of the circle and r is the radius. Of the equations given, only $(x + 4)^2 + (y + 3)^2 = 36$ has a center at $(-4, -3)$ and a radius equal to one-half of 12, or 6. In choice F, the signs of both coordinates of the center are wrong, and the right side should be the square of the radius, not the diameter. Choice G is incorrect because the radius on the right side is not squared. Choice J is incorrect because the 3 should be added, not subtracted, on the left side, and the right side should be the square of the radius, not the square of the diameter. Choice K is incorrect because the 3 should be added on the left side and the right side should be squared.

· ·

SOLIDS

Cubes, boxes, and cylinders are among the most common solids you will see on the ACT Mathematics test.

Solid	Illustration	Surface Area Formula	Volume Formula
Cube		$SA = 6s^2$	$V = s^3$
Rectangular Box		$SA = 2(lw + lh + wh)$	$V = lwh$
Cylinder		$SA = 2\pi r^2 + 2\pi rh$	$V = \pi r^2 h$

Use the information provided in the chart to solve this problem.

. . . .

A cube has side length s. A new cube is formed whose sides are three times as long as the original cube. Which of the following statements is true?

A. The volume of the new cube is 3 times the volume of the original cube.
B. The volume of the new cube is 9 times the volume of the original cube.
C. The volume of the new cube is one-third the volume of the original cube.
D. The volume of the new cube is 27 times the volume of the original cube.
E. The volume of the new cube is 81 times the volume of the original cube.

The correct answer is D. First, determine expressions for both cubes and then compare them. The volume of the original cube is $V_{original} = s^3$. The length of a side of the new cube is $3s$. So, the volume of the new cube is $V_{new} = (3s)^3 = 27s^3$. Comparing the two formulas, we see that the volume of the new cube is 27 times the volume of the original cube. So, choice D is the correct answer. Choice A is incorrect because *each* side is tripled and so the volume increases by a factor larger than 3. Choice B is incorrect because this would be the amount by which the surface area increases, not the volume. Choice C is incorrect because the new cube is larger than the original cube and so cannot have a smaller volume than the original cube. Choice E is incorrect because instead of cubing each side to find the volume of the cube, it instead assumes you raise each side to the fourth power.

RIGHT TRIANGLE TRIGONOMETRY

The **trigonometric functions** are used to identify the lengths of sides of a right triangle when you are given one side and one angle (instead of two sides). Consider the following right triangle in the figure below:

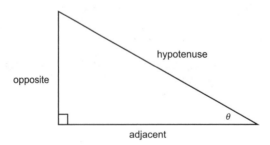

The following table lists how these functions are defined within the topic of **right triangle trigonometry:**

Trigonometric Function	Definition
Cosine	$\cos\theta = \dfrac{\text{adjacent}}{\text{hypotenuse}}$
Sine	$\sin\theta = \dfrac{\text{opposite}}{\text{hypotenuse}}$
Tangent	$\tan\theta = \dfrac{\text{opposite}}{\text{adjacent}}$
Secant	$\sec\theta = \dfrac{\text{hypotenuse}}{\text{adjacent}} \left(= \dfrac{1}{\cos\theta}\right)$
Cotangent	$\cot\theta = \dfrac{\text{adjacent}}{\text{opposite}} \left(= \dfrac{1}{\tan\theta}\right)$
Cosecant	$\csc\theta = \dfrac{\text{hypotenuse}}{\text{opposite}} \left(= \dfrac{1}{\sin\theta}\right)$

TRIGONOMETRIC FUNCTIONS

Take a look at the graphs of $f(x) = \sin(x)$ and $g(x) = \cos(x)$ for $0 \le x \le 2\pi$:

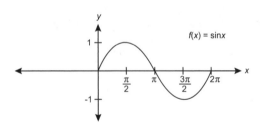

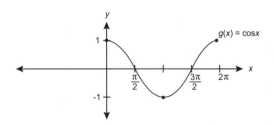

Now that you know what these look like, you know what a sine or cosine graph will look like at other intervals. The graphs on the intervals $2\pi \le x \le 4\pi$, $4\pi \le x \le 6\pi$, etc., are identical to the graph above; that means these functions are **periodic.** The **period** is the length of the smallest interval that can be used to produce the graph by replicating what it looks like on that interval or abutting intervals of the same length. Here, in both cases, the period is 2π.

- The period of $f(x) = \sin(Bx)$ and $g(x) = \cos(Bx)$ is $\dfrac{2\pi}{B}$.

- The amplitude of a periodic function equals $\dfrac{\text{maximum value} - \text{minimum value}}{2}$.

- The amplitude of $f(x) = A\sin(Bx)$ is $|A|$.

Test your understanding with the following question.

· ·

What is the period of the graph of $y = -3\cos\dfrac{x}{4}$?

   F. $\dfrac{\pi}{2}$

   G. π

   H. $\dfrac{\pi}{4}$

   J. 8π

   K. 2π

The correct answer is J. The graph of $y = \cos x$ has a period of 2π. However, if you graph $y = -3\cos\dfrac{x}{4}$, the period increases by a factor of 4 to get $8\pi \left(\dfrac{2\pi}{B} = \dfrac{2\pi}{\frac{1}{4}} = 8\pi \right.$. Note that the coefficient of the cosine, -3, affects only the amplitude, not the period.

· ·

TRIGONOMETRIC IDENTITIES

There are many trigonometric identities that are useful for simplifying expressions involving trigonometric functions, or determining the sine or cosine of an angle when the other value is known. The following are the most commonly used identities:

Name	Identity
Pythagorean Identity	$\cos^2\theta + \sin^2\theta = 1$
Periodicity Identities	$\sin(2n\pi + \theta) = \sin(\theta)$, where n is an integer $\cos(2n\pi + \theta) = \cos(\theta)$, where n is an integer
Symmetry Identities	$\sin(-\theta) = -\sin(\theta)$ $\cos(-\theta) = -\cos(\theta)$
Complementary Angle Identities	$\cos\left(\dfrac{\pi}{2} - \theta\right) = \sin\theta$ $\sin\left(\dfrac{\pi}{2} - \theta\right) = \cos\theta$
Double-Angle Identities	$\sin(2\theta) = 2\sin\theta\cos\theta$ $\cos(2\theta) = \cos^2\theta - \sin^2\theta$

Solving Trigonometric Equations

To solve trigonometric equations, you must remember the values of the trigonometric functions of the standard angles:

x	$\sin(x)$	$\cos(x)$
0	0	1
$\dfrac{\pi}{6}$	$\dfrac{1}{2}$	$\dfrac{\sqrt{3}}{2}$
$\dfrac{\pi}{4}$	$\dfrac{\sqrt{2}}{2}$	$\dfrac{\sqrt{2}}{2}$
$\dfrac{\pi}{3}$	$\dfrac{\sqrt{3}}{2}$	$\dfrac{1}{2}$
$\dfrac{\pi}{2}$	1	0
π	0	−1
$\dfrac{3\pi}{2}$	−1	0
2π	0	1

Let's quickly work through this next question together.

What are the first two nonnegative solutions of cos (3x) = 1?

Using the table above, you can see that in order for the solution to be 1, the expression in the parentheses must be equal to 0 or 2π. So, any value of x for which $3x = 0$ or 2π is a solution of this equation. Therefore, $x = 0$ and $x = \dfrac{2\pi}{3}$ are both solutions.

SUMMING IT UP

- **Whole numbers** are the "counting numbers": 1, 2, 3, 4,.... A whole number greater than 1 whose only factors are the numbers 1 and itself is called **prime;** if it has other factors, it is called **composite.** The **prime factorization** of a number is writing it as the product of only prime numbers. **Integers** are whole numbers, their negatives, and zero.

- A **fraction** is a quotient of whole numbers (denoted $\frac{a}{b}$, where $b \neq 0$). The **reciprocal** of any fraction $\frac{a}{b}$ can be computed by flipping the fraction to get $\frac{b}{a}$. To add or subtract fractions, you must first find a common denominator. When multiplying, simply multiply numerators and denominators. When dividing, find the reciprocal of the divisor to turn the calculation into multiplication.

- When adding or subtracting decimals, line up decimal points. When multiplying or dividing, calculate as whole numbers, then count the total number of spaces after each decimal point in the original numbers and place the decimal point that many spaces in from the far right of the product.

- Use of the **order of operations** to simplify an arithmetic expression: parentheses, exponents, multiplication, and division from left to right and finally addition and subtraction from left to right.

- If b and n are natural numbers, then $b^n = \underbrace{b \times \ldots \times b}_{n \text{ times}}$. The result of raising any nonzero real number to the zero power is $1 (a^0 = 1)$. When multiplying terms with the same base being raised to powers, just add the powers; when dividing, subtract. When raising a term that is already raised to a power to another power, multiply the powers.

- If the terms of a sum or difference of radicals have the same radical parts, just add or subtract the coefficients—you cannot combine different radical parts.

- To convert from decimal form to percent form, move the decimal point two units to the right and affix the % sign. To convert from percent form to decimal form, insert a decimal point two units to the left and drop the % sign.

- To compute x% of y, convert x% to a decimal and multiply by y.

- Linear equations are equations in which the variable is raised to the first power, like $6x = 167$ and $34(n-1) = 1,278$. To solve, first simplify the equation by clearing fractions; then use the order of operations and the distributive property of multiplication to simplify both sides of the equation; finally, isolate the variable on one side. If you perform an operation on one side, you MUST perform the same operation on the other.

- The **absolute value** of a, denoted $|a|$, measures the distance between a and 0 on a number line.

- An **algebraic expression** is an arithmetic combination of terms, like $4x - 7z$. If two terms have the same "variable part," they are called **like terms.** All rules and properties of arithmetic apply to algebraic expressions.

- An **outcome** is the result of a single trial of a probability experiment; the collection of all outcomes is the **sample space.** The **probability** of an event A, denoted by $P(A)$, is a number between 0 and 1, inclusive, that describes the percent chance that event A has of occurring.

- The equation of a line can be given in **standard form,** $Ax + By = C$, or **slope-intercept form,** $y = mx + b$, where b represents the y-intercept and m represents the slope of the line (the change in y-value per unit change in x-value). If m is positive, then the graph of the line rises from left to right; if m is negative, it falls from left to right.

- If you have a point (x_1, y_1) on a line and you know its slope m, then the **point-slope form** for the equation of this line is $y - y_1 = m(x - x_1)$.

- Two lines are **parallel** if the slopes are equal and are **perpendicular** if the product of the slopes is -1.

- When adding or subtracting **rational expressions,** first find a common denominator. When multiplying or dividing, first factor all expressions and cancel common factors to the numerator and denominator.

- A **complex number** is a number of the form $a + bi$, where a and b are both real numbers and $i^2 = -1$.

- You can solve **quadratic equations** (of the form $ax^2 + bx + c = 0$) using factoring or the quadratic formula $\left(x = \dfrac{-b \pm \sqrt{b^2 - 4ac}}{2a} \right)$.

- If the radicand $b^2 - 4ac$ is positive, there are two distinct real solutions; if it is equal to 0, there is one real solution; if it is negative, there are two complex solutions.

- When solving **linear inequalities,** switch the inequality sign whenever both sides of the inequality are multiplied by a negative real number.

- A **system of linear equations** is a pair of linear equations involving x and y that must be satisfied at the same time—the solutions must fit in both equations to be correct. Solve systems by using the elimination method or the substitution method.

- The distance between two points $P(x_1, y_1)$ and $Q(x_2, y_2)$ is $\sqrt{(x_2 - x_1)^2 + (y_2 - y_1)^2}$. The midpoint of the line segment with endpoints $P(x_1, y_1)$ and $Q(x_2, y_2)$ is the point with coordinates $\left(\dfrac{x_1 + x_2}{2}, \dfrac{y_1 + y_2}{2} \right)$.

- In a **function,** each input x has a corresponding y-value. The **domain** of a function is the set of all values of x that can be substituted into the expression and yield a meaningful output; the **range** of a function is the set of all possible y-values attained at some member of the domain. Perform arithmetic operations on functions in the same manner you would perform operations on real numbers.

- The **x-intercept** of a function f is a point of the form $(x, 0)$. You determine the x-intercepts of a function by solving the equation $f(x) = 0$. The **y-intercept** of the function f is the point $(0, f(0))$.

- An **acute angle** measures between 0 and 90 degrees; a **right angle** measures 90 degrees; an **obtuse angle** measures between 90 and 180 degrees. **Complementary angles** sum to 90 degrees; **supplementary angles** sum to 180 degrees.

- All triangles obey the **Triangle Sum Rule** (the sum of the measures of the three angles in any triangle must be 180 degrees) and the **Triangle Inequality** (the sum of the lengths of any two sides of a triangle must be strictly larger than the length of the third side).

- Use the **Pythagorean theorem** ($a^2 + b^2 = c^2$) to determine the side lengths of right triangles.

- Two triangles are **congruent** if all three corresponding pairs of angles are congruent and all three corresponding sides are congruent.

- The **perimeter** of a region is the "distance around" and is computed by adding the lengths of all segments/curves forming its outer boundary; the **area** of a region in the plane is the number of unit squares needed to cover it.

- The **radius** of a circle is the common distance r by which points on the circle lie from the center. The **diameter** is twice the length of the radius. The circumference of a circle is $2\pi r$ or πd. The area of a circle equals πr^2.

- $\cos\theta = \dfrac{\text{adjacent}}{\text{hypotenuse}}$, $\sin\theta = \dfrac{\text{opposite}}{\text{hypotenuse}}$, $\tan\theta = \dfrac{\text{opposite}}{\text{adjacent}}$

- The graphs of sine and cosine are **periodic.** The **period** is the length of the smallest interval that can be used to produce the graph by replicating what it looks like on that interval on abutting intervals of the same length.

- The period of $f(x) = \sin(Bx)$ and $g(x) = \cos(Bx)$ is $\dfrac{2\pi}{B}$.

- $\cos^2\theta + \sin^2\theta = 1$, $\sin(-\theta) = -\sin(\theta)$, $\cos(-\theta) = -\cos(\theta)$

CHAPTER 5
THE ACT® READING TEST

OVERVIEW

- Test Overview
- ACT® Reading Strategies
- ACT® Reading Test Question Types
- The Social Studies Passage
- The Natural Sciences Passage
- The Humanities Passage
- The Literary Narrative/Prose Fiction Passage
- Summing It Up

After the English and Math tests, and the scheduled break, it's time to tackle the ACT Reading test. Reading is always the third test you'll see on test day, after math and before science. The ACT Reading test is a 35-minute assessment consisting of 40 multiple-choice questions that are divided among four text passages. Unlike the English test, which assesses your writing and editing skills, the ACT Reading test measures how well you read, understand, and interpret information given to you in a passage you've (probably) never seen before.

In this chapter, we'll cover each passage type and the question types you're likely to see on test day.

TEST OVERVIEW

The ACT Reading test is divided into four thematic sections/passage types: Social Studies, Natural Sciences, Humanities, and Literary Narrative/Prose Fiction. Each subsection can pull texts from these subject areas:

Theme	Potential Subject Areas	
Social Studies	Anthropology Archaeology Biography Business Economics	Education Geography History Political science Psychology Sociology
Natural Sciences	Anatomy Astronomy Biology Botany Chemistry Ecology Geology Medicine	Meteorology Microbiology Natural history Physiology Physics Technology Zoology
Humanities	Architecture Art Dance Ethics Film Language	Literary criticism Music Philosophy Radio Television Theater
Literary Narrative/Prose Fiction	**Literary Narrative:** Short stories Novels Memoirs Personal essays	**Prose Fiction:** Short stories Novels

In each of these four subsections, there will be a passage (or two shorter, related passages) followed by a set of 10 multiple-choice questions. In cases where there are two passages in the section, the questions may deal with one or both of the passages. The ACT Reading test doesn't test memorization skills or specific grammar rules. Test makers are more interested in how you read and interpret on the fly.

If you look at official ACT scores, you might notice that the Reading score is broken into two subscores: Social Studies/Sciences and Arts/Literature. Both of these sections carry equal weight—50% of your Reading score—so there's no need to prioritize any of the thematic sections over the others. No passage type is more or less difficult than the others, and you can expect easy and difficult questions with each passage type.

Remember: On the ACT Reading test, you're not expected to be an expert in social studies, science, literature, or the humanities. Instead, you'll be asked to read a passage that you probably haven't seen before and make decisions based entirely on the text in front of you.

NOTE: Cramming facts, dates, and vocabulary ahead of time won't help you on the ACT Reading test, but you know what will? Knowing what types of questions to expect and having a plan of attack for tracking down the answers in any passage.

The ACT Reading test questions will ask you to:

- Identify main ideas.
- Locate details within a passage and make decisions about what they mean.
- Make comparisons within a passage (or between two passages that you're given).
- Identify relationships within the passage (sequence of events, the flow of ideas, cause-and-effect).
- Figure out the meaning of words, phrases, and sentences based on the context.
- Draw conclusions and make inferences about the themes and details presented in the passage.
- Analyze the author's tone, purpose, or style.

ACT® READING TEST STRATEGIES

You're going to face 35 minutes, 4 passages, and 40 questions. You definitely need a game plan to get through this section. One of the best prep moves you can make is to know ahead of time how to attack the passage reading. Passages can range from 350 to 1,000 words, so in order to maximize your time, you need to get through any passage quickly.

Formulating Your Reading Plan of Attack

Time is definitely of the essence on the ACT Reading test. You need time to read each passage at least once and answer 40 questions, all within 35 minutes. It sounds like a game show, doesn't it? Like any well-prepared contestant on a game show, you should have a strategy for go time.

- **Read or skim through the passage once,** underlining and making notes about themes, topics, any details or character points that jump out at you. You may not need all of these notes later, but they can help lead you back to the info you need, after you start digging into the questions. If you're taking the test online, use scratch paper to make your notes.

- **Skim the questions** to see what you'll need to find in the passage. Make a special note of words like *except*, *most*, or *least*, because missing those directions could net you a wrong answer.

- **Answer any big-picture questions first,** since those are likely fresher in your mind after your first read-through.

- **Go back to the passage to confirm information.** If the question gives you a specific paragraph or line reference, great! If not, your notes should help you move back through the passage with ease. It can be tempting to rely on your short-term memory, but it's always better to do a quick confirmation that the passage says what you *think* it said.

As you read through the passage initially, here are the key areas where you should focus your notes:

- Topic (on both the passage and paragraph levels)
- The writer or narrator's purpose
- Characters
- Opinions expressed by the writer or characters

These are the areas that are likely to show up in the questions. And even if they're not tested directly, they can help you zoom in on the right parts of the passage once you've moved on to the questions.

One last tip for your reading plan: You don't need to tackle the passages in the same order as the test presents them. You're working against the clock, so you want to do this as efficiently as possible. If literature is your strongest area, tackle that passage and question set first before going back to the others. This way, you can breeze through your strong points, then go back and have time for the others. The last thing you want to do is spend most of your time on a problematic passage, only to be crunched for time when you come to a passage you like.

 If you're not sure what your reading strong points are, take a couple of timed practice tests and see which passages took up the most time and which ones were easier for you.

ACT® READING TEST QUESTION TYPES

The questions you'll see on the ACT Reading test fall into six different categories:

1. **Main Idea questions:** What is the main topic or theme of the passage?
2. **Detail questions:** What does a particular detail say about the passage?
3. **Vocabulary-in-context questions:** What is the meaning of a word or phrase, based on the words around it?
4. **Function and Development questions:** What effect does this information have on the passage?
5. **Inference questions:** What information is implied by the passage?
6. **Relationship questions:** How do details or characters compare or contrast with others in the passage? What are the cause-and-effect relationships in the passage? What is the sequence of events?

You might see some overlap in these areas—for example, a question about a cause-and-effect relationship might ask you to make inferences about the text. However, these categories represent the overall question structure. Let's take a quick look at each question type and how to tackle it on test day.

MAIN IDEA QUESTIONS

Main idea questions are pretty straightforward. They want you to be able to identify or infer—you guessed it—the main points or themes of the passage. Think of them as the "big-picture" questions, since you're asked to make an assessment of the passage as a whole. There's no special wizardry involved in this kind of question—you can often find the main idea in the first paragraph of the passage or at the very end of it. The trick is to be able to find it fast and to make sure that the rest of the passage supports that choice.

Here are some examples of how main idea questions might look on test day:

The main idea in this passage is:

- **A.** that owning a pet is difficult.
- **B.** how great it is to own a pet.
- **C.** that owning a pet is not worth the trouble.
- **D.** how glad the author is that he adopted a cat.

The central theme of the passage concerns the:

    F. narrator's struggles to fit in at a new school.
    G. feelings of all teenagers.
    H. best way to make new friends.
    J. teacher shortage at Memorial Hills High School.

Which of the following most closely represents the main idea of the passage?

    A. Aaron Burr should not be treated like a pure villain.
    B. Alexander Hamilton and Aaron Burr had a long and complicated history together.
    C. America's founding fathers did not get along.
    D. Alexander Hamilton should stay on the ten-dollar bill.

All of these questions boil down to, "What is the point of this piece of writing?" Still, for each different passage type, the main idea questions may look a little different. In Natural Sciences, Humanities, and Social Studies passages (a.k.a. the nonfiction passages), the main idea will almost always be the argument that the author is making in the passage. In nonfiction passages, you should be able to look at the introductory and concluding paragraphs to get a sense of what the main idea is.

In the Literary Narrative/Prose Fiction passage, the main points are related to the central conflict in the story and how that affects characters or other parts of the passage. Because this passage is likely to be an excerpt from a novel or short story, it's less likely to have the introduction + argument + clear conclusion structure that you could expect from a nonfiction passage on a specific topic.

Topic vs. Theme

One important thing to keep in mind with the main idea questions is that topic and theme aren't necessarily the same thing—and these big picture questions might ask you about both. The topic is usually pretty straightforward: *What is this passage about?* The themes can be a little trickier: *What is the message or lesson of this passage?*

Given that you only have 35 minutes to answer the 40 questions (not to mention the time it takes to read the passages themselves), it can be very easy to gloss right over that distinction. Make sure you read the questions carefully, and make sure you're identifying the correct part of the passage—the topic or the theme.

 Think of a topic as the subject of the passage. Think of the theme(s) as the concepts behind the subject.

Here is an example:

Which of the following themes is most closely supported by the second paragraph?

- **F.** The narrator's search for a spouse
- **G.** That the narrator has been unsuccessful in his relationships
- **H.** That marriage isn't necessarily as great as the narrator thinks it will be
- **J.** That marriage is every bit as fulfilling as the narrator thinks it is

Looking at the answer choices, you can narrow it down right away if you note that the question is asking for a theme, not a topic. (Instead of answering the question, "what is the author's main point?" you're answering the question, "what is the author's bigger message here?") Choices F and G are topics, while choices H and J are messages. Then, having eliminated two potential answer choices, you'd go back to the passage and see which option is best supported by the excerpt. The strongest answer-choice candidates will have multiple support points throughout the passage. For example, if the author talks frequently about marriage, then you can make a mental note that this is a potential main topic or theme. While you're reading the passage, you should feel free to make quick underlines or margin notes that will help you go back and search for information later.

 It's important to be as specific as possible when naming a main topic or theme. If you're torn between two answer choices, err on the side of the more specific answer.

Remember: It's not enough to find information that you *think* is the main idea. You also need to check the passage for details that support your answer choice. The "close enough" choice may not be the right one, so you should always pick the answer choice that's most fully supported by the passage.

Detail Questions

Most ACT Reading test questions fall into the category of detail questions. If main idea questions are the big picture, detail questions are the little picture. The ACT wants you to zero in on a very specific part of the passage instead of looking at the passage as a whole. This is where your close reading skills come in handy. If you've marked up your passage on your first pass-through, you can use those marks as a roadmap to get back to the details you need. For example, if you made a note (mental or written) that the second paragraph is about clown fish, and the question is asking about fish habitats, you can skip back to that fairly easily.

 The test may not always give line references to help you find information. You might need to pinpoint info within a paragraph or at several points in the passage.

Detail questions deal with the nitty-gritty information and how it's presented. In these questions, the test will usually ask you to identify a specific detail in a passage or paragraph. These questions are the most straightforward ones you'll see in the ACT Reading test—it's really just about retrieving information and connecting it to the best answer choice. However, like all of the question types, there are easy detail questions and hard detail questions. An easy one might ask you to find a very clear detail that supports the main idea of the passage. More difficult questions might ask you to find a minor detail that's buried in a dense part of the passage or to restate a detail that wasn't very clearly stated in the passage itself. Again, this is where your quick reading notes come in handy as a trail of breadcrumbs back through the passage.

Detail questions often look like these examples:

According to the passage, the US space program's original intent was to:

A. go to the moon.
B. establish an international space station.
C. earn money for the US government.
D. catch up to the USSR's space program.

Based on the passage, the primary purpose of Mary's fundraiser was to:

F. raise money for a veterans' charity.
G. get attention for Mary's blog.
H. throw a party.
J. recruit volunteers.

The passage establishes all of the following EXCEPT:

A. Shirley Temple Black was the first child actor to be elected to Congress.
B. Shirley Temple's movies are regaining popularity.
C. Kids today don't understand movies about life in the 1930s.
D. Child actors rarely go on to have successful careers as adults.

All of these questions ask you to be able to recall (or re-find) the information given in the passage. No tricks, no advance knowledge necessary—just the ability to go back to the passage and find the information. Don't overthink detail questions: If you're clear on what the question is asking (again, look out for words like *except*, *most*, and *least*) and you've located the information, mark your answer choice and move on.

You can work through detail questions quickly using these fast review questions:

- **Question 1:** What is the question asking?
- **Question 2:** Can you eliminate any of the choices?
- **Question 3:** Where is the information?
- **Question 4:** Which remaining answer choice fits?

Let's walk through the questions you can ask to answer a detail question, if the answer isn't clear right away.

Question 1: What is the question asking?

Make sure you're clear on what information is necessary to answer the question. Again, look out for words like *except*, *most nearly*, and *least*, because they tell you if you're looking for a single detail or need to rule out other details.

Question 2: Can you eliminate any of the choices?

There may be at least one obviously wrong choice, based on your first read-through of the passage. See if you can rule out any answer choices right away before you go back to the passage.

Question 3: Where is the information?

Detail questions may not give you line or paragraph information, so you'll need to be prepared to skim the passage until you find key words or ideas.

Question 4: Which answer choice fits?

After you've located the right part of the passage, match it up with the answer choices and pick the one that best fits the question. Sometimes, you may need to choose between two similar-sounding answers—**always go with the more specific option.**

 ALERT: If you can't find the answer to a detail question within 30 seconds, it's time to cut bait, eliminate any wrong answer choices you can, make a guess, and move on. It's not worth derailing your entire test strategy if you're stuck on a single detail question.

Detail questions are especially important in the nonfiction passages, because facts (and interpretation of those facts) often make up most of the content in these passages. The information could be complicated or layered, so you need to pay extra attention to details in the Natural Sciences, Social Studies, and Humanities passages.

VOCABULARY-IN-CONTEXT QUESTIONS

Unlike detail questions, vocabulary-in-context questions require you to make a judgment call. These questions will ask you to determine the meaning of a challenging word, based on the passage. These fall into two basic areas:

1. Common words that have multiple potential meanings

2. Difficult words that you may not have seen before

In both cases, you need to look carefully at the sentence the given word is in and possibly the paragraph or passage as a whole to figure out the correct meaning. You are not required to memorize lots of complex vocabulary or be able to recall that info on the spot. Rather, you'll always have the information in front of you to make an educated guess about the correct answer. It's the same set of skills that you use to find details in the passage—only this time, you're looking for details to draw your own conclusion.

Vocabulary-in-context questions may give you line references and send you to a specific sentence to define a word. These are pretty straightforward. If you don't recognize the word or its meaning by sight, you skim the passage until you find the noted line or paragraph and look at the surrounding words. At that point, either the meaning will be clear to you or you'll at least be able to eliminate some of the answer choices.

An example of this type of vocabulary question:

As it is used in line 45, the word *egregious* most nearly means:

- **A.** complicated.
- **B.** shocking.
- **C.** compelling.
- **D.** comforting.

Vocabulary-in-context questions might also ask you to summarize or paraphrase the meaning of a word or idea in the passage. For example:

Based on the passage as a whole, which of the following words would best describe Tiny Tim's relationship with his father?

- **F.** loving
- **G.** antagonistic
- **H.** apathetic
- **J.** distant

The best and quickest way to answer these vocabulary-in-context questions is to do a basic find-and-replace mission. You can do this two different ways:

1. Find the word/phrase in the passage, as indicated in the question. Insert a blank where the current word is and substitute a word of your own choosing. Then, find the closest answer choice that matches your substituted word.

2. Take each answer choice (at least the ones you couldn't eliminate right away) and quickly reread the sentence with each answer choice inserted into the sentence. The one that makes the most sense is the winner.

Both options are fairly quick; if you find yourself stumped, don't spend a lot of time on these vocab questions. Make your best guess and move on.

Beware of "close enough" answer choices! The ACT often uses words that have multiple meanings and throws in subtle differences in meaning to trip you up.

FUNCTION AND DEVELOPMENT QUESTIONS

After detail questions, the next most frequently asked on the ACT Reading test are function questions. Function questions ask you what a particular word, phrase, sentence, or paragraph does within the passage. Development questions are a variation on function questions—they ask you to figure out how the given information relates to the structure of the passage as a whole (i.e., how the author uses it to develop a theme or idea). Instead of vocabulary in context, think of function and development questions as action in context.

When answering function and development questions, ask yourself, "How does this text serve the purpose of the overall paragraph or passage?" Purpose is at the heart of every function and development question.

Remember the questions we used to answer detail questions? You can use that process for function and development questions as well:

- **Question 1:** What is the question asking?
- **Question 2:** Can you eliminate any of the choices?
- **Question 3:** Where is the information?
- **Question 4:** Which remaining answer choice fits?

Here are some of the types of function and development questions you're likely to see on test day:

The main purpose of the second paragraph is to:

- **A.** show how the narrator feels about Paris.
- **B.** tell the reader what food in Paris is like.
- **C.** show how the narrator feels more comfortable in Paris than in his home country.
- **D.** compare Paris with Buffalo, NY.

The author uses the information about lions in the fifth paragraph to:

- **F.** compare the narrator's family to wild animals.
- **G.** show how human and animal nature can be similar.
- **H.** contrast the lions' behavior with Andrew's behavior.
- **J.** suggest that the party should have taken place at the zoo.

In terms of developing the narrative, the rain imagery in the fourth paragraph primarily serves to:

- **A.** emphasize the theme of loneliness.
- **B.** provide a contrast with the narrator's statement about his feelings.
- **C.** support the writer's main argument that the weather can affect mood.
- **D.** contrast with the sun mentioned in the first paragraph.

It can be tempting to answer questions based on what you think the rest of the book, short story, or article might say. Resist that urge! The passages are typically excerpts from a larger work, but all of the information you need to answer the questions is right in front of you. Don't make assumptions about what the author might have said in the larger book, essay, or short story. If the information isn't in the passage or isn't directly supported by information in the passage, it might as well not exist—work with what you have in front of you.

INFERENCE QUESTIONS

Inference questions require you to take information and run with it. As with function and development questions, all the source information you need is right there in the passage—you don't need to apply facts or data of your own.

Inference questions ask you to take information from the passage (possibly a specific line or paragraph) and draw a conclusion about what that information means. Unlike function and development questions, these won't ask you to make decisions about what purpose a particular word, phrase, or section has in relation to the whole passage. Instead, you'll use your judgment to draw conclusions about what the author is trying to say in the passage. Basically, an inference question is the roundabout version of a detail question—except you supply the detail.

Look out for these words and phrases that tell you you're dealing with an inference question:

- *suggest*
- *infer*
- *imply/implication*
- *conclude*
- *assume*

These words tell you right away that you're not hunting for specific details in the passage, but rather for information that supports a particular point.

Inference questions can pop up in any ACT Reading passage, but expect to see them most often in the Literary Narrative/Prose Fiction passages. The nonfiction passages (Natural Sciences, Social Studies, and Humanities) all present specific information and might not be as concerned with the subtle development of themes or characters.

Some examples of inference questions you might see on test day:

It can be reasonably inferred from the passage that the narrator's favorite school subject is:

- **A.** history.
- **B.** math.
- **C.** physics.
- **D.** biology.

Based on the passage, it is likely that the author would most nearly agree with which of the following statements?

    F.   There is not enough funding for green energy initiatives.

    G.   There is already too much funding for wind energy.

    H.   Solar energy is not a valid alternative energy resource

    J.   The United States should lead the way on the search for alternative energy sources.

Inference questions can ask you to make generalizations about any number of things in the passage: meaning of words/phrases, theme, purpose, tone, function, or the author/narrator's intentions. The ACT doesn't require you to be psychic about what an author meant to say, but you should be able to find information in the passage to support your answer choice. Some of the hardest inference questions on the ACT will be attached to complex passages and will need you to understand information and draw conclusions based on multiple points in at least one passage.

To tackle inference questions, let's try a modified version of our reading analysis question list.

Question 1: What is the question asking?

This type of question is asking you to make a conclusion about the author's perspective and rephrase it.

Question 2: Can you eliminate any of the choices?

There may be at least one obviously wrong choice, based on your first read-through of the passage. Because this a judgment call and not a straight detail answer, it's okay to rely on your instincts. Skim the choices to see if any of them just feel wrong based on your initial read.

Question 3: Which answer choice fits?

Try reading the first sentence of each paragraph. This can be useful in helping you estimate where each answer choice might be found.

If your approach is to answer the questions out of order instead of pushing through chronologically, it's a good idea to work on the big picture/main idea questions first. That way, you've got a good sense of what's going on in the passage and that could trigger the "Aha! That's what the author is saying" moment when you get around to the inference questions.

RELATIONSHIP QUESTIONS

Relationship questions are a variation on inference questions in that they want you to draw conclusions about how characters or pieces of information are related within the passage. Relationship questions are most concerned with cause and effect, the sequence of events, and compare and contrast.

Cause and Effect

How does one detail or event impact another? Cause-and-effect relationships are often used to create broader meaning or emphasize bigger themes by drawing a line between events that may not seem related. Here is an example:

According to the passage, why did Deenie really miss the bus?

- **A.** She stayed up too late the night before and slept through her alarm.
- **B.** She wanted to miss homeroom and avoid seeing Marcia.
- **C.** The bus came earlier than usual.
- **D.** She didn't want to go to school at all.

In this example, you can infer from the word *really* in the question that the answer is not necessarily a stated detail from the passage, but possibly a conclusion you need to make based on other information in the passage (like Deenie's feelings about going to school in general).

Sequence

What happened and when? How does this affect the meaning of the passage? Passages might not have straight linear stories to tell. This is especially true in Literary Narrative/ Prose Fiction, where the timeline might be subtle or complicated by a narrator's telling of the story. When you do your initial passage read, make a note of what happens and try to create a quick mental timeline of these events or steps.

Sequence questions can look similar to cause-and-effect questions, in that both need you to understand *why* something is happening. It could be a motivation (which goes back to cause and effect), or it could be an event. For example:

According to the passage, the challenger's campaign likely failed because:

- **F.** she was unpopular with voters.
- **G.** she didn't have enough petition signatures before the deadline and didn't appear on the ballot.
- **H.** she was caught on video saying she didn't really want to be mayor.
- **J.** the current mayor declared victory in the race.

In this question's passage, there's likely a story behind the challenger's loss of the election. Your job is to find that story and determine when things happened and which piece had the most impact on the election.

 TIP Some passages may have sequences based on priority or significance, rather than factual order of events.

Compare and Contrast

How do details compare and contrast with others in the passage, and what does that mean for the passage as a whole?

Compared to the narrator, how does Chloe feel about the new neighbors?

- **A.** skeptical
- **B.** warm and welcoming
- **C.** excited
- **D.** angry

To answer a question like this one, you need to know how the narrator feels about the neighbors, and then locate direct details (or implied information) about Chloe, so that you can decide how the two perspectives line up.

Compare-and-contrast questions are especially important if you come across "paired passages" in the Literary Narrative/Prose Fiction passage. (More on that later in the chapter!) Because there will be two passages to grapple with, you'll need to be able to locate and understand similar details in two passages that may have totally different information and styles.

Some of the more challenging and time-consuming ACT Reading test questions might offer you a set of options labeled with Roman numerals, then ask you to make a decision about how those numbered options are related for your answer. For example:

Based on the passage, the author believes that which of the following are essential habits of successful people?

- I.   Getting 8 hours of sleep
- II. Having a nutritious breakfast
- III. Always saying yes to trying new things
- IV. Having firm personal boundaries

- **F.** I, II, and IV
- **G.** I, II, and III
- **H.** IV
- **J.** III and IV

Answering these questions requires a little bit more footwork than your average reading question, because you need to a) figure out what the question is really asking, and b) determine the relationships between the Roman numeral options before you can even hope to answer the question. Your plan of attack for these questions:

1. Quickly read the options.
2. Compare and contrast, determine the sequence of events, or figure out if there's a cause-and-effect relationship.
3. Skim the passage to find information that supports each option.
4. Choose the combination that works best with the information you have.

As always on the ACT Reading test, the most specific answer is the one you want to choose. Make sure the passage backs up each part of your answer choice.

Now that you're familiar with the question types you'll see on test day, look at the different passage types you'll see.

THE SOCIAL STUDIES PASSAGE

The social studies passage (sometimes informally known as the social science passage) is a nonfiction passage that presents information in the history or social science fields:

Anthropology	The study of people and societies
Archaeology	The study of ancient and recent human history through physical evidence
Biography	a narratives about the life of a specific person
Business	The study of commerce and trade
Economics	The study of the production, consumption, and transfer of wealth
Education	The study of teaching
Geography	The study of the physical features of the earth, as well as human populations
History	The study of past events and their effect on the world
Political Science	The study of government and politics
Psychology	The study of the human mind and behavior
Sociology	The study of human society and social relationships

The Social Studies passage is usually an excerpt from an **article, report, nonfiction book, essay, or textbook.** Looking at the list above, it's a pretty broad list of potential topics, so don't even try to be an expert in these areas before test day. Remember: **All the information you need will be in the passage itself.** You won't need to have any knowledge of Spanish-American relations or military history in general to answer questions about a historical essay about the Spanish-American War.

For the Social Studies passage, it's important to use the close reading skills we talked about earlier in the chapter. The passage may have a lot of details to keep straight—and in areas like history, political science, or economics, relationships like cause and effect, sequence, and comparison might be crucially important. So when you do your initial read of the passage, start by thinking about the context of the passage. When was it written? What is the author's probable perspective? What is the author trying to accomplish with this information—informing the audience or making an argument?

It's also important to consider the characters involved. The Social Studies passage may not have the same kind of characters that you'd find in a Literary Narrative/Prose Fiction passage, but the excerpt could very well be a profile of a famous figure and his or her contributions to society, so the focus of the questions will be different. Because they deal with historical figures and the author is writing a profile rather than a story, perspective questions about a Social Studies passage will focus on the subject, not the writer.

Social Studies passages are likely to ask you questions along these lines:

- Whether an author would agree with a particular statement, based on the information presented in the passage
- How information from the passage affects or describes the subject of the passage
- The subject's point of view (if it's a person)
- How events or ideas impact the main arguments or themes of the passage

Now that you have a sense of what's involved in the Social Studies passage, let's take a look at a sample passage and questions.

· ·

This passage is excerpted from *The Declaration of Independence* by Thomas Jefferson.

In every stage of these Oppressions We have Petitioned for Redress in the most humble terms: Our repeated Petitions have been answered only by repeated injury. A Prince, whose character is thus marked by every act which may define a Tyrant, is unfit to be the
5   ruler of a free People.

Nor have We been wanting in attention to our British brethren. We have warned them from time to time of attempts by their legislature to extend an unwarrantable jurisdiction over us. We have reminded them of the circumstances of our emigration and settlement
10 here. We have appealed to their native justice and magnanimity, and we have conjured them by the ties of our common kindred to disavow these usurpations, which would inevitably interrupt our connections and correspondence. They too have been deaf to the voice of justice and of consanguinity. We must, therefore, acquiesce in the necessity,
15 which denounces our Separation, and hold them, as we hold the rest of mankind, Enemies in War, in Peace Friends.

We, therefore, the Representatives of the United States of America, in General Congress, Assembled, appealing to the Supreme Judge of the world for the rectitude of our intentions, do, in the Name, and
20 by the Authority of the good People of these Colonies, solemnly publish and declare, That these United Colonies are, and of Right

ought to be Free and Independent States; that they are Absolved
from all Allegiance to the British Crown, and that all political connection between them and the State of Great Britain, is and ought
25 to be totally dissolved; and that as Free and Independent States, they
have full Power to levy War, conclude Peace, contract Alliances,
establish Commerce, and to do all other Acts and Things which
Independent States may of right do. And for the support of this
Declaration, with a firm reliance on the Protection of Divine Providence,
30 we mutually pledge to each other our Lives, our Fortunes and our
sacred Honor.

1. Which of the following statements is supported by the passage?
    A. The author is interested in working closely with the British government to
    find a solution to this conflict.
    B. In many political conflicts, there comes a point where war is a necessary choice.
    C. The colonies will still continue to pay taxes to the British crown.
    D. The United States is not interested in establishing its own economy.

The correct answer is B. The last sentence of the second paragraph ("We must, therefore,
acquiesce in the necessity, which denounces our Separation, and hold them, as we hold
the rest of mankind, Enemies in War, in Peace Friends") states that the United States
already sees Great Britain as a potential enemy in war. Choice A is incorrect because the
entire passage outlines the reasons why the colonies can no longer go along with British
rule. Choice C is incorrect because in paragraph 3, the author states that all connections
to Britain should be dissolved and that the United States should be able to establish its
own commerce (which also eliminates choice D).

2. Based on the context of the passage, the word *unwarrantable* (line 8) most
    nearly means:
    F. justified.
    G. unjustifiable.
    H. peaceful.
    J. angry.

The correct answer is G. The author is listing his grievances against the British crown,
which means it's unlikely that "justified" (choice F) is the correct answer. Choice G fits
with the angry tone the writer establishes with words like *tyrant* (line 4). Choice H is
incorrect because the passage suggests that the relationship between Britain and the
colonies is anything but peaceful; and choice J is incorrect because, although the writer's
tone is angry, there's no indication that Britain is acting with anger.

3. The sentence, "We, therefore, the Representatives of the United States of
    America, in General Congress, Assembled, appealing to the Supreme Judge of
    the world for the rectitude of our intentions… solemnly publish and declare,
    That these United Colonies are, and of Right ought to be Free and Independent
    States," marks a shift in the passage from _____ to _____.

A. a rejection of unfair power; acceptance of Britain's terms for the colonies
B. anger; optimism
C. independence; dependence
D. dependence; independence

The correct answer is D. In this sentence, Jefferson is putting an exclamation point on his argument that because the United States has been treated so badly by Britain, the time has come to break the ties. Choice A is incorrect because it suggests that Jefferson is embracing British rule, not rejecting it. Choice B is incorrect, because although it's possible that the author is optimistic about the United States' future, there's not really anything in the passage to support this choice. Choice C is incorrect because it's the exact opposite of Jefferson's goals: he sees the colonies' relationship to Britain as abusive and controlling and wants the colonies to move away and create their own economy and government. Choice D explains that relationship perfectly.

....

THE NATURAL SCIENCES PASSAGE

The Natural Sciences passage is a nonfiction passage that presents historical or current factual information about the hard sciences. It draws from these content areas:

Anatomy	The study of the human body
Astronomy	The study of space, celestial objects, and the universe
Biology	The study of living organisms
Botany	The study of plants
Chemistry	The study of substances and matter
Ecology	The study of the environment
Geology	The study of the earth's physical structure
Medicine	The study and treatment of disease and health
Meteorology	The study of the weather
Microbiology	The study of microscopic organisms
Physiology	The study of the body
Physics	The study of the properties of matter and motion

Technology	The study of applying scientific knowledge for practical purposes
Zoology	The study of animals

The Natural Sciences passage is usually an excerpt from an **article, report, nonfiction book, essay, or textbook.** The topics may include ones you've covered in school (biology, chemistry, Earth science, physics) but can also include specific branches of specialized study. It can be a little confusing, because isn't there already an entire science test on the ACT? There is indeed, but that test focuses on scientific thinking and logic, while the Natural Sciences passage is more concerned with your ability to read about science and understand what's written. If you've never been a whiz in the laboratory scene, no need to panic. You don't need a science background or Einstein's theory of relativity in your back pocket. All you need are those reading comprehension skills you already have (or are working on).

The Natural Sciences passage is more similar to the Social Studies passage than anything else, because both present factual information to be understood and interpreted by the reader. There's no complex data to decode, just narratives about science or discussions of specific events or findings in the science world. You won't be interpreting charts or graphs and drawing your own conclusions about the scientific process. Rather, it's more like reading a magazine article about an advance in physics or a profile of a Nobel Prize winner.

Here's a quick cheat sheet on the Science test vs. the Natural Sciences reading passage.

- **The ACT Science test:** You will interpret data presented to you.
- **The Natural Sciences Reading passage:** You will analyze *how* data is presented to you.

Although you can expect any question type to come up in the Natural Sciences passage, it's unlikely (though not impossible!) that you'll be asked to discuss theme or character development. However, you should definitely be prepared to field questions in these areas:

- Specific detail questions
- Whether a statement can be backed up within the passage
- What argument the writer is making
- Making inferences about the information presented

Let's look at a sample Natural Sciences passage and some sample questions.

. . . .

This passage is an excerpt from "2014: The Year of Concentrating Solar Power,"
a report produced by the United States Department of Energy.

Across the nation, solar energy is taking off, with more Americans
"going solar" every day. And, it's not just solar panels popping up on
the rooftops of homes; Americans are starting to adopt other forms
of solar energy as well. Concentrating solar power (CSP) is a technology
5   that harnesses the sun's energy potential and has the capacity to
provide hundreds of thousands of customers in the United States
with reliable renewable energy—even when the sun isn't shining.
The United States is particularly well suited for CSP because it leverages
the nation's abundant solar energy resources, particularly in the
10 sun-drenched southwestern states. Every day, more energy falls on
the United States—in the form of sunshine—than the country uses
in an entire year.

The year 2014 marks a significant milestone in the history of
American solar energy. Through sustained, long-term investments
15 by the United States Department of Energy (DOE) and committed
industry partners, some of the most innovative CSP plants in the
world connected to the United States electricity grid in 2013, and
five plants of this kind are expected to be fully operational by the
end of 2014. One of them is the largest CSP plant in the world; another
20 represents a first-of-its-kind in energy storage technology at commercial scale in the United States. Collectively, these five CSP plants
will nearly quadruple the preexisting capacity in the United States,
creating a true CSP renaissance in America.

By many measures, the solar energy industry has been one of
25 the fastest growing industries in the United States over the last five
years. By the end of 2013, the United States had more than 13 giga-
watts of installed solar capacity—nearly 15 times the amount installed
in 2008 and enough to power more than 2 million average American
homes.

30   DOE's SunShot Initiative—launched by the Office of Energy
Efficiency and renewable Energy's Solar Energy Technologies Office
in 2011 as a national effort to make solar energy fully cost competitive
with traditional energy sources by 2020—has played a critical role
in solar energy's recent success. The SunShot Initiative's investments
35 support innovation in solar energy technologies that are aimed at
improving efficiency and reducing the cost of materials, as well as
making it easier, faster, and cheaper for homeowners, businesses,
and state, local, and tribal governments to "go solar." Technology

innovation is not the only area where DOE is contributing to the
40 growth of solar in America. Through its Loan Programs Office (LPO),
DOE is helping to finance the first deployments of innovative solar
technologies, such as CSP, at a large scale. Projects employing technologies that are successfully demonstrated at a small scale with
minimal large-scale applications often face difficulty securing the
45 necessary capital for the initial commercial deployments. By providing
loan guarantees for commercial-scale projects using these newer
technologies, DOE reduced the projects' financial risk enabling new
private investment in the CSP market.

1.   According to the passage, all of the following are goals of the SunShot Initiative
     EXCEPT:

     A.   improved efficiency.
     B.   cheaper materials.
     C.   ease of use for homeowners.
     D.   Congressional legislation.

The correct answer is D. In the fourth paragraph, the author lists improved efficiency
(choice A), cheaper materials (choice B), and ease of use (choice C) as goals for the
SunShot initiative. There's no mention of Congressional legislation here or anywhere
else in the passage, so choice D is the exception and the correct answer. Remember,
always check for words like *EXCEPT* in the questions!

2.   Which of the following statements best explains the writer's perspective on
     solar energy?

     I.   Its time has passed as an alternative energy source.
     II.   Businesses and government should pay more for solar energy
           than homeowners.
     III. Solar energy is the energy source of the future.
     IV.   Other countries are better suited for solar energy than the United
           States.

     F.   I and II
     G.   III only
     H.   IV only
     J.   I, II, III, and IV

The correct answer is G. The first sentence of the passage states that solar energy is
"taking off," so that eliminates statement I and any answer choice that includes it (choices
F and J). Statement II is not supported by any information in the passage; in paragraph
4, the author talks about how government can work *with* businesses and homeowners,
but there's no indication that he or she thinks that one specific group should foot the
bill. So you can eliminate any answer choice containing II (choice J). Statement III is
supported by the very first sentences of the passage (and not undermined anywhere

else in the passage), so the correct answer will contain statement III. That means choices G and J, and we've already eliminated choice J. Choice G is the correct answer.

3. Based on the passage, you can infer that:

   A. wind energy has less potential than solar energy.
   B. the author thinks the United States should do more to adopt solar energy.
   C. private companies should be driving the solar energy adoption initiative.
   D. Japan is interested in embracing solar energy as well.

The correct answer is B. The topic of the piece, as stated in the very first sentence, is that solar energy is really taking off in the United States. There's no mention of wind energy anywhere in the passage, so choice A is incorrect. You can infer the author's support for solar energy based on his or her approach to the topic, but since he or she doesn't mention wind energy, you can't compare it with solar energy here. Choice B is correct because the author emphasizes that there are already a number of solar initiatives in the works, and makes the statement that "the United States is particularly well suited for CSP," suggesting that there's potential for more growth. Choice C is incorrect because the passage is primarily about the U.S. government's role in developing solar energy in the country. Choice D is incorrect because there's no information in the passage about Japan at all, let alone its approach to solar energy.

4. According to the passage, the DOE expected which of the following to happen by the end of 2014?

   F. The United States would be completely energy-independent, thanks to solar energy.
   G. The largest CSP plant in the world would be active in the United States.
   H. European countries would embrace the same solar energy initiatives.
   J. The United States would kick off nuclear power initiatives as well.

The correct answer is G. Paragraph 2 directly states that the DOE expected that the new, largest CSP plant in the world would be opening in 2014.

. . . .

THE HUMANITIES PASSAGE

The Humanities passage is kind of a hybrid of the Social Studies and Literary Narrative/ Prose Fiction passages: it's nonfiction (like social studies), but can also be crafted in a literary way to tell a story (like literary narrative/prose fiction). Informally, it's the non-fiction prose section, where narrative is often as important as specific details. This means that in this section, you should be on the lookout for questions that ask about tone and point of view along with the standard detail questions, main idea questions, inference questions, function questions, etc.

Humanities passages may come from any of these topic areas (essentially, philosophy and the arts):

- Architecture
- Art
- Dance
- Ethics
- Film/Film criticism
- Language
- Literary criticism
- Music
- Philosophy
- Radio
- Television
- Theater

The passages themselves might be taken from memoirs, personal essays, biographies, or articles. The passage could range from scholarly work (like a philosophical essay) to pop culture (an essay about the films of a specific director or the effect of a TV show on culture). The Humanities passage is fairly similar in structure to the other nonfiction passages (natural sciences, social studies), so let's dive in with a look at a sample passage and questions.

· ·

This is an excerpt from *Beethoven*, a biography of the composer by George Alexander Fischer. In it, the author discusses the teacher-student relationship between Ludwig von Beethoven and Franz Joseph Haydn.

Closely following his arrival in Vienna, Beethoven began studying composition with Haydn, applying himself with great diligence to the work in hand; but master and pupil did not get along together very well. There were many dissonances from the start. It was not in
5 the nature of things that two beings so entirely dissimilar in their point of view should work together harmoniously. Beethoven, original, independent, iconoclastic, acknowledged no superior, without having as yet achieved anything to demonstrate his superiority; Haydn, tied down to established forms, subservient, meek, was only happy when
10 sure of the approbation of his superiors. His attitude toward those above him in rank was characterized by respect and deference; he probably expected something similar from Beethoven toward himself. Haydn was then at the height of his fame, courted and admired by all, and his patience was sorely tried by the insolence of his fiery
15 young pupil. He nicknamed Beethoven the Grand Mogul, and did not have much good to say of him to others. The pittance which he received for these lessons was no inducement to him, as he was in receipt of an income much beyond his requirements. The time given up to these lessons could have been better employed in composing.

20 Haydn and Beethoven, however, were in a measure supplementary to one another as regards the life-work of each. Haydn paved the way for Beethoven, who was his successor in the large orchestral

forms. He and also Mozart were pioneers in the field which Beethoven made peculiarly his own. Haydn also directed Beethoven's attention
25 to the study of Händel and Bach, whose works Beethoven always held most highly in esteem. It is true that Beethoven, even in the old Bonn days, was familiar to some extent with the works of these masters; but his opportunity for getting at this kind of music was limited in Bonn. Vienna, the musical center of the world at that time,
30 was, as may be supposed, a much better field in this respect.

The lessons to Beethoven continued for a little over a year, or until Haydn left on another visit to England in January of 1794. So eager was he for advancement, that he took lessons from another teacher at the same time, carefully concealing the fact from Haydn.
35 Beethoven always maintained that he had not learned much from him.

Strangely, Haydn had no idea at this time or for some years after that his pupil would ever amount to much in musical composition. He lived long enough to find Beethoven's position as a musician firmly established, but not long enough to witness his greatest triumphs.

1. Which of the following statements best characterizes the relationship between Beethoven and Haydn?

A. They were close friends and confidantes.

B. They never got along very well, despite their similar talents.

C. Beethoven and Haydn had a long and productive teaching relationship.

D. Haydn was jealous of Beethoven's talent.

The correct answer is B. Choice B is supported by details in every paragraph of the passage: both Beethoven and Haydn are described as great composers, but the first paragraph talks about how different their personalities were; the second paragraph presents their complementary careers as an unexpected event, given their unhappy collaboration; the third paragraph talks about Beethoven leaving Haydn's lessons behind; and the fourth paragraph talks about how Haydn never expected Beethoven to amount to much. All of this information supports choice B as an inference. Choice A is incorrect because all of the supporting details in the passage suggest the opposite of their friendship. Choice C is incorrect because the third paragraph says explicitly that they only worked together for about a year. Choice D is incorrect because there's no indication that Haydn was jealous of Beethoven, just that he didn't like Beethoven.

2. Based on the context, the word *approbation* (line 10) most nearly means which of the following?

F. rejection

G. disapproval

H. approval

J. independence

The correct answer is H. The sentence that contains *approbation* tells you that Haydn was "meek" and "subservient". That suggests that he did not have a bold or independent personality (choice J). *Subservient* also suggests that Haydn would not actively seek rejection (choice F) or disapproval (choice G) from others, but approval (choice H). If you find that the context words (like *subservient*) are also unfamiliar to you, look for root words that could help you. In this case, from the *serv* part of *subservient*, you could make a logical decision that serving is part of the definition.

3.   Which of the following most closely represents the main idea of the passage?

   A.   Talented individuals might not work well together if they have different personalities and perspectives.
   B.   Composers do not get along with other composers.
   C.   Composers have much to learn from one another.
   D.   Beethoven would have been better off working with Mozart instead of Haydn.

The correct answer is A. The passage spends a lot of time telling the reader how different Beethoven and Haydn were, especially in the second paragraph. If you combine that with the second sentence (which explicitly says, "master and pupil did not get along together very well"), you can extrapolate that the overall theme of this excerpt is that challenges can come from two talented-but-different artists working together. Choice B is too general—there's nothing in the passage that suggests that all composers would have the same relationship. Choice C is incorrect because it's also a very vague statement, without much specific support from the passage. Choice D is incorrect because no supporting details in the passage suggest that Mozart would have been a better choice as a mentor.

· ·

THE LITERARY NARRATIVE/PROSE FICTION PASSAGE

Despite the name, the Literary Narrative/Prose Fiction passage isn't just fictional stories and characters. Although prose fiction passages come straight from novels or short stories, literary narrative passages can be excerpted from novels, short stories, personal memoirs, or other forms of storytelling. Think of this passage as the broad "literature" one. It's also usually the longest: the passage can be anywhere from 350 to 1,000 words.

NOTE: On test day, you will see either a literary narrative OR a prose fiction passage. You should be prepared for both types, but you won't see both within the same test.

Paired Passages

The format for the Literary Narrative/Prose Fiction passage is pretty much the same as the other three passage types—with one exception. The ACT has started including "paired passages" in this section, which means that instead of one long passage + 10 questions, sometimes there are two much shorter passages + 10 questions. (Don't worry: The number of questions is always the same, no matter what!) Not every ACT test session includes a set of paired passages, but you should definitely be prepared to see them in the Literary Narrative/Prose Fiction subsection, just in case.

When answering questions for paired passages, don't get too caught up in combing both passages for information, because you still need to answer the same number of questions regardless of the passage type. Keep an eye on your time!

The main difference isn't the format so much as the complexity. Now you have two separate pieces of writing to read and process in the same amount of time in which you'd usually tackle one passage. You can expect three general question types with paired passages:

1. Passage A questions
2. Passage B questions
3. Passage A + Passage B questions

Your game plan for paired passages really depends on how you work through questions best—in order, or jumping around. However, with the paired passages, you might find it easier to attack the single-passage questions first, then move on to the questions that will make you go back and forth between the mini-passages. That way, you have a pretty good sense of what passage A is about and what passage B is about before you try to fit them together.

The paired passages will always be related somehow—linked by theme, topic, or author. You don't need to worry about getting two entirely unrelated pieces of writing that you'll need to figure out how to compare.

For example, here are some of the types of questions you could expect to see on a paired passage ACT:

Compared to Passage A, the tone of Passage B is . . .

It can reasonably be inferred that the narrator of Passage A is _____, while the narrator of Passage B is _____.

Compared to the relationship in Passage A, the relationship in Passage B could best be described as . . .

As with standard passages, all the info you need will be in the passage (or at least the information you need to make inferences).

Let's try a sample Literary Narrative/Prose Fiction passage and some sample questions.

This is an excerpt from the novel *Anne of Green Gables*,
by Lucy Maud Montgomery.

Anne went to the little Avonlea graveyard the next evening to
put fresh flowers on Matthew's grave and water the Scotch rosebush.
She lingered there until dusk, liking the peace and calm of the little
place, with its poplars whose rustle was like low, friendly speech, and
5 its whispering grasses growing at will among the graves. When she
finally left it and walked down the long hill that sloped to the Lake
of Shining Waters it was past sunset and all Avonlea lay before her
in a dreamlike afterlight—"a haunt of ancient peace." There was a
freshness in the air as of a wind that had blown over honey-sweet
10 fields of clover. Home lights twinkled out here and there among the
homestead trees. Beyond lay the sea, misty and purple, with its
haunting, unceasing murmur. The west was a glory of soft mingled
hues, and the pond reflected them all in still softer shadings. The
beauty of it all thrilled Anne's heart, and she gratefully opened the
15 gates of her soul to it.

"Dear old world," she murmured, "you are very lovely, and I am
glad to be alive in you."

Halfway down the hill a tall lad came whistling out of a gate
before the Blythe homestead. It was Gilbert, and the whistle died on
20 his lips as he recognized Anne. He lifted his cap courteously, but he
would have passed on in silence, if Anne had not stopped and held
out her hand.

"Gilbert," she said, with scarlet cheeks, "I want to thank you for
giving up the school for me. It was very good of you—and I want
25 you to know that I appreciate it."

Gilbert took the offered hand eagerly.

"It wasn't particularly good of me at all, Anne. I was pleased to
be able to do you some small service. Are we going to be friends
after this? Have you really forgiven me my old fault?"

30   Anne laughed and tried unsuccessfully to withdraw her hand.

"I forgave you that day by the pond landing, although I didn't
know it. What a stubborn little goose I was. I've been—I may as well
make a complete confession—I've been sorry ever since."

"We are going to be the best of friends," said Gilbert, jubilantly.

35   "We were born to be good friends, Anne. You've thwarted destiny
enough. I know we can help each other in many ways. You are going

to keep up your studies, aren't you? So am I. Come, I'm going to walk home with you."

Marilla looked curiously at Anne when the latter entered the kitchen.

40 "Who was that came up the lane with you, Anne?"

"Gilbert Blythe," answered Anne, vexed to find herself blushing. "I met him on Barry's hill."

"I didn't think you and Gilbert Blythe were such good friends that you'd stand for half an hour at the gate talking to him," said Marilla
45 with a dry smile.

"We haven't been—we've been good enemies. But we have decided that it will be much more sensible to be good friends in the future. Were we really there half an hour? It seemed just a few minutes. But, you see, we have five years' lost conversations to catch up with, Marilla."

1. Based on the passage, you can conclude that:

   A. Anne is devastated over Matthew's death.
   B. Anne and Gilbert will be enemies again in the future.
   C. The beautiful evening has softened Anne's feelings toward Gilbert.
   D. It was Anne's fault that she and Gilbert were enemies.

The correct answer is C. Although the scene of the passage is set in a cemetery, there is no information about Matthew's death, or Anne's reaction to it. She may have been devastated at the time, but none of the info you have in the passage supports choice A. Choice B is incorrect because all of the supporting details in the passage suggest otherwise: Gilbert believes that he and Anne will be good friends and put their previous problems behind them. Choice C is correct because the passage spends the entire first paragraph talking about how lovely the evening is and how it affects Anne. With the sentence, "The beauty of it all thrilled Anne's heart, and she gratefully opened the gates of her soul to it," you can make the connection that because Anne feels happy and open, she's more willing to talk to Gilbert. Choice D is incorrect because although there's no specific information about what caused Anne and Gilbert to be enemies before, Gilbert suggests that the "fault" was his own.

2. The author uses the cemetery imagery at the beginning of the passage in order to:

   F. suggest that death is sad.
   G. emphasize that although sad things happen, life is still beautiful.
   H. show that Anne's cheerfulness is disrespectful to Matthew.
   J. give Gilbert an excuse to talk to Anne.

The correct answer is G. As in question 1, the cemetery is a setting, but not really a platform for talking about death itself. Instead, the author chooses to emphasize the loveliness of the evening, rather than focus on the sadness of Matthew's death. Therefore, choice F is not really supported by the passage. Choice G is a much better choice, because it mentions the push-pull tension between the once-sad setting and the happiness that Anne feels there now. Choice H is incorrect; from the passage, we don't know enough about Matthew to know whether he would think Anne's sense of peace and happiness is disrespectful to his memory. Choice J is incorrect because the cemetery itself has nothing to do with the reason Gilbert and Anne talk.

3. What is the main theme of this passage?

    A. forgiveness
    B. spending an evening talking with a friend
    C. coping with death
    D. a description of Anne's day

The correct answer is A. Anne and Gilbert talk about forgiving each other, and then at the very end of the passage, Anne re-emphasizes that the point of her conversation with Gilbert was that they will no longer be enemies. There's support throughout the passage for choice A. Choices B and D are incorrect because they're really topics, not themes (concepts). Choice C is incorrect because despite the setting, the passage doesn't really talk about death.

SUMMING IT UP

- The **ACT Reading section** is divided into four sections, or passage types: **Social Studies, Natural Sciences, Humanities, and Literary Narrative/Prose Fiction.** For these multiple-choice questions, you'll be asked to identify themes, details, relationships, and meanings from each passage. You'll also be asked to draw conclusions based on the information you're given. All the info you need will be in the passages themselves—no need for outside expertise!

- While you read each passage, take quick notes and focus on big pieces like topics, themes, characters/narrator, and major ideas expressed by the author.

- **Main idea questions** ask you to identify the primary topics or themes of the passage. Topics describe what the passage is about. Themes are the messages or lessons of the passage. Make sure you're clear on which one the question is asking you to identify.

- **Detail questions** ask you to confirm very specific information in the passage, often without a line reference. Always make sure your answer choice is *fully* backed up by the passage.

- In **vocabulary-in-context questions**, you'll need to choose the best meaning for a word or phrase based on the context in the passage. No need to memorize a ton of vocabulary words—you should be able to figure out the meaning instead of knowing it by heart.

- **Function and development questions** want you to determine what a particular detail or theme is doing in the passage. How does this information relate to the passage as a whole?

- For **inference questions**, you do the heavy lifting. You need to take information given in the passage and make decisions about characters or themes.

- **Relationship questions** ask you to analyze how characters, events, and details are related. Cause-and-effect questions ask you to make a conclusion about how characters or events affect one another. Sequence questions ask you to determine the order in which things happened or the priority that the author sets for them. Compare and contrast questions want you to take information from different parts of the passage, and make a decision about how they're related. Remember: All the information you need is in the passage, so make sure that your answer choice is supported by the information you have in front of you.

- The **Social Studies passage** is a nonfiction excerpt from a book, essay, article, report, or textbook, with a focus on history, business, or the social sciences. With this passage, you should be prepared to answer questions about the author's perspective, the relationship between details and information in the passage, and how details and events impact the author's main arguments or themes.

- The **Natural Sciences passage** is a nonfiction excerpt drawn from articles, reports, books, essays, or textbooks about the sciences. It's different from the Science section of the ACT because the Natural Sciences passage focuses on interpreting science narratives rather than scientific data. Some of the more common questions within the Natural Science passage include specific detail questions, questions about the author's argument, and inference questions about the information presented.

- The **Humanities passage** is a nonfiction excerpt that relates to philosophy and the arts. It's slightly different from Social Studies in that the passage is kind of a hybrid narrative—it's factual information, but often presented in a more literary way. In this section, expect to find questions about the author's tone and POV, along with the same kind of detail, main idea questions, inference questions, and function questions that you'd find in the other nonfiction passages.

- The **Literary Narrative/Prose Fiction passage** is the literature-based passage—expect to see an excerpt from a novel or short story. The most common questions are about the tone, the author/narrator's point of view, relationships between characters and events, details, and inference questions about themes and details. In this passage, you might also encounter two shorter paired passages, where you'll be asked to compare and contrast information between the two.

CHAPTER 6
THE ACT® SCIENCE TEST

OVERVIEW

- Test Overview
- Data Representation: Reading and Analyzing Scientific Figures
- Research Summaries: Understanding and Analyzing Scientific Experiments
- Conflicting Viewpoints: Reading Comprehension, Science-Style
- Summing It Up

The ACT Science test examines your ability to think like a scientist, rather than your ability to recall science facts. While the test makers presume that you have at least three years of natural science course experience when you take the exam, you could still actually do relatively well on the exam without too much background knowledge! You just need to know what to expect, and that's where this chapter comes in.

The pages that follow will explore the basic strategies you can use to make reading and understanding science passages easier. We'll talk about the different passage types you'll see on test day and the question types that accompany them and show you how to recognize key details that will make answering questions second nature.

TEST OVERVIEW

Overall, the ACT Science test contains 40 questions, which you must complete in 35 minutes. At first glance, this may seem stressful, as you have less than a minute to spend on each question, but having some familiarity with the structure of the exam, the types of questions you'll see, and strategies you can employ will keep you on course and allow you to get through the test without panicking.

With regard to content, the ACT Science test covers biology, chemistry, physics, and earth and space sciences. Again, no one expects you to be an expert in any of these fields. All of the factual information you need to know to earn a high score on the exam is found directly in the passages you are given.

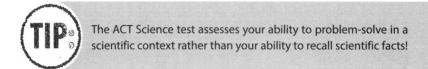

TIP The ACT Science test assesses your ability to problem-solve in a scientific context rather than your ability to recall scientific facts!

However, you will find it easier to read the passages, and will be able to make your way through them faster, if you have a familiarity with basic science concepts within each content area. When it comes to reviewing your high school science, focus on the most basic concepts in each field. For example, in biology, focus on biomolecules and the subunits that make them up, such as proteins composed of amino acids. In chemistry, understand the difference between reactants and products. In physics, make sure you know something about gravitational acceleration and oscillatory motion. In earth and space sciences, know the difference between planetary revolution and rotation and the different types of rocks. For the most part, key vocabulary will be spelled out for you in the ACT Science test, or you will at least be given enough background information to figure out definitions.

There are three types of passages (and accompanying questions) that you will encounter on the ACT Science test:

1. Data Representation

2. Research Summaries

3. Conflicting Viewpoints

Data Representation passages and questions focus on your ability to understand and analyze graphs and figures. **Research Summaries** also involve data analysis, but they additionally emphasize experimental procedures and logic behind the experiment. **Conflicting Viewpoints** provide you with two or three arguments on a particular phenomenon and mostly test your reading comprehension skills, namely your ability to recall information, compare and contrast the arguments, and draw inferences.

Of the 40 questions that appear on the ACT Science test, there are roughly 15 Data Representation questions based on three passages, 18 Research Summaries questions based on three passages, and 7 Conflicting Viewpoints passages based on one passage. We will go through each passage type to delve into its structure, typical associated questions, and strategies.

So when all is said and done, the real goal of the ACT Science test is to test your ability to solve problems in scientific contexts. Can you read and understand scientific information? Are you able to reason through experimental procedures? Can you analyze data? By the time you get through this chapter, you should be able to answer "yes" to all of these questions, and you will be armed with the knowledge to tackle any science passage or question that could be thrown your way.

DATA REPRESENTATION: READING AND ANALYZING SCIENTIFIC FIGURES

Data Representation passages generally make up 30-40 percent of the ACT Science test and focus on your ability to interpret scientific figures and use them to draw conclusions. Each Data Representation passage will begin with an introduction, which can range in length from a sentence or two to a few paragraphs. The introductory text is where you will find important vocabulary related to the topic of interest, along with information about the experiment or study upon which the presented figure is based.

The figure itself is the most important part of any Data Representation passage. Figures might include graphs, scatterplots, experimental setups, or data tables. Regardless of what is thrown at you, your job will be to look at the figure, determine what it is telling you, note patterns or trends in the data, and draw conclusions about them. You will, in many cases, be given multiple kinds of figures, though usually no more than two or three.

What makes Data Representation passages notable is that if the scientific principles discussed in the introductory text are confusing, **the figures themselves can usually tell you everything you need to know.** Graphs and data tables will provide you with any independent or dependent variables, which can help to clarify the scientific question posed by the scientist.

Each Data Representation passage is followed by approximately five questions that test a number of important skills that you will use—even in other passage types. The most common question types you will encounter following Data Representation passages will ask you the following:

- Do you understand the data presented in the figure?
- Can you analyze graphs?
- Can you draw conclusions based on the presented data?
- How valid are the presented data?
- What future work could be performed next in the context of the results?

We will go through each of these question types and focus on important vocabulary associated with each that will help you to successfully address them.

Do You Understand the Data Presented in the Figure?

The first goal you should have when tackling a Data Representation passage is to identify the **scientific question,** which presents the purpose of the experiment. Often, the scientific question will be directly stated in the introductory text that precedes a figure, but regardless, make sure you understand the data you will be looking at as soon as possible. If you misunderstand the scientific question, you might be inclined further down the road to select incorrect answers to questions about conclusions and future work, for instance, so identifying the scientific question is important.

Another feature you may encounter in the written introduction, and which can help you to pinpoint the scientific question, is the **hypothesis**—an educated guess about an experimental outcome. Questions that follow a Data Representation passage may ask you to select a logical hypothesis, or a hypothesis of the scientist may be given directly. Either way, a sensible hypothesis for a scientific question must address the appropriate variables, which set the parameters for the experiment.

The **independent variable** is the condition that the scientist alters during the experiment, and the **dependent variable** is the condition that the scientist measures during the experiment. For example, if you are testing the effect of pesticides on pea plant growth, the absence or presence of pesticides is the independent variable, while pea plant height might be the dependent variable. If these variables are not obvious based on the introductory text, you can often figure out what they are based on the provided figure. The headers of a data table and the axes of a graph are two extremely common places to find independent and dependent variables. On a graph in particular, you can usually find the independent variable on the horizontal x-axis and the dependent variable on the vertical y-axis.

NOTE: You're unlikely to ever encounter a 3D graph on the ACT Science test, but if you do, the z-axis is the axis that would project out of the page at you.

CAN YOU ANALYZE GRAPHS?

Your ability to analyze graphs will be tested throughout the ACT Science test, so let's go over some of the more common features of graphs you should recognize in any presentation. **Linear graphs** form straight lines, while **exponential graphs** form curved lines that either increase or decrease in slope at steady rates. Positive graphs increase from left to right, while negative graphs decrease from left to right. A horizontal line has a slope of zero, while a vertical line has an undefined or infinite slope.

Many graphs will include a **legend,** which is a key that can be used to interpret the graph. Axes will almost always be labeled and can accordingly provide you with information about the independent and dependent variables for a given experiment.

More Complicated Graph Types

Parabolas are symmetrical graphs shaped like the letter U, while **hyperbolas** are curves that approach but never reach invisible lines called asymptotes—this isn't a math test, so you're unlikely to see either of these graph types, but keep them in the back of your mind on the off chance you do.

Linear and exponential graphs are probably the most common graphs you'll see. A common graph type is the **scatterplot,** which has an *x-* and *y*-axis, along with data points marked that associate particular *x-* and *y*-values. Sometimes, lines are used to connect data points in a scatterplot. Another common graph type that deviates from the axis-based graphs you may be used to is the **pie chart,** which can be used to show the percentages of a total that are occupied by components of the whole.

Depending on whether you prefer to work with visuals or numbers, you might prefer data tables to graphs, or vice versa. A good strategy to employ in this case would be to convert one to the other. For instance, if you prefer visuals and are given a data table, use the margins of your test to sketch a graph. In contrast, if you're given a graph and would rather work with numbers, organize a simple data table, estimating numbers from the figure as needed. It may seem like a giant time suck, but really—it's worth the extra minute or two to get the information into a format you can work with comfortably.

CAN YOU DRAW CONCLUSIONS BASED ON THE PRESENTED DATA?

You can practically guarantee that every Data Representation passage will be followed by a question that asks you to draw a conclusion that expresses the key take-home message based on trends in the data. At this point, you've already done the hard part by figuring out the variables and reading the figures. Now your job is simply to identify any patterns or trends in the data and frame a conclusion in the form of a statement that describes these trends. This is usually a fairly straightforward question type, but you might see variations in which you have to apply conclusions to a related scenario or predict a result that was not specifically measured in the experiment. These questions take your data analysis to the next level. But they are not trick questions, so try your best to answer the questions as simply as possible, without confusing yourself.

HOW VALID ARE THE PRESENTED DATA?

There are a number of ways to assess data validity, but scientists often rely on statistical methods. Such methods can help one to determine the **accuracy** and **precision** of a set of data. The following table defines these terms and describes the relevant statistical means for determining them:

Term	Accuracy
Definition	How close a measured number is to a known standard or value
Mathematical Indicator	Percent Error = $$\left| \frac{\text{Known Value} - \text{Measured Value}}{\text{Known Value}} \right| \times 100\%$$ $$\text{Mean} = \frac{\text{Sum of Values from All Trials}}{\text{Number of Trials}}$$
Analysis of Mathematical Indicator	A lower percent error indicates that a measured value is close to the actual value; a lower percent error therefore indicates higher accuracy. The mean, or average, is the "measured value" you should use for a given trial set.
Term	Precision
Definition	How close a set of measured numbers is to one another for the same repeated experiment
Mathematical Indicator	**Standard deviation** describes how far the numbers in a set of trials are from their mean. It is a fairly complicated calculation, and you will never have to perform it on your own, but it is worthwhile to know what it means.
Analysis of Mathematical Indicator	A lower standard deviation indicates that the numbers are generally close to the mean; therefore, a lower standard deviation indicates higher precision.

It is worth noting that **outliers,** data values that deviate drastically from the norm, can affect your mean for a trial set. The appearance of an outlier data value in a trial might mean that an error occurred in the trial, since the number is so different from the other numbers. As such, increasing the number of total trials performed for an experiment improves the validity of the data because you are more likely to have many unflawed trials, making it easier to identify potential outlier data values.

Questions that ask you about data validity might ask you directly to assess accuracy or precision based on the numbers from the figure you've been given. You might also be asked to suggest an error that might have occurred during the experiment and affected measured values or to recommend a way to improve the experiment in order to increase data validity. As we have just noted, increasing the number of trials is always a surefire way to improve data validity for a given experiment.

WHAT FUTURE WORK COULD BE PERFORMED NEXT IN THE CONTEXT OF THE RESULTS?

In the real world of scientific research, the data obtained in one experiment or set of experiments will lead to another experiment or set of experiments. Scientists perform experiments to learn something new or to confirm something they thought they knew, so relevant follow-up experiments might include a similar experiment that tests a different but relevant variable, or perhaps an entirely new experiment that will contribute useful knowledge to the topic of study.

You won't have to come up with new experiments off the top of your head; however remember, this is a multiple-choice exam. Often, you will be provided with a goal for future experimentation, and you will have to choose an experiment that accomplishes this goal, ensuring that you've selected an experiment that addresses the appropriate independent and dependent variables. Process of elimination is very useful here, as you can eliminate choices that incorrectly identify one or both of these variables.

As we will see later in this chapter, Research Summaries questions often also test this skill, so thinking about future work based on current data is definitely a useful skill. Fortunately, it is really just based on logic and your understanding of the scientific method.

POTENTIAL PITFALLS IN DATA REPRESENTATION PASSAGES AND QUESTIONS

The table below describes a few potential common obstacles you could encounter in Data Representation passages and questions, along with some tips for overcoming them.

Potential Pitfall	Useful Tips
Difficult terminology	• When you encounter a challenging vocabulary word in a passage, re-read the text to see if the word is defined directly in the text. • If the word is not directly defined, use your reading comprehension skills—look for words and phrases around the difficult term to see if they can help you make an educated guess about its meaning. • Look at the provided figures. Do they offer any hints about the meaning of the word? • Check out the questions and see if the definition of the word is required to answer them. If it isn't, don't hesitate to move on!
Extraneous information	• Don't focus too much on historical information, widely known background information, or other unnecessary text. Instead, hone in on text related to the scientific question, experimental variables, and the provided figure(s).
Unexpected results	• Don't assume you know the answer to a given scientific question. Use the data to look for trends and draw conclusions, even if the data look different than you would have expected. • If unexpected results are provided, keep an eye out for potential built-in design flaws in the experiment or consider errors that may have occurred that would provide these results. You may encounter a question later that asks you to think about either of these potential flaws.
Unusual figures	• While most of the data you'll see will be straightforward and formatted recognizably, you may encounter unusual presentation styles for data, such as maps or 3D graphs. Focus on the key features, namely identifying the independent and dependent variables, as this will help you to see how these variables are related visually on the figure.

Data Representation: Example Passage and Questions

Now it's time to take a look at a Data Representation passage. Read the following passage and then answer the questions that follow, keeping in mind the key tips we've already covered in this chapter.

. . . .

Embryo implantation is a tightly regulated step during the establishment of pregnancy, and disease can result if implantation goes awry. The mouse gene *ndrg2* and the local microRNA of *ndrg4*, miR-3074-5p, were recently implicated in mouse embryo implantation, so a group of scientists decided to test whether or not the *ndrg4* gene itself is involved in embryo implantation.

Experiment 1

The scientists first determined the levels of uterine *ndrg4* expression in the uteri of newborn mice during the various postnatal developmental stages using quantitative PCR (qPCR) to detect the mRNA produced by the *ndrg4* gene. Expression levels were calculated relative to the expression of beta-actin, which is expressed the same regardless of pregnancy or development. The error bars represent standard deviations based on the three trials performed per stage:

Uterine *ndrg4* expression in the postnatal mouse developmental stages (W = # weeks old)

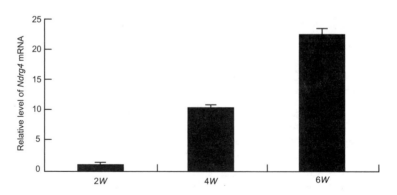

Figure 1

Experiment 2

The scientists then used qPCR to detect uterine *ndrg4* expression during early pregnancy in the uteri of parental mice. Expression levels were calculated relative to the expression of beta-actin, which is expressed the same regardless of pregnancy or development. The error bars represent standard deviations based on the three trials performed per bar:

Uterine *ndrg4* expression during early pregnancy in mice (D = # days of pregnancy, IS = implantation sites, NI = non-implantation sites

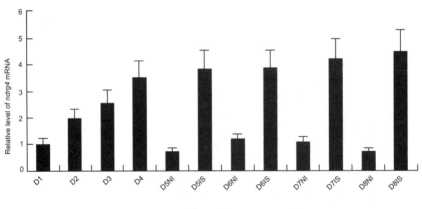

Figure 2

On average, what was the approximate expression of *ndrg4* relative to beta-actin after six days of pregnancy at implantation sites in the parental uterus?

A. 1.1
B. 3.9
C. 4.2
D. 22.0

The correct answer is B. According to Figure 2, the bar for D6IS shows that after six days of pregnancy, the expression of *ndrg4* was approximately 3.9-fold higher than that of beta-actin at implantation sites. Choice A is incorrect because this is the approximate expression of *ndrg4* relative to beta-actin after six days of pregnancy at non-implantation sites, according to Figure 2. Choice C is incorrect because this is the approximate expression of *ndrg4* relative to beta-actin after eight days of pregnancy at implantation sites. Choice D is incorrect because this is the approximate expression of *ndrg4* relative to beta-actin after six weeks of postnatal development, according to Figure 1.

The dependent variable in Figure 2 is the:

  F. amount of *ndrg4* DNA relative to beta-actin DNA.
  G. number of weeks after birth.
  H. of *ndrg4* mRNA relative to beta-actin mRNA.
  J. number of days of pregnancy.

The correct answer is H. The dependent (measured) variable in Figure 2 is the amount of *ndrg4* mRNA relative to beta-actin mRNA. Choice F is incorrect because the passage indicates that qPCR measures mRNA, not DNA. Choice G is incorrect because it represents the independent variable in Figure 1. Choice J is incorrect because it represents the independent variable in Figure 2.

Which of the following conclusions is supported by the data collected in these experiments?

  A. *ndrg4*, expressed minimally in mice uteri at birth, increases in expression throughout development, and in parental uteri, expression is higher at embryo implantation sites than at non-implantation sites.
  B. *ndrg4*, expressed significantly in mice uteri at birth, decreases in expression throughout development, and in parental uteri, expression is higher at embryo implantation sites than at non-implantation sites.
  C. *ndrg4*, expressed minimally in mice uteri at birth, increases in expression throughout development, and in parental uteri, expression is lower at embryo implantation sites than at non-implantation sites.
  D. *ndrg4*, expressed significantly in mice uteri at birth, decreases in expression throughout development, and in parental uteri, expression is lower at embryo implantation sites than at non-implantation sites.

The correct answer is A. Figure 1 shows that *ndrg4* barely expressed at all at birth in mice uteri before rapidly increasing in expression. This eliminates Choice B and Choice D, which indicate the opposite. Figure 2 shows that *ndrg4* expression is always higher at implantation sites than at non-implantation sites for any given number of days of pregnancy. This allows for the elimination of Choice C. Choice A correctly describes both of these trends.

Which of the following describes an additional experiment that could be performed to confirm the results from Figure 2?

F. Fix and process pregnant mouse uteri; boil the uteri to denature any proteins or enzymes present; and visualize the uterus using a fluorescence microscope.

G. Fix and process pregnant mouse uteri; incubate the uteri with fluorescent labeled primers that *ndrg4* DNA; and visualize the locations and quantities of the *ndrg4* gene throughout the uteri using a fluorescence microscope.

H. Fix and process pregnant mouse uteri; incubate the uteri with fluorescent labeled antibodies that target the uterine lining; and visualize the uterine lining throughout the uteri using a fluorescence microscope.

J. Fix and process pregnant mouse uteri; incubate the uteri with fluorescent labeled antibodies that target the NDRG4 protein; and visualize the locations and quantities of NDRG4 protein throughout the uteri using a fluorescence microscope.

The correct answer is J. Choice F is incorrect because nothing notable will show up on a fluorescence microscope without a fluorescence tag. Choice G is incorrect because the location and quantity of DNA tells nothing about expression; expression relates to mRNA and subsequent protein production. Choice H is incorrect because this choice is unrelated to the *ndrg4* gene and NDRG4 protein; you will simply see the uterine outline when observing this under a fluorescence microscope. Choice J is correct because this method will allow you to see where in the uterus (i.e., implantation vs. non-implantation sites) the NDRG4 protein is localized, as well as relative quantities of the protein throughout the uteri.

. . . .

RESEARCH SUMMARIES: UNDERSTANDING AND ANALYZING SCIENTIFIC EXPERIMENTS

The largest portion of the ACT Science exam, about 45–55 percent, is made up of Research Summaries, which test your ability to read and understand experimental protocols and analyze data. Research Summaries, like Data Representation passages, start with a written introduction that provides background information, such as important vocabulary terms, relevant scientific principles, and specific details about the experimental topic. Then, you will see an explanation that describes the experiment performed. Using this information, you should be able to identify the independent and dependent variables, as well as any constants and control trials, which we will cover in a moment.

Because Research Summaries describe the experiment itself in addition to the data, these passage types tend to be longer and more in-depth than Data Representation passages, which focus primarily on the figure(s) of interest. Sometimes, Research Summaries will include an illustration of the experimental setup to help you picture it. After the experimental description, you will be given the data, which can again include a data table or graph or some combination of these. You could also be given a textual description of the obtained results. In rare cases, you could be given a conclusion but, in most cases, you can count on a question or two that asks you to look at the data and draw a conclusion yourself.

NOTE: Research Summaries passages generally make up 45–55 percent of the ACT Science test and focus on your ability to read and understand experimental protocols and interpret scientific figures and use them to draw conclusions.

Based on what you now know about Research Summaries, it may be clear why these occupy the largest part of the exam: in the real world of science, Research Summaries are everywhere. They are most obviously found in scientific journals, but you can also find Research Summaries in mass media and textbooks. ResearchSummaries are geared toward providing you with a solid look at an experiment and the data the experiment yielded. The six or so questions that follow Research Summaries focus on both of these areas.

Let's go through each of these question types and focus on important vocabulary associated with each that will help you to successfully address them.

- Can you identify the scientific question and a logical hypothesis for this experiment?

- Do you understand the underlying scientific principles and techniques employed in this experiment?

- Can you analyze the experimental data?

- What conclusions can you draw based on the experiment and the data?

CAN YOU IDENTIFY THE SCIENTIFIC QUESTION AND A LOGICAL HYPOTHESIS FOR THIS EXPERIMENT?

We already covered the concepts of identifying the scientific question (or purpose) and hypothesis (or educated guess) about the experimental outcome when we discussed Data Representation questions, so we won't go into too much depth again here. The key to defining the purpose or to choosing a logical hypothesis for an experiment always lies in the determination of the independent and dependent variables for the given experiment. Use the background information you've been given to ask yourself what the experiment is testing for, what the significance of the results will be, and why this topic was chosen in the first place as the subject of scientific research. Research Summaries tend to focus more on experimental background and details with extra information about techniques and how they work, so you will have plenty of context from which to determine the relevant variables.

A Note About Hypotheses

Hypotheses are commonly, though not exclusively, framed in the "If . . ., then . . ." format. The first clause, following "If . . ., gives the proposed cause of the prediction, while the second clause, following "then . . .," gives the prediction itself, or the effect.

Choosing a possible hypothesis for a given experiment does not necessarily mean the hypothesis correctly guesses the outcome; the most important feature of a logical hypothesis is the inclusion of the correct independent and dependent variables. Scientists guess incorrectly all the time, and it is often most interesting when an experiment provides results that are not exactly what you might have expected at the start.

Questions that ask you about the scientific question may ask you to select a statement of purpose from four provided choices, or you could be asked to come up with a new scientific question for future work based on the data with which you've been provided. Questions that ask you about the hypothesis may ask you to choose a logical hypothesis based on provided background information, in which case you will want to pay attention to whether or not the cause and effect in the hypothesis are logical and make sense; again, remember that hypotheses do not always correctly predict an experimental outcome, but if they use the correct variables and are logical, they can still be appropriate answer choices.

Do You Understand the Underlying Scientific Principles and Techniques Employed in This Experiment?

The most significant difference between Data Representation and Research Summaries passages is the inclusion of an experimental protocol that describes the methods used in the lab to investigate the scientific question. The majority of techniques you see on the ACT Science test will be straightforward and easy to understand, but occasionally, you will come across completely new techniques you've never heard of. The good news here is that the **passages give you enough information to figure out what is going on in the experiment**. More good news: These passages won't be pages and pages long, so the techniques cannot be insanely complicated.

TIP The key to understanding difficult techniques is reading comprehension, namely, using the words and ideas you do understand in a passage to help you understand those words and ideas you do not understand.

Questions based on experimental design will often ask you to identify the basic features of the experiment, including the independent and dependent variables, constants, and controls. **Constants** are variables that stay the same for all experimental runs, regardless of any changes made to the independent variables. **Controls** are trials that minimize the effect of the independent variable. There are two types of controls: positive and negative. **Positive controls** are trials that will definitely give you a positive result. **Negative controls** are trials that will definitely give you a negative result.

For example, if you are testing the effect of a new antibiotic on *E. coli* bacterial growth on LB nutrient plates, your negative control will be a plate lacking antibiotics, on which the bacteria should survive, and your positive control will be a plate containing an antibiotic to which *E. coli* is known to be sensitive, on which the bacteria should not survive. Constants in this experiment include the type of bacteria (*E. coli*) and the use of LB nutrient plates for all experimental runs.

Not all experimental design questions will be so straightforward, though. For example, you may be asked to critique an experiment, note possible sources of error, suggest improvements to the experiment, or indicate a possible alternative method. These questions are a bit more challenging because they are not simple recall questions; you really have to understand the passage and choose an answer that is not spelled out for you already. Questions like these usually rely on your ability to use reason and logic, so simply be sure you're choosing answers that make sense.

Can You Analyze the Experimental Data?

As you can probably tell at this point, there is a lot of overlap between the skills required for Data Representation and Research Summaries passages and questions. We covered data analysis already, but let's review the key points:

- Data analysis questions will require you to be able to understand the presented data, work with and analyze a variety of graphs, use the data to draw conclusions, assess the validity of the data, and propose future research based on the results presented in the passage.

- In order to understand the data, you should be able to identify the variables, constants, and controls based on the textual and graphical clues presented.

- In working with graphs, you should know the basic graph types, how to interpret them, and what kinds of patterns or trends you should be looking out for (e.g., linear vs. exponential).

- You will be asked to draw conclusions by applying the presented data in order to answer the scientific question. Assessing data validity requires you to evaluate the accuracy and precision of the results.

- Finally, future research can be proposed based on improving the presented experimental design or moving in a new (but relevant) direction. While questions about future work in Data Representation questions will be grounded in the interpretation of the presented data, questions about future work in Research Summaries questions may emphasize the experimental details more because this information is provided to you in addition to the use of the presented data.

What Conclusions Can You Draw Based on the Experiment and the Data?

We've previously covered the concept of drawing conclusions for Data Representation questions, and the same principles apply to Research Summaries. As noted before, your goal when considering conclusions is to use the presented data to answer the scientific question, and you can do this by noting any patterns or trends in the data and using them to relate the independent and dependent variables. Conclusions are the end goal of scientific research, and their goal is to state the significant findings of the research without going into too much technical or quantitative data. When you draw conclusions, you demonstrate that you are capable of thinking like a scientist because you know how to use measured numbers to answer a question of interest. A bonus with Research Summaries is that you have extra experimental data available to you, which can be helpful to your understanding of why the experiment was performed the way it was performed.

Potential Pitfalls in Research Summaries Passages and Questions

The following table lists a few potential common obstacles you could encounter in Research Summaries passages and questions, along with some tips for getting past them.

Potential Pitfall	Useful Tips
Passage skimming	<ul><li>Passage skimming may be useful in Data Representation questions because the figure is the star of the show, but passage skimming can be detrimental in Research Summaries because the text often provides crucial information.</li><li>As you read the passage, take notes in the margins, noting the scientific question, independent and dependent variables, constants and controls, and any key terminology to which you may want to refer later. Writing down key details will help you remember the main ideas of the passage, and they will point you in the right direction if you're looking back through the passage for a specific detail later on.</li><li>Don't rush on Research Summaries questions! Incorrect distracters will include key words to throw you off track, so make sure you understand what you're reading.</li></ul>

Potential Pitfall	Useful Tips
Implying information that has not been provided	This is very similar to the aforementioned "unexpected results" pitfall, which certainly falls in this category. Here we extend the "don't assume anything" warning to experimental protocols: • Don't assume that a given step or control was included if it isn't stated directly in the passage. For instance, if the passage states that an experiment was performed and no error bars are given, don't assume that multiple trials were performed. Instead, recommend multiple trials if a question asks for an improvement to the experiment. • If something major seems to be missing from a protocol in a Research Summaries passage, there will almost always be a question that addresses it. Use reason and logic to choose the most appropriate answer.
Unfamiliar techniques	• Test takers will vary widely in techniques to which they have or have not been exposed. If you come across an unfamiliar technique, use your reading comprehension skills to try to understand it, focusing on words and ideas in the passage that you do understand to help yourself grasp the technique you don't understand. • Use the graph or data table to help you identify variables for the technique. Remember, the axes of a graph will almost always directly state the independent and dependent variables.

RESEARCH SUMMARIES: EXAMPLE PASSAGE AND QUESTIONS

Now let's see what the setup of a passage and question set will look like on the ACT Science test. Read the passage below and answer the questions that follow.

. . . .

A group of scientists recently identified a natural clay mixture called CB that has antibacterial activity against a broad spectrum of bacterial pathogens. The scientists were interested in investigating the effect of clay mixture composition on *in vitro* antibacterial activity.

Experiment 1

The scientists first tested the antibacterial effect of 10% clay mixture suspensions in deionized water on the survival of *E. coli* and MRSA bacteria after 24 hours of exposure of the bacteria to the clay mixture sample. Four CB samples were tested (CB07, CB08, CB09, and CB10), and bacterial viability was determined by finding the number of colony forming units (CFU) per unit volume for each sample. Each sample was tested three times, and the average data were plotted in Figure 1, along with standard error bars:

Viability of *E. coli* (A) and MRSA (B) after 24-hour exposure to 10 percent CB clay mixtures in deionized water.

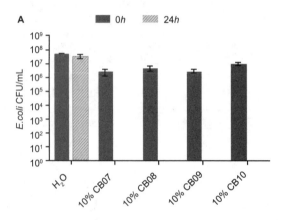

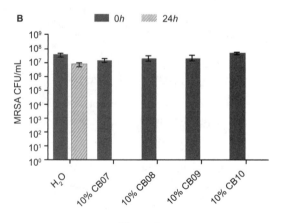

Figure 1

Experiment 2

The scientists then repeated the experiment with leachates from each mixture to see if they exhibited antibacterial activity. Clay mixture leachates were prepared by mixing and then centrifuging each 10% clay suspension to separate soluble and insoluble fractions. The aqueous (soluble) fractions were sterilized and were the leachates used to test viability. Their data are shown in Figure 2, again with all trials performed in triplicate.

Viability of *E. coli* (A) and MRSA (B) after 24-hour exposure to 10 percent CB clay mixture leachates in deionized water.

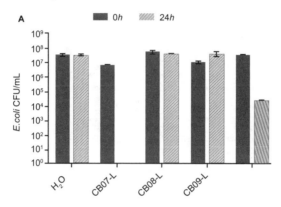

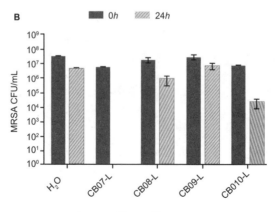

Figure 2

Experiment 3

Finally, the scientists tested the viability of *E. coli* and MRSA with several selected leachates from Experiment 2 at different pHs. Some samples received ion supplements (IS) and were supplemented with Fe, Co, Ni, Cu, and Zn. Their data are shown in Figure 3, again with all trials performed in triplicate.

Viability of *E. coli* (A) and MRSA (B) after 24-hour exposure to 10 percent CB clay mixture leachates in deionized water at various pHs and in the presence or absence of ions.

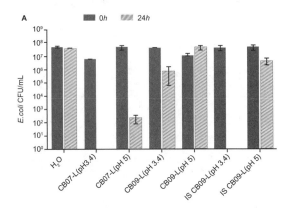

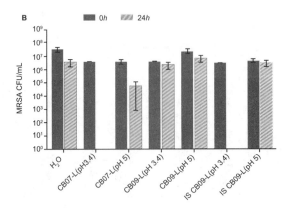

Figure 3

For all three experiments, the trials with deionized water alone serve as a(n):

    A.   constant that remains the same throughout all trials of the experiment.

    B.   independent variable that is altered by the scientists throughout the experiment.

    C.   positive control that demonstrates bacterial inability to survive in the absence of clay.

    D.   negative control that shows bacterial viability in the absence of clay.

The correct answer is D. The deionized water trials are indeed negative control trials that demonstrate the survival of bacteria when they are unaffected by clay mixtures or leachates. Choice A is incorrect because a trial or trial set cannot be a constant, but also because deionized water alone is not used for all trials of the experiment. Choice B is incorrect because the clay type, not each water trial specifically, is the independent variable. Choice C is incorrect because a positive control would use a sample that is known to cause antibacterial activity.

On average, how many CFU/mL of MRSA were present after the 24-hour incubation with CB08 leachate?

    F.   0

    G.   between 10^4 and 10^5

    H.   between 10^6 and 10^7

    J.   between 10^7 and 10^8

The correct answer is H. Figure 2B shows that the bar for CB08-L falls somewhere between 10^6 and 10^7. Choice F is incorrect because this is the number of CFU/mL of MRSA present after the 24-hour incubation with 10% CB08. Choice G is incorrect because this is the number of CFU/mL of MRSA present after the 24-hour incubation with CB10-L. Choice J is incorrect because this is the number of CFU/mL of MRSA present before the 24-hour incubation with CB08-L, as well as the number of CFU/mL of E. coli present before and after the 24-hour incubation with CB08-L.

Why were CB07 and CB09 leachates from Experiment 2 specifically selected for use in Experiment 3?

    A.   Both leachates gave approximately the same high bacterial viability data in Experiment 2 and would therefore be comparable in Experiment 3 if they reacted differently to the ion supplements and pH changes.

    B.   Both leachates gave approximately the same strong antibacterial results in Experiment 2 and would therefore be comparable in Experiment 3 if they reacted differently to the ion supplements and pH changes.

    C.   The leachates serve to contrast one another with ion supplements and pH changes in Experiment 3 because CB07-L was highly antibacterial in Experiment 2, while CB09-L was minimally antibacterial.

    D.   The leachates serve to contrast one another with ion supplements and pH changes in Experiment 3 because CB09-L was highly antibacterial in Experiment 2, while CB07-L was minimally antibacterial.

The correct answer is C. For both *E. coli* and MRSA, CB07-L and CB09-L gave vastly different results in Experiment 2, so choices A and B can be eliminated. As far as characterizing those vastly different results, CB07-L was highly antibacterial because Figure 2 shows that all bacteria alive at the start of the experiment were no longer viable after 24 hours in CB07-L for both types of bacteria. CB09-L, in contrast, was minimally antibacterial because, according to Figure 2, most of the bacteria alive at the start of the experiment were alive after 24 hours; in fact, there were more *E. coli* after 24 hours than at the start of the experiment. This allows for the selection of choice C over choice D.

Which set of conditions provided the CB09 leachate with the greatest antibacterial activity?

- **F.** Low pH and no ion supplement
- **G.** High pH and no ion supplement
- **H.** Low pH and ion supplement
- **J.** High pH and ion supplement

The correct answer is H. According to Figure 3, for both *E. coli* and MRSA, the lower pH and presence of ion supplement completely depleted viable bacteria. In contrast, the other three conditions described by choices F, G, and J provided significantly lower antibacterial activity, as most of the bacteria present initially were present after 24 hours.

. . . .

CONFLICTING VIEWPOINTS: READING COMPREHENSION, SCIENCE-STYLE

Approximately 15–20 percent of the ACT Science test will be composed of Conflicting Viewpoints passages and questions. This section, easily the shortest of the three, tests your ability to read and understand scientific arguments and relate them to one another. On a typical ACT Science test, you will almost always see one Conflicting Viewpoints passage accompanied by seven questions.

NOTE: Conflicting Viewpoints passages make up 15–20 percent of the ACT Science test and test your ability to read and understand scientific arguments and relate them to one another.

A Conflicting Viewpoints passage consists of a brief introduction, followed by two or three arguments that are related to the topic described in the introduction. Figures may or may not be included to supplement the arguments. The kinds of arguments you might encounter will often be hypotheses or theories—a common theme on the ACT Science test, as you might have gathered! Again, a hypothesis is an educated guess based on minimal evidence. By contrast, a **theory** is usually substantiated by more experiments and observations than a hypothesis. The provided arguments will almost always give some kind of supportive evidence, which may or may not be convincing.

Within these arguments, it will be important to distinguish between **fact**, statements that are demonstrated to be true, and **opinions**, which reflect the personal feelings of an individual. Occasionally, you might be provided with snippets of research in which students describe experiments that support opposing conclusions or different experiments that support the same conclusion.

The key to tacking Conflicting Viewpoints passages and questions is to use reading comprehension skills, which we have already discussed for the other two question types but are perhaps most applicable here. You won't be responsible for data analysis when it comes to Conflicting Viewpoints passages and questions. Instead, you should read through the passage, jot down notes, circle keywords, and take note of important supporting evidence, because your main job will be to understand and recall information from the arguments, as well as to relate the passages to one another and to real or hypothetical evidence. Make sure you are clear on the basic view or stance discussed in each argument. Questions that accompany Conflicting Viewpoints questions will ask you the following:

- Can you recall specific details from the viewpoints?
- Can you compare and contrast the viewpoints?
- Can you make logical inferences to connect the viewpoints with one another or with external data?

Let's now go through each of these question types and explain how you can successfully address them.

CAN YOU RECALL SPECIFIC DETAILS FROM THE VIEWPOINTS?

The most straightforward Conflicting Viewpoints questions will merely ask you to recall information from the viewpoints. These answers can usually be found directly in the passages, stated outright—although sometimes information may be implied by statements found directly in the passages. An important tip here is to pay attention to detail: it is likely that many distracter answer choices in these questions will be true statements, but you have to make sure that the answer you select is both true and actually relevant to the question posed.

Understanding the viewpoints will not require extensive background knowledge of the topics at hand, although you may better understand a topic if you have seen it before. Fortunately, since this passage type is largely based on reading comprehension, you won't have to be an expert on any topics encountered here to do well. As described earlier, use reading comprehension skills to understand difficult vocabulary or ideas by reading around the confusing part of a passage in order to find hints that can clue you in to the meaning of that portion of the passage. Of the seven questions that accompany a Conflicting Viewpoints passage, as many as three or four may be based on recall, so take advantage of these straightforward questions!

Can You Compare and Contrast the Viewpoints?

A number of questions that follow a Conflicting Viewpoints passage (often three or four) will ask you to compare and contrast the provided viewpoints. Questions like these are often a bit more difficult because you will have to relate the viewpoints to one another, but they are far from impossible.

While arguments in Conflicting Viewpoints passages will often argue opposite points, you can still draw comparisons between them. Maybe they use the same evidence for different purposes, or perhaps it is possible that both arguments are valid in light of one another. This is where note-taking in the margins is especially helpful; if you've been highlighting key pieces of evidence per argument, finding evidence in common might not be so difficult because you'll have it marked or even rewritten in your own words.

Contrasting the two arguments works in just the same way, and you can use the same approach here. Take notes on each argument, honing in on key words and supporting evidence. When comparing the arguments, you look for evidence in common between the arguments. When contrasting the arguments, you want to find evidence in each passage that exclusively supports that viewpoint, or better yet, evidence that actually refutes the other viewpoint.

Beware!

Common distracters in compare-contrast questions include true statements that are irrelevant to the question, choices that represent a similarity when you are looking for a difference (or vice versa), and statements that are true and relevant but do not answer the question at hand.

Can You Make Logical Inferences to Connect the Viewpoints with One Another or with External Data?

Inference-based questions are probably the most in-depth kind of question you'll see in the Conflicting Viewpoints portion of the ACT Science test because they require you to look beyond the information directly presented to you. Inference-based questions may ask you to connect or relate the viewpoints to each other or to relate data to one or both of the viewpoints. These answers are unlikely to be found directly in the passages, so a quick re-read of the passages won't suddenly reveal them. Instead, it will be important to gain a solid understanding of the basic premises of the viewpoints, and then consider how the question at hand fits in with those premises.

The first kind of question you might see will ask you to relate the viewpoints to one another. This is primarily where you will be asked about whether the viewpoints are mutually exclusive, namely whether or not they can both be true. Some pairs of arguments will directly oppose each other and therefore cannot coexist, but other pairs of arguments might be able to coexist because they are arguing slightly different points, or perhaps they are looking at a question in two different but equally valid ways.

The second kind of inference question is often more common because it can be included rather easily for any Conflicting Viewpoints passage, regardless of the arguments made within them. You may be given a statement that describes real or hypothetical data, and you will be asked to analyze the data in light of the two viewpoints. For example, if you are given a piece of data, you may be asked to indicate whether it supports the basic premise of the first argument, the second argument, both arguments, or neither argument. How does the data fit in (or not) with each presented viewpoint? Alternatively, you may be asked to choose the piece of data from among a set of options that supports one, both, or neither of the arguments.

It doesn't matter which type of inference question you see—as long as you understand the basic premise of each presented viewpoint, you should be able to determine how any introduced data fit in with each.

POTENTIAL PITFALLS IN CONFLICTING VIEWPOINTS PASSAGES AND QUESTIONS

The following table describes a few potential issues you could encounter in Conflicting Viewpoints passages and questions, along with some tips for overcoming them.

Potential Pitfall	Useful Tips
Focusing on minute details on the first read-through	• When you're reading viewpoints, focus on the big picture initially—don't try to memorize everything. Take notes about the main ideas, the most important evidence, or key vocabulary words. • If you focus too much on minute details that you'll have to refer back to when you get to the questions, you'll be wasting time that you could be using to answer other questions or double-check your work.
Confusing the distinct passages	• If a question asks you about a particular viewpoint, regardless of whether or not the question is straightforward, make sure you refer back to the appropriate viewpoint. This may seem obvious, but confusing the passages is an error more common than you might think, and the test-makers know it! • The best way to avoid this pitfall is to simply check your work. Look at the question stem and make sure you're focusing on the viewpoint it addresses.

Potential Pitfall	Useful Tips
Falling for distracters that contain key words	• Noting and defining key vocabulary words is extremely useful for understanding any passages on the ACT Science test. However, if you just pick out key words without understanding why they're important, you could fall for a common trick employed by the test-makers. • Test makers will often throw relevant vocabulary words into incorrect distracters to tempt you to choose the options. As a strategy, use those key words to help you choose the correct answer. If a question is asking you about Viewpoint 1, and a key word in one of the choices appears only in Viewpoint 2, you may be able to eliminate that choice. • The key to avoid falling for distracters that contain key words is to make sure you understand what you're reading. You can't rely entirely on the presence or absence of particular words because the test makers can use that reliance to lead you astray.
Failing to find textual support for answers	• Conflicting Viewpoints passages are essentially reading comprehension passages in the science field, so finding textual support to confirm answers to questions is of utmost importance. The only way you can be fairly confident in an answer to a Conflicting Viewpoints question is if you find textual support for that answer in the passage itself. • Don't just pick an answer because it sounds good, or because it seems like a sufficient answer to the question—make sure your answer makes sense in the context of the passages and has textual support. Well-written distracter choices are meant to throw you off track in exactly this way!

CONFLICTING VIEWPOINTS: EXAMPLE PASSAGE AND QUESTIONS

Now it's your turn once again. Read the Conflicting Viewpoints passage set below and answer the questions that follow.

. . . .

The phlogiston hypothesis and oxidative combustion theory are two arguments that at one point or another were widely accepted to explain what happens when a substance undergoes combustion, or burns.

Viewpoint 1

Every combustible substance is composed of an undetectable substance called phlogiston. When a substance burns, phlogiston is liberated, and the core of the substance is left behind as a residue, called *calx*. This means that air is essentially the receptacle for phlogiston. Even rusting iron loses its phlogiston, returning to its elemental state. When objects burn, they lose mass, which can be explained by the loss of phlogiston, and the remaining object is usually different in appearance after it has been burned. Phlogiston cannot be directly detected.

Viewpoint 2

When objects burn, they undergo combustion, releasing heat and light. Combustion usually involves oxygen (though there are variations on this concept). A combustible object reacts with oxygen and forms gases from a solid. A loss in mass is observed in a burning object because solid material has undergone a chemical change to be converted into gaseous material, so the mass of gas around the object increases. When a hydrocarbon burns, for example, carbon dioxide and steam form. Antoine Lavoisier demonstrated experimentally that when one captures the gases produced by a burning object, the overall mass of the system actually increases, suggesting the input of a chemical (i.e., oxygen) to drive the reaction. Lavoisier tested phosphorus and sulfur, as both substances burn readily. Furthermore, the appearance of a burning object changes due to the chemical reaction taking place.

In Lavoisier's experiments, he tested the combustion of:

A. rusting iron.
B. phosphorus and sulfur.
C. phlogiston.
D. hydrocarbons.

The correct answer is B. Rusting iron, described in choice A, is incorrect because Viewpoint 1 merely provides this as a sample process for the application of the phlogiston hypothesis. Choice C is incorrect because Viewpoint 1 describes phlogiston as the substance released from a burning object. Choice D is incorrect because hydrocarbons are noted as an example in Viewpoint 2 of a chemical that combusts to release carbon dioxide and steam, but this is not in reference to Lavoisier's experiments. Viewpoint 2 indicates specifically that Lavoisier tested the combustion of phosphorus and sulfur because both burn readily.

Which of the following pieces of evidence do both viewpoints use to support their respective arguments?

    F.   When a solid object burns, the masses of the solid and surrounding gas decreases.

    G.   Carbon dioxide and steam are released when an object burns.

    H.   The appearance of an object changes when it burns.

    J.   Phosphorus and sulfur burns readily.

The correct answer is H. Both viewpoints note an appearance change in a burning object; while Viewpoint 1 points to phlogiston release as the reason for this appearance change, Viewpoint 2 indicates that a chemical reaction is responsible for the appearance change. Choice F is incorrect because it is only true of Viewpoint 1; while both viewpoints agree that the mass of a burning object decreases, Viewpoint 2 indicates that the mass of the surrounding gas increases due to gas formation during the chemical reaction. Choice G is incorrect because Viewpoint 1 states that phlogiston is released during combustion, not carbon dioxide and steam. Choice J is incorrect because it provides information used in Lavoisier's experiment but is not used as evidence for either viewpoint.

A key distinction between the viewpoints is that:

    A.   Viewpoint 1 describes the release of a substance that cannot be detected, while Viewpoint 2 describes the release of a substance that can be detected.

    B.   Viewpoint 2 describes the release of a substance that cannot be detected, while Viewpoint 1 describes the release of a substance that can be detected.

    C.   Viewpoint 1 includes no qualitative evidence, while Viewpoint 2 does.

    D.   Viewpoint 2 includes no quantitative evidence, while Viewpoint 1 does.

The correct answer is A. Viewpoint 1 describes phlogiston release but indicates that phlogiston cannot be detected, while Viewpoint 2 describes gas release and even indicates that Lavoisier was able to measure this gas release. This points to Choice A and eliminates choice B. Choices C and D are incorrect because both viewpoints include qualitative evidence, or non-numerical/observable evidence. For example, both viewpoints describe the loss of mass of a particular object when it burns, as well as its change in appearance throughout the duration of the process.

. . . .

SUMMING IT UP

- The ACT Science test covers biology, chemistry, physics, and earth and space sciences. You should be familiar with the sciences covered in your high school classes, but all of the factual information you need to answer all the questions will be in the passages.

- **Data Representation** questions ask you to understand and analyze graphs and figures; **Research Summaries** emphasize experimental procedures and logic behind the experiment; **Conflicting Viewpoints** provide you with two or three arguments and ask you to recall information, compare and contrast the arguments, and draw inferences.

- In Data Representation passages, the introductory text is where you will find important vocabulary related to the topic of interest, along with information about the experiment or study upon which the presented figure is based.

- The figure or figures are the most important part of any Data Representation passage—they usually tell you everything you need to know. Your first step is to look at any given figure, determine what it is telling you, note patterns or trends in the data, and draw conclusions about the data.

- Your first step is identifying the **scientific question**, or the purpose of the experiment. Finding or formulating your own **hypothesis**, or educated guess, about an experiment's outcome, is an important part of understanding the data presented to you.

- The **independent variable** is the condition that the scientist alters during the experiment, and the **dependent variable** is the condition that the scientist measures during the experiment. On a graph, you can usually find the independent variable on the horizontal *x*-axis and the dependent variable on the vertical *y*-axis.

- Most Data Representation question sets will feature a question asking you to draw a conclusion that summarizes data trends. As you read the passage and analyze the graphs, always take note of any patterns you see!

- Always take note of **outliers**, data values that deviate drastically from the norm. If one is present, data may be skewed. If you notice an obvious outlier, there is sure to be a question about it on the exam.

- Like Data Representation questions, first approach **Research Summary** questions by identifying the scientific question, independent and dependent variables, and the constant and control trials. **Constants** stay the same for all experimental runs, regardless of any changes made to the independent variables. **Controls** are trials that minimize the effect of the independent variable.

- Research summary questions usually ask you to read all about an experiment and eventually make a prediction about what will happen—you are always looking to create or find a hypothesis. A hypothesis does *not* have to be correct—the only rule is that it must contain the proper independent and dependent variables.

- Research Summaries often describe complex experiments, but keep in mind that you are always given enough information in the passage to figure out what is going on in the experiment.

- Conflicting Viewpoints passage sets feature a brief introduction followed by two or three arguments related to the topic described in the introduction. Arguments can be presented as hypotheses or theories. Unlike a hypothesis, a **theory** is usually backed up by more experiments and observations. Your main goal in reading these passages is to understand and recall information from the arguments, as well as to relate the passages to one another and to real or hypothetical evidence.

- Conflicting Viewpoints will feature evidence for you to consider. Within these arguments, it will be important to distinguish between **fact**, statements that are demonstrated to be true, and **opinions**, which reflect the personal feelings of an individual.

- Many of the questions that accompany Conflicting Viewpoints passages will ask you to compare and contrast the different arguments. As you read, take notes on each argument and jot down key words and supporting evidence. When comparing the arguments, look for evidence in common; when contrasting the arguments, find evidence in each passage that exclusively supports that viewpoint or refutes the other viewpoint.

- Inference-based questions require you to look beyond the information directly presented to you and connect or relate the viewpoints to each other, or to relate data to one or both of the viewpoints. As you read, aim to gain a solid understanding of the basic point of view of each viewpoint, and then consider how the question at hand fits in with each separate premise.

CHAPTER 7
THE ACT® WRITING TEST

OVERVIEW

- Why You Should Take the ACT® Writing Test
- Test Overview
- How the ACT® Writing Test Is Scored
- The ACT® Writing Test: A Closer Look
- Planning Your Essay
- Writing Your Essay
- Reviewing Your Essay
- Summing It Up

We know you're short on time to prepare for the ACT, and, considering this is an optional section of the exam, chances are you may not be spending a great deal of your time and effort preparing for this test section. This makes logical sense, but if you're taking this section of the exam (perhaps it's a requirement of one of the colleges you're applying to) and want to earn a great score, this chapter will help you prepare as quickly and efficiently as possible.

NOTE: For comprehensive information regarding the ACT, visit the official ACT website: ***www.act.org.***

This chapter is designed to take you quickly through the ACT Writing test, including how it's structured and scored, and what official ACT essay readers are looking for in an essay. You'll get just what you need to set yourself up for a great score:

- Quick coverage of what to expect when you take the ACT Writing test
- No-nonsense advice for improving your writing abilities, attacking essay prompts, and using your time well to plan and construct a solid essay
- Effective writing practice and review with a sample prompt and model essays at various score levels to compare your work against
- Proven test strategies to help you craft an essay that demonstrates a solid understanding of the four writing domains on which your work will be judged

WHY YOU SHOULD TAKE THE ACT® WRITING TEST

There are two strong reasons to consider taking the ACT Writing test:

1. Although the Writing test is an *optional* component of the ACT, it may be a requirement of a college or university that you're applying to; and

2. You're a great writer and want the opportunity to showcase your skills on this important test.

Do Your Research

As you thoroughly research your target schools, make sure you know their individual admissions requirements regarding ACT Writing test scores. You have a few options:

- Contact schools directly.

- Ask your high school counselor for information.

- Use the College Writing Test Requirements Search Tool on the official ACT website (***https://actapps.act.org/writPrefRM/***) to see which schools require or recommend that you take the ACT Writing test.

If you're reading this chapter, it's safe to assume that you've made the decision to take this test, and you're definitely in the right place—we'll get you in great test-taking shape *fast*!

TEST OVERVIEW

The ACT Writing test is a 40-minute essay-writing task designed to:

- Assess your English-language writing capabilities

- Gauge your ability to respond thoughtfully and persuasively to a provided topic

- Measure your analytical ability

- Test your ability to develop ideas using logical reasoning and craft a well-structured piece of argumentative writing

In order to achieve a good score on the ACT Writing test, you'll need to use the writing skills you've acquired throughout your academic career, including English language writing conventions, to craft a compelling argumentative essay that responds to a provided essay prompt.

Writing essays is a skill like any other, and practice is the key to success. The best preparation for writing an essay that earns the highest possible score is as follows:

- Understand the format of the test, including essay prompts, perspectives, the essay task, and test directions.
- Understand the key areas (domains) on which your essay will be graded.
- Understand what the official ACT essay readers are looking for in a great essay by reviewing model essays at various score levels.
- Practice writing argumentative essays—from quick idea brainstorming to structuring and editing your work—all within the 40-minute time limit that you'll face on test day.

In addition to the writing assignments you'll tackle in your classes, make the most of your time between now and test day to polish your writing abilities.

The ACT Writing test can be taken on all six of the official national test dates (which include the United States, US territories, Canada, and Puerto Rico), as well as the five official international test dates and special or arranged test dates (visit the official ACT website for additional test scheduling information).

The ACT Writing test *does not* affect your scores on other ACT subject area tests or your overall composite score. However, the *only* way to receive an English Language Arts (ELA) test score is by taking the ACT Writing test.

The test is taken using a pencil (remember to bring a few sharpened, non-mechanical #2 pencils with you on test day), and you'll write your essay on paper provided to you by the test administrator. If you require specific test accommodations, please visit the official ACT website for additional information.

Recent Test Enhancements

The ACT Writing test has undergone some changes recently. Here's a quick rundown of recent enhancements that you should be aware of:

- **Increased time for essay planning and writing.** Previously, test takers had 30 minutes to plan and write their essays. Test takers now have 40 minutes to do so.

- **More comprehensive scoring.** The test now provides scoring in four writing proficiency domains: **Ideas and Analysis, Development and Support, Organization,** and **Language Use and Conventions.**

- **More guidance and structure for essay planning.** The test now features prewriting guidance for structuring and crafting a written response (more later in this chapter).

- **Wider range of subjects.** Previous essay prompts focused mainly on school-based subject matter. Now, essay prompts will draw from a wider array of engaging subjects and topical issues.

- **Broader topic perspectives provided.** Testtakers will get three diverse perspectives on the issue provided in the essay prompt, allowing for a more multifaceted analytical engagement.

- **More reflective of real-world topic discussion.** Previously, students provided a response to the issue provided in the prompt. Now, their responses are built alongside, and in dialogue with, varying perspectives.

HOW THE ACT® WRITING TEST IS SCORED

Your essay will be a response to a writing prompt based on a carefully chosen topic, which will be presented alongside three distinct perspectives, each of which suggests a certain way of thinking about the specific issue.

A high-scoring ACT essay will accomplish the following goals:

- Examine and assess the perspectives given
- Declare and explain your own perspective on the issue
- Discuss the relationship between your perspective and those given

As you plan and structure your essay, your unique perspective on the issue can agree with any of the three perspectives provided, agree partially, or be completely distinct.

High-Scoring Essay Formula

An essay that achieves a high score will:

- Demonstrate a well-developed, clear, and confident position on the issue with appropriate support
- Use careful analysis, solid reasoning, sound ideas, excellent grammar, and compelling examples

---

THE FOUR WRITING PROFICIENCY DOMAINS

Your essay will be scored by two separate (and highly experienced) certified ACT essay readers in four specific writing proficiency domains. Your score in each domain will range from 1 to 6, with 6 being the best possible score.

Sharpen Your Debate Skills!

Great debaters are typically successful on the ACT Writing test. Why? Because they have a great deal of practice arguing their points of view on a wide range of topics.

Sharpen your debating skills in preparation for test day. Stay aware of issues and current events that people are talking about, and make it a point to engage others in conversations (and debates) about them as often as possible.

Getting comfortable arguing your perspective on a range of issues is valuable practice—and one of these issues just might be the foundation for your essay prompt when you take the ACT Writing test!

Let's take a closer look at each domain.

---

1. Ideas and Analysis

This domain measures how well you can critically analyze a provided prompt and diverse array of perspectives on a given topic.

An essay that receives a score of 6 in this domain will demonstrate an excellent understanding of the topic and provide a compelling, relevant argument that reflects your distinct perspective, including:

- Effective critical engagement with perspectives
- Nuance and purpose-driven precision
- Excellent depth and contextual insight on the topic
- Thoughtful analysis of the prompt issue(s) and implications of the writer's perspective

2. Development and Support

This domain assesses your ability to craft an effective written argument with sound ideas, solid reasoning, a clear rationale, and thoughtful support.

An essay that receives a score of 6 in this domain will demonstrate a clear flow of thoughts that reflect a solid stance on the issue provided in the prompt, with compelling support in defense of your perspective, including:

- A deep and insightful level of effective idea development to promote understanding
- Skilled reasoning and use of relevant and varied support to strengthen perspective

3. Organization

This domain measures your ability to carefully and thoughtfully organize your ideas to create a convincing, coherent, and well-structured essay.

An essay that receives a score of 6 in this domain will demonstrate a solid understanding of essay structure and an effective flow of ideas from introduction to conclusion, including:

- A skilled ability to capably organize ideas into a cogent piece of writing
- An effective and insightful central narrative theme that unifies the text
- A thorough understanding of standard essay structure and flow, including effective transitions between sentences and thoughts

4. Language Use and Conventions

This domain measures your ability to effectively utilize English-language writing principles, including spelling, vocabulary, grammar, syntax, and language mechanics.

An essay that receives a score of 6 in this domain will demonstrate a clear, polished, and effective piece of writing that reflects a mastery of language use and conventions, including:

- Skillful deployment of standard English language principles
- Excellent use of varied and engaging vocabulary and sentence structures
- A clear, authoritative, and effective voice and tone
- Few or no errors in grammar, mechanics, and syntax

 Don't underestimate the importance of making a strong first impression on ACT essay readers with a killer introduction and leaving them wanting more with an unforgettable conclusion.

SCORING YOUR ESSAY

The two readers who will be scoring your essay will provide a score from 1 to 6 in each of the four writing proficiency domains.

Your total **domain score** for each of the four areas will be the sum of the two scores and will range from 2–12 (if the scores of the two readers in any domain area differ by more than one point, a third reader will be used to resolve the discrepancy).

Your domain scores will reflect the essay readers' impressions of your abilities as follows:

- **Score 6:** Your essay demonstrates a highly effective skill level in this domain area.
- **Score 5:** Your essay demonstrates a well-developed skill level in this domain area.
- **Score 4:** Your essay demonstrates an adequate skill level in this domain area.
- **Score 3:** Your essay demonstrates some developing ability in this domain area.
- **Score 2:** Your essay demonstrates a weak or inconsistent skill level in this domain area.
- **Score 1:** Your essay demonstrates a deficient skill level in this domain area.

The test readers will calculate your individual domain scores based on the following ACT scoring rubric:

Score Level	Score 6
Ideas and Analysis	**Essay demonstrates:** • Effective critical engagement with perspectives • Nuance and purpose-driven precision • Excellent depth and contextual insight on the topic • Thoughtful analysis of the prompt issue(s) and implications of the writer's perspective
Development and Support	**Essay demonstrates:** • A deep and insightful level of effective idea development to promote understanding • Skilled reasoning and use of relevant and varied support to strengthen perspective
Organization	**Essay demonstrates:** • A skilled ability to capably organize ideas into a cogent piece of writing • An effective and insightful central narrative theme that unifies the text • A thorough understanding of standard essay structure and flow, including effective transitions between sentences and thoughts
Language Use and Conventions	**Essay demonstrates:** • Skillful employment of standard English language principles • Excellent use of varied and engaging vocabulary and sentence structures • A clear, authoritative, and effective voice and tone • Few or no errors in grammar, mechanics, and syntax

Score Level	Score 5
Ideas and Analysis	**Essay demonstrates:** • Productive critical engagement with perspectives • Purpose-driven precision • Depth and contextual insight on the topic • Commendable analysis of the prompt issue(s) and acknowledgment of the implications of the writer's perspective
Development and Support	**Essay demonstrates:** • A commendable level of idea development to deepen understanding • Solid reasoning and use of relevant and varied support to strengthen perspective
Organization	**Essay demonstrates:** • A solid ability to capably organize ideas into a cogent piece of writing • A solid central narrative theme that unifies the text • A commendable understanding of standard essay structure and flow, including effective transitions between sentences and thoughts
Language Use and Conventions	**Essay demonstrates:** • Commendable employment of standard English language principles • Strong use of varied and engaging vocabulary and sentence structures • A capable and effective voice and tone • Few or no errors in grammar, mechanics, and syntax

Score Level	Score 4
Ideas and Analysis	**Essay demonstrates:** • Critical engagement with perspectives • Noticeable clarity and purpose • Insight on the topic • Analysis of the issue(s) in the essay prompt
Development and Support	**Essay demonstrates:** • A good level of idea development that provides clarity • Good reasoning and use of relevant and varied support to strengthen perspective
Organization	**Essay demonstrates:** • An ability to organize ideas into a coherent piece of writing • A central narrative theme that demonstrates a real effort to unify the text • A good understanding of standard essay structure and flow, including evidence of clear transitions between sentences and thoughts
Language Use and Conventions	**Essay demonstrates:** • A good use of standard English language principles • Use of varied and engaging vocabulary and sentence structures • A good attempt to establish voice and tone • Some errors in grammar, mechanics, and syntax, which may occasionally impede meaning

Score Level	Score 3
Ideas and Analysis	**Essay demonstrates:** • A limited engagement with perspectives • Noticeable clarity and purpose • Some discernible insight on the topic • Some analysis of the issue(s) in the essay prompt
Development and Support	**Essay demonstrates:** • Some general but simplistic idea development • Some evidence of reasoning in an attempt to clarify argument
Organization	**Essay demonstrates:** • An attempt to organize ideas into a piece of writing with a basic structure • A grouping of ideas in some logical order • An attempt to provide a structure and flow between sentences and thoughts that the reader can follow
Language Use and Conventions	**Essay demonstrates:** • An attempt to employ standard English language principles, with occasional errors • An attempt to display some varied range of vocabulary and sentence structures, though errors are present • A discernible voice and tone, though largely hard to discern • Noticeable errors in grammar, mechanics, and syntax that impede meaning

Score Level	Score 2
Ideas and Analysis	**Essay demonstrates:** • A weak engagement with perspectives • Limited clarity and purpose • Deficient insight on the topic • Poor analysis of the issue(s) in the essay prompt
Development and Support	**Essay demonstrates:** • Weak or deficient idea development • An effort to offer reasoning in an attempt to clarify argument, though largely ineffective or off target
Organization	**Essay demonstrates:** • A weak organization of ideas and deficient structure • Ideas are weakly ordered, adversely affecting comprehensibility • A largely ineffective attempt at providing sound structure and flow between sentences and thoughts
Language Use and Conventions	**Essay demonstrates:** • A deficient attempt to employ standard English language principles, with several noticeable errors • A weak or deficient vocabulary range and basic, often flawed, sentence structures • A weak, ineffective voice and tone, largely hard to discern • Several obvious errors in grammar, mechanics, and syntax that strongly impede meaning

Score Level	Score 1
Ideas and Analysis	**Essay demonstrates:** • No engagement with perspectives • Lack of clarity and purpose • No insight on the topic • Lack of analysis of the issue(s) in the essay prompt
Development and Support	**Essay demonstrates:** • An absence of appropriate idea development • No appropriate or discernible effort to offer reasoning in an attempt to clarify argument
Organization	**Essay demonstrates:** • No organization of ideas and a lack of basic structure • A lack of thoughtful order of ideas, severely affecting comprehensibility • An unsuccessful attempt at providing sound structure and flow between sentences and thoughts
Language Use and Conventions	**Essay demonstrates:** • No attempt to deploy standard English language principles, with serious errors • A very basic and often erroneous use of vocabulary and many serious errors in sentence structure • A largely absent or indistinct voice and tone • Serious and widespread errors in grammar, mechanics, and syntax that profoundly affect meaning and comprehension

Your final test score is the average of the four domain scores (ranging from 2–12) on the essay—the highest possible score you can earn on the Writing test is 12. You'll also receive a scaled English Language Arts (ELA) score ranging from 1–36.

 The colleges that recieve your ACT score report will also be able to view your complete ACT Writing test essay. Keep this in mind as you craft your essay.

THE ACT® WRITING TEST: A CLOSER LOOK

Let's move quickly and review each piece of the ACT Writing test. It's worth your time—even if you don't have much of it—to understand what you'll encounter on this test. Remember, being prepared and well-informed are among your two best test-taking tools!

THE ESSAY PROMPT

You'll be given a prompt from which you'll craft a thoughtfully constructed, well-written, and compelling essay that will reflect your perspective on the issue presented.

Again, the essay prompt can be based on a wide range of topics, so the best way to prepare for a perfect score is to *be prepared for anything*.

As you start to tackle the essay prompt, make sure you read it *at least* twice.

- **Your first read-through** should focus on digesting the information provided. Make sure you know exactly what the issue being presented is and what you're being asked to address in your essay response. Don't rush into furiously writing your essay without first knowing what it should cover!

- **Your second read-through** should confirm that you're completely clear on the essay task at hand and should also be an opportunity to start brainstorming ideas that you plan to include in your essay.

Slow Down!

Don't race off into writing your essay right after reading the prompt. If you want to achieve a high score, your essay will include a critical analysis of the three perspectives provided alongside the essay prompt and task.

Here's a sample essay prompt, in the format you'll encounter on test day:

> **Free Public Transportation for Everyone?**
>
> Efforts have been made to convince local and state governments and policymakers that public transportation systems should be both expanded and made free all across the United States. Free public transportation could potentially convince people to rely less on their own personal vehicles and more on public forms of transit, many of which are embracing more environmentally friendly forms of hybrid and electric technologies. But free public transportation could also potentially put an undue strain on local and state budgets, likely leading to cuts in other important services or increased taxes. The ongoing concerns about the environment and the potentially negative economic impact should fuel this debate for some time to come.

Let's quickly break down how you should handle the prompt you'll encounter on test day.

1. **Carefully read the entire essay prompt** before moving forward. Notice that the sample prompt presents a controversial topic designed to stimulate your thinking. A high-scoring essay will reflect a thorough understanding of the topic and will address it within a well-structured written response.

2. **Think critically about the prompt.** Consider the sample prompt here. You're being asked to analyze the relative pros and cons of making public transportation free and more accessible for people. You're presented with a brief overview regarding how this could theoretically affect the environment or the economy. Start building your own perspective on the issue and assess how the information provided aligns with your thoughts.

Note taking: After reading the prompt at least twice, don't go into full essay planning mode just yet. Consider taking a few notes during and immediately after your second read-through if something important or relevant crosses your mind that you think would fit well into your essay or help you structure and organize your response.

Okay, once you've carefully analyzed the essay prompt, and perhaps written down your preliminary thoughts and ideas, you're ready to move on to the three perspectives provided.

THE ACT ESSAY PERSPECTIVES

On test day, you'll be given three varying perspectives on the issue provided in the essay prompt. You'll need to carefully consider each of these three perspectives as you plan and construct your essay, and your final piece of writing should reflect a thoughtful analysis of each, integrated with your own well-developed perspective.

As you analyze the three ACT essay perspectives, think about how each **complements** or **detracts** from *your* thoughts on the issue.

Reading the various perspectives provided alongside the essay prompt should get your argumentative and creative wheels turning. The ideas flowing through your mind at this stage will likely serve to structure the core of your written response.

This is a great opportunity to take some quick notes and capture your thoughts. At this stage, your brainstorming notes might be a simple list of ideas that you think may prove useful later on when you're planning your essay. Or, you might be the type of student who needs to add more structure to the notes.

Consider making some general columns in which your notes can be added.

A few suggestions:

- Make notes columns for "My Perspective," "Competing Perspectives," and "Miscellaneous Ideas," and use these general categories to organize your thoughts.

- Make notes columns that correspond to the basic structural elements of essays: "Introduction," "Body Paragraphs," and "Conclusion." Use these categories to manage your ideas.

The last thing you want to have happen on test day is to complete the Writing test only to realize that you left out key points in your final essay. Choose a strategy that works best for you!

Let's take a look at three perspectives on "Free Public Transportation for Everyone?"

Read and carefully consider these perspectives. Each suggests a particular way of thinking about the notion of making all public transportation free and more accessible.

PERSPECTIVE ONE

Communities, cities, and states nationwide should quickly embrace the notion of providing free public transportation to all citizens. The benefits that would come from such a visionary initiative—cleaner environments, healthier citizens, clearer and better roads and traffic, more accessible travel options for those who need it most—are clearly worth the budgetary reorganization that would need to occur to accommodate the costs. People who don't have their own vehicles and have extremely limited funds will be able to explore new job opportunities and commute to work, take care of important errands, and have greater mobility—it's hard to argue that this is not a worthwhile endeavor. Government institutions at all levels are overdue for reorganization and streamlining, which would go a long way to help fund this program. People across the country already pay a great deal in taxes, and they should have access to more tangible, life-changing benefits such as this one.

PERSPECTIVE TWO

There's no such thing as a free lunch—or a completely free public service program like public transportation. An effort to both expand and make free public transportation would take a huge amount of bureaucratic mobilization, effort, and money that would have to come from somewhere. It would force governments to either cut the budgets of other programs—possibly more important and widely beneficial ones—or raise already high taxes, thus negating the idea that this is a free public utility. Public transportation isn't very expensive as it is, and it isn't something that benefits everyone, so time, energy, and money should be reserved for programs that have a more immediate and urgent public benefit.

PERSPECTIVE THREE

Every program that could potentially benefit a wide and diverse population deserves consideration. It would be a challenge to proclaim that free and expanded public transportation would not provide some level of societal benefit to a segment of the population that could likely benefit from expanded services, and this is an initiative that should be carefully discussed and reviewed. However, due to the significant cost involved in enacting such a program, a blanket implementation is both an unrealistic and hasty notion. Instead, this initiative should be carefully and thoughtfully discussed, reviewed, and analyzed by individual government entities, policymakers, and community activists, and citizens should have a forum for voicing their opinions on whether or not to implement such a program. Issues revolving around need, budgeting, available resources, and mobilization of a free public transportation program are different all over the country, and this program should be considered within the specific context of each community, city, or state.

As you read these perspectives, think carefully about how each point of view might complement—or contrast—your own perspective on the issue of free public transportation for everyone. Again, it may be a good idea to take some notes and capture your thoughts on each perspective.

- If you think that free public transportation for everyone is a great idea, you'll likely start thinking about how your ideas align with those in Perspective One and begin formulating an argument why Perspective Two represents a flawed way of thinking.

- Maybe you think that free public transportation is a bad idea and are eager to argue against it—if so, you'll likely take the opposite approach and argue in favor of Perspective Two.

- If you think there are merits to both perspectives, are hesitant to make a general proclamation, or have alternative ideas regarding public transportation, you may align most closely with Perspective Three and argue against the narrow focus of Perspectives One and Two.

TIP Remember—a great piece of writing that fails to *fully* address the essay prompt and task will *not* earn you great scores on test day.

Okay, so we have our quick initial approach for analyzing essay prompts and carefully considering each of the three perspectives. For the sample prompt and perspectives provided, you should have some idea about how they align with your specific point of view (and perhaps you have some helpful notes that will serve you well when planning and structuring your own essay). We're ready to move forward!

THE ACT ESSAY TASK

Bottom line: Be sure to read the essay task *carefully*—the readers of your essay will be checking to make sure it capably addresses the task provided. A strong essay simply cannot leave any aspect of the task unaddressed.

Read the following essay task for "Free Public Transportation for Everyone?"

Essay Task

Write a unified, coherent essay in which you evaluate multiple perspectives on the idea of free public transportation. In your essay, be sure to:

- Analyze and evaluate the perspectives given.
- State and develop your own perspective on the issue.
- Explain the relationship between your perspective and those given.

Your perspective may be in full agreement with any of the others, in partial agreement, or wholly different. Whatever the case, support your ideas with logical reasoning and detailed, persuasive examples.

At this point, you've read the essay prompt and considered your take on the issue alongside the three perspectives provided, and you're fully aware of the essay task. You likely have some ideas that you'd like to use in your writing.

The next step is to move forward and structure your essay!

PLANNING YOUR ESSAY

Since you're short on prep time, we'll start with a quick acknowledgement: There's no single, proven method for essay planning that works for everyone. A great approach is to think about strategies that have worked for you in the past.

Do you like to write an outline or plan in your head? How do you like to brainstorm ideas? There's no reason to "reinvent the wheel" for the ACT—use the writing strategies that have proven themselves to work well for you, using the strategies, tips, and advice in this chapter to help guide you through.

Although your essay will be unique and reflect your own distinct perspective on the issue provided in the prompt, an effective piece of argumentative writing should follow a basic structure.

Let's do a quick review.

INTRODUCTION

The introduction of your essay is your opportunity to make a strong and lasting impression on the essay readers. Use your essay opening to grab the reader's attention, confidently introduce your thoughts on the topic, and explain why you think it's an important issue worth exploration. Consider the following tools for starting your essay:

- a memorable and relevant quote from a noted figure
- an emotional and impassioned connection between you and the central issue of the essay prompt
- an intriguing question posed to your readers

A strong essay introduction can really keep readers interested in what you have to say. A weak introduction can be a challenge to overcome and can make it difficult for you to keep readers engaged.

Make every effort to introduce the central idea or thesis of your essay *as early as possible*. With limited time to craft your essay on test day, you should make readers aware of your main idea quickly and allow yourself ample time to develop adequate and convincing support in the body of your essay.

Body

The body paragraphs of your essay—and any essay that achieves a good score—should include the following:

- a thoughtful analysis of the essay prompt and task
- effective idea development that supports your central thesis
- a comprehensive analysis of the three perspectives provided and how they complement or contrast with your own distinct perspective

A high-scoring ACT essay will be a comprehensive and memorable piece of writing that covers the three perspectives provided while strengthening your own central thesis regarding the issue in the essay prompt.

Conclusion

Just as important as a strong introduction is ending your essay with an unforgettable conclusion. Remember, you want to leave a positive and lasting impression in the minds of official ACT essay readers.

Make sure the conclusion of your essay does the following:

- neatly ties up the ideas you've provided in your essay
- reasserts the importance and value of your central position on the topic
- includes relevant and insightful ideas for further exploration

Consider using the strategies mentioned earlier for creating a powerful introduction when developing your essay's conclusion: a memorable and relevant quote, an emotional personal connection that demonstrates your passion toward the main issue, or a provocative question can help you conclude on a high note.

And don't forget—a truly great argumentative essay not only fiercely supports a specific point of view, it also capably acknowledges and addresses alternate and competing viewpoints.

Brainstorming and Taking Notes

Taking notes as you brainstorm can be an effective initial strategy as you prepare to structure, organize, and develop your essay.

Don't waste time crafting grammatically perfect sentences out of your brainstorming notes—remember, the clock is ticking as you take the ACT, and you'll need to make the most of the time allotted.

Your notes should simply be a rough collection of relevant thoughts that arise as you analyze the essay prompt, perspectives, and task.

These early notes can serve in the following key ways:

- They can be developed into the polished, carefully organized, and compelling ideas that will make up your essay.
- They can stimulate your thinking about new ideas for your piece.
- They can help you remember to include key information and ideas in your essay, which could potentially get lost as you work to finish your essay in the time allotted.
- They can help you prune out unnecessary ideas that won't serve to strengthen your piece.

Your essay notes don't have to include only the things you may want to include in your final essay. They can also include:

- relevant questions you'd like to explore (and eventually answer!)
- ideas about structure and organization
- general writing notes to yourself

NOTE: We suggest you spend *no more than 10 minutes* brainstorming, taking notes, and planning your essay before you start writing your first draft. This is where practice before test day comes in handy.

Get comfortable with a time formula that works best for you. Determine if the "10 minutes preplanning/30 minutes writing and editing" approach works for you, and don't be afraid to tweak it if necessary!

Let's take a look at a sample brainstorming list for "Free Public Transportation for Everyone?"

The following list mirrors the basic structural elements of an essay: introduction, body paragraphs, and conclusion. Remember, how you approach brainstorming and note taking should reflect the strategies that have worked for you thus far in your academic career. There's no need to change what works for you!

Introduction ideas

- *Free public transportation is potentially a good idea*
- *Why is this a good idea?*
  - *Individual benefits*
  - *Societal benefits (long term/short term)*

- Potential challenges/roadblocks
- Who decides if it's a good idea?
  - Give everyone a voice on the issue
- Should this be handled on a national or local scale?
- Personal story (how it helped my uncle)

Body paragraph ideas

- Benefits (brief mention)
  - Helping those who need rides
  - Improved mobility for life's needs
  - Cleaner air/environment
  - Reduces traffic
  - Less reliance on fossil fuels
- Potential negatives
  - Expensive (where will money come from?)
  - Lots of effort
  - Not everyone benefits
  - Better ways to spend public money
- Can work in places where budget and infrastucture allow
  - Should be decided after careful review/analysis/voting?
- Should not trigger defunding of other projects or higher taxes
- Discuss related problems
  - Cars/gasoline too expensive
  - Not enough money for socially responsible programs
- How would I influence this policy?
  - What would I change or keep the same?
- Alternative ideas
  - Private corporate sponsorship (good PR, like sponsoring a sports stadium)
  - Incentives for using public transportation (tax break, etc.)
  - Free volunteer car share

Conclusion ideas

- *Realistic possibilities/limitations for free public transportation programs*
- *Should be approached slowly/carefully, not nationally*
- *Supplement with alternative programs*
- *Reiterate importance of this issue, for all of us and future generations*

You can see that by using this method, an essay response is already starting to loosely take shape. The list includes thoughts that can be further developed into effective essay sentences, as well as questions to help stimulate new ideas.

Consider your notes your initial essay blueprint or outline, which you can refer to as needed when you move past the brainstorming phase and begin writing. Your notes can help keep you on track and ensure that all of your ideas are incorporated into your final essay.

After you've taken approximately 10 minutes to develop a general plan or outline for your essay, take a deep breath and pick up your pencil—because you're ready to start writing your first draft!

WRITING YOUR ESSAY

Now that you know what to expect on the ACT Writing test and have a solid initial plan of attack—including a careful analysis of the essay prompt, perspectives, and task, as well as brainstorming, outlining, and taking notes—you're ready to dive into writing your own essay!

We're going to use "Free Public Transportation for Everyone?" to practice developing, writing, and polishing an ACT essay. Find a quiet place to work, get a pencil and some paper, set a timer for 40 minutes, and let's get started.

Take the first 10 minutes to reread the material provided and think about this issue. Use the following space to brainstorm ideas that will help you construct your final work, or feel free to use a separate notebook or scratch paper.

 Students who get great ACT essay scores are more than just smart—they have practiced and have gotten comfortable with working in test-like conditions and are equipped with confidence on test day.

Remember, the key to effective practice is to be honest and serious about using the time allotted to complete this section of the test. You'd likely be able to develop an impressive and high-scoring essay on nearly any topic if given unlimited time to write— the key to success on the ACT exam is to do just that *in 40 minutes*.

Brainstorming ideas for:
"Free Public Transportaion for Everyone?"

Introduction

_____
_____
_____
_____
_____
_____
_____
_____
_____
_____
_____

Body Paragraphs

_____
_____
_____
_____
_____
_____
_____
_____
_____
_____
_____

Conclusion

_____
_____
_____
_____
_____
_____
_____

At this point, you've used approximately 10 minutes to brainstorm, outline, and construct a solid list of relevant ideas, thoughts, and questions for further exploration, which will help form the core of your essay—consider this time well spent!

A few quick reminders that bear repeating, because when the clock is ticking and stress levels are high, we often forget the most fundamental things first.

Your essay should:

- Reflect your distinct perspective on the issue provided in the prompt.
- Follow basic rules of essay structure, including an introduction, supporting body paragraphs, and a conclusion.
- Thoroughly addresses the prompt and task.

Now it's time to use your remaining 30 minutes to craft and edit your essay.

What's the most effective way to use this time? Again, this is completely up to you and how you like to work, but we suggest the following:

- 20–25 minutes to write your first essay draft
- 5–10 minutes to edit your work, making sure it's polished and free of errors

---

Defend Your Viewpoint

When writing your essay, don't be afraid to be provocative. Too often, students choose to write from a perspective on the essay task that they *think* the official ACT readers will want to read, even if it doesn't match their actual beliefs. This could result in an essay that lacks passion and conviction and may adversely affect your final score.

Don't be afraid to write from a perspective that may seem controversial—your essay will be judged on how well you develop and support your ideas, not on whether the readers agree with your point of view.

. . . but Don't Let Passion Prevail!

On the other hand, you may encounter a topic that you feel passionately about and want to eagerly dive into writing and impress the test readers—until the test time is up and you're left with an unpolished, disorganized piece of work.

Remember, this is a test of your ability to craft a well-organized, argumentative essay that reflects a mastery of English language mechanics and conventions, not just an opportunity to show off how much you know on a given subject.

Even if you encounter the *perfect* essay task on test day, don't forget to pace yourself properly, allowing yourself time to carefully plan, organize, structure, develop, and edit your writing into an effective piece of work in 40 minutes.

It's time to craft your first draft and edit your essay now. Make sure your writing environment is quiet and free from distractions, you have enough pencils and paper, as well as an accurate timer, and best of luck!

Editing Your Essay

Once you've written a competent first draft of your essay, ideally you'll have 5–10 minutes left on the clock to review and polish your work. This isn't a lot of time, so you'll have to make the most of every minute left available to you.

Remember, one of the four primary domains that your essay is going to be scored on is Language Use and Conventions, so you'll want to convince the official readers that your essay demonstrates the following:

- **Skillful use of standard English language principles:** Make sure that your work follows sound principles of English language writing.

- **Excellent use of varied and engaging vocabulary and sentence structures:** Your work should demonstrate a masterful command of vocabulary and use of compelling and varied sentence types.

- **A clear, authoritative, and effective voice and tone:** Your essay should be a confident, passionate, and convincing assertion of your perspective on the topic provided.

- **Few or no errors in grammar, mechanics, and syntax:** Nothing is sadder than an essay that's full of great ideas, but also full of misspellings and grammatical errors. The editing phase is the ideal time for you to make sure your work is free from errors in grammar, mechanics, and syntax.

ACT Writing Test: Use Your Time Wisely

Use this guide to make the most of your time on test day:

Total test time: 40 minutes
Brainstorming: 10 minutes
Essay writing: 20–25 minutes
Editing and revising: 5–10 minutes

REVIEWING YOUR ESSAY

Now that you've written and edited your essay and your 40 minutes are up, we know what you're thinking: *How did I do? Does my essay deserve a good score? Are there areas I need to improve on between now and test day?*

A great way to get a sense of your own work is to compare it to sample essay responses that received varying scores in each of the four writing domains.

When you review the following sample responses and scoring analyses for each domain, think about how your essay stacks up. Consider things that the sample essays do particularly well, areas that could use improvement, and how your essay compares in each of the primary writing domains. Feel free to take notes, and use them to continue to analyze and improve your writing.

SAMPLE ACT ESSAY: SCORE 6

Ideas and Analysis:	Score = 6
Development and Support:	Score = 6
Organization:	Score = 6
Language Use and Conventions:	Score = 6

Recognizing the inherent value of an idea that benefits others, and perhaps not yourself, is a noble measure of selflessness. Making public transportation free for everyone, and expanding the program so that those who need it most can rest assured that there is help available when they desperately need it, is the sort of progressive public utility that I believe deserves serious consideration. It is the very type of public good that rests at the heart of the American ideal: A program that recognizes a real need of its citizens; calls for collective mobilization, effort, and sacrifice to meet that need; and is something that we work on together to realize, because we understand that the true measure of a society can best be determined by how its least fortunate are treated.

Convincing others about the core benefits of free public transportation is likely not an uphill battle. It's hard to imagine how even the most hardened of individuals could not recognize that free public transportation would provide desperately needed mobility options for those who need it most, for those who often may have a disability or live in remote or inconvenient areas and for whom the cost of a bus or train ticket might not be as affordable as you or I blithely assume. Imagine the following everyday, real-world scenarios: having to hunt for a new job or commute to a job opportunity far away, having to go to a hospital for care or a pharmacy for medicine, or having to buy groceries or visit a sick friend or relative. Now let's strip away some of the advantages you may enjoy that make these obligations seem routine and forgettable: imagine not being able to afford a car, or not being able to drive, and having no one around who can drive you. Imagine not having any money to cover the cost of public transportation, or maybe there's no transportation close to you. What do you do? These everyday chores don't seem so easy anymore, do they? Now imagine that this describes you or someone you know, perhaps a friend or relative? It isn't so difficult to see how we all may benefit from free public transportation.

The real truth is that even if this scenario doesn't resonate with you, we all benefit from expanded use of public transportation anyway. Reducing the number of cars on the road helps reduce the level of harmful vehicle emissions that hurt the environment and pollute the air we all breathe. An expanded public transportation program could require the use of low-emission vehicles that take advantage of eco-friendly electric or hybrid technology. Fewer cars would also mean less reliance on fossil fuels and gasoline, less traffic to contend with, and less wear on roads, which would save local and state governments money on infrastructure repair. Would you argue that these aren't things that would benefit everyone?

Yes, making public transportation free for everyone wouldn't be free to implement. Such an ambitious proposal would need to be backed up by significant planning, effort and mobilization—which is not free. But just because it will have a price tag attached to it doesn't mean it isn't a good idea. Progressive governments and policymakers should think of new and innovative ideas for funding this program. Increased ridership should translate to increased ad revenue, and new and creative ways to implement ad space, both print and digital, should be explored. In addition, private sponsorship can be pursued; much like bike share programs and sports stadiums across the country, corporations can be courted to sponsor public transportation initiatives, and be given a wealth of free and desirable ad space—and great PR in return. Great minds with forward-thinking ideas can really serve to think of new ways to help offset the costs involved in implementing this bold initiative.

My Uncle Shelly would have benefitted from a free public transportation program. A carpenter and fiercely independent man his entire adult life, when he turned 58 he suffered an accident that made driving and working impossible for him. He was forced to retire early and live on an extremely tight budget. If there were free public transportation available to him he would've been able to handle his daily responsibilities and retain some measure of his independence. But there wasn't. He was forced to sell his home and move in with us, and was dependent on my parents to drive him to wherever he needed to go. Being dependent on others has not been easy for my uncle. All around this country are individuals just like my uncle—proud individuals who have contributed to society and who would like to retain their independence and mobility—and this program would help them do just that. Don't these people deserve this much? Doesn't everybody?

The following is an analysis of the sample essay in each of the four domains that your ACT essay will be scored on. Use this to identify areas of strength and weakness in your own writing, which will help you structure an effective essay writing skills improvement plan and get ready test day.

Scoring Explanation

Ideas and Analysis: Score = 6

This essay provides a compelling and engaging argument for implementing free public transportation wherever possible. The ideas presented are both well considered and nuanced, with a thoughtful analysis of the benefits and challenges involved in initiating such a program (including costs, effort, and mobilization). The author offers some fresh, innovative concepts for funding ("private sponsorship can be pursued; much like bike share programs and sports stadiums across the country, corporations can be courted to sponsor public transportation initiatives") and makes an earnest plea for "great minds with forward-thinking ideas" to address the main challenge involved in implementing such a large program on a wide scale. The author also develops a personal connection to the issue at hand (Uncle Shelly); the overall result is an impressive, passionate, and stirring call for action.

Development and Support: Score = 6

The author of this essay does an excellent job of developing a moving and effective essay in support of his or her view that free public transportation is both a noble and worthwhile pursuit and provides an exemplary level of support to bolster the argument. The author fortifies his or her argument with convincing coverage of the many ways free public transportation benefits a society, wisely choosing to make the distinction that those of us who may never use public transportation will still benefit, and addresses potential detractors head on with bold ideas for overcoming possible challenges and an earnest plea that "just because it will have a price tag attached to it doesn't mean it isn't a good idea." The overall level of sophistication and care demonstrated in developing this essay results in a wholly persuasive and effective piece of writing.

Organization: Score = 6

It's apparent the writer of this essay has a strong command of the basic principles of essay structure and was able to effectively deploy them in service of his or her position on the issue of free public transportation—from the introductory salvo asking us to recognize the inherent value of public services that we may not even benefit from ("a noble measure of selflessness") to the closing plea to consider what each of us deserves from the society we help to perpetuate and advance. A strong introduction, body paragraphs that offer a well-reasoned review of both sides of the issue alongside additional insight to address potential roadblocks, a moving and emotional conclusion, and a holistic approach to idea generation result in a very successful essay.

Language Use and Conventions: Score = 6

An impressive display of effective vocabulary and varied word choice is evident throughout the piece, and sophisticated sentences and transitions clearly indicate a high level of writing proficiency. The writer was able infuse a great deal of passion into his or her essay and captures the reader's attention from beginning to end. The essay is largely free from errors, resulting in a highly polished and provocative piece.

> When crafting your essay, think about "above and beyond" ideas that can enhance your work. Fresh, innovative thinking about the essay task—as long as it doesn't veer off topic—can really impress official ACT essay readers.

SAMPLE ACT ESSAY: SCORE 3

Ideas and Analysis:	Score = 3
Development and Support:	Score = 3
Organization:	Score = 3
Language Use and Conventions:	Score = 3

Public transportation is a big part of people's lives. Some people really like taking public transportation and need it, and some people just don't like it very much. There are people who need it a lot but just don't have much money for it, and these people should not be forced to pay for it, and other people should be able to ride for free too. It should really be free.

If they make all trains and buses free, then people will have things much easier for them. In places, when its important. They will be able to take the bus to go to work and they will be able to go shopping, food and clothes and things they need, and also visit the people that are important to them. If they have no money they couldn't be able to do this and they'd have to save up money or just stay home. The air will also be better of there are less cars on the roads and we will all be able to breathe easier and better and plants and trees will be better too. They should, have buses and trains everywhere, so people who live very far away can ride it too. We should all be able to get to where we need to go without going broke, even if it's near or very far away.

If you don't think that public transpartation should be free then your very lucky because you don't need to worry about money and have enough or a car to take you where you need to go, and that's great. But you should think more about those people who don't have as much money as you and things should be made easier for them. It also helps you if less people use cars and the air is much better to breathe, so even if you don't take busses and trains things will be better for you if its free. Yes it will cost money to do this but good things cost money and this is important and a good thing to spend the money on. Theres money for other things too anyway?

> *In conclusion, I think free public transportation is a very good idea and it should be done for everybody. Everyone will benefit from it, so people who cant afford it will, be able to get rides to wherever they need to go, and those who don't use it will have better air to breathe and less traffic on the road to have to deal with, so its good for everybody. Something that's good for everybody should always be done as soon as possible.*

Scoring Explanation

Ideas and Analysis: Score = 3

It's evident that the author of this piece made an attempt to generate topic-appropriate ideas regarding free and accessible public transportation; however, there is a lack of real depth and insight to lift this piece to a higher score. The author focuses on the merits of free public transportation ("If they make all trains and buses free, then people will have things much easier for them.") with relatively rudimentary analysis. There is very little thought given to arguments against free public transportation beyond acknowledging that some people may not agree with ("If you don't think that public transportation should be free then your very lucky because you don't need to worry about money and have enough or a car to take you where you need to go, and that's great."), and that it will cost money ("Yes it will cost money to do this but good things cost money"). The end result is an essay that stays on track and addresses the prompt and task, but one that would really benefit from additional effort and thought about the relative pros and cons of public transportation, the arguments on both sides, and fresh ideas to offset the critics and demonstrate original thought and real insight.

Development and Support: Score = 3

The author's argument remains at a very general level, with a simplistic array of thoughts that warrant additional development in order to become a truly compelling essay. Although the ideas provided reflect a specific and recognizable point of view regarding free public transportation, the piece would be more effective if it offered additional support for the ideas presented. The author's central claim is that free public transportation is a good idea, and he or she does offer some very general ideas why (helps those who need mobility options, cleaner air, less traffic), but doesn't go any deeper than that. Even less idea development is offered for the opposing viewpoint; failure to take on and confidently address opposing viewpoints is a hallmark of an argumentative essay that is adequate at best. The author would greatly benefit from stepping back and more deeply weighing the merits and disadvantages of this proposed initiative—what are the potential challenges and roadblocks of free public transportation? How could this feasibly be implemented on a large scale? How can the critics be convinced that the initiative is truly worth it?

Organization: Score = 3

This is an appropriately ordered essay response to the prompt and task provided. There is an introduction that, although lacking an impressive level of insight, makes the author's point of view clear ("It should really be free"). Body paragraphs exist that address perspectives for ("If they make all trains and buses free, then people will have things much easier for them.") and against ("If you don't think that public transportation should be free then your very lucky because you don't need to worry about money and have enough or a car to take you where you need to go, and that's great.") free public transportation, albeit on a very basic level. The conclusion reasserts the author's basic central claim that free public transportation is a good idea, but lacks the sort of original creative thought or passion that makes better essays more memorable. A less mechanical and more interconnected piece of writing that ties together the ideas in each paragraph, leading to a more cohesive and blended piece of writing, would achieve a higher score.

Language Use and Conventions: Score = 3

The quality of writing in this written response reflects a basic grasp of English language, with simplistic sentence construction and transitions, leading to an adequate but lackluster essay. The ideas present are clear and straightforward but are somewhat hampered by a few misspellings (*everwhere*, *transpartation*), errors in construction (sentence fragment, etc.), and errors in punctuation. The word choice lacks sophistication as well. Overall, the author clearly would benefit from additional development in this proficiency domain.

SAMPLE ACT ESSAY: SCORE 1

Ideas and Analysis:	Score = 1
Development and Support:	Score = 1
Organization:	Score = 1
Language Use and Conventions:	Score = 1

I think public transpration is good, its something that I used to use more than now that I have a car or my friends can pick me up and give me rides to places. They help people go places, busses and the trains, and they cant let people, not get on as long as they have the money to pay, and you don't need a car or able to afford one and that's the best part of it. When I went, to school in junior high and I needed to get to school I took the school bus but hated it because I didn't have somone to drive my there! We can for it. When my mom wasn't working she will take me to the mall and my friends house and she will usuale pick me up when, I got to come home for the day. I don't rember the bus being free when I used to take it but when I was really small I don't, think my mom had to pay for me or my brother to have to ride the bus until I was much older. I think that people should have a ride when they, need one, and they should ask someone they know to ride them or if not there should be a bus or something to take them where they need to go or what else can they do?

Scoring Explanation

Ideas and Analysis: Score = 1

This low-scoring essay suffers from a profound lack of topic-relevant ideas and analysis that relates to the essay prompt and task. The few scattered ideas that the author does provide fail to address the issue of whether or not public transportation should be made free for all individuals; rather, the ideas veer off course and instead discuss his or her thoughts on public transportation in general ("I think public transpration is good, its something that I used to use more than now that I have a car or my friends can pick me up and give me rides to places."). There is no indication of the author's point of view on making public transportation free. The overall result is an off-topic and ill-conceived piece of writing that falls far from the mark.

Development and Support: Score = 1

The author of this ineffective and weak piece of writing offers a poorly developed response to the essay prompt and is, at best, a tangentially relevant reply to the topic at hand (focusing on the author's thoughts on public transportation in general and not on whether it should be made a free public service). The thoughts that are offered lack depth or insight, and support is minimal or nonexistent. Since the author quickly goes off topic and remains there, the little support that the author does offer ("I think that people should have a ride when they need one and they should ask someone they know to ride them or if not there should be a bus or something to take them where they need to go or what else can they do?") fails to bolster a response that effectively addresses the essay task.

Organization: Score = 1

This scattered and largely disjointed piece of writing lacks effective organization and structure. There is no clearly discernible introduction that ushers in the author's point of view, no body paragraphs that develop and support his or her central thesis, and no effective conclusion that wraps up the author's key points. Instead, the author provides an incoherent and meandering response that is a loose collection of random thoughts on public transportation and transportation in general ("When I went to school in junior high and I needed to get to school I took the school bus but hated it because I didn't have someone to drive my there"), which lacks authority and fails to live up the task.

Language Use and Conventions: Score = 1

The author of this piece would have been well served to review and edit his or her work; the essay response is an unpolished response with serious errors in language use and conventions, including run-ons ("I don't remember the bus being free when I used to take it but when I was really small I don't, think my mom had to pay for me or my brother to have to ride the bus until I was much older."), fragments ("We can for it."), misspelled words (*transpration*), and incorrect use of punctuation (i.e., comma usage). The level or errors in this piece seriously detract from the effectiveness of the response and only serve to keep it from appropriately meeting the essay task.

SUMMING IT UP

- **Analyze and understand the prompt material:** We know you're eager to get started writing, but before you do, analyze the instructions, the essay prompt, the perspectives, and the essay task carefully. Be sure you fully understand the issues presented in the prompt material and know exactly what you're being asked to write about.

- **Use what you know:** The essay prompt that you'll encounter on test day can be based on a nearly unlimited array of topics. Since you won't know what topic you'll see, the best way to prepare is to stay aware of issues and current events taking place around you and in the world.

- **Use your time wisely:** You'll have 40 minutes to plan and write your essay. Use this time efficiently. Practice planning and writing essays in the time provided, using an approach that you've practiced before test day (we recommend 10 minutes of brainstorming, 20–25 minutes of writing, and 5–10 minutes of editing). Come to test day with a good idea of a writing pace that works for you.

- **Plan carefully:** When you feel the pressure and clock ticking on test day, your first instinct may be to begin quickly and write furiously, to get as much down on the pages before the end of the test. Resist this urge. Instead, take a few minutes to think critically about the issue and plan. Creating an outline can help you properly structure your essay and save you time in the long run.

- **Write purposefully:** Use the writing techniques and strategies that have worked for you in the past as you craft your essay. Establish a clear perspective and focus for the reader, and craft compelling, well-structured sentences that support your argument and address the essay prompt and questions provided, as well as the implications and potential consequences of your ideas.

- **Structure your work effectively:** Don't forget that the structure and polish of your final essay is being scored alongside the quality and content of your ideas. Make sure that your essay adheres to the rules of proper essay structure, with an introduction, body paragraphs, and conclusion that stay on target.

- **Efficiency and clarity are crucial:** Remember that you only have a total of 40 minutes to analyze the essay prompt, perspectives, and task and write your complete polished response. Saying the same thing over and over again is not time well spent. Avoid redundancy in your final essay—an efficient piece of writing that stays on task, covers all of your points, and highlights your distinct perspective is the best approach on test day.

- **Avoid tired and overused words and phrases:** Your essay will not be the only one that the official ACT essay readers will be evaluating. If you're vying for a good score, be mindful of your writing decisions—try to avoid tired, well-worn clichés and phrases and use varied, creative word choices and sentence structure throughout your piece in an effort to dazzle your readers.

- **Edit your work:** Save a few minutes to review and edit your work after writing your essay. Think about the four writing domains that your essay will be scored on as you review your work:

- Does your essay present a wealth of compelling ideas and nuanced analysis in response to the prompt?

- Are the ideas in your essay fully developed, and do they contain sufficient support to bolster your perspective?

- Is your essay well-structured and organized?

- Do you effectively adhere to established English language principles and mechanics in your essay? Avoid common test-day essay mistakes, including sentence fragments, run-ons, reliance on passive voice, and inappropriate pronoun shifts.

- Have you swept for errors, proper word choice, grammar, sense, and sentence usage?

- **Practice is essential:** Use the study time you have available to practice writing essays on a variety of subjects. Choose a topic that's getting a lot of news attention or, better still, work with a writing partner who'll help you choose writing topics and who can also review your work. If you can find a reader who's capable of reviewing your work along the four domains and providing helpful critical feedback, that's even better!

Bottom line: Make the most of the time you have between now and test day—no matter how long it is—to get plenty of practice with the ACT Writing test and build your essay writing skills. If you carefully practice and prepare, you'll put yourself in the best position possible to achieve a great score!

NOTES

NOTES

NOTES

NOTES

NOTES